Augsburg

DURING THE

Reformation Era

An Anthology of Sources

AUGSBURG

DURING THE

REFORMATION ERA

An Anthology of Sources

Edited and Translated,
with an Introduction, by

B. Ann Tlusty

Hackett Publishing Company, Inc.
Indianapolis/Cambridge

15 14 13 12   1 2 3 4 5 6 7

For further information, please address
  Hackett Publishing Company, Inc.
  P.O. Box 44937
  Indianapolis, Indiana 46244-0937

  www.hackettpublishing.com

Cover design by Abigail Coyle
Interior design by Elizabeth L. Wilson
Composition by William Hartman
Printed at Data Reproductions Corporation

Library of Congress Cataloging-in-Publication Data
Augsburg during the Reformation era : an anthology of sources /
edited and translated, with an introduction by B. Ann Tlusty.
        p. cm.
    Includes bibliographical references and index.
    ISBN 978-1-60384-841-1 (pbk.) —
    ISBN 978-1-60384-842-8 (cloth)
    1. Augsburg (Germany)—History—16th century—Sources.
  2. Augsburg (Germany)—Social conditions—16th century—
  Sources. 3. Augsburg (Germany)—Church history—16th
  century—Sources. 4. Reformation—Germany—Augsburg—
  Sources. I. Tlusty, B. Ann, 1954–
    DD901.A92A83 2012
    943'.375031—dc23   2012019287

For Jack and Mikey

Preface

As I write this Preface, most of the documents upon which these translations are based are no longer available in the city archive in Augsburg that has been their home for more than a century. In early 2010, the archive was forced to choose between removing the documents for an indeterminate period of fumigation and leaving them to be consumed by an infestation of bread beetles that had already caused considerable damage. Access to this valuable collection will remain limited for some years to come. This catastrophe followed only months after the city archive of Cologne, which housed another of Germany's richest collections of medieval and early modern documents, collapsed upon itself as the result of careless construction on a nearby subway, taking down with it millions of pages of irreplaceable bits of history.[1] These are only two of the sad stories affecting Europe's largely unexploited collections of manuscripts, which have over the centuries also suffered the effects of war, fire, mold, disinterest, pigeon droppings, and periodic processes of selective thinning (generally referred to as "weeding") that did not always anticipate the interests of future generations of readers.

Such losses are all the more painful to the historian, not only because most of these records exist only in one copy but also because the people whose voices they preserve often appear only once among them. Thus the fragile record of countless lives, having survived for hundreds of years, can be extinguished entirely in an instant or a season. As much as we would hate to lose the first editions of works of great statesmen or the correspondence of the leading religious reformers in a similar disaster, their work and their voices would at least survive in myriad subsequent editions and, more recently, digitized copies. Most of the records reproduced here, however, exist only as a single manuscript and are being published for the first time.

Of course, this small selection represents much less than the tip of an iceberg. For the social historian, it is this multiplicity of voices that is the stuff of history; for only by understanding the negotiations that went on among all members of society can we deconstruct the major events, mentality shifts, and institutional changes that shaped the modern world. These cultural fragments should be of special interest to

---

1. Most, although not all, of Cologne's collections have been recovered and are undergoing a lengthy process of restoration. Many will remain damaged even if readable. Two lives were also lost in the collapse.

English-speaking readers because it was so often these ordinary voices that articulated challenges to the old order. Public discourse in early modern city streets regularly tested the limits of restrictions on freedoms that are still being negotiated today—freedoms of speech, religion, and assembly; the right to bear arms; rights of petition and redress; freedom from cruel and unusual punishment; legal rights for ethnic minorities; and personal freedoms, including the right to choose marriage partners, to live in accordance with sexual preference, and to drink alcohol. All of these struggles find expression in these pages.

I am very grateful, therefore, for the opportunity to provide at least this small collection of voices to English-language readers, and for that I thank Hackett Publishing and, especially, Rick Todhunter for his patience and support. I would also like to express my gratitude to the staff at the Stadtarchiv Augsburg, all of whom were most helpful under the worst of conditions. Without their willingness to be flexible, this book would not have been possible. As always, the staff at the Staats- und Stadtbibliothek Augsburg also proved professional and helpful at every step. Helmut Graser spent many hours helping me to decipher the nuances of my Early New High German texts for the best possible expression in English, and a number of my students shaped the work in various ways, first inspiring its beginning by their eagerness to learn more about early modern life, and then helping the manuscript find its final form with their helpful feedback on earlier drafts. Finally, many friends and colleagues, including two anonymous peer reviewers, provided advice and feedback along the way. Some even passed on their transcripts of documents otherwise currently out of reach. Although it is impossible to name everyone here, you know who you are—my sincere thanks to all of you.

B. Ann Tlusty
Lewisburg, PA

Contents

Chapter Five. Work and Trade

Chapter Six. Sports, Entertainments, and the Control of Leisure

Chapter Seven. Ethnicity

Chapter Eight. Ritual and Ceremony

Chapter Nine. Magic and Popular Religion

Chapter Ten. Dealing with War and Catastrophe

General Introduction

The work of a new generation of social historians has changed the way we think about and teach the period of Reformation in Europe. Most historians now understand the reformation process as involving people at all levels of society, with political and religious change depending on negotiation and consensus among different social groups. As a result, the majority of historical treatments of the Reformation since the 1980s consider not only the ideas of the reformers but also their reception among the general populace. Dozens of monographs and anthologies have appeared during the past two decades that utilize archival sources such as court records, civic ordinances, sermons, supplications, and chronicles to reevaluate the relationship of religious and political thought to the lives of early modern Europeans. In recent years, these trends have affected the way that we teach the history of the Reformation at the college level and also have influenced more general surveys of European history. Topics such as marriage and family, social and gender identity, ritual, class, ethnicity, and the relationship between religion and magic are now standard fare in European survey textbooks. The goal of this collection is to present the life of the people of one city in the immediacy possible only with rare documents of social history. Although some key excerpts from published sources are included for context, I have avoided incorporating extracts from well-known works easily available in English elsewhere. A reading bibliography of additional primary sources located at the end of the volume will point interested students to many such works.

Choosing a limited number of sources from among the many possibilities available to the social historian is never an easy task. Many difficult decisions had to be made in order to keep this book at a reasonable length, and, undoubtedly, others would have chosen differently. My goal in selecting this particular collection was to illuminate as clearly as possible the lives of ordinary people in a period of extraordinary upheaval. Naturally, much of what was written down and archived resulted from unusual circumstances—due to an arrest, a complaint, a major event, or an institutional change. The task of the social historian faced with such sources is twofold: to identify the historical significance implicit in the record of events, and also to tease out the context of ordinary life that can be glimpsed behind the scenes. Along with telling a story of Reformation, resistance, and war, then, these records reveal much about the daily round of townspeople at all levels of society and in circumstances both common and uncommon. Here we observe early modern townsfolk from various levels of society not only expressing discontent and challenging their authorities but also working, playing games, and making merry; getting married and having sex (not necessarily in that order); squabbling, debating, and coming to blows; gathering to chat in pubs, churches, homes, and the streets; dabbling in magic and dealing with illness—in short, living their lives on their own terms and in accordance with their own worldview.

Aside from making selections with an eye for illuminating life in an early modern city from the perspective of its citizens, I also gave preference to a number of sources that have been treated in recent work by important historians of the period. A bibliography of works of secondary literature consulted and suggestions for further reading, arranged by chapter, will aid students interested in further exploring the context of these sources.

Although Augsburg may not be as well known to many English readers as Munich or Berlin, the choice to focus on this Swabian city to tell the story of the Reformation would hardly have surprised anyone who lived through it. To begin with, it was in the south German cities that the Reformation initially took hold, and it was in Augsburg specifically that many of the most important political events of the sixteenth century took place. Among them were the three major Imperial Diets of 1518, 1530, and 1555, at which the dictates of the Lutheran faith (The Augsburg Confession) and religious peace (The Peace of Augsburg) were ultimately worked out. Between 1518 and 1555, the people of Augsburg came into regular contact with ideas associated with various religious factions, including the more radical groups (i.e., Zwinglians, Schwenkfelders, and Anabaptists)[1] along with Lutherans and Catholics. These ideas were communicated from the pulpits and debated in letters and petitions, locally produced pamphlets, and in the streets, and the major legal and cultural shifts they precipitated affected the lives of Augsburg's citizens for the next century. The fact that for most of this period, the city remained biconfessional, meaning that both of the recognized Christian faiths or confessions (i.e., Catholics and Lutherans) were allowed to worship within its walls, provides an unusual opportunity to explore the relationship between Catholics and Protestants among common folk as well as among clergymen and council members.

1. Zwinglians were followers of the Swiss reformer Ulrich Zwingli (1484–1521); Schwenkfelders were followers of the spiritualist reformer Caspar Schwenkfeld (c. 1589–1561); Anabaptists were members of a radical movement believing in adult baptism (forerunners of modern Amish, Mennonites, and Baptists).

Concentrating on a single city provides a clearer picture of relationships between people, events, and institutions than can more general source books that cover greater geographical territory. Claims to greater comprehension in such collections are typically offset by their tendency to lack cohesion, requiring each source to be treated in isolation and with little context. While any one of the sources presented here can stand alone as a topic for discussion, they combine to tell a comprehensive story of one city's struggle to maintain balance in a turbulent world. Augsburg is an interesting case study for this purpose not only due to the events that took place there but also because of the city's status during the Reformation era as a major center of banking, artistry, and printing. During the sixteenth century, Augsburg was one of Germany's largest and most prosperous cities. As the home of Europe's wealthiest financiers; a major manufacturing center for textiles, gold- and silver-smithing, armor, and scientific instruments; and the largest producer of German-language books in the empire, the city was a hub not only of international finance and trade but also of ideas. These factors combine with Augsburg's unrivaled archival collections to make it an ideal setting for looking at the period of Reformation and post-Reformation from the bottom up.

Like other free imperial cities, Augsburg was an independent entity within the Holy Roman Empire of the German Nation, a complex political body covering large parts of Central Europe until 1806. Because the title of emperor was not hereditary, but dependent upon election by a group of powerful electoral princes (the *Kurfürsten*), the emperor himself never consolidated absolute rule throughout the empire. Instead, he shared power over the more than 300 autonomous political entities that it comprised with territorial princes, bishops, lords, city oligarchies, and other local rulers, who had local authority over taxes, dues, and the courts. Defense systems also remained primarily in the hands of local rulers, along with internal policing. In the free imperial cities, the rights to make and enforce law as well as to collect taxes and dues were relegated to local, self-governing councils, typically dominated by the town's most powerful families.

Good policing, to early modern governments, meant enforcing both public and moral order. Thus secular rulers exerted influence over many aspects of daily life now considered private. The councils of all German towns produced a plethora of decrees, regulations, and ordinances that provide rich details about life in the city. These prescriptive sources, however, present only part of the story. Those who violated local laws could expect to face one of a number of lower or upper courts, all of which also left detailed records. For minor infractions such as getting into fights, exchanging insults, or going out to the countryside to drink untaxed wine, a visit to a lower court and a fine of a gulden or two would normally suffice. Drunkards, vagrants, and other unruly persons arrested after hours often spent the night in the "Fool's House," in Augsburg a low cage located next to the council house where the delinquent would be subject to ridicule while waiting to be brought before the officials. For graver offenses defendants were questioned by the councilmen themselves. Depending on the circumstances, very serious crimes could lead to banishment or corporal punishment. Questioning under torture, which could permanently affect the honor of the accused, was reserved for capital crimes.

Records produced in the process of arrests and interrogations provide some of the most colorful and detailed sources for the social historian. Naturally, one must be careful not to assume that everything reported by a defendant under interrogation was the truth, any more than every accusation made by local authorities was valid. But the negotiations that took place between questioners and questioned in these cases reveal a great deal about the concerns and norms that governed the conversation on both sides.

Also valuable for identifying the interests of ordinary citizens are supplications. Every early modern subject had the right to present petitions of grievances to their authorities, and supplications were also regularly presented in support of relatives arrested for a crime. Normally, such documents were prepared by a professional notary or scribe; thus they include much that is formulaic. But even if the arguments made therein may have been influenced by professional advice, the goal of the supplication was to represent the concerns of the petitioners who commissioned them, and many of their assertions were formulated in a unique voice. Petitions appear in trial records, guild disputes, debt negotiations, and complaints of all sorts, and are often accompanied by the responses of experts consulted in the case (e.g., guild masters, medical or legal authorities, or other offices that the city council considered responsible for the matter at hand). These records combine with excerpts from sermons, city chronicles, council minutes, military records, and other cultural artifacts produced in the normal course of life in the city (including a number of documents written by ordinary citizens in their own hand) to provide us with glimpses into the lives of those people whose voices are so rarely heard in standard treatments of the period.

The organization of this book around ten specific themes is intended only as a suggestion for how the sources might be used. Any number of additional topics could be explored by gathering together sources from different chapters (e.g., medicine, crime and punishment, gender, protest). Themes introduced within the chapters can also be augmented by sources from elsewhere in the book. The reader is referred to the index for identifying these connections along with additional themes of study.

Early Modern Conventions and Editorial Principles

The guiding principle in translating these texts into English was to make them readable without entirely sacrificing the style and flavor of the originals. Not all Early New High German words and phrases can be precisely rendered in English, and not every word is unambiguous in meaning, or even readable. Translating requires flexibility and, invariably, some precision must be sacrificed in the interest of clarity and manageability. Space limitations also require that many documents appear as excerpts; thus summaries of information appearing elsewhere in the document are enclosed in square brackets. Passages omitted are indicated by a series of periods (. . .). Within the source texts, square brackets are also used to enclose clarifications and other changes from the original made for the sake of clarity or brevity. Explanations for specific terms likely to be unfamiliar to many readers and identifying information for key individuals and events appear in footnotes.

Certain repetitive terms and phrases that might seem odd to the modern reader require some explanation. My decision to translate directly the standard third-person phrase "an Honorable Council," regularly used in correspondence from the ruling city council to indicate itself, was made for the sake of maintaining at least one aspect of early modern conventions of status. On the other hand, I have shortened most of the lengthy titles and obsequious closings that early modern custom required for commoners petitioning to their rulers. A typical supplication, for example, might begin, "Noble, well-born, steadfast, able, honorable, and wise Lord Mayors, Burgomasters, and an Honorable Council of this laudable Imperial City, your imperious gracious and auspicious Lords, we herewith apply to your steadfast and most diligent wise and gracious Lords." Depending on the status of the petitioner and the notary's style, these lists of ingratiating titles and expressions of humility could be repeated half a dozen times in a single-page petition. Most of these lengthy formulaic expressions have thus been abbreviated with some variation of [Your Lords] or, as appropriate, [Your humble servant].

Readers will also note that many words and phrases are preceded or followed by a formal apology (here rendered by the modern equivalent "pardon the expression"). The original phrases represented by this term, often expressed in Latin and taking a variety of forms ("without offense," "with modesty," "with reverence," "by permission," "with honor," etc.), signify an expression of regret by the speaker (or more likely, the scribe) for mentioning things with unpleasant or indecent associations. Such apologies typically not only accompany curse words, words denoting sexual behavior or intimate body parts, and references to dishonorable people but also appear with words that can create associations with bad smells, such as animals or shoes. These attempts by the scribe to distance himself from inappropriate speech appear only rarely in the earlier sixteenth century but increase in regularity with time, revealing increasing sensibilities on the part of elite townspeople to language considered crude or inappropriate.

Also posing a potential problem for many modern readers are German titles and offices that do not have exact English equivalents. In some of these cases, translation decisions depend less upon the word at hand than on the political context in which it is used. I have followed established convention as much as possible in interpreting such titles (translating *Vorgeher,* for example, as "leader" in an informal context, but as "Principal" when referring to guild leaders, etc.). A specific local problem in translation arises from the ambiguous use of the terms *Bürgermeister* and *Stadtpfleger,* either of which could refer to the city governors (i.e., mayors, of which there were always two), and in this context, the relationship of these offices to Augsburg's particular political situation bears explaining. During the reign of Augsburg's guild-based government (1368–1548), one of the two city *Bürgermeister* was elected from among the guild masters, and the other was always a member of the highest order of urban elites, a class of gentry known in the cities of the Holy Roman Empire as "patricians."[2] In 1548, Emperor Charles V, as the victor in the Schmalkaldic War, disbanded the guild government and broke the powerful guilds down into smaller crafts. The new constitution that Charles imposed upon the city reinstated the older term *Stadtpfleger* (literally "city caretaker") and limited the office to members of the patriciate. The title of *Bürgermeister,* however, remained in use for the overseers of an administrative office responsible for much of the day-to-day business of the city. Thus I have translated *Bürgermeister* as "mayor" up until 1548, and subsequently as "Burgomaster." After 1548, the term *Stadtpfleger,* as the city's highest office, is translated as "mayor."

Dates in early modern texts can also be ambiguous. Many are rendered not by number but by the name of a saint's day, especially in less formal texts such as chronicles. Designation of saints' days varied

---

2. See Chapter Three for more on rank and privilege among the patrician class.

based on local traditions, and some names appear more than once on the yearly calendar. Where ambiguities existed, I have based decisions on the local calendar of the Augsburg diocese and logical relationships to seasons or other surrounding events.

Understanding Early Modern Currency

When encountering a reference to a monetary amount in a document from a past era, it is natural for students to ask, "How much is that, exactly?" Just what it meant, for example, for a craftsman to pay a fine of "a gulden or two," as noted above in connection with court records, is difficult to say. Most ordinary craftsmen appear to have paid such fines without serious problems, although occasionally in installments over several weeks. A poorer craftsman earned about a gulden a week in the early sixteenth century, while a city guard or piper (also at the lower end of the earning scale) earned approximately 1½ gulden per week in the 1580s. Incomes for mid- to upper-level city officials ranged from 130 to 200 gulden per year in the later sixteenth century. Since most middling craftsmen were independent tradesmen, their incomes probably varied considerably. There are a number of sources included in this collection that reflect prices and incomes (especially documents 1.1, 5.11, 5.12, 10.1, and 10.10). To help in interpreting these amounts, local currency values are provided below. All must be considered approximate, since coin values changed in relation to one another throughout the period; both the pfennig and the schilling, in particular, are very difficult to pin down:

> 1 gulden = 60 kreuzer, or 15 batzen, or 20 schilling, or 420 heller
> 1 gulden = around 210 pfennig, with variation (at the beginning of the sixteenth century), later (during the seventeenth century) somewhat standardized at 240 pfennig
> 1 batzen = 4 kreuzer or 14 pfennig
> 1 kreuzer = about 3.5 pfennig in coin[3]
> 1 schilling (also called a groschen or a plappart) = 3 kreuzer (10½ pfennig, later 12 pfennig) or 21 heller
> 1 heller = ½ pfennig
> 1 thaler (Reichsthaler) = 90 kreuzer, or 1½ gulden

---

3. Or 4 *Rechnungspfennig* (accounting pfennig), which was never an actual coin, but an abstract currency value.

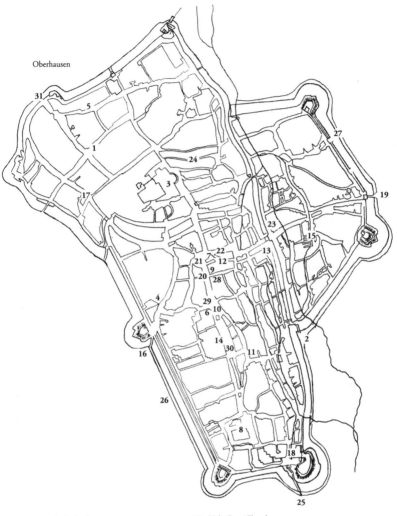

Oberhausen

1	At the Cross
2	Bird Gate
3	Church (Cathedral) of Our Lady
4	Church of St. Anna
5	Church of St. George
6	Church of St. Mortiz
7	Church of St. Peter
8	Church of St. Ulrich
9	Council House
10	Dance House
11	Dominican Church
12	Fish Market
13	Franciscan Church
14	Frugger Palace
15	Fuggerei
16	Gögginger Gate
17	Holy Cross Church
18	Hospital
19	Jacob's Gate
20	Patricians' and Merchants' Drinking Rooms
21	Perlach Square
22	Perlach Hill
23	Pilgrim's Hospital
24	Priests' Lane
25	Red Gate
26	Rosenau Shooting Grounds
27	Stephinger Gate
28	The irons
29	Weavers' Hall
30	Wine Market
31	Wertach Bridge (Beggars' Bridge)

Map of Augsburg during the Reformation Era. Copyright © B. Ann Tlusty

Chapter One
Popular Responses to Reform, 1520–1554

The separate identities of the Protestant and Catholic denominations, normally referred to as "confessions," did not appear on the scene fully conceptualized in 1517 even in published tracts of reformers, let alone in the minds of the people. Confessional identities and what they meant in terms of church practice were worked out over the course of the sixteenth century in a process that involved not only churchmen but also secular governments and laypeople.

Social historians studying the early modern period in Europe have for decades concerned themselves with the role of the populace in shaping political change, often using terms like "reception" and "history from below" to focus attention on the collective negotiating power of the general populace during periods of upheaval. The fact that lasting political change more often grew out of a consensus between authorities and populace than as a result of strictly top-down decisions is by now a widely accepted paradigm. The Reformation in Augsburg provides an ideal model for examining this process. It was in the towns that the evangelical movement found its most fertile ground, according to some historians because of the attraction to many townspeople of the communal principles inherent in the new teaching. But as the sources in this chapter make clear, the way that people received the new ideas and put them into practice did not always coincide with what the reformers had in mind. Augsburg's residents were not passive receptacles for the ideas of preachers and reformers, but chose their own paths in reaction to new ways of thinking about the church. Some resisted or supported change with great passion, and others went through a period of experimentation in their attempt to cope with the confusing array of messages they were receiving.

This chapter begins with the volatile events of 1523 and 1524, during which new ideas were being discussed and disseminated not only among theologians and preachers but also wherever ordinary people gathered to talk. Religious debates broke out in church, in the street, and in pubs and homes. The large-scale protest of 1524 and the arrests that followed are related to the series of bloody uprisings generally known as the German Peasants' War (1524–1525), which also included urban unrest such as that illustrated here. Partisan preaching polarized the debates as battle lines were drawn between the confessions. During this transitional phase, records of arrest tended to focus on general challenges to authority rather than specific religious doctrines, although some civic ordinances were very specific about church practice.

In 1537, the Reformation process came to a head in Augsburg with the election of Mang Seitz and Hans Welser as mayors, both of whom were strongly influenced by the ideas of Ulrich Zwingli and Martin Bucer.[1] From then until 1547, Augsburg's government was dominated by Zwinglian-style insistence on strict moral and religious discipline, and Catholics faced arrest and interrogation for leaving the city to engage in Catholic ceremonies. But punishment in such cases does not seem to have gone beyond a warning, the language of which concentrated on the violation of the council's decree more than on matters of personal belief.[2]

For many Augsburg citizens, however, obedience to authority took a backseat to their concern over their souls. For others, economic and political concerns were at the forefront. Common people regularly expressed dissatisfaction with the authorities over exploitive taxes, wasted government resources, suppression of guild rights, and other issues of temporal concern, all of which became caught up in the politics of religion and the struggle for spiritual power.

There was one religious doctrine that was punishable in its own right, namely Anabaptism. Unlike those who practiced various interpretations of Catholic, Lutheran, or Zwinglian teachings, Anabaptists were harshly treated just for carrying out the dictates of their faith, which included adult baptism. Rejection of infant baptism was viewed as heretical not only by the Catholic Church but also by most of the evangelical reformers. Perhaps more of a concern to local authorities was the fact that many Anabaptists rejected oaths of fealty to a worldly power. This meant that they would not be bound to honor their oath of citizenship. In some cases they also refused to bear arms for civic defense or to pay local defense taxes. Although few Anabaptists in Augsburg adhered to these more radical views, the movement in general appeared threatening to city leaders, who assumed that loyalty to outside powers would lead to civil disobedience.

This fear naturally appeared all the more justified after the events in Münster in 1534–1535, when radical Anabaptists gained control of the city and established complete authority there in a regime that

---

1. An important reformer in Strasbourg known for his tolerant views and his attempts to mediate between Zwingli and Luther over matters of doctrine, especially concerning the Eucharist.

2. Cf. document 8.3.

included experimentation with polygamy and communal property. Abandoning the pacifist stance held by many Anabaptists, the radical regime in Münster took up arms against its enemies and waged a bloody war against local dissenters. These events served to intensify the determination of both Catholics and Protestants to stamp out what they understood as a subversive sect. As a result, many historians have been left with the impression that those drawn to Anabaptism in the sixteenth century were either particularly pious, or extremely zealous, and that they were made into martyrs wherever they went. In fact, however, many of those accused of Anabaptism in Augsburg were less than fervent about their beliefs and were willing to recant rather than face banishment, after which they were left in peace. Those who would not recant in some cases faced harsh punishments such as whipping and branding. Unlike rulers in many other German and Austrian territories, however, Augsburg was comparatively lenient in that it refrained from executing Anabaptists, a fate that met those in the Swabian territories outside its walls even after they recanted.

Naturally, the popular reactions represented here did not occur in a vacuum. The people of Augsburg were exposed to the new teachings in a variety of ways. Perhaps most influential were the sermons of charismatic preachers, some of which have been excerpted here and in other chapters. Excerpts from more authoritarian voices have been included as well, primarily in the form of ordinances. But townspeople also had other sources for information. The invention of the printing press during the fifteenth century led to an explosion of new kinds of information. Along with instructive literature (including moral and religious tracts) and an abundance of printed laws and ordinances, the late fifteenth and early sixteenth centuries saw the advent of a genre of print intended primarily for diversion. Luther and his followers quickly became adept at combining religious instruction with entertainment, producing satirical broadsheets and pamphlets aimed at a wide audience. Many of these combined anti-Catholic texts with pictures, sometimes exploiting crude imagery in order to catch the viewer's attention and ensure that the message was easy for anyone to interpret.

Even pamphlets without pictures were likely to reach a fairly large audience. Augsburg's populace would have had ready access to the explosion of Reformation pamphlets appearing during the early sixteenth century, for nearly one third of the 10,000 or so such prints that appeared between 1518 and 1530 was produced in Augsburg's printing shops. A fair number of the city's residents would also have been able to read them. Recent scholarship suggests that literacy levels in early modern towns have generally tended to be underestimated, with some data indicating a populace that was nearly one third literate in the early sixteenth century and going up. General literacy was also being encouraged by Protestant theologians, who encouraged all Christians to learn to read the Bible.

Not all of those who could read could also afford to purchase books and pamphlets, but the audience for such texts was undoubtedly larger than just those who were able to pay for them, or even those who could read them, for reading aloud was a popular form of sociability and entertainment. Public houses were a natural choice for reading and discussing the latest broadsheets, ordinances, pamphlets, and sermons. Ideas picked up in church and at the tavern were then passed on by word of mouth throughout the streets and homes of the city. The conversations presented in this chapter's selection of sources represent only a tiny fraction of the lively debates that went on at all levels of society and in all corners of the city during the first decades of the sixteenth century.

I. Unrest in the City

1.1 Witnesses to Claus Hirschman, Bishop's Spy in the Church of St. Anna[3]

Claus Hirschman, who was a constable, or beadle, in service to the Bishop of Augsburg, caused suspicion when he appeared at a church service in the Church of St. Anna. St. Anna's pastor Johann Frosch was at the forefront of reformed ideas in Augsburg. Following Frosch's Sunday sermon on October 22, 1523, an argument broke out in the church in which parishioners of St. Anna accused Hirschman of being there as a spy for the Bishop. Hirschman was subsequently detained, and a number of witnesses were questioned about the incident. Most of those whose statements are extracted here are not identified beyond their name. Most likely they were local artisans.

QUESTIONING OF WITNESSES

On the 28th day of October, 1523
Simprecht Hoser testifies that on last Sunday, which was the 22nd, he went to hear the sermon in St. Anna and was listening to the morning

---

3. Stadtarchiv Augsburg (hereafter StadtAA), Urgicht Claus Hirschman, October 28–December 8, 1523.

service from the gallery. Looking down into the church, he saw the beadle, [Claus] Hirschman, with a group of people standing around him and arguing. He went down and approached them. The beadle was saying that he was there [at St. Anna] on behalf of his Gracious Lord [i.e., the Bishop], and then [Christoph] Herwart[4] said, "God is the Lord." To this, the beadle responded, "My Gracious Lord [the Bishop] is My Lord, and you are also My Lord," to which Herwart said, "I am not your Lord." The beadle then said, "Why do you then allow yourself so often to be accused of being a Lord?" And Herwart said, "The Devil should thank anyone who accuses me of being a Lord," and with that he walked away. Otherwise Hoser didn't hear Herwart say anything else.

Marx Miller said the same as Hoser, adding that as he approached, the beadle was speaking in very heated tones and threatening or pointing with his finger, but he [Miller] doesn't know what he was saying. Herwart then came up and grabbed the beadle's finger, and said, "Speak to them with your mouth and not with your hands." To that the beadle responded that whatever he did, he did on the orders of his Gracious Lord [the Bishop], to which Herwart said, "We have one Lord and that is God." Otherwise his testimony is the same as Hoser. . . .

The customs official N. Haug testified as the others did regarding Herwart. As he approached them, he heard a woman say to the others, "He says his Gracious Lord [the Bishop] gave him his orders. He admits himself that he is a snitch." The women and the beadle were yelling at each other, and some called the beadle a snitch, others a rogue, and others assailed him with other insults. But he [Haug] doesn't know them. As they were thus fighting with one another, Herwart sent Haug to the mayor to request that he order the guard to escort the beadle out of the church unharmed. This Haug did. And when he came back into the church, Haug said to the beadle, "Dear man, why is it necessary for you to get involved in such a dispute in the church? Do you want to end up on the butcher's block?"

Lucas Kreler, goldsmith, testifies as did the others in regard to Herwart. The beadle spewed out a lot of heated words. Kreler also went up to them and said to the beadle, "My dear Hirschman, why are you putting

---

4. The Herwarts (also spelled Herwort or Hörwart) were an influential patrician family in Augsburg who were early supporters of the Reformation. Christoph Herwart was a deacon of the church and the brother of Georg Herwart, who would be elected mayor in 1538.

yourself in danger by getting mixed up in this matter?" To which the beadle responded that he was there because he was supposed to observe the pastor [Johann Frosch], for his Gracious Lord [the Bishop] had ordered it. Kreler then asked what the pastor had preached that was inappropriate, and the beadle said, "The pastor preached that if Christ were now to return to earth, the Pope and Emperor would turn him in and send him off to be crucified, as the Pharisees did." At this [Kreler] left and reported it to Father Frosch, but found it was not the case that he had preached this. So he went back to the beadle and said, "Dear man, how is it that you twist the pastor's words so?" To which the beadle said, "What did I say?" And Kreler repeated to [Hirschman] the words as he had said them. But Hirschman denied it. So Kreler asked the people standing around if he had not said it, and many of them said yes, that the beadle had spoken as noted above. The beadle insisted that this wasn't what he had said; rather, he meant the pastor had preached that one no longer had to obey the Pope, or the Emperor, or the Bishop. To this Kreler answered he was still doing the pastor an injustice, for the pastor had not preached this. And with some other words he walked away from the beadle. . . .

Jorg Rumel, weaver, testifies as did the others in regard to what he heard from Herwart. . . . As they were speaking thus with the beadle, a young woman forced her way into the crowd and said to the beadle that (pardon the expression) she shits on him and his Gracious Lord. Herwart was no longer standing with them at the time, but had left.

Felix Hofherr's wife called the beadle a snitch, among other words, and the beadle said, "Run along, my pretty woman,"[5] to which she said, "The pretty women [i.e., prostitutes] are in the priest's houses." Then another woman said, "The Bishop takes in 1,500 gulden a year from such women. I know of no greater pimp in the land than the Bishop. Go on and tell him that too, just as you tell him everything."

Among other words being exchanged, it also happened that Baumgartner's servant said to the beadle, "One must be more obedient to God than to the Bishop," to which the beadle said, "No, I have to be more obedient to the Bishop than to God, because I get 100 gulden a year from him."

5. A euphemism for a prostitute.

1.2 A Decree against Iconoclasm[6]

An Honorable Council of this city of Augsburg, along with the imperial bailiff, earnestly direct and command that no one in this city or its realm abuse or insult the images, coats of arms, paintings, and other monuments that hang or stand in the churches, churchyards, or anywhere else by besmirching them, or otherwise damage or break them, without the knowledge and approval of the authorities. [Otherwise, the perpetrator will face] punishment, depending on the circumstances, on their goods, body, and life. . . . Decreed on March 19, 1524.

1.3 Chronicler Clemens Sender Describes the Protest of 1524[7]

Clemens Sender (1475–c. 1537) was a monk in the Dominican monastery of St. Ulrich and a humanist in the tradition of Conrad Peutinger. His chronicle, which concentrates primarily on events in Augsburg during his lifetime, reflects his suspicion of the new religion.

On the 13th of April [1524], during the night, the shoemaker Jorg Nässlin and his servant besmirched, despoiled, and ruined with cow blood all of the plaques in the churchyard and cloister at the Church of Our Lady,[8] which were put there in memory of the dead and were decorated with figures, crucifixes, the Mount of Olives, Our Dear Lady Mary, and images of the saints. This shoemaker then hid out for three days, afterward turning himself in for his mischief. He was banished from the city for one year; but shortly thereafter he was let back in, and became even more Lutheran than he was before.

On Saint Sixtus' Day [August 6], during the eighth hour of the morning [i.e., between 7:00 and 8:00 AM], around 1,300 men took it upon themselves to gather at Perlach Square in front of the council house and plead to the council to keep the Franciscan friar [Johann Schilling],[9] who was their Lutheran preacher, in his post. For the council here had

6. Staats- und Stadtbibliothek Augsburg (hereafter SuStBA), 2°Aug.10. 2. Abt. fol. 49.

7. *Die Chronik von Clemens Sender von den ältesten Zeiten der Stadt bis zum Jahr 1536*, 156–59. In *Die Chroniken der deutschen Städte* (hereafter CDS), vol. 23 (1894).

8. The city cathedral.

9. A popular friar and preacher at the Franciscan Church and monastery (Barfüsserkirche).

forced [Schilling] to leave town. Their reason [for sending him away] was that the city council in the town of Gmünd had banished him from there because of his rebellious sermons, and also because he had often abandoned his order and behaved no better than a mercenary soldier. While he was inciting rebellion in Gmünd, he lived an unchaste life and was full of wine daily. Then he did the same thing in Augsburg, and kept company with others of the same sort, preaching according to their counsel and suggestions. While he was at it, he did not forget his personal interests, in a short time taking in around 600 gulden.

The council answered that they would look into [the petitioners'] demand faithfully, and until such time as they found another appropriate preacher, they would appoint Doctor Urbanus Rhegius[10] to the position. With this answer, the men who had been sent to the council by the rebellious crowd left quietly. The council assumed the rebellion was already over and done with, and began to deal with other matters in council, meanwhile sending Ulrich Rehlinger and Conrad Herwart to inform Doctor Urbanus [Rhegius]. As they were sitting in council, they started to get worried, and Mayor Hieronymus Imhoff comforted them with these words: "My Lords and fellow councilmen, put all your fears aside, for our people are too obedient and pious to do anything to the council. So be of good cheer!" He had not even finished his words of comfort when a rebellious cry went up outside. The mayor went out and asked what the reason was for such a clamor, to which they replied, "In a word, we want the Franciscan friar to remain our preacher!" And they requested of the council that they allow Christoph Herwart to speak on their behalf and address the council. And so it happened.

Since the rebellion would not be quieted or quashed unless they were given the Franciscan friar as a preacher, this was agreed upon, and the council assumed [the crowd] would quiet down and be grateful. A little while afterward, a rebellious cry was once again raised on the market, which startled and frightened the council. They were afraid to open the windows, and watched secretly through the cracks to see what the mob was doing, not daring to leave the room. The mob sent to the council for the third time, requesting now that no one be punished for gathering and making demands, for their intentions were good. In the twelfth hour [i.e., between 11:00 and 12:00], Doctor [Conrad] Peutinger, on the council's orders, gave this answer: "The council will take it in the spirit in which it was meant if they go home peacefully." Afterward [the councilmen] sat in council until one o'clock.

10. Humanist theologian and priest at the cathedral (cf. documents 1.8 and 4.2).

On St. Lorenz evening [August 9], the council gave a secret order during the night that all their commanders and officers appear at the council house at 6:00 AM with their armor and weapons, as if they were going to war. And so it was done. Then the council occupied the council house and the Lords' and Merchants' Drinking Rooms[11] with the officers. And on this day all the commanders and officers also had to repeat their oath to protect and support the council. . . .

On the 15th of September, the council had two weavers, Hans Kag and Hans Speiser, beheaded on Perlach Hill between the council house and St. Peter's Church. They were both sixty years old and were the captains and ringleaders of the mob in the recent rebellion. And it was announced that they were condemned to death because they were blasphemers, and that on St. Hilary's Day[12] [August 12], they had acted in opposition to the council and to the common good. They were taken quietly out of the irons,[13] and the alarm bell was not rung so that the plebeians wouldn't again become rebellious. They were not given communion in the irons, rather a mass was read to them there. Hans Speiser did not want to receive the sacrament unless it was given in both kinds [i.e., both bread and wine, in the Protestant tradition]; this the council did not want to do, so that he died without it. But Hans Kag took it in devotion in one kind.

1.4 Hans Kag and Hans Speiser, Executed for Rebellious Talk in 1524[14]

Hans Kag and Hans Speiser were only two of a number of men who gathered to present demands to the city council in August of 1524. Concerned about the general state of unrest throughout the empire (the German Peasants' War), the council made an example of the two weavers by beheading them as ringleaders in the uprising. As is the case with many interrogations from the early sixteenth century, the questions Kag and Speiser are answering here have not survived, and can only be inferred from their responses.

---

11. The Drinking Rooms were the social and political centers of elite society (see Chapter Three).

12. St. Hilarie et sociae.

13. A jail built along the hill beside the council house (*Eisenberg*, "Iron Hill") in which prisoners were locked as punishment.

14. StadtAA, Urgichten Hans Kag and Hans Speiser, September 11–14, 1524.

Witness statement from an anonymous "snitch"

Last St. Magnus Day [September 6] at Regitzer's,[15] they were sitting together in a group of six, namely with Hans Speiser, Paul Kirschner, the cardmaker on crutches, Ambrose Eitel, and he himself (N.).[16] Hans Kag started things by saying, "Although we have to lie low for now, it won't be longer than until Christmas, and then we'll go for it with full force." He also said, among other things, "*Eiya,* to goddamn hell with all the fat cats." Thereupon Hans Speiser said, "*Eiya,* if we did it like they did in Austria back then—there they threw them out of the windows." Paul Kirschner said, "It would serve them all goddamn right." The crippled cardmaker said, "If I were as straight as any other, then I'd know what to do, but as it is I must keep my silence."

Interrogations of Hans Kag

On September 11, 1524, Hans Kag was questioned without torture.

To the first question: He says that he didn't say anything other than, "Come Christmas, we will elect those who aren't against God's Word to the Twelve[17] and as guild masters. Others we have among us [i.e., guild masters] are against God's Word."

To the second question: The reason he said it is that Ulrich Richsner has a daughter who married a monk, and the weaver's guild doesn't want to tolerate him [in their guild], although it can be proven that they are pious, honorable people.[18] But before this, they put up with illegitimate children, and these are still among them [in the guild].

To the third question: He only said this because Polinger, a weaver, and two others came up to him on Perlach [Square] and told him that the guild won't accept the monk, Richsner's son-in-law, which upset him. And it seemed strange that the guild had accepted those born illegitimately, and now won't tolerate pious people.

To the fourth question: He doesn't know who the two people were with whom he spoke, and he has otherwise not bothered about it. He was not plotting anything . . . [and] he never had in mind taking any action against an Honorable Council. . . .

---

15. Hans Regitzer, publican at the Golden Eagle on Hinterer Perlach (located just behind the council house).

16. "N." for no name (the anonymous snitch).

17. Guild representatives in the Large Council, the city's lower governing body.

18. On the Reformation debates about clerical marriage, see Chapter Four.

All of this was admitted without torture, as noted above.

Once again [he was] questioned severely.

After being hoisted [on the strappado] three times without weights,[19] and again three times with the smaller weights, he says nothing other than what is above.

On the 12th of September 1524, Hans Kag said without torture,

On St. Magnus Day he, Paul Kirschner, Speiser, and the limping cardmaker were at Regitzer's for a beer, talking about this and that, and among other things he said, "We need to lie low until Christmas, until we get [Lord Mayor Rehlinger] on our side. He'll take up the banner and then we can go for it. . . ." What moved him to say this was the fact that he heard from Ulrich Richsner that someone had fired a gun at the monk at the Franciscan Church [Johann Schilling]. The shot came from a painted house across the moat (where they used to cast guns), while the monk, the *praepositus,* and another young monk were sitting in his room at table. And the shot only missed going into the room and killing [Schilling] by a little, perhaps a hand. So he said that if Mayor Rehlinger were in office, he would have prevented it. He thinks it was Speiser who said, "If we treated them like they did in Austria, then we'd throw them out of the windows." Anyway someone said it; and it wasn't the cardmaker, or Kirschner, or the other guy, so he has to assume it was Speiser who said it.

On the 12th of September, 1524, [Kag first responds that he knows nothing to a series of unknown questions]. Afterward he is tortured [on the strappado] without weights three times, and says that one day after the people were at the council house, he saw My Lord Mayor Georg Vetter entering Stephinger Gate, and wanted to reprove him, with goodly words and in a brotherly way, to give up his whore. He also wanted to bring charges against this mayor before the council, because he (Kag) once was involved with a case of manslaughter, which cost him a lot of money. And Mayor Vetter was in a position to prevent this, but he didn't. So Kag wanted to accuse him. He and three other people also wanted to beat up the guild master Prigel, because they were once at his house having some wine and he called them rogues and scabby weavers.

---

19. The strappado worked by raising the accused off the floor by his or her arms, which were tied together behind the back, putting great stress on the shoulders and usually dislocating them. The pain was intensified by hanging weights on the defendant's feet (see the illustration in document 1.5).

[Here the sign +0+, see below]. He and others named hereafter had planned together that after Christmas, they would petition to the council together with the publicans to do away with the drink tax.[20] And if it didn't work, then, if he had his way, they would demand it with force. That was his intent, and those named hereafter were his accomplices: Christian Beiss, Speiser, Caspar Pfahler, [and] Raphael Weber. He can't think of anyone else to name right now, but will think about it and come up with some more by tomorrow. . . .

September 14, 1524, Hans Kag [was] questioned without torture.

He stakes his life on it that he is not aware of having made the remark about taking up the banner. But he was remiss in not asking that the cardmaker and Haug be questioned, and requests now that these two be interrogated. If they say so, then he must have said it, but what he said above was out of fear of being tortured. And if Speiser said this of him, then he is doing him wrong. . . . And as he does not want to admit anything, all of his former testimony is read back to him. He confesses to everything up to the sign [+0+], and then says he lied. Afterward, upon further questioning without torture, he simply stuck to all his former testimony. Thereupon he was taken away from the Lords.

STATEMENTS BY HANS SPEISER

[On September 13, 1524, Hans Speiser responds mostly negatively to a series of unknown questions, without torture.]

. . . Upon further questioning he admits that he said, "In Austria they beheaded ten or twelve people. There they tried to throw them out of the windows." But he wasn't referring to the council or anyone else here. He was drinking beer at Regitzer's on St. Magnus' Day with Paul Kirschner, Hans Kag, the limping cardmaker, and Augustine Haug.

Upon severe questioning, tortured twice without weights, he says that he thinks Kag said, "By Christmas things will change," meaning the guild elections, in other words that they would get rid of the guild master by voting him out.

Tortured again without weights, he says in sum that since that Saturday [August 6] when the people were at the council house, he has neither talked about the situation nor heard anyone talking about it, except for the part about the guild master as above.

20. Excise taxes on alcoholic beverages were high and very unpopular.

Afterward, being tortured once with smaller weights, he admits that he said that about Austria, but only meant it harmlessly, and he was drunk on beer. After being hoisted twice more with the small weights, he says they said nothing at all about a plot other than that they wouldn't elect the guild master again.

Afterward he also testifies that he heard more than once around town about the articles that were supposedly made at Has', but he was never in the house. He heard about it on Perlach, in front of the slaughterhouse, and during drinking bouts, and they had nothing else in mind than to petition to the council to agree to [the articles] willingly for the sake of the craftspeople. He and others also planned to meet again in order to petition to the council, as noted above. And if it was not successful, they planned to leave peacefully. He can't really name his collaborators. . . . If they force him [with torture] he will say what they want, and also name people and denounce them, but he will be doing them wrong. . . .

Under threat of torture, [he] says that if the council had not agreed to their petition in respect to drink taxes, the size of measures, merchants, the Burgrave, and the clerics, it was their intent to achieve it with force and without their consent, regardless of the consequences. He can't say with whom he planned this, for he honestly doesn't know them, and if his father, brother, or brother-in-law were among them he wouldn't protect them, but honestly report and name them. He really doesn't know them. It was a lot of young people from among the artisans, whom he doesn't know personally.

A WITNESS DESCRIBES KAG'S REBELLIOUS NATURE

Christian Beiss, weaver, September 25, 1524

At the time that the [Lords'] Drinking Room burned down,[21] he and Kag got into a disagreement and struck each other on the sidewalk by the inn at the Cross,[22] now occupied by the innkeeper called Simerwirt. The fight started over a girl during a dance. Because of this incident, Kag has since then often threatened to strangle him, for Kag has always been a nasty, rebellious person, for which reason he has avoided his company and as far as he knows has not drunk with him in four years.

21. The house on Perlach Hill that housed the Drinking Room burned down in 1488 and was subsequently rebuilt.

22. At the Cross (*Auf dem Kreuz*) is a street behind the Cathedral Quarter, named after Holy Cross Monastery.

To the second question he says, he reached a settlement with Kag over the incident described above about eight days later with the mediation of some journeymen. He thinks they agreed that neither should seek vengeance against the other, but [the details] escape him because of how long ago it was. Since then he has avoided Kag and as far as he knows has not had a drink with him in four years, aside from possibly having ended up in the same company by chance.

1.5 The Strappado, from the Sixteenth-Century Law Code *Layman's Mirror: On the Proper Administration of Civic and Capital Law* by Ulrich Tengel (Illustration)

The Strappado. From Ulrich Tengel, *Layen-Spiegel: Von rechtmässigen ordnungen in Burgerlichen vnd peinlichen regimenten* (Augsburg, 1509), fol. T3r. By permission of the Staats- und Stadtbibliothek Augsburg.

1.6 Demands of the Protesters in 1524[23]

Although references here and in the interrogations were to twelve articles, only nine have survived.

In N. Has the mason's house, they decided to approach the council again and to present twelve articles, and to spread news of this around.

First, that the two preachers at the cathedral and the Dominican Church should be put out of the city.

Second, the old measure [of beer and wine] should be reinstated.[24]

Third, the Burgrave should not be given anything that belongs to the Bishop and the clerics.

Fourth, the clerics should no longer be paid ground rents.

Fifth, beer should be brewed as it was years ago, and there should be no excise tax on it.

Sixth, all [trading] companies should be done away with, and everyone should trade for themselves.

Seventh, the furrier in the irons should be let go.[25]

Eighth, the clerics should pay property taxes and excise taxes.

Ninth, if the council does not want to agree, then they would demand it by force.

1.7 The Interrogation of Anna Fassnacht[26]

Anna Fassnacht was interrogated for seditious talk following the uprising of 1524. In part, her complaint targets paying outsiders to stand guard in the city, while poor local citizens capable of guarding their own hometown go hungry. Again, the questions are missing from the trial transcript.

On September 15, 1524, Anna, Hans Fassnacht the weaver's wife, upon being confronted with her deeds and duly questioned without torture, says:

---

23. Wilhelm Vogt, "Johann Schilling der Barfüsser-Mönch und der Aufstand in Augsburg Jahre 1524," *Zeitschrift des historischen Vereins für Schwaben und Neuburg* 6 (1879), 1–32, Beilage IV.

24. The standard measure for serving beer and wine in public houses had been reduced in 1474, while excise tax per measure remained unchanged.

25. The demand was to release a furrier named Kiessling, who was being held captive for life for threatening to stab the mayor and other officials after beating his wife with a club.

26. StadtAA, Urgicht Anna Fassnacht, September 15–March 10, 1524.

At St. Anna in the church before the sermon, as she recalls it was fourteen days ago next Sunday, she said, "Why don't they let poor people stand guard that don't earn more than a batzen per day? It would be better than taking on outsiders. Where would they get the money for it, though? If it were their money, then it would make sense. And they could take the guard money and buy grain and lard with it."

She was born in Kempten, and Barbara on the corner by St. Anna was her sister.

The money for guards comes from drink taxes, from inspection fees,[27] from property tax, and defense taxes.

If [the councilmen] are going to behave in an ungodly fashion, then the good people of the community would be as good as a council.

September 19, 1524: [Presumably a statement from a witness to Anna's behavior in the church:] Anna Fassnacht said before and after the sermon in St. Anna, "Nothing will happen unless the commoners do it. They now have guards—if only one took the same money and bought grain and lard with it," meaning that it should go to the poor. "They are told to run to the council house when the alarm bell rings,[28] as if they were running to the granary." She further said, "If our men won't do anything about it, then we women will have to do something, for they are making deals under the table. That has to stop in the future. The people will also find out what they are up to (meaning that our men must also sit up there someday [in the government]). *Ei*, they should all get leprosy. . . ."

[Tortured first with thumbscrews and then the strappado, Anna Fassnacht repeats her previous testimony.] She doesn't know what she meant by this talk other than that she would rather see what they are paying outsiders go to the locals, rather than to strangers.

Judgment: Anna, the wife of Hans Fassnacht, who was locked in the irons, took an oath because of her evil seditious slander to stay outside of the city and not come within a six-mile radius around it for the rest of her life, and was thereupon escorted out of town.

---

27. Fees charged by the city from craftspeople for inspecting and certifying their wares. Fassnacht was most likely asked where she thinks the money to pay guards comes from.

28. Reference to laws requiring all local men to defend the city in emergencies. See document 10.7.

II. Fiery Preachers

1.8 Of Serfdom or Servitude: Advice from Godly Laws on How Lords and Their People Should Behave as Christians. Preached by Doctor Urbanus Rhegius in Augsburg, 1525[29]

Urbanus Rhegius' sermon on worldly servitude came as a response to the series of bloody uprisings generally known as the German Peasants' War. Rhegius' sermon was in two parts: the first considered the condition of subjects, and the second provided advice for rulers. In the excerpt from the first part presented here, Rhegius follows Lutheran teaching in explaining the idea of Christian freedom in spiritual rather than worldly terms. Luther's argument that all people belong to one "estate" under God was meant as an attack on the Catholic idea of a privileged "spiritual" estate of clergy, not a call for doing away with social difference. Power within the Christian estate, he explained, should be exercised in accordance with one's worldly office.

It is being asked in light of the Gospels if servitude or serfdom should be tolerated among Christians, who are all born of one earthly father and reborn of one Heavenly Father, and who are all made evangelically free through the blood of Christ. To this question, I answer that the holy Scripture tells us what to say to Lords and servants. . . .

We are all born of Adam as children of wrath, with no difference in our natural origins. We Christians are then born again in water and in spirit, and in this rebirth we become the children of God. . . . Nonetheless, afterward there is a great difference in how the gifts of God, the Holy Spirit, are distributed among mankind. For one is given more than the other, as it pleases God. But only sweet faith sets apart the sons of the kingdom from the sons of damnation.

We are also all priests in Christ, and may appear before God by the power of this priesthood, pray for one another in the spirit of faith, proclaim the kingdom of heaven, and bring our offering of the cross and our praises. But our king's realm is not of this world. He reigns in matters of heaven and the spirit . . . so that the kingdom of the faithful is not a visible, temporal kingdom here on earth, rather a spiritual kingdom of faith. . . .

---

29. From Urbanus Rhegius, *Von leibaygenschaft oder knechthait / wie sich Herren vnnd aygen leüt Christlich halten sollend / Bericht auss gotlichen Rechten . . . Durch D. Urbanum Regium zu Augspurg gepredigt 1525*, c. 1525.

Therefore a believer in Christ is completely free and a Lord of all things, and can and should at the same time be a servant of all people and subject to everyone. For Christian freedom is of the spirit, and should not be a smokescreen for the flesh and unrestrained wickedness. For that reason, civic servitude or serfdom, through which a Christian is subject and bound to a physical person for taxes, tolls, rents, veneration, or whatever else such servitude may entail, may well stand beside evangelical freedom in our kingdom.

[Rhegius then provides numerous examples of pious slaves and masters from the Old and New Testaments.]

Thereby a pious Christian should consider that bondage and servitude were established because of sin, so that he may bear them as a scourge of God. For he professes to be a poor sinner, as he should, and therefore should accept his father's discipline as does an obedient child, and not flee from it. . . .

[In the second chapter of his sermon, Rhegius admonishes those placed in a position of authority to rule with love, wisdom, and in fear of God, as good Christian rulers rather than tyrants.]

1.9 Trying to Silence Otmar Nachtigal, Priest at St. Moritz, for Inflammatory Anti-Protestant Preaching: Entries from City Council Minutes[30]

On Monday, the seventh day of September 1528, an Honorable Council, via their council scribe Martin Hayden, notified the Doctor of Theology and current pastor of St. Moritz [Otmar Nachtigal] of the following report and order: Namely, he has undoubtedly not forgotten that an Honorable Council sent one of their honorable peers and entreated him to avoid, keep away from, and cease preaching that which can lead to and serve to incite rebellion, insurrection, and discord. This he offered and agreed to do. Although an Honorable Council assumed he had complied with this order, he can himself easily perceive from his sermons whether or not he actually did. Thereupon an Honorable Council, for good cause, notified him that he should stay off of and avoid the public streets for a period of time, until an Honorable Council

---

30. StadtAA, Ratsprotokolle 15, 1520–1529, 189r–92r.

revokes the order, at their pleasure. This he should understand as well meaning and for his own good rather than his detriment.

Upon hearing this, Doctor Nachtigal, having understood the notification and an Honorable Council's order, was more than a little surprised that he should stay off the streets and wished to know the reason for it. But he is happy to stop preaching. He had been ready for some time to foreswear preaching, but his Lord the Fugger did not want to permit this, rather pressed him to continue preaching.[31]

Upon this, the council scribe [Hayden] said that the Honorable Council's order was not that [Nachtigal] should abstain from preaching, but that he should stay off the public streets and not use them. Thereupon Doctor Nachtigal said he was prepared to comply with an Honorable Council's order, but asked of [Hayden] if he could not have a day or two to get his things in order. To this [Hayden] replied that he was only delivering an Honorable Council's order, and it was not in his power to allow him anything. He knows well where to get permission. To this Doctor Nachtigal thanked me [Hayden] for the message and we parted ways. [This occurred] on the same day, in St. Moritz's Church, with no one else present.

On the twelfth day of September 1528, an Honorable Council once again sent their council scribe to Doctor Otmar Nachtigal to notify and remind him of that which had been arranged with him last Monday in St. Moritz's Church on the council's behalf, and namely, that he gave his word to an Honorable Council's representatives to refrain from that which can lead to rebellion, discord, and insurrection. This an Honorable Council, after all, expected to be obeyed. However, [Nachtigal] did not comply with it (as he himself knows), rather acted in violation of it, and did not keep his word. And he also recently accused several people in his sermon as heretics. This grave matter came to an Honorable Council's notice, giving them good reason to order him to stay off of the public streets in this city, and leaving them no choice. An Honorable Council then again notified and reminded [Nachtigal] of this order and that it was still in force, which he should understand as more for his own good than to his detriment, and should follow so long as an Honorable Council favors it.

Thereupon Doctor Nachtigal answered that, since he is preaching and acting in obedience to His Imperial Majesty and his published

---

31. The wealthy Fugger family patronized the preacher at St. Moritz.

Edict [of Worms],[32] he is more than a little surprised that an Honorable Council should forbid him to walk the streets, and allow those preachers who preach and act in violation of the edict to walk them. And although it is true, as he admits, that he called a number of [Protestant] preachers heretics, he does not remember preaching anything that would have caused any trouble or insurrection and rebellion. For His Imperial Majesty in His Majesty's edict also called these preachers heretics. And it is also clear that these pastors' sermons would be much more likely to cause rebellion and insurrection. But ultimately he is ready and willing to comply with an Honorable Council's order.

On that day [September 15, 1528], the matter with Doctor Nachtigal was settled through Count Gabriel von Ortenburg and Lord Jorg Truchsess, Lord Georg Vetter, Lord Hieronymous Imhof, Lord Ulrich Rehlinger (the new and old mayors) and Doctor [Conrad] Peutinger on behalf of an Honorable Council by allowing Nachtigal back on the streets, but with the understanding that he will conduct himself in a friendly and not an offensive manner, and cease preaching at St. Moritz for now.

This all came about because this Doctor [Nachtigal] incriminated the other preachers here as heretics from the pulpit on Sunday, the sixth of September. Supposedly he said other things as well, which will be investigated.

1.10 Defense of the Augsburg Preachers against a Letter from Doctor Martin Luther[33]

In 1533, Luther took offense with the claim of the Augsburg preachers that he agreed with their teachings, which he condemned as too Zwinglian. Luther wrote a letter to the Augsburg council demanding that they prohibit Augsburg's preachers from capitalizing on his name or he would openly condemn them in a public writing. These excerpts are taken from the local preachers' response to Luther's attack.

Grace and peace from God the Father through our Lord Jesus Christ. Farsighted, honorable, wise, Auspicious, and Imperious Lords, some days ago, a copy of a letter that Doctor Martin Luther wrote to the

---

32. Reference to Emperor Charles V, who had forbidden Lutheran teaching and condemned Luther as a heretic in the Edict of Worms in 1521.

33. StadtAA, Literaliensammlung, Reformationsakten 1, ad 1533 Okt. 16, "Verteidigung der Augsburger Predikanten auf das Schreibens Dr. Martin Luthers" (copy).

council was delivered to us by Lord Mayor Ulrich Rehlinger, on [Your Lords'] behalf, for us to examine, so that we could let [you] know what our thoughts are. We are most grateful to [Your Lords'] fatherly loyalty for not keeping this reproach from us (it having occurred without our knowledge and behind our backs), and instead requesting an appropriate response. This we provide [here] summarized into six points:

First, Doctor M. Luther writes that it appears to him that we maintain and claim in the pulpit and otherwise that we agree with those from Wittenberg on the doctrine of the holy and most worthy sacrament of the body and blood of our Lord Jesus Christ. To that we say that we strive fervently to be in agreement with Doctor M. Luther and the church of Wittenberg, and all of the faithful, not only as concerns this point of the worthy sacrament of the true body and blood of Christ, but in all beneficial doctrines that emanate from the true and certain word of God, and are in accordance with the faith. For what we present to the community of God is nothing but the pure Gospel. . . .

Since, however, a difference of opinion has arisen between Doctor M. Luther and other evangelical servants over the sacrament [of the Eucharist], we carefully considered the writings of both sides with an open mind, and concluded that it is only a fight over words. For both sides profess that what they present to the faithful is the presence of Christ's body and blood in the Eucharist. We thus eschewed all disagreements, and warned everyone to keep out of them. For it is not the way of the community of God to quarrel, especially at the holy Lord's Supper, at which we gather in the greatest of love and unity in order to remember the death of Christ. . . . What would be more damaging than this—at the Supper of Love (as the ancients called it), to tear love apart? . . .

Second, Doctor M. Luther writes that we so mince our words in respect to the Holy Sacrament that one could get either opinion out of them, and we don't straightforwardly present a single point of view. Answer: This he writes in response to an unfounded report from those who made this claim about us, for he has never listened to us, and the opposite will be found in our published Catechism. For in it we do not mince words, nor do we present our outlook so obscurely that one could take either opinion from it—rather, we state one opinion so straightforwardly that anyone can well see what it is (as he himself subsequently noted). . . .

Third, [Luther] explains that it is truly a grave matter to let the common man go about with false opinions, the one believing this and the other believing that, while both of them with their separate and opposing beliefs listen to the same word and attend the same sacrament.

Answer: We teach the pure, true faith in our Lord Jesus Christ, the foundation, the prophets, and the apostles according to the content of the holy Scripture. We draw on the words of Christ as he mandated his holy Lord's Supper, as they were recorded by the holy Evangelists and Saint Paul, and also let them stand in their correct and natural meaning. Therefore it is true, as Doctor M. Luther writes, that one hears only one word from us. But we are not aware that people are coming to the sacrament in separate and opposing beliefs (as he was told), nor can we know this, because neither we nor anyone else can see into the hearts of the people. That only God, the knower of hearts, can do. We do not bestow faith, nor should we or do we wish to govern the faith of another. . . .

We present the Word of the Lord faithfully and admonish each person to look into himself before partaking of the Bread of the Lord and drinking the Lord's Drink, so that he is not guilty for the body and blood of the Lord. But whether our admonishment bears fruit after we cultivate and plant it is not the result of our efforts, or within our power, rather due to God, who is the one who causes it to blossom. And whoever thereupon comes to the Lord's Supper, we do not see as Lutheran or Zwinglian, but as a disciple of Christ, whom Luther serves just as we do. . . .

Fourth, [Luther] accuses us of basically seeing in the Holy Sacrament of the body and blood of Christ nothing more than mere bread and wine, and presenting only that to the people, etc. To this we say that we are being unfairly treated by Doctor M. Luther or whomever is falsely representing us to him, as [Your Lords] can conclude from the confession of our faith regarding the Holy Sacrament that we presented to [you]. Not only that, but as often as we have celebrated the Lord's Supper here, we have openly stated our belief before the community of God, and no one has ever heard from us that we teach or hold that we are giving the Christians merely wine and bread in the Eucharist, rather that it is the true body and blood of Christ. This we openly state in our published Catechism with these words: "Here we see that Christ takes the bread and the wine, his body and his blood." Therefore we profess and believe that in accordance with the words of Christ, the bread and the wine (and not in, beside, or with the bread, as some have added to the words of Christ) are the true body and blood of Christ, but in mystery. That is, as Luther says in his confession, in sacramental essence and unity. . . .

These words [this is my body, etc.] we declare before the congregation and admonish them to believe firmly. We also leave them undistorted and unchanged, in their natural and proper sense and as Christ meant them, for they should not and cannot be changed by any person. This doctrine of the Lord's Supper we keep not under the name and deed of Luther, as he incorrectly claims, but under the name of Christ. . . .

Fifth, [Luther writes], he knows all too well that we teach Zwinglianism. Answer: We teach neither Lutheranism nor Zwinglianism, rather [we] remain in the simple teaching of our Lord Jesus Christ, who is not only our master, but that of Luther and Zwingli as well.

It would have been more appropriate for Doctor M. Luther to write to us first to give an account of our beliefs before he disparaged us by bringing charges to [Your Lords] based on some allegations, a fact that we present to [Your Lords] only for further consideration. We must accept the fact that he threatened to bear witness to this before God and all the world by publishing it, although we are comforted in that we provided no grounds for this, other than that he perhaps put too much faith in some people who reported this to him behind our back, rather than asking or questioning us. . . .

Sixth and last, he is amazed that we can be so bold as to pride ourselves in using his name and doctrine, when (as he writes) we are a foe of his doctrine and name. Answer: Either he is wrong, which is surely not the case, or once again he was falsely informed. For we did not lay claim to his name, other than once or twice quoting him, [because] one should not become followers of any person. We preach Christ the crucified, not Luther, and are opposed to every sect that in human fashion falls into zealousness, quarrelsomeness, and discord. We have as little interest—yea, much less interest—in being Lutheran or Zwinglian, or being called Lutheran or Zwinglian, as we have in being Paulian or Appolean.[34] We have freed ourselves from the Pope and human doctrine, God be praised, in order that we no longer have to put ourselves into servitude to man. . . .

In respect to his additional claim that we are foes to his doctrine and name, we say that although we do not label ourselves with his doctrine and name, or anyone else's, still we are no foe to it. But we do not wish to be bound to his or any other person's doctrine. We are happy to oblige his request that an Honorable Council see to it that we do not lay claim either to his doctrine or to his name, for we have not boasted of his or another human name up to now, and do not wish to do so in the future. Rather, we want to boast of the name of our master, which is neither Zwingli nor anyone else (as Luther claims of us), but the one Christ, Lord and master of us all.

34. Reference to 1 Cor. 1:12 ("One of you says, 'I follow Paul'; another, 'I follow Apollos.' . . ."), in which the faithful are admonished not to quarrel over leadership but remain united in Christ.

This we wished to present to [Your Lords] simply so that an Honorable Council sees that Doctor M. Luther is unfair to us in his letter. For it is not our belief that mere bread and wine is received by the faithful in the Lord's Supper, as is explained above, rather we profess before God and everyone that the Bread of the Lord and the drink in the Supper of the Faithful is the true body and the true blood of Christ . . . not just as a symbol, but in truth. . . .

[Your Lords'] devoted servants to the Gospel
Sebastian Mayer
Michael Weinmar
Bonifatius Wolfart
Michael Keller
Wolfgangus Musculus
Johannes Held
Wolfgangus Haug
Johannes Ehinger
Leonhardus Regelius
Jacobus Dachser

1.11 Attempts to Tone Down Heated Sermons, 1554[35]

The period between Emperor Charles V's occupation of Augsburg during the so-called Armored Imperial Diet of 1548 and the recognition of both religions with the Religious Peace of Augsburg in 1555 is referred to as "the Interim." During this phase, Catholicism again dominated in the city. This decree, published shortly before the Peace of Augsburg was concluded, demonstrates the concerns of the council about hotheaded preaching further polarizing the confessions in a volatile climate.

Past events and daily experiences make it obvious to everyone what utility and good follow from peaceful and friendly cohabitation, and what detriment as well as ruinous harm and damage to the soul, body, honor, and goods must be expected (and has so often occurred in large communities) as a result of disagreeableness, envy, and hate. . . . An Honorable Council, in accordance with its office, is bound to support everything that serves the honor of God and the welfare of this city. . . . However, it has come to the council's attention that, among other things, the

---

35. StadtAA, Literaliensammlung, Reformationsakten, April 20, 1554, Vertrag an die Herren Predikanten.

preachers in the cathedral have been employing heated and harsh words from the open pulpit. [Therefore, to prevent further anger and hate, the council has] worked together with the Lords of the cathedral chapter, and managed to get them to offer to counsel their preachers to strive from now on toward appropriate modesty, and to avoid heated insults entirely. Likewise, an Honorable Council has renewed its charge to the booksellers to cease selling all kinds of slanderous and defamatory books from either of the religions. . . . Thus it is the request and fatherly admonishment of an Honorable Council that you heretofore do your part to use appropriate restraint, [and] diligently admonish the common man to due obedience and brotherly love. . . .

III. Establishing Protestant Discipline

1.12 Punishment of Anabaptists, 1528[36]

The "new sect" of Anabaptism was forbidden in Augsburg in 1527 in a decree that outlawed practicing it, meeting about it, teaching it, or harboring Anabaptist preachers and teachers.

April 16, 1528
Elizabeth Wollschager of Augsburg, Anna Schuster of Hirblingen, and Barbara Dötz from Scheuringen, in violation of an Honorable Council of this city of Augsburg's decree, did meet and gather here at a suspicious time and in a suspicious place, along with others. And they also did not want to swear allegiance to this city upon said council's order. Therefore the council, out of mercy nonetheless, decided and determined that they should be beaten out of the city with rods, and move six miles away, not coming near here again nor returning to this city or its territory for the rest of their lives. All heed this warning.

January 22, 1528
Benedict Klain and Blasy Daniel, both from Augsburg, who are here on the pillory,[37] did in violation of an Honorable Council's public decree house and support secret preachers and Anabaptists, and provided them with food, drink, and cover, and they congregated and assembled. Thus they acted disobediently and in violation of their legal authorities and

36. StadtAA, Urgichten K5, 1528.

37. A pillory was a defaming platform (in Augsburg located on the side of the council house) where delinquents stood while their crimes and sentences were announced publicly by a town crier.

the ban on Anabaptism. Therefore an Honorable Council, and out of mercy nonetheless, decided and determined that they both should be beaten out of the city with rods, be sworn over the Lech [River] and also over the Danube, and should not come back over for the rest of their lives. All heed this warning.

1.13 Statement of Agnes Vogel, Interrogated for Anabaptism, 1528[38]

On May 14, 1528, Agnes, the wife of soldier Paul Vogel, from Augsburg, says under questioning without torture,

She was rebaptized before St. Michael's Day[39] by the tailor Hans Leopold, in the upstairs room of a public house in Wellenburg. Also baptized at that time was a village boy that she doesn't know. She was moved to this baptism by the preachers here, for she went to their sermons for a good four years, while one preached this and the other that. One saw a symbol in the sacrament and the other would have it be flesh and blood. Thus they preached against one another, and made her all confused, so that she didn't know what to believe, and so she wanted to hear the others as well. For this reason she went out to Wellenburg with the shoemaker Simbrecht Widenman's wife and Rispin Pötin, and listened to the afore-noted Leopold's sermon. Based on what he taught her and what he showed her in the Scriptures, she believed that if she followed him, she would be saved, and as noted above, she let herself be baptized. Before that she was never at a meeting, and also never knew or heard of any leader, and she also didn't know if Leopold was a leader or not. . . .

Her husband doesn't know anything about her being rebaptized, and was not happy that their landlady, Mrs. Hafner, came to see her. And if her husband had found the leader in the house he would have thrown him down the stairs. . . .

1.14 Religious Debate in the Street, 1529[40]

This extract concerns a disagreement over religion that broke out while a group of neighbors were gathered in front of armory officer Georg Zeindlweber's house to sit and talk at the end of their workday. The group

38. StadtAA, Urgicht Agnes Vogel, May 14, 1528.

39. September 29 of the previous year (1527) (Michaelis archangelus). The first council decree making Anabaptism illegal was not issued until October 11 of 1527.

40. StadtAA, Urgicht Georg Zeindlweber, June 12, 1529.

included a number of men of different trades along with several of their wives and maids. The argument broke out between Zeindlweber, who was a gunsmith and the officer in charge of the local armory, and Heinrich Meckenloher, a city guard. Presented here is only one of a number of witness statements taken from several neighbors after Zeindlweber was arrested for blasphemy.

On the 12th day of June 1529, Peter Sölber, goldsmith, testified that as he came up to [the armory officer Georg Zeindlweber][41] and [Heinrich] Meckenloher, the armory officer said, "The princes are meeting in Nuremberg; they'll make a new [Berthold] Aichelin[42] to stop them from hanging people like that" [i.e., for their religious beliefs]. Then the armory officer told Meckenloher that he carries a rosary so that Aichelin won't catch him, and trusts in God that they will now pass a measure so the people will no longer be hanged. And eventually, among other talk, it happened that Meckenloher said that he wished that everyone would do unto him as he does unto others, for that is how he treats everyone. To this the armory officer answered, "So you're a saint, come on and let me kiss your feet!" and he reached for Meckenloher's feet. [Sölber] doesn't know what Meckenloher said then. Then the armory officer said that he found it odd that they always go after the poor Christians that way, and poor Christians have to be sacrificed just because of little errors of faith. "Why don't they go after the Jews?" [the armory officer said]. "The Jews actually say that Mary was a whore and Christ was a bastard."

To this Meckenloher responded, "If I heard this from a villain of a Jew, then I would stake my life on the fact that he wouldn't say it again! He'd have to teach me a thing or two, or I him." Upon these words, the armory officer became angry, because he thought that Meckenloher had insulted him as a villain. Thereupon Meckenloher repeated that if he heard it from a villain of a Jew, he would do as described above. But he hadn't heard it from a Jew, but from a Christian, for he held the armory officer for a Christian.

After this the armory officer started in and said, "Dear Heinz, if you or I were to die, it would be the same as if a fly should shit on the wall, for God is so almighty, that if you or I die, he can make another Meckenloher or armory officer. He made the whole world, so he can do

41. Throughout the case, Zeindlweber is referred to only as *Zeugwart* (i.e., "the armory officer").

42. Reference to Berthold Aichelin, a provost who served the Swabian League and was known for executing hundreds of peasants during the Peasants' War.

away with it and make another. It's not our problem. If we die in faith, we'll be saved. If we die without faith, then it means nothing, the same as fly dirt (pardon the expression)."

Then they both started talking about Mary again, and how the Jews say that she must have been a whore, and Christ a bastard. The armory officer said to Meckenloher, "If you want to be such a Jew-slayer, then go down and slay Master Michael [Keller];[43] he says openly that the mass is knave's work and meaningless."

To this Meckenloher answered, "I don't want to slay anyone, for if Master Michael talks a lot, then he'll have to answer for it."

The armory officer responded, "*Ei,* but you're a Jew fighter, you want to kill the Jews, why not him too? The Jews say openly that Mary was a whore, and Christ a bastard. And yes, she WAS a whore, and Christ WAS a bastard!" And it is Sölber's opinion that the armory officer spoke these words so heatedly to Meckenloher in order to get Meckenloher to come after him, because he had before insisted so strongly that if he heard such a thing from a Jew, that he wouldn't let him get away with it. For the armory officer said three times at least, "Yes, yes, yes, she was a whore," and Meckenloher answered, "I won't stay here any longer, for where one steals the honor of the Mother of God and insults her, I will not stay." And with that he stood up and made to leave.

As he did so, the armory officer called after him (pardon the expression), "Like shit, she is God's mother! She's the Devil's mother," and the armory officer further said to Meckenloher, "*Ei,* go on in the Devil's name, you warped ninny or rogue! Let's just forget whether or not you could run me through the street with the Devil, or I you with the Gospel." Meckenloher said, "*Ei* deliver us from the Devil, we have nothing to do with the Devil!" The armory officer then said to Meckenloher's wife, "The Devil is in him, he's on his back, he's talking through him," to which the woman responded, "*Ei,* he has nothing to do with the Devil," and the armory officer said, "Yes, he's sitting on his back, he is talking through him."

Upon this he, Sölber, led Meckenloher away. And then the armory officer stood up, reached for his weapon, and yelled after Meckenloher, "Some fighter you are, what Peasants' War have you been in, how many have you killed, you cripple? I'd like to knock you on your back with a stone, some Jew-killer you are!" But Meckenloher did not respond with

43. Reference to Michael Keller (Cellarius), radical follower of Zwingli and pastor at the Franciscan Church in Augsburg from 1524 to 1544. Keller was a popular preacher and was influential in Augsburg's Reformation process. His anti-Catholic sermons raised the ire of local Catholics.

a single word—perhaps he didn't hear it, since Sölber was leading him home. And thus they separated.

1.15 Chronicler and Brewer Georg Siedler[44] Describes the Reforms of 1537[45]

1537. On Monday, the 8th of January, there was a council election, and Hans Welser became mayor, a brash young man who would make a better military officer than mayor. Immediately upon taking over the mayoral office and powers, on the 17th of January, he called together the Large Council[46] and did away with the mass. And then right on the 18th, he began with the civic workmen to tear down all the altars, paintings, panels, lamps, and more in all the churches in the city, starting with Our Lady and then St. Ulrich, St. Moritz, and other churches. He compelled the clergy to become citizens, and to accept their civic duties and take an oath of citizenship, which some did. Some didn't, and they soon left the city. Right afterward on the 22nd of July [sic], on the orders of an Honorable Council, all Roman Catholic holidays were denounced from the pulpits, and only Christmas, New Year's, and Annunciation Day were to be celebrated.

1.16 An Honorable Council of the City of Augsburg's Decree to Establish a Christian, Disciplined, and Decent Life[47]

The rules laid down in this unusually harsh ordinance, representing the Zwinglian ideal, were short lived.

September 11, 1541
An Honorable Council of the laudable imperial city of Augsburg has observed and wishes to point out how unworthy and reprehensible it is,

44. Augsburg brewer and chronicler Georg Siedler (1559–1619) was privileged as a child to attend school to learn not only German but also Latin. He kept his unique record of city events from around 1597 until shortly before his death in 1619. Siedler relied on earlier chronicles and other records for events that occurred before his lifetime.

45. StadtAA, Chroniken 20, Chronik von Siedler, 1055–1619, 95r.

46. A lower governing body made up primarily of guild masters, which provided support for the higher ("Small") Council. After 1548, the Large Council was also dominated by elites.

47. SuStBA, 2°Aug.324 Band 2, Nr. 5.

in all areas of human life, to bear a title in name only, and not truly to demonstrate it by deeds. This is especially the case when it comes to the honor of God, the welfare of mankind, and proper order. Indeed, when one considers that we strive to be Christians and pride ourselves with leading a godly life, what would be more appropriate for us, more than for any other race of man, to prove our name and faith before God and the world with hope, love, humility, patience, discipline, honor, and all decency. . . .

But based on the way we behave and have been spending our lives for many years now, it is unfortunately apparent that there has never been more excessive eating and drinking, feasting and splurging, vanity, disloyalty, lying, envy, hate, lack of trust in God, offending of our neighbors, avarice, usury, cursing, swearing, blasphemy, lack of faith, and, in general, all manner of vice and vanity being practiced everywhere by young and old as there is now. And now that we have been given plenty of warning, the justified anger of God has come upon us all, the small, poor, miserable remaining lot of Christianity. Many kingdoms, lands, and people are taken from us, and an innumerable flock of innocent Christians are wretchedly being sent into eternal slavery like beasts. In some cases they are being horribly murdered, without sparing women and children, small and big, or old and worn-out people, and hands are being washed in their blood. We have been repeatedly visited with plague, famine, and sorrow in a short period of years; and now, in addition to other plagues, the Turk, the true scourge of God, the new Attila and Maximinus, is nearing us again with all his power. Just recently, the Christian army in Hungary suffered a bitter and severe defeat; and even more lament and misery is at our door and will soon be upon us. But who can really wonder? . . .

Therefore, an Honorable Council, as the orderly authority, recognizes its duty, in order to honor almighty God, to look into this and see if the vice and vanity can be somewhat reined in, if not entirely done away with, and an improvement made. [The council thus] decrees, orders, wills, and proclaims that henceforth, each and every citizen, resident, and subject of this city, young and old, male and female, rich and poor, with no exceptions, will until further notice hold no dance, whether at weddings, engagements, or otherwise, openly or secretly. There will be no courting with string instruments, singing, piping, or drumming in the streets, whether during processions to church or otherwise. And everyone should also refrain from all cheering, yelling, and screaming, and from indecent or shameful songs, gestures, and talk, on the streets and inside.

Likewise, all musicians, waffle sellers,[48] acrobats, and ridiculous, wanton comedians or dancers should stay out of the inns and guildhalls.

As well, everyone should abstain from excess and luxury in dinner parties and meals, and abide by the limits set by the Discipline Ordinance—that is, keep it to four courses or dishes.

And because drinking to conclude contracts has been found to be most detrimental and harmful, henceforth no contract drink may be drunk over any kind of goods or sale. But it is not herewith forbidden to give or receive a reasonable cash tip to seal the contract.

Likewise, because the Discipline Lords[49] have already ordered that the vice of drunkenness be harshly punished, henceforth this should be enforced with even more diligence than before. And whoever displays evidence and appearance of drunkenness, whether by words or actions, should be taken to the Fool's House without fail, or otherwise be penalized appropriately.

And so that those drunkards who sit in public houses daily, uselessly wasting their money, and letting their wives and children go without, have all the less opportunity for their debauched lifestyle: No publican should allow drinking bouts before midday either on holidays or workdays, whether in guildhalls or in public houses, inside or outside of this city. And they should not allow any wine to be served before the clock has struck one. And once it is one o'clock, the publican may sell and serve wine, but no longer than until the clock strikes three.[50] Then he should immediately settle with the guests and serve no more wine or allow any more drinking or lingering at table. However, the honorable principals of the guilds may hold their conventions, meetings, and customary drinking bouts[51] in accordance with tradition, although in moderation. But all after parties are herewith forbidden.

In addition, no citizen or resident may leave the city in order to drink within a radius of two miles around the city, nor host any drinking bout outside of town.

An Honorable Council also herewith renews all of their previous ordinances and laws regarding gambling, blasphemy, vanity, usury, slander, idleness, going for walks and gambling during the sermon, and

48. Boys who sold waffles or *Oblaten* (wafers) had a reputation for loud voices and impoverished circumstances.

49. Lords or judges appointed to hold court over violators of discipline ordinances.

50. The experiment with a two-hour serving time ceased to be enforced within the year; by 1553, closing time had returned to the traditional 9:00.

51. *Schenke*, i.e., drinks served to welcome new journeymen and for other ritual purposes at guild meetings.

everything else that has been decreed (and in some cases included in the Discipline Ordinance),[52] and reminds and orders everyone to adhere to them, on pain of the established penalties or worse, as often as anyone violates these rules. All heed this warning and avoid punishment.

An Honorable Council in its fatherly role expects as well that every House Father and householder, as well as all those who have reached the age of reason, will themselves recognize that they should diligently listen to the preachers of God's Word, continue with fervent prayer to God . . . practice brotherly Christian love for one another, and observe how horribly Sodom and Gomorrah were punished with consuming flames when they persisted in their sins, while the Ninevites, as repentant, penitent people, were mercifully spared from the threatened punishment. . . . Amen.

1.17 Decree Posted at the City Gate to Attend Sermons on Holidays[53]

An Honorable Council of this laudable city of Augsburg has already openly decreed that henceforth, no one should be found on holiday mornings strolling, playing games, or chatting on the squares or in front of the gates. Therefore it is the earnest command, will, and order of the well-considered Honorable Council that the guards under the main gates write down the names of all persons who go in or out of the gates on holiday mornings between 7:00 and 9:00. If they don't know them, they should ask them their name. These they should take immediately after midday to the Lord Mayor currently in office and hand them over, so that appropriate measures can be taken against these disobedient citizens in accordance with the above-noted decree. Decreed by an Honorable Council on Thursday, May 24, 1543.

---

52. Reference to the Discipline Ordinance of 1537, excerpted in document 4.4.
53. SuStBA, 4°Aug.1021 4 Band 1 Abt., Nr. 4.

Chapter Two
Enforcing the Peace of Augsburg

Taking the dictum *cuius regio, eius religio* (whose realm, his religion) as a guiding principle, the Religious Peace of Augsburg that was concluded in 1555 gave rulers throughout the Holy Roman Empire the right to determine whether their subjects should practice the Catholic or the Lutheran faith. Under the terms negotiated by the Emperor, Augsburg remained biconfessional, required to tolerate both religions. The city council expressed their commitment to religious peace by noting in that year that "one does not feel burdened by the coexistence of two religions in Augsburg."[1] Augsburg thus became one of only a handful of biconfessional towns that allowed their citizens to choose between the two accepted religions, while government was shared by members of both faiths. For a time, the matter appeared to be settled.

As illustrated in Chapter One, the people of Augsburg had been debating the relative merits of various religious doctrines for decades; and if their debates were at times heated, there is also ample evidence of interconfessional marriage and regular socialization between Catholics and Protestants throughout the sixteenth century. Tensions between the two confessions grew, however, as religious preferences became more and more entwined with both local and international politics. This period of German history is often defined by historians in terms of a process of "confessionalization," during which social identities were consolidated along confessional lines and "Catholic" and "Protestant" developed into sociopolitical as well as religious labels.

Among the populace, debate over religion by now was moving away from questions of church practice and theology and focusing increasingly on the perceived political agenda of the rival religion. In Augsburg, many Protestants were angered by the new civic constitution imposed upon the city by Emperor Charles V in 1548, which placed the bulk of the power in the hands of Catholic patricians. Protest from the disenfranchised Lutherans took the form of graffiti, printed and handwritten pamphlets and slander sheets, and oral communication including seditious songs, public insults, and rumors. The complaints recorded in many of the arrests for these violations reflect a popular view among

1. Wolfgang Zorn, *Augsburg: Geschichte einer europäischen Stadt* (Augsburg, 2001), 257.

Protestants that the Catholic-dominated council was exploiting its power by imposing unfair taxes and suppressing the power of the guilds. Nostalgia for the old government, which had given much greater political power to the guilds, thus came to be framed in terms of Protestant solidarity.

Meanwhile, the government followed a policy aimed primarily at peace and stability, censoring materials deemed inflammatory or liable to cause "resentment and harm" rather than specifically addressing matters of religious doctrine. Even as the terms of the Religious Peace were being worked out, the council was issuing warnings to local clergy to use restraint in the pulpit and preach in the interest of "peaceful and friendly cohabitation" rather than inflaming "envy and hate" with heated words (see document 1.11). Council decrees also exhorted booksellers to resist selling texts or images that were insulting to either religion, eventually subjecting all locally printed matter to approval by censors. Texts deemed heretical, including those espousing Calvinist, Anabaptist, or Schwenkfeldian views, remained illegal.

Despite their obvious interest in stability, tensions clearly existed among the members of the city council themselves, perhaps even more intensely than within the populace at large. Among all of Europe's wealthy elite, politics often revolved around family connections and marriage networks, and this was the case in Augsburg just as it was elsewhere. The fact that a few powerful Catholic families seemed to be consolidating government power in their hands was a sticking point for many Lutherans. The situation was exacerbated by news of violent events occurring in France and the Netherlands. The highly publicized massacres of Protestants known as the "St. Bartholomew's Day Massacre" (Paris, 1572) and the "Spanish fury" (Antwerp, 1576) gave local Protestant preachers fuel for fiery anti-Catholic sermons.

Among the most inflammatory were the sermons of the superintendent Doctor Georg Müller (also called Mylius), particularly in response to the city council's adoption of the new Gregorian calendar in Augsburg in 1583. Named for the current Pope, Gregory XIII, and pronounced into law by the Catholic Emperor in 1582, the new calendar was in fact a reasonable correction to the flawed Julian calendar, observation of which had gradually caused the celebration of religious holidays to be out of synch with the astronomical year. But to many Protestants, it naturally appeared as if the Pope was now dictating the observance of religious holidays. If the Pope controlled shifts in time, what would be next? The charismatic Doctor Müller aimed much of his vitriol at the Jesuits (members of the staunchly Catholic Society of Jesus), whose influence in the city had initially been supported by a major donation for the founding of a Jesuit school (St. Salvator) provided by Augsburg's wealthiest family, the Fuggers. Also at issue were controversial church appointments: in early 1584, the Catholic-dominated government broke with previous tradition by appointing two Protestant pastors of their own choosing rather than following the recommendation of the Lutheran Church Council. Both government and populace were increasingly polarized by the public debate over these issues. As a security measure, the city took on additional soldiers, one contingent of which was under imperial command. This further raised the ire of some citizens.

Things came to a head in the early summer of 1584, when city leaders finally decided to remove Müller from his post and secrete him out of the city. Word of the removal of Müller leaked out, and a riot resulted. Reacting to rumors of impending anti-Protestant violence that had been circulating for months, crowds of local citizens gathered in the streets, many of them armed. Although the crowd was dispersed with scarcely any bloodshed,[2] the council found itself on the defensive in the wake of this event. Facing both armed insurrection from its people and possible intervention by the Emperor, who had an interest in containing the unstable situation, the city council members called up a citizens' committee with representatives from each of the three social estates (patricians, merchants, and commoners) to negotiate a solution. Tension was diffused by means of a compromise that allowed the Lutherans to celebrate the upcoming Pentecost holiday according to the old calendar but required them to follow the new one from then on. The Protestants on the city council then agreed to accept the calendar in return for a sworn oath by the council not to otherwise interfere with the Protestant religion. Many of those who had taken a stance against their government were treated harshly during questioning, and some were banished for their disobedience. The creation of martyrs was prevented, however, by a series of pardons granted by the Emperor's representatives. Once again, rulers chose the path of stability rather than religious zeal.

But they could not turn back the clock. Not only in Augsburg but also throughout the Holy Roman Empire and beyond, resentments grew as the line drawn between the confessions became increasingly visible. The discontent was exacerbated by a series of economic crises, largely the result of inclement weather that adversely affected agricultural

2. Shots were fired from the windows of homes during the riot, one of them striking the imperial bailiff in the arm. Reports are conflicting on whether others were hit, but none report more than one fatality.

production.[3] Thus, by the time the series of destructive conflicts known as the Thirty Years' War began in 1618, there was more than enough bitterness on both sides to fan the flames of military violence.

While the two forms of Christianity recognized by the Peace of Augsburg vied for power and influence throughout the empire, alternate belief systems also continued to push for recognition and religious freedom. The interrogations of goldsmith David Altenstetter and the Schwenckfeld-leaning furrier Martin Künle provided here suggest that quiet contemplation of alternate ideas was still possible despite the apparent pressures to conform along confessional lines that characterized the post-Reformation period. This testimony survives as witness to the multiplicity of forms of individual religious expression that continued to characterize Reformation-era debates. Ultimately, the most successful challenge to Catholicism and Lutheranism would be Calvinism, finally recognized in 1648 as a legitimate confession within the German lands.

I. Enforcing the Peace through Censorship

2.1 Decree on Slanderous Songs, June 14, 1579[4]

An Honorable Council of this holy imperial city of Augsburg has learned that a few seditious persons are having all kinds of frivolous, derisive songs and writings composed and distributed, read, and sung among the citizens. But such things are not only in direct violation of the law and the Holy Imperial Recess; they are also wrongful in and of themselves, and give cause for all manner of resentment and harm. Therefore, an Honorable Council earnestly demands and desires that everyone refrain from such things here in this city, and commit no more violations of this sort. For if an Honorable Council should find out, sooner or later, that anyone dared to make, distribute, or sing scandalous writings and songs that mock, deride, or humiliate another, in violation of this warning and prohibition, the council will not hesitate to take earnest and certain action against the offender or offenders, if necessary through corporal punishment or otherwise as appropriate for the violation. And they will also see to it that sufficient evidence is acquired against the violator. All heed this warning to protect themselves from harm.

---

3. Cf. Chapter Ten.

4. StadtAA, Evangelisches Wesensarchiv 1561, Öffentliche Anschläge und Verrufe, 1490–1599, Tom 2.

II. Opposition to the New Calendar

2.2 Letter of Protest Circulated in the Fall of 1583[5]

According to the Augsburg chronicler Georg Kölderer (1576–1607), about 150 copies of this pasquinade were circulated in the city, some of them posted on the council house and other prominent spots (see the trials of Gedeon Mair and Christoph Widenman for more on this incident).

We the people of this community have been observing for a long time, My Lords, what sort of peace the Pope's false new calendar is keeping in the city of Augsburg and whether it is not trying to make a papal city out of it. If [this calendar] is not done away with, then we of the community will be strong enough to take action. We ask our Lords to think about this in order to protect themselves from harm, so that we can continue to live together in peace. If things heat up, then it will be the problem of those who helped set the fire, lay and cleric: in particular the children of the Devil, the Society of Anti-Jesus.[6] We will help them demolish what they have built together with their supporters. May God and the Christian authorities prevent this.

2.3 Trials for Spreading Dangerous Rumors in the Fall of 1583[7]

Interrogations of Gedeon Mair

On Monday, the 7th of November 1583, Gedeon Mair, interrogated without torture, responded as follows:

1. What is his name and where does he come from? His name is Gedeon Mair. He is a local citizen.

2. What does he do for a living? He supports himself as a cabinet-maker and maker of spindles.[8]

---

5. StadtAA, Urgichten zum Kalenderstreit, Jonas Losch, September 3–9, 1583; Chronicle of Georg Kölderer, transcribed in Benedikt Mauer, *"Gemain Geschrey" und "teglich Reden": Georg Kölderer—ein Augsburger Chronist des konfessionellen Zeitalters* (Augsburg, 2001), 178–79.

6. A play on words: Instead of *Jesuiter* (Jesuits), the word here used is *Jesuwider* (anti-Jesusites).

7. StadtAA, Urgicht Gedeon Mair, November 7–15, 1583; Urgichten Georg Eiseloer and Christoph Widenman, November 10, 1583; Strafbuch 1581–1587, 102r–v.

8. Or screws (meaning not clear).

3. It is known that he has for a long time, and in more than one place, been spewing out all kinds of evil talk about the authorities, which is easy to prove. Therefore he should willingly testify as to what he said against the government in each case, or else the executioner will get it out of him the hard way. It has indeed been going around among the people that Lord Mayor Rehlinger intended to have the Imperial Guard close the craftspeople's shops on Simon and Judas Day, and that Lord Marcus Fugger had also agreed to it. For Mair's part, whenever he heard it, he would answer that he didn't believe such a thing about the authorities. He doesn't remember anything else.

4. What evil things in particular did he say regarding the guards? He doesn't remember.

5. Since he and everyone else well knows that the guard is maintained in the interest of keeping peace and tranquility and for the good of the city and its citizens, and that this is done upon the orders of the authorities, why does he oppose them in spite of this with so much unnecessary, evil, nasty, and punishable talk? He didn't spread evil talk, although he did from time to time say that the guards are not set up the way they were before. When he was in the watch, they used to go about in groups. Now they stand around and let only one or two make the rounds, which he himself has seen.

6. One is well aware that a few weeks ago, he went around to more than one spot saying unjustly that the Duke of Bavaria, the Bishop of Augsburg, both mayors, and the priests' lackeys in the council made a pact with one another to fall upon the congregations in their churches and the others in their houses, and to murder them all. Where and why did he say this? He had better testify willingly than under torture. He told a clockmaker who lives in Froenmiller's house that he had heard that the Duke of Bavaria and the Bishop of Augsburg, supposedly the city's protectors, had agreed with My Lords [i.e., the council] that they want to force everyone here into one religion. And this is the reason he said this to Cossman Moll, carpenter, and to the smith at Brueggel's bathhouse. But they said that they didn't believe they would really do it.

7. Did he invent this great and shameful outrage against the authorities himself, or hear it from others, and from whom? He doesn't remember from whom he heard it. He will give it some thought, since it doesn't occur to him right now, but he assumes that he came up with it on his own out of anger.

8. It is also known that he said to the citizens that they should strap on their weapons and remain armed and ready. Therefore

he should explain exactly what he meant by this. **Against whom should the citizens arm themselves or be ready?** Because this talk was going around, he said to a few craftsmen that they shouldn't go to the sermon unarmed, so that if they are fallen upon in church they can defend themselves. In the same way, he himself was also asked by his neighbor why he wasn't wearing a weapon.

9. What did he intend to incite among the citizens by doing this? It was so that if someone started some kind of trouble in the church, they could put it down.

10. Did he not have in mind getting the citizens agitated against the government and starting a rebellion in the city? He should tell the truth, for he can't believe that this rebellious talk could lead to anything other than rebellion and insurrection. This never entered his mind.

11. Who instructed him in this, and with whom did he discuss these things? Says as above. He doesn't remember any more.

12. What kind of agreement did they make about it, and where did they hold their meetings? He agreed with his closest neighbors that if any trouble started, they would stay in their houses, or if the alarm bell was rung, they would run directly to their lane captain.[9] But they didn't hold any meetings about it.

13. Who else is also involved in this? He doesn't know of anyone who spoke badly against the authorities.

14. Why would he offend the Lord Mayors and other councilmen with such baseless derisive slurs, and on top of this with shameless, made-up, false insults and abuses? And this against the [councilmen] who, at their own expense, invest so much effort and work daily for the sake of the city and the citizenry? If he has done anything against the authorities, he begs for the sake of God for forgiveness, and not to take it so seriously.

15. Is he not bound and obligated by oath to the Lord Mayors, Burgomasters, and an Honorable Council, like all other citizens? Says yes.

---

9. Mair's testimony here is intended to mirror exactly the requirements of civic duty. Civilian militia duties in the sixteenth century were organized by neighborhood. Each quarter of the city had a "quarter captain," usually resident in the quarter and of elevated social status, who commanded a group of lieutenants or "lane captains" normally responsible for overseeing ten neighboring houses each. The entire system was under the command of the Captain of the Guard, a full-time military officer. For more on lane captains and defense procedures, see document 10.7.

16. Why then does he not give the least consideration to this oath, rather violates it with deliberate presumption? If he has violated it, then he asks for forgiveness.

17. Does he not know what the punishment is for rebellion and oath-breaking? He does.

18. Who wrote the letter that was recently found posted on the council house, on the irons, and on St. Anna's Church? He knows nothing about this.

19. Did he not hang this letter himself, and on whose orders? He didn't do it. Begs for mercy and forgiveness, and in view of the fact that he has five children and that he is an ill man, to let him out of the jail.

On Wednesday, the 9th of November, 1583, Gedeon Mair responded to the accompanying questions without torture as follows:

1. Because he has not yet told the real truth, the order has been given to get it out of him through torture. So he should behave accordingly and protect himself from further measures.

2. What caused him to say as if it were fact that the Lord Mayors planned with the help of the Bishop and the Duke of Bavaria to suppress the one [Lutheran] religion, when it is only a shameful fiction, and this idea never entered the thoughts of the Lord Mayors? After the reminder [to tell the truth], he says in response to the second question that he heard it from the peasants who come in from Bavaria and were buying bread at the baker Obmair. They said that the Duke of Bavaria, the Bishop, and My Lords would bring everyone here to the Catholic religion. Therefore he repeated it, and didn't think it would be so damaging to him.

3. Did he not invent this himself, and then spread it around among the citizens as the truth, and why? He heard it from the peasants, as he said above, but he doesn't know their names.

4. Didn't he hope through such lying, false invention to turn the citizens against their government, and to cause a riot in the city? That never entered his head.

5. Who advised and helped him in this? No one.

6. Has he heard this and other such talk from anyone else, and from whom? He didn't hear it from anyone except what the peasants said, as above.

7. Why would he attack the Lords in the council with such denigrating, insulting words? He didn't mean to be insulting.

**8. Since he himself admitted that he warned the citizens to arm themselves, and go to church armed, one would like to know what

his intentions were. He only said to some of his neighbors that because everyone is going around armed, then they should also not go to the sermon without arms, so that they can respond to any trouble that might easily come up, in light of the fact that such trouble also occurred during the imperial diet. But he didn't mean this as an attack on the authorities.

9. Did he not intend to start a riot, and then go looting through the houses of well-off citizens? Says he never had this in mind.

10. How could he think this would work, or who offered him council, help, and assistance? He did not for his part encourage any riot, and thus also did not get any promise of support from anyone.

11. Who posted the letter on the council house, on the irons, and on St. Anna's Church? He really doesn't know.

Upon that he was hoisted [on the strappado] without any weights, and left to hang a good while. Then he testified that a Jacob[10] Widenman, who is a shoemaker by trade . . . also told him that the Duke of Bavaria, the Bishop, and My Lords have made an agreement to put the preachers out of the city and establish a single religion here. And [Widenman] said that when the tumult starts, he wants to see to it that he also kicks up a row, and kills someone as quick as anyone else.

And once when they were talking about this matter on Smithy Lane, one person, Wurstle the gunsmith, was heard to say, "If they want to use the Imperial Guards to shut up their shops, as people are saying, then he himself would help stop the authorities and turn them away." Otherwise he did hear another gunsmith, who he thinks is called Rem, say that all of those on Smithy Lane have made a pact, and if they try to close the shops, they would defend themselves, for they have weapons and guns in their houses. And some have stockpiled up to six or seven loaded guns in their shops, as well as stones and similar things in the houses.

Upon this he was hoisted again with two weights attached, and then said that he had also heard from Wurstle and Rem that the grocers and others who have their shops up by Schwalbeneck and up to the slaughterhouse had made a pact with those on Smithy Lane to stand together if they should close up the shops, and not to leave one another's sides. As he heard it, the majority of the common citizens were in on the pact. Peter Eiseloer, instrument-maker by the Kress Mill, was going around to the shops and saying that they should stick together, which he said to [Mair] himself. [Eiseloer] also said and planned that once they were

10. Mair misidentifies Christoph Widenman as Jacob, and Georg Eiseloer as Peter.

stronger, and had overcome the guards, then they would fall upon Lord Mayor Rehlinger in his house, and see if he has the power and authority to force this upon the citizens. This he heard from Peter Eiseloer, Rem, and Würstle. And they also said they would attack Marcus Fugger and the other council members in the same way.

And although four weights were attached to him as a threat, further torture was stopped in view of his sixty years of age and because he is rather weak in person. After this he further testified that the above-named Widenman also said that when the ruckus began, he wanted to be in the middle of it [when] they overran the monks and papists and slew them. And that he wanted to help to overrun the Jesuits and to tear down and burn their building. And that he himself wanted to assist in attacking the Lord Mayor and Council Lords and hanging them from the city hall.

During the imperial diet when he was still in the watch, he heard once at night from several guards in the Pfründhof that the Colonel told them when he recruited them that they should join up with the watch, and here they would profit from their own Dutch War. And when sooner or later it came to a riot, if they are assigned to the better houses, they should kill everyone, and thus come into a good booty. He doesn't know who any of them were though, because it was dark. Begs for mercy.

SUPPLICATION FROM GEDEON MAIR'S WIFE

Noble, well-born, steadfast, farsighted, honorable, and wise Lord Mayor, Burgomaster, and an Honorable Council, Gracious Imperious and Auspicious Lords. My husband, Gedeon Mair, maker of spindles, was taken to the jail last Saturday because of his talk, about which I and all of his friends and relations are greatly saddened. For aside from this incident, he has always and in all ways behaved obediently, and was a member of the local guard for seventeen years. And he is a bit crazy in the head and at times not very prudent.[11] Therefore, I submit my humble devoted appeal and plea [to Your Lords] not to understand my husband's thoughtless talk to be as serious as it sounded, rather to take his lack of judgment into account, to replace austerity with mercy, and to release him from the jail out of compassion, so that he can support

---

11. Mair's guild masters noted in a separate petition that they had "credible evidence that he [Mair] is sometimes not right in the head, as several pieces of his skull were taken out of it, which occasionally leads him to have a lot of strange thoughts."

me and my five little children without resort to poor relief, as he has up to now. For this mercy I, together with my little children, will plead to God day and night [for your sake. Your humble devoted] Anna Mair, the imprisoned Gedeon Mair's wife, November 10, 1583.

INTERROGATIONS OF CHRISTOPH WIDENMAN

On Thursday the 10th of November 1583 Christoph Widenman responded without torture to the accompanying questions as follows:

1. What is his name and where does he come from? His name is Christoph Widenman. He is a local citizen.

2. What does he do for a living? In his youth he learned the shoemaker's craft, but afterward served Lord Gudacker von Starnberg in Austria for several years as a silver chamberlain. Two years ago he got married here. Since then he has been back in service to his Lord [Gudacker], and only returned around Easter, but now is planning to open a tap house. And meanwhile his brother David has been providing him with board.

3. What kind of evil rebellious talk did he recently engage in? He doesn't remember any.

4. It is known that he said that the Bishop of Augsburg, the Duke of Bavaria, and the Lords in the council have made an agreement to suppress the [Lutheran] religion. So he might as well testify willingly as under the martyr whether he invented these shameful lies by himself, or from whom he heard this? Denies vehemently having said this. Upon further prompting, however, says that he did say this to Gedeon Mair, but he didn't hear it from anyone, rather would have made it up himself.

5. It is known that he said that when the trouble starts, he wanted to jump in with gusto, kill the monks and priests, and hang the mayors and other councilmen from the city hall. Therefore he should explain what led him to say this? He did say to Mair that when the ruckus began, he would defend himself as well as he could, and help to attack the monks, priests, and Jesuits, and to kill them. As far as the councilmen go, he said to Mair something along the lines of, "If the authorities didn't do right and trouble started, he would himself help to throw them out of the city hall," but this slipped out of him because of thoughtlessness, and he never had in mind doing it for real. Requests therefore for the sake of God that an Honorable Council not take this so seriously, and be merciful to him.

6. What did he tell Gedeon Mair and others about this? This he testified to above. Pleads for mercy. He has at all times from his youth onward behaved uprightly and honorably, and didn't consider the consequences of this talk.

Christoph Widenman should be questioned under torture and the truth brought from him.

On Friday the 11th of November 1583, Christoph Widenman answered willingly under earnest threat to the accompanying interrogation as follows:

1. Because he didn't give the real reason for his evil rebellious talk, he should willingly confess to this again and not give reason for more severity.

2. Why did he invent what he said to Gedeon Mair, namely that the council here was going to suppress the [Lutheran] religion, and to whom else did he say it? After the warning, he responds to the second question that he did say this to Gedeon Mair, but it happened out of thoughtlessness, and he didn't say it to anyone else. If he had he would admit it.

3. Did he not intend to incite the citizenry and community to rebel, and to enrich himself during the riot? This wasn't his intention at all.

4. Why was he planning to help throw the councilmen out of the city hall, and said so to Gedeon Mair? He said this too, but he was drunk, and not in command of his judgment.

5. Does he think that this is the thanks that the authorities deserve for the many efforts, worries, and labors that they bear on behalf of the city? He is sorry that he blurted out such evil talk, and because this was not really his intent or opinion, pleads for God's sake for mercy. And he adds that if he should ever say this again or anything similar, that he should be punished mercilessly.

6. Who wrote the letter that was hung a few days ago on the city hall, on the irons, and on St. Anna's Church? He knows nothing about it, except that he heard from Gedeon Mair that such a letter was found, but he couldn't tell him who hung it up.

7. Did he not write it or hang it up himself? Says no.

As he did not want to admit anything else willingly, he was at first hoisted up [on the strappado] without weights, but didn't confess. Then he was hoisted a second time without weights, and said he would confess. This however he did not do. Afterward he was also lifted up with two weights, and after the torture, admitted that approximately eight days ago at the gate to St. Anna's Church, on the way to the imperial bailiff, there was a letter posted, which he saw at around five o'clock in the morning but did not read. He assumes it was the letter he heard about later from Gedeon Mair. But when he was threatened and asked again, he said he hung up the letter himself, and that Gedeon Mair told him about it, and said he would find the letter beside the gate. After this he was hoisted up again with four weights, and then he testified that Mair didn't know about this placard or letter, and that he wrote it himself and hung it up. After this he was further asked what was in the letter, to which he answered he didn't write it, but he hung it up, and he found it by the gate at St. Anna, as Mair told him he would. And he only said he wrote it because of the torture. Then he also said that he didn't hang up the letter, rather only confessed to it so they would stop the torture. He also said he had never seen the letter. And because the longer he talked the more inconsistent he became, and he said that what he said before the torture was the truth, but what he testified during and after the torture about writing and hanging this letter was because of the pain and did not happen, he was spared further torture. Pleads for mercy.

[On the following Monday, Mair and Eiseloer were placed face-to-face and questioned, and Mair retracted what he had said of Eiseloer.]

Punishment records for Mair, Widenman, and Eiseloer

Gedeon Mair and Christoph Widenman from Augsburg spewed out rebellious talk, as if one wanted to suppress the Augsburg Confession here, but they made it up themselves. And in addition, they planned to help throw the authorities out of the council house, without any cause on the authorities' part. Although they have thus forfeited their lives according to the law, an Honorable Council decreed out of mercy that the two of them be beaten with rods and banished from the city for life.

[Gedeon Mair snuck back into the city in May of 1599 and was banished again.]

Georg Eiseloer, locksmith and local citizen, was accused by Gedeon Mair of speaking rebelliously about the authorities, and of going around to the shops and counseling the citizens to stick together. Therefore he was put in the jail. But because he did not confess to this, and Mair himself later retracted the charge, he was let go upon a promise to return if necessary.

2.4 Punishments of Participants in the Riot of 1584[12]

These two brief excerpts are representative of dozens of participants who were interrogated in the summer of 1584.

June 7, 1584: Jorg Schmid, tailor, citizen here, was arrested by the city bailiff [during the riot] just because he was wearing a sword. Because there was nothing illegal about this, an Honorable Council decreed that he be released without charge.

June 16, 1584: Georg Halbritter, tailor from Augsburg, armed himself and went to the square during the recent riot, and afterward claimed that his lane captain Adam Pfleger had told him to, which resulted in Pfleger also being arrested. Because this was false testimony, an Honorable Council decreed this day that Pfleger should be released, but Halbritter should be banished from the city. (On August 28, 1584, Halbritter was pardoned upon the intercession of His Imperial Majesty's commission.)

2.5 Inquisition by the Imperial Commission in the Summer of 1584[13]

In August following the riot of 1584, a delegation commissioned by the Emperor subjected all of the members of the citizens' committee to a closed inquisition. Not all questions were put to every one of those questioned, but they were all sworn to secrecy. In most cases, the responses of the committee members leave little doubt as to their religious preference.

1. Lord Hans Fugger, Baron of Kirchberg and Weissenhorn, patrician:
Because a few years ago, great strife and mistrust appeared in this city, what, as far as the witness knows, is the reason for it? He doesn't know of anything to report except that some preachers who were too hotheaded and turbulant in the pulpit, and especially Doctor Müller, agitated the community, so that there was reason to fear that it would finally lead to a revolt. This he heard from some adherents to the Augsburg Confession; for his part he has not attended [Müller's] sermons.
Who is the author and instigator of this disobedience? He heard that the rebellion originated among those of the Augsburg Confession.

---

12. StadtAA, Strafbuch 1581–1587, 122v–23v.

13. StadtAA, Reichsstadt, Kalenderstreit 5 (alte Archivsignatur 28), Bericht der kaiserlichen Kommission, 129r–174v.

What reason did the citizens have for this? He believes that the reason is due to the mischief and poverty of some, who like to see things stirred up.

Who encouraged and supported the citizens? He can't really say, except that no upright person was among them.

What does each of them have or know of to complain about this government? He doesn't know what complaints others have. He has nothing to complain of, rather has the highest of praise for the government.

Has [the government] ever impeded the Augsburg Confession here in their teaching and what follows from it in the churches, or in any way interfered with it or obstructed it? Absolutely not.

Has anyone ever openly complained to the government about this, and what answer were they given? What the preachers presented to the common man, the people believed, especially that they wanted to take their preachers and religion away, which embittered them against the authorities.

Has the council also ever burdened the citizenry here with unusual taxes, duties, and contributions, and when and how did this happen? Does the person being questioned have any complaint against this government, and why? Speaking for himself, he has not been burdened. The tax on drinks was lowered in 1582, because it had at other times been raised.

Does he not know that there was a plot here calling for a change in the government? Who made it and who else was involved with it? Doctor Müller wanted to have one foot at the council house and the other in the pulpit, so he collected a group of followers among the citizens and the council.

Does the person being questioned want to work with and support this government, and help it reestablish and keep the general peace? To the last question, yes, to the best of his ability.

2. David Weiss, patrician [most of the delegation members were asked only these four questions]:

1. The dispute that arose here and has been going on for some time appears to suggest that a change in the government was the aim. Does the person being interrogated know anything about this? And what does he know, and from whom, and was he involved in the plot? No, he knows nothing at all of a plan to make a change in the government, only that Emperor Charles [V]'s ordinance is not being adhered to as regards the religion of the people in either the Privy

Council or the entire council. And that in the first, second, and third ranks, among the thirty-one councilmen, Lord Mayor Rehlinger has sixteen that are his relatives. And since 1576, [Rehlinger] has governed pretty much alone, along with Doctors Tradel and Laiman, whom he follows and listens to too much. For Lord Marcus Fugger took the other office of mayor only so that [Rehlinger] could take it over entirely, as [Fugger] defers to [Rehlinger] in everything. [Weiss] thinks [Fugger] should be let go, to remain in the Privy Council, and Lord Rehlinger be given another colleague.

2. Have the authorities ever impeded, interfered with, or hindered the teachings and practice of the Protestant religion? When, in what points, and how did this happen? If things remained as they had been up to now, then he for his part would have no complaint . . . [but] they have been noticeably impeded by the removal of the four former councilmen and the church elders, and because preachers were appointed who are not of the Augsburg Confession, and also because they are trying to force upon them new, unusual directives. Before, the church elders searched for [new] preachers, examined them in the council of ministers, and presented them to an Honorable Council. Now the mayors do it, and even Doctor Tradel himself, whose religion isn't known, since he doesn't go to any church and doesn't take communion.[14] The preacher [Johannes] Ehinger, who was most recently appointed based on Doctor Tradel's recommendation, is such an unlearned man that he isn't qualified to be here. He, David Weiss, could preach better than this Ehinger. The commoners are complaining because every citizen is duty bound to pay property taxes, and then they find out that all the Fuggers together have an arrangement to pay only 2,000 gulden. This deal was just extended and prearranged for another year without the required prior knowledge of the council. Any other citizen who owns more than 150,000 or 160,000 gulden has to pay an established tax, namely 600 gold gulden, and there is no Fugger here who can't also pay that much. And the Lord Fuggers also bought a lot of houses, tore them down, and made pleasure gardens out of them, through which living spaces for the poor citizens were reduced and taken away. In the Privy Council a lot of things are handled by only a few people without the knowledge of the entire council, which is not the least of the annoyances, and also shows the great lack of trust the council has for him and other citizens.

---

14. Georg Tradel, council advocate, was officially a Protestant, thus seen as a traitor by others of his religion.

3. Does the person being questioned himself have a complaint against the local authorities, and what is it? This is understood from the above.

4. Is he prepared to share benefits and burdens with this government, as he took an oath to do, and to show them due obedience, to help in restoring the civic peace, and to support it to the best of his ability? Yes, he will lay down his life, honor, goods, and blood for the authorities. The mistrust began with the new calendar, because Lord Mayor Rehlinger wanted to govern everything alone with Doctor Tradel and Doctor Laiman. And in particular, Doctor Tradel is the major instigator of all the trouble and unrest, which practically the entire city is complaining about. No source of money is beneath him; he takes it everywhere he can get it. Tradel will drive a lot of honor-loving citizens out of the city who can no longer stand for his rule and his hostile agitation, and he, Weiss himself, won't be able to bear nor tolerate it anymore, but will have to give up his citizenship and settle elsewhere. [He] requests of the Lord Commissioners that they try to put an end to this great, destructive mistrust and reinstate peace, tranquility, and unity, so that all parties can continue to stay together and live side by side.

From the delegation of commoners, responding to the same questions
3. Sigmund Zoller, innkeeper:

1. Nothing, from start to finish.

2. He knows nothing about it. The common man said that some psalms would be changed, but it was nothing.

3. Nothing.

4. He has always done so and will continue to do so as long as he lives. He has enough to do with running his inn, and hasn't concerned himself with anything else. If it were possible that the four [council] Lords who were replaced could be reinstated, he would praise and thank God.

4. Endres Zelling:

1. He knows nothing about it, and hasn't heard anything of it.

2. None at all.

3. Not as far as he is concerned.

4. Yes. It is his opinion that the lack of good sense among the people is the cause of the unrest, for they don't know what their Christianity is. Otherwise they would know how to treat their authorities. According to what he heard from others, the preachers were preaching that one could not accept the calendar without violating one's conscience.

2.6 Revised Defense Orders for City Captains, 1584[15]

Copy of that which was presented to the quarter and lane captains on June 10 by Lord Mayor Ilsung, on the orders of the Lords of the Privy Council.

The quarter and lieutenant captains, who are called lane captains, should be earnestly directed and ordered on behalf of the council not to call up any of the citizens, or call them to arms, without an Honorable Council's orders or the striking of the alarm bell.

No matter what happens, they should stay in their houses and not come out without specific orders of the authorities. And if they observe others gathering, they should earnestly warn them against it.

If crowds should assemble, whether by day or by night, and whether small or large, they should immediately report it to the Burgomaster in accordance with their civic duty.

They should also inform the citizens that anyone appearing in arms and armor[16] without orders or a request from the authorities, and causing or joining in a tumult, should and will be seriously punished.

No one should injure an Honorable Council's soldiers and guards, who have been taken on for the defense and protection of the citizenry, with abusive insults or threats of arson or attacks, thus inciting disturbances and further consequences, on pain of serious penalty. Instead, they should rest assured that an Honorable Council, with their guard, will defend and protect their citizens from violence and attacks.

2.7 Georg Müller Describes the Process of Confessionalization in Augsburg[17]

Because [as a result of the Religious Peace of 1555] both religions were assured that they would be left unhindered in their practice and were completely freed of any danger of being repressed or driven out of the city by the opposition, all distrust and anxiety in the hearts of the citizens immediately ceased. For some years, they lived together so trustingly that both sides intermarried regularly, called on one another as godparents, and joined and served one another at weddings, funerals,

---

15. StadtAA, Militaria 194, June 10, 1584.

16. Reference to military arms and armor (helmets, breastplates, pole arms, and loaded guns). The right to wear swords and daggers was not restricted.

17. Excerpted from Georg Müller, *Augspurgische Händel, So sich daselbsten wegen der Religion / vnd sonderlich jüngst vor zwey Jaren im werenden Calender streit mit Georgen Müller D. Pfarrer vnd Superintendenten daselbst zugetragen* (Wittenberg, 1586).

and social and business events with merry banqu[...]
of the churches and pulpits, not the least sign of [...]
among the citizens.

In this atmosphere of trust, it also happened [...]
much attention to the council elections. Sometir[...]
the upper hand and were a majority in the cou[...]
Catholics; but either way, no one on either side [...]
or suffered any disadvantage. . . .

After this nonpartisan government and general sense of confidence among the citizens had lasted for several years, God in righteous judgment (undoubtedly for no other reason than because of the collective sins of the city, such as conceit, vanity, fornication, usury, and the like) deigned that his corrupting scourge, the Jesuits, should quietly and treacherously settle themselves in this city. . . . At once, beginning in around 1564, nearly everything about this way of life and the mutual trust started to turn around. For the Jesuits not only began immediately to break up engagements between Catholics and Protestants but also pressured those [Catholics] who were already married to a Protestant incessantly from the pulpit, and especially during confession, to get their Protestant spouse to become Catholic, if not amicably then otherwise. . . . [They also pressured] masters and artisans to lay off their servants and apprentices if they did not want to convert to Catholicism, and told the Catholic citizens not to hire Protestant craftsmen . . . and in short, they began with great zeal to turn every proper Catholic against the Lutherans as if they were the worst kind of heretics—or even as if they were dogs and beasts. And the worst of it was that they impressed upon those in government that it would be contrary to their conscience to vote for a Lutheran in the council. . . .

[In 1576] on Exaudi[18] Sunday, I was interpreting for my congregation the customary chapters 15 and 16 from the Gospel of John about the persecution and killing of the apostles. And in explaining the prophecy of Christ, I noted that this can happen to Christ's church at any time . . . as recently occurred in France; and as a reference to the reason for it, I added: "The fault lies mostly with Jesuits and others of their sort, who have turned bitter the hearts of the pious rulers with their bloodthirsty excitations. As an example, not long ago, a godless hack published an admonishment to our pious Emperor to put on his sword and hunt down the Lutheran heretics." . . . A few days after this sermon, I was called to appear before the mayors in the presence of the

---

18. The sixth Sunday after Easter (i.e., the last Sunday before Pentecost).

t elders, and asked if I had blamed the Jesuits for pushing the
chs into shedding blood, causing the bloodbath in Paris,[19] and
ting a book in which His Imperial Majesty was admonished to hunt
down Lutherans with the sword. When I answered that I did not dispute the substance of this, although the circumstances were somewhat
skewed, [the mayor told me] that he did not permit writing and printing
such books in Augsburg . . . [and] as such things meanwhile only lead to
resentment, I was hereby being told and warned to be quiet about such
matters in the pulpit.

[Müller then lists a number of insults to Protestants by the Jesuits
and abuses of power by the Catholics in the council, claiming that the
two confessions are not treated equally in the city.] . . . From all of this
it is obvious that the fight about the calendar is as much the result of
pure malice and coercion on the part of the Catholics, as [resistance]
is necessary for survival among the Protestants. . . . If the council, or
more to the point the mayor, believed that the new calendar should be
introduced in Augsburg, he should have asked ahead of time in both
churches if and how this change would work. Then there would have
been all the less reason to be concerned about ill will and guile from any
side. But since the mayor pulled the new calendar out of his shirt without warning . . . and what they hashed out in silence among themselves
a few days before was decided and concluded in a snap, this looked too
suspicious, and not everyone can accept that it was well meant. . . .

III. Continuing Debate

2.8 Interrogation of Sabina Preiss for the "Müller Song," 1588[20]

*The song Preiss is accused of singing here told the story of Müller's
banishment from Augsburg, and the resulting riot, from the
Protestant perspective.*

On Wednesday, the 13th of January 1588, Sabina Preiss answered willingly to the accompanying questions, under earnest threat, as follows:

**1. What is her name and where does she come from, and also
how old is she?** Her name is Sabina Preiss, she is from Augsburg, and
doesn't know her age. She appears to be about 24.

19. I.e., the St. Bartholomew's Day Massacre of 1572.
20. StadtAA, Urgicht Sabina Preiss, January 13, 1588; Strafbuch 1588–1596, 2v.

2. How long she has been in the hospital? It has now been one year since she went in.

3. Because she is still young and strong of body, why does she burden the hospital, and not support herself with serving and handwork? Because of her [afflicted] limbs, she is a miserable wretched person. She has been in the Pilgrim's Hospital[21] and Plague House, and the hospital father is well acquainted with her affliction and misery.

4. Did she not sing a song about Doctor [Georg] Müller in the hospital the other day? Yes, she did.

5. Did the hospital father not take this song away? Says yes.

6. She should report truthfully who gave her this song. Her brother Hans Georg Preiss, weaver and local citizen, had it, and she asked him for it. He gave it to her at her request.

7. Where was this song printed? She couldn't say, for it isn't in there. She doesn't know where her brother got it.

8. Does she not know that such texts are forbidden here, and that a number of people have been punished for it before? No, she hadn't heard that, and didn't know anything about it. If that happened then it must have been before she came in.

9. Why then, in spite of this, did she not only carry this song around with her but also sing it publicly? She didn't sing it out of any malice, rather it happened as follows: When she first came to the hospital, her room mother told her she had to say her prayers just like the others. Thereupon she answered, "If she knew the prayer they said in the hospital, she would be glad to pray." Then the room mother asked if she could read, and she said that she can read print a little. So the room mother said, "Oh my, my son has a song about Doctor Müller. I'll bring it to you and you must read it to me." This she also did, and so it happened. When she had been in the hospital for barely four weeks, the room mother thought she should learn the song by heart, so left it with her for around eight or nine weeks. Then she asked for it back, and gave it back to her son, and [Preiss] was unable to learn it, for there were very difficult words in it. Plus she was ill in the meantime. Because the room mother thought she ought to know it by heart by then, but she didn't, the room mother was not at all happy about her having it for so long and still not having learned it. Afterward, on St. Martin's night [November 11], the room mother's son Hans Borst, a weaver, was dining with his mother. And then another person as well, called Beürle, who is a weaver

---

21. Pilgrim's hospital (*Pilgerhaus,* lit. "pilgrim house") was originally intended for housing pilgrims but by 1600 operated as a hospital with more than 480 beds. The Pilgrim House was subordinate to the Office of Poor Relief.

and used to be in the guard here, was also visiting his daughter in the hospital. And both Beürle and the room mother's son started to discuss the old and new calendar. She, Sabina Preiss, said that they should let the discussion over the calendar be, and sing a nice song instead. Then the room mother said to her son, "Sing us the Doctor Müller." And her son did. That's all that happened. Only from his singing did she notice that it was the same song she had seen a while back at her brother's. Therefore she went to her brother and asked for it, as above, and only got it nine days before Christmas. She didn't carry it around anywhere, and didn't give it to any other person, rather kept it to herself. What the men were discussing, she honestly couldn't say, other than that the old one, who had been going to the current sermons, started to say about the new calendar that one should keep it as it used to be. What the other said in response she couldn't know. She right away made the request as above [that they sing a song instead].

10. How did she expect to get away with this without punishment? She didn't understand it, and had never heard of it before. She was once a seamstress in Doctor Müller's house, but never heard about this song. Nonetheless she asked the room mother if one was allowed to sing the song, and [the room mother] said it wasn't forbidden in the hospital. Requests mercy, and appears simple and unsuspicious.

[Preiss was banned from the city, allowed back in to recover from an illness in January of 1589, and then finally pardoned four months later.]

2.9 Interrogation of David Altenstetter and Martin Künle for Unconventional Religious Thinking[22]

INTERROGATIONS

On Friday the 4th of December, 1598, the following [persons], questioned separately, responded willingly under earnest threat to the accompanying questions as follows:

David Altenstetter
  1. What is his name, from where, and how old is he? Says he is a local citizen and he is forty-eight years of age.
  2. What does he do for a living? He is a goldsmith by trade, and that is what he does.

---

22. StadtAA, Urgichten David Altenstetter, Potiphar Künle, and Martin Künle, December 4–7, 1598; Strafbuch 1596–1605, 65v.

3. What is his religion, and to which confession does he profess? He should testify truthfully. He has in the matter of religion thus far been free, for although he was born in a Catholic town, afterward he lived in Switzerland, where the Zwinglian faith is practiced. But since coming here he has at times listened to the preachers of the Augsburg Confession, and at times also listened to the Catholic preachers. In particular, he and Master Johann Spreng[23] have listened to Father Gregor, the current cathedral preacher, more than the others. But he doesn't really adhere to either one or the other of the confessions. If he has to profess to one of them, he would take the Catholic, but he would have to take the necessary instruction in it.

4. How it happens that he has for many years not visited the churches of the Augsburg Confession, and what does he find wrong with it? Says as above. He is sometimes in the churches of the Augsburg Confession, but more often in the cathedral, because the Catholic religion is somewhat more attractive to him, and he likes the cathedral preacher better than the preachers of the Augsburg Confession.

5. Why does he not approve of the churches, teachings, and ceremonies of the Augsburg Confession and the local ministry, rather disparages them? He leaves the churches, teachings, and ceremonies of the Augsburg Confession alone, and doesn't wish either to praise or to rebuke the local ministry. He has thus far been free in the matter of religion, and has not really professed one or the other, and repeats his above testimony.

6. What does he think of the holy sacraments, especially baptism? At this time, and until God gives him further grace and knowledge, he believes that there are two sacraments, namely baptism and the Eucharist. He also believes that the sacrament of baptism is necessary for achieving salvation, as he received this sacrament once in his childhood and never again. And, had God granted him children, he also would not have wanted to deny them. And in general, he also believes that the holy sacraments are mysteries of God.

7. Since he doesn't attend any church or sermon, what does he do on Sundays and holidays? Or where does he hear sermons? Says here again what he said above in response to the third question. But it is true that there were times on Sundays and holidays that he went neither to one church nor to the other, rather either stayed at home or, when he ran into some company, went for a walk inside or outside of the city, which happened a lot during the summer.

23. Johann Spreng (1524–1601), Augsburg notary, Meistersinger, and translator.

8. Do he and others not gather in special places on Sundays and holidays? Where and in what places? And how many years has it been going on? He knows and can swear an oath to the fact that he has no such community that gathers on Sundays or holidays to hear a sermon or to read, and if they find otherwise, he forfeits life and limb.

9. Have they not been gathering for many years nearly every Sunday and holiday in Altenstetter's house between 7:00 and 8:00 AM, and also in his garden, which he acquired from My Lords?[24] **Hasn't Altenstetter been hosting and permitting such assemblies and congregations the whole time?** He has never held or allowed any such assemblies or congregations of this sort in his house or in his garden, and it surprises him to hear that he has come under the authorities' suspicion for such a thing. But he could perhaps well imagine where this came from, and recounts that a year ago last summer, on a Sunday, Master Johann Spreng and Martin Künle, furrier, both came to his house together in the morning between seven and eight o'clock because Spreng had made a testament for himself in which he named Altensteter and Künle as executors. And because it was to be sealed afterward, he wanted to read it to the two executors in his, Altenstetter's, house. But because some members of his household were underfoot and at home in the house, this could not be handled appropriately. Therefore he took them to his garden, and the said testament was then read in the presence of the three of them [and signed the next day, again in the garden]. And afterward they had a drink. He cannot remember any other gathering that was held in his house or garden, other than that occasionally on a Sunday or holiday he and others played bowls and drank in his garden. And he can only think that it must have been because of the above-described incident that the suspicion suggested by the question fell upon him.

10. Who are all these people? He should, in accordance with his duty of citizenship, report the names of those who so congregate, and hold nothing back. For even though it is already known, one wants to hear it from him. To this question he repeats the answer above. He knows of no other gathering or meeting, other than once in a while good friends came to his garden, which he acquired from My Lords only two years ago, to enjoy a drink or a walk.

11. What do they do together? Which books and rites do they use? What do they read or preach, and who does it? This he explained above, namely they occasionally played bowls, had drinks, and played board games. They did not otherwise give sermons, read, or participate in ceremonies.

---

24. I.e., bought or rented from the city.

12. How did they come to such opinions? Who instructed them in it, and what is the basis for it? Says he is innocent.

13. Do they not meet yearly in April or May and in the fall outside of the city in the woods, and hold special sermons from up in the trees? Where does this occur, and who does it? He knows nothing of this and has never in his life seen it, let alone been present and participated.

14. Are maidens and women also to be found there, and who are they? Knows nothing of these things.

15. What do they mean by this, and where did it come from? 16. He should testify in detail and truthfully what else they do at such assemblies, and hold nothing back, so that it is not necessary to get it out of him the hard way. 17. Is he aware of other such assemblies of this and other religions that are being held here? Where? When and by whom? And who all attends? And what do they do there? Since he has never been present at such things and knows nothing about it, he also cannot say anything about it.

18. Is this not meant to disparage the local ministry and churches of the Augsburg Confession? He doesn't know.

19. Does he not know that, in accordance with the law and the civic oath, all gatherings and congregations are forbidden, even if nothing bad happens there? He doesn't know.

20. How should one take the fact that he not only violated this law, but allowed and abetted such gatherings in his house and garden?

21. What was he looking for in this or trying to achieve? And who provided him with help, counsel, and instructions? From the above testimony his innocence will be apparent.

22. Does he not know that only two religions, the Catholic and the Augsburg Confession, are allowed here? He knows this.

23. Does he not know that such sects are also not tolerated in other towns, especially in imperial cities? He knows it, but has no other city in which he is thus complicit.

24. Why he then behaved in violation of this? Repeats what he testified above.

25. Does he wish to give up his erroneous ways? He knows of no error in which he participates and repeats his answer to the third question above.

26. Did he not think this would come out into the open, and how did he think he would get away with it without punishment? He was not worried about anything he was doing. Requests a merciful and swift release because he has necessary work to do for the Emperor.

Martin Künle's responses to the same questions

1. Says he is a local citizen, sixty-five years of age.

2. He is a furrier and that is how he supports himself.

3. He sometimes goes to the churches of the Augsburg Confession, but not scrupulously, and he has been known to read Schwenkfelder and Lutheran books at home. He has also listened to the sermons of the current cathedral preacher, Father Gregor. Notes in addition that he likes the Schwenkfelder teachings best, because they require more than others a Christian life and piety.

4. He has never completely professed to this church [i.e., the Augsburg Confession], rather often attended the sermons on Sundays, and also for weddings and funerals.

5. He has not disparaged [the Augsburg Confession], and no one has ever heard that from him. He has not turned anyone at all away from it, not even the members of his household.

6. He believes foremost that there are two sacraments, namely baptism and the sacrament of the altar [i.e., the Eucharist]. There might be more of the sacraments, but as a layperson he can't say anything about that, because he isn't that familiar with them. And baptism in particular he considers to be the entrance into Christendom, and he also believes that babies should be baptized, just as he had all of his children baptized.

7. When he didn't attend the sermon, he was at home reading, or otherwise handling business that he saved to do on those days.

8. He doesn't know about such meetings or congregations, and has never been at one, and no one has ever come to his place for this reason, for he knows well that it is strictly forbidden by My Lords . . . [professes innocence to remaining questions].

Second interrogation

On Monday the 7th of December 1598, the following two people willingly responded to the accompanying questions, separately and under earnest threat, as follows:

David Altenstetter

1. It is known that he did not tell the whole truth, therefore he should do it now and not give cause for harsher measures. 2. Since he himself just admitted that he is committed neither to the Catholic religion nor to the Augsburg Confession, he should be clear about what religion he then professes. After being presented with the first article, he responds to the second: Because the theologians of the Catholic Church and the Augsburg Confession are extremely antithetical to one another, he has been in agreement with neither one nor the other, rather has been free. And at home he has read all kinds of Christian books, as for example the Taulerum,[25] the Imitation of Christ,[26] the Paraphrase of Erasmus,[27] and then an old Bible that was printed in Nuremberg 100 years ago. Aside from that, he has sometimes attended the Catholic and at times also the Lutheran Church and listened to their preachers, as previously testified. And although he occasionally hears something he doesn't like in both places, that doesn't mean that he hasn't heard a lot of good preached in both churches that he really liked and that made sense to him, especially from Father Gregor the cathedral preacher, as well as some years ago from Father Nas at St. Ulrich, whom he often listened to then. And he hopes that he won't be forced to one or the other religion too quickly, rather that he will be given some time so that he can listen a little better, especially to Father Gregor, and give some thought to the Catholic religion. But if this is forbidden to him, he would have to profess to the Augsburg Confession, because he hasn't yet had enough instruction in the Catholic Church. But he requests to have some more time to be free, until he learns some more.

3. Since he knows that only two religions, the Catholic and the Augsburg Confession, are allowed here, neither of which he professes, but he also just testified that he is not aware that he adheres to any error, he should profess clearly his confession or belief. He isn't sure which of these two, namely the Catholic or the Lutheran religion, he will entirely accept or to which he will profess. Other than these religions, he has never belonged to any other sect.

4. It is known, and can be proven if necessary, that he and his fellow believers hold special meetings on holidays and Sundays between seven and eight o'clock in the morning, and that they have taken place many times morning and afternoon. Therefore he should tell the truth and hold nothing back. He says once again as he testified before that he has never been to such gatherings in his life, and would like to know who it is who has been at such meetings with him and who can say this about him. He can't testify otherwise if it costs him life and limb.

---

25. The writings of fourteenth-century theologian John Tauler.
26. Thomas à Kempis.
27. *Paraphrase of Erasmus upon the New Testament.*

5. Who are his fellow believers and what [do] they do and practice during their meetings? Also, what does their belief consist of? He can say nothing about this, for he knows nothing of it. And otherwise as regards his own faith, he testifies as above.

6. Are not Doctor Kneulin, Doctor Carl Widenmann, Heggenauer, Notary Sembach Spreng, Potiphar Künle, Georg Schemburger, and others as well often at his place, and do they not share his opinion? And what are the names of all these men and women? These are all his good friends, but they have never all or in part gathered together for the sake of religion or discussed anything about it, and this will not be found of them.

7. Because his peculiar faith is not tolerated here, is he willing to stay away from it and let himself be instructed? He has no peculiar faith, but adheres in some bits to the Catholic religion and in some to the Augsburg Confession. And he would be happy to be guided and instructed in the truth, as he has already suggested. Requests thereupon a gracious release, and notes as well that he has always and in every way behaved in accordance with his civic duty and has never opposed the authorities, rather he provided manly defense against others who raised their weapons against the authorities in the rebellion, with more than a little danger to himself. This he can prove in detail with numerous people, and has already done so before through the late Lord Mayor Anton Christoph Rehlinger and others.

Martin Künle's response to the same questions

1., 2. After being read the first article, he says in response to the second question that it is in fact true that he has professed neither the Catholic religion nor the Augsburg Confession, in spite of the fact that he has heard sermons in both churches. In particular, he has not entirely left the Augsburg Confession, though if he is to tell the truth, then he has to say that Schwenkfelder's books, writings, and faith appeal to him the most.

3. He likes the Schwenkfelder beliefs best.

4. He has never been at such [irregular religious] gatherings, and also knows nothing about them. And what he has read in the Schwenkfelder books and writings, he did so alone and quietly by himself, and did not even tell his household about it. He notes that some of his people and household members are Catholic (among them his mother's sister), and some go to the Lutheran Church, and he doesn't keep them from it. He diligently enjoins them to go, to which they can give witness. And he notes that in case he is in error, he is leading only himself into error, and has taken no one with him.

5. He knows of no one who shares his faith, and there have also been no meetings at which he could be found in which religion was practiced. This he asserts most strongly.

6. He knows all of these people, but they have never gathered together and held meetings for the sake of religion and faith in his presence, and he knows nothing to say about it.

7. As soon as he is set free he will talk to the preachers here about the matter, and if they can lead him to an improvement over what he has thus far believed or understood, then he will be happy to follow it and act accordingly. He only requests that he be given some time, about a month, in view of the fact that he has a lot of work at the moment and is a widower as well, and has no help at home. And he requests in addition a merciful release.

THE FOLLOW-UP REPORT

June 25, 1609
Upon merciful order of both Lord Mayors, we the undersigned, both currently Burgomasters in Office, summoned David Altenstetter, goldsmith, who appeared in my, Albrecht von Stetten's, normal interrogation room today after the morning sermon at around ten o'clock. He was first reminded that he was arrested along with others in 1598 under strong suspicion that he had turned to a sectarian teaching, but that in accordance with his request at the time, he was let go upon an agreement to reappear if called. Altenstetter offered at the time, among other things, that insofar as he was in error regarding the matter of religion, he would inform himself and be instructed. Thus one now wants to know which religion he adheres to and professes at this time. To this he avowed that he professes only the evangelical religion, which is usually called Lutheran, and that he still attends the same church and sermons, and thinks that with God's help he will stick with it.

In regard to the fact that he wrongly came under evil suspicion before, his testimony in his interrogation record will show that there was only a misunderstanding in his case in respect to the aforementioned meetings. So for now we accepted his report and testimony, and let him leave again.
June 24, 1609
Your magnificence
Dutiful
Albrecht von Stetten
Philip Endris

Punishment record

December 8, 1598. David Altenstetter, goldsmith, and Martin Künle, furrier, both local citizens, followed erroneous and sectarian teachings, bringing suspicion upon themselves that they were holding secret meetings and gatherings. Therefore they were arrested. But as they did not confess to attending meetings, and then offered to better inform themselves, an Honorable Council today decreed that, upon their request and an agreement to appear again if requested, they should be released.

Note. On the orders of both Lord Mayors, Altenstetter was questioned on June 25, 1609, by both Lord Burgomasters in Office, Albrecht von Stetten and Philip Endris, about his religion and confession, to which he avowed that he professes to the Evangelical Confession that is called Lutheran, attends the sermons of the same, and wishes to remain with it. This is in accordance with both Lord Burgomasters' written report, which is to be found with the interrogation record of Altenstetter and *consortium*. Künle, however, has already died.

2.10 Ban on Assembly during the Imperial Occupation, 1629[28]

As part of the hostilities of the Thirty Years' War, imperial troops occupied Augsburg between 1629 and 1632 and temporarily forced the populace into Catholicism (see Chapter Ten).

An Honorable Council here in Augsburg is particularly displeased to have been informed that many local citizens and residents are insolently allowing themselves of late to gather in great numbers in certain places in order to publicly preach, sing, and participate in other activities that have been forbidden on His Imperial Majesty's orders. This is in violation of their solemn oath sworn to God and the authorities to completely refrain from all gathering, congregating, and assembling, and also to remain loyal, heedful, and obedient to the Lord Burgomasters and an Honorable Council, or their appointed representatives, and to dutifully comply with all of their orders and bans. And it is also in violation of the most recent Imperial Order on the abolishment of the practice of the Augsburg Confession and the resulting proclamations and decrees.

Also, when they are asked to disband by the authorities, they contemptuously continue what they are doing in spite of it, and physically resist the bailiffs. And on top of that, they are heard to say defiantly

---

28. SuStBA, 2°Aug.10. 2. Abt., Nr. 475a, 29.11.1629.

and disobediently that no one is going to stop them without trouble. This assembling and demonstrated disobedience could easily bring civic peace and welfare into ruin, and lead to dangerous rebellion, tumult, and bloodshed.

[Thus an Honorable Council again orders everyone to] refrain from all public gatherings of this sort, or others that are also forbidden (such as singing at funerals), and to subject themselves in every respect to the will of the emperor. And they are to remember the oath that they have taken and their obedient duty, and not give cause for more stringent measures. For in the interest of peace and the general welfare, as well as out of respect for the Emperor and authority, an Honorable Council has resolved once and for all to observe this vigilantly, and make such an example of violators, regardless of who they are, that others will certainly take it seriously.

2.11 Interrogation of Thomas Schueler, Weaver, for Practicing Lutheranism during the Imperial Occupation, 1630[29]

On Tuesday, October 8, 1630, Thomas Schueler, weaver, in the jail, testified to and answered the accompanying questions under earnest threat as follows:

1. What is his name, where is he from, and how old is he? 2. What does he do for a living? His name is Thomas Schueler. He's a local citizen and a weaver by trade, around forty years old.

3. How often has he been arrested, and why? When he was still single he was once placed in the irons for fighting and not reporting it. Otherwise never again until now.

4. Do certain people not congregate in his house every Sunday and holiday for whom he gives or reads a sermon, and afterward sing with one another? Who are these people? And how long have they been having these meetings? What has he profited from it? Not on all Sundays and holidays, but occasionally on Sundays, starting about five or six weeks ago, a few of his neighbors have come to visit him without him having asked them to. Specifically, Hans Roühardt, sack carrier; Euphrosina, a cartier's wife; Appolonia Baderin; and a widow were at his house. He read them something of the Gospels and the book of meditations, and afterward they did some singing, which

---

29. StadtAA, Urgicht Thomas Schueler, October 8, 1630.

he was prompted to do by devotion and the Holy Spirit. He didn't gain anything from it or ask for anything.

5. Does he not read or preach so loudly that not only the people on the street in front of the house often stop but also the neighbors can clearly hear everything? And after he completes his sermon, do not he and his listeners, along with the neighbors in their houses, all sing loudly together? Since his home is not far up from the ground, it may well be that they could be heard, and also that others sang along with them in their own homes.

6. Does he not know that, in accordance with the abolishment of the practice of the Augsburg Confession here, such secret congregations and sermons in hidden corners are forbidden, and instead His Royal Majesty has earnestly commanded that Sundays and holidays be spent in church listening to the public sermons? He didn't understand that the prohibition of the practice of religion meant that one could not sing Christian prayers and psalms at home, or read the Gospels and the meditations. That's all he did. Otherwise he observes the Imperial Command in dutiful honor.

7. Why then did he act in violation of this? And will he and his obey the Imperial Order to go to the Catholic Church from now on? He didn't think that it would attract such a crowd, and that he would get in trouble for it; otherwise he wouldn't have done it. He will be glad to cease doing it from now on. Otherwise he hopes that God will arrange everything for the best. Begs otherwise for mercy and to be released. . . .

Thomas Schueler should be released and put out of the city.
Decreed in the Senate, October 10, 1630.

2.12 A Gospel Parody, 1631[30]

This parody was found on the person of Augsburg citizen Hans Fürst, guard at Jacob's Gate, who claimed to have gotten it from a Nuremberg weaver.

A nice Gospel, aimed at all worldly and clerical lay and get laid brothers as a useful consolation

Today's Gospel on dickedy Thursday[31] out of Genitals 24 Cowtail 8, Luke first and Lick last.

30. StadtAA, Urgicht Hans Fürst, May 21, 1631.

31. *Gzumpeten* (dickedy)—a crude play on "Gelumpeten" or "raggedy" Thursday, the Thursday before Shrovetide (*Lump* means "rag"; *Zump* means "male member").

The holy Bishop of St. Anna was led into a cloister by the Abbess of St. Stephan in order to tempt him. And when he had spent forty days and forty nights therein, he found that holy matrimony was good. And the Abbess came and said unto him, If thou be the Bishop of St. Anna, command these nuns that they should all be made Lutheran. And he said, It is also written, thou shalt not tempt the Bishop of your Lord. And she again brought him into another convent, and put him before all the nuns, and said unto him again, If thou be the Bishop of St. Anna, then command that all these nuns should be made secularized. For it is written, be fruitful and multiply. And he answered and said, It is also written, Thou shalt live in chastity and discipline, and not encourage your Bishop to fornicate. And nothing would help, so she took him into her own beautiful room and showed him all her riches, pearls, jewels, chains and treasures, cunt and tits, and the breasts of her lovely tender young body and said unto him, All of this I will give thee if thou therefore wilt fall down and cover me. And he said unto her, *Ei,* come here, you lovely and well-formed creature, for it is written, that two and two and not three should be together. And he quit being clerical and slept with the Abbess. And when the other nuns, monks, and priests saw this, they came forth and served him, and did it also, *etc.*

Chapter Three
A Society of Orders

According to a pervasive philosophy that influenced European thought from the Middle Ages until the Enlightenment, all of God's creations on earth were arranged in a great "chain of being" that reached from the basest mineral up through the highest form of earthly life, humankind. At the bottom was the inanimate class (minerals), followed by plants, then animals, then man. Above man in the chain was the heavenly sphere with its hierarchy of angels and, of course, God at the top; and beneath the lowest element were the depths of hell. A natural hierarchy existed within each of these categories as well. Among the minerals, gold was on a higher plane than brass, diamonds higher than gold. Animals with only a sense of touch but no other faculties, such as shellfish, were lower on the chain than fish and insects, which in turn were below animals such as dogs and horses. The angels, who embodied pure reason and spirituality, also existed in a hierarchy of orders.

Early modern philosophy placed human beings at the center of this system. With their feet in the clay of a corrupted earth and their souls reaching out for salvation, humans were the only beings endowed with both the physical senses shared by beasts and the intellect that otherwise existed only among angels. Thus they metaphorically incorporated the entire chain of being. This idea of a "Divine Hierarchy" underpinned notions of social hierarchy as well, expressed in terms of "orders" or "estates." In theory, humans were arranged into three such estates. The first of these consisted of the clergy, whose role it was to pray, providing a link between humankind and the divine. The second estate was the nobility, whose role was to defend and govern. Finally, the third estate—that of the commoners who made up the vast majority of society—was bound to work, providing nourishment for the entire system.

Within each of these estates, of course, additional hierarchies existed, which by the sixteenth century were characterized by a complicated system of rank and privilege. This was as true of the church hierarchy (pope, cardinal, bishop, abbot, etc.) as it was of the nobility (king, prince, duke, count, etc.). Most problematic for the theory that shored up this system was the increasing stratification of the so-called commoners, especially in the towns. The land-based feudal notion of a third estate dedicated to agricultural production in the form of peasant labor had little relevance to the reality of economics in sixteenth-century towns, which were dominated by trade and production. The rise of a wealthy class of nonnoble urban elites challenged the basis of the earthly hierarchy. Thus it comes as no surprise that it was in the towns (especially those in Switzerland and the south of Germany) that the most radical attacks on church hierarchies also originated.

In the German towns, the social hierarchy was topped by a wealthy class of urban gentry called patricians, with the governing council usually dominated by a few powerful families. Many patricians had family ties to the nobility and a few had noble titles, although the majority were not of noble status. Second in the town hierarchy were the merchants, whose wealth challenged and often surpassed that of the patricians, although they did not share their elevated social status. The names of patricians and merchants were invariably identified in the documents with the title *Herr* or *Frau,* which in modern German would simply be "Mr." or "Mrs.," but in the context of the early modern social system are best rendered as "Lord" and "Lady." No such titles appear in connection with those of the "commons," who made up the rest of the town population.

Each of these groups in turn was also characterized by a sociopolitical hierarchy and sometimes unrelated variations in wealth. The greatest disparity existed among those of the artisan classes, whose members ranged from the wealthy goldsmiths and fur traders who occasionally intermarried with members of the Merchants' Society, to impoverished craftsmen partially dependent on alms. Below the artisans in status were day-laborers, servants, and the beggars and vagrants who made up the ranks of the truly poor.

As the shift from a land-based society to an economy based increasingly on trade in manufactured goods made differences in social rank less obvious, those in a position of power worked harder to create institutions that shored up their position of status and privilege. To distinguish themselves from commoners, for whom membership in a formal guild or craft was a condition of citizenship, first the patricians and then the merchants established exclusive, club-like "societies" that defined their privilege. The Patricians' ("Lords'") Society and the Merchants' Society were both identified by membership in a private drinking hall, which also provided space for exclusive socializing. So-called sumptuary legislation, or luxury laws, issued during the sixteenth and seventeenth centuries (here represented by wedding and clothing ordinances) further delineated social difference by limiting displays of wealth to those of a certain status. These and other ordinances and documents normally identified patricians and merchants by referring to them directly as "those belonging to the Drinking Room Societies," or for short, "those of the Rooms."

Wealth in this civic society was overwhelmingly concentrated in the hands of the richest citizens, with 80 percent of all taxable property in Augsburg belonging to less than 5 percent of the taxpayers at the dawn of the sixteenth century. In fact, 30 percent of all of the city's assets was controlled by only twenty-two people. Little had changed a century later.[1] Those at the top of this financial and social hierarchy, however, had both a civic duty and a Christian obligation to provide for those at the bottom, for the poor served the rich as a stimulus for Christian charity, an example of humility, and a deterrent to wasteful living. In both Protestant and Catholic areas of Europe, reforms in poor laws enacted during the Reformation era increasingly made providing for the poor a civic rather than an individual obligation.

But the poor were not all equally entitled to the benefits of civic poor relief. A theoretical distinction separated those considered "deserving" from those who were "undeserving." In the first category were persons assumed to bear no fault for their circumstances, such as elderly widows, orphaned children, disabled persons, and others apparently incapable of work. In the latter group, deemed undeserving of alms, were the so-called sturdy beggars—healthy men and women whose lack of means was assumed to result from idleness and wasteful living. In practice, this distinction often translated into resident beggars versus vagrants and other nonresident wanderers.

Augsburg provided for its deserving poor not only in the form of alms but also through civic institutions. Various kinds of hospitals offered care for the sick and infirm, at the same time isolating those with contagious disease from the rest of the populace. In 1572, Augsburg established the first public orphanage in Germany, where needy children found not only shelter and sustenance but also indoctrination to a life of collective discipline and productive labor. Perhaps most innovative of all was the establishment in the early sixteenth century of the social housing development now known as the Fuggerei, where deserving poor from local families were housed in a walled community of more than 100 well-built, individual homes with gardens. Founded by fabulously wealthy Jacob Fugger "The Rich," the Fuggerei remains in operation today as a monument to the early modern idea that providing

---

1. In 1610, 86 percent of the city's wealth was in the hands of 7 percent of the population.

for the poor not only is good for the soul but also serves to promote social stability and order.

I. Enforcing Status

3.1 Clothing Ordinance, 1582[2]

Social and economic stratification among commoners continued to increase over the course of the early modern period. By the second half of the seventeenth century, the four classes of subnobility represented here had expanded to six.

An Honorable Council of this laudable city of Augsburg would like nothing better than to see each of the citizens and residents here behaving in accordance with their estate when it comes to clothing and adornments, and avoiding unnecessary expenses. However, the council has noted for some time now that luxury in clothing and adornments among some people has so taken the upper hand that one can hardly tell one estate from the other. . . . Therefore, [the council] has composed the following ordinance. . . .

First, regarding the men and women of the Lords' Room

The men of the Lords' Room should not be allowed to use anything better than marten as a lining, but are allowed to dress in velvet, silk, damask, and that of lesser value. Their clothing should not be embroidered, however, and they are forbidden to wear swords with gilded pommels, hilts, or chapes,[3] all on pain of 10 gulden for each offense. . . . Otherwise, they may well wear gold chains, jewels, pearls, bracelets, rings, and brooches in accordance with their custom.

So far as the honorable ladies and maidens of the Lords' Room are concerned, they may wear marten back fur, but nothing better. Otherwise they should dress as they have traditionally, but without embroidery and decorative stitching, on pain of 10 gulden. Velvet shoes and slippers, however, are herewith forbidden. . . . Otherwise they may well wear velvet caps, gold bonnets set with pearls (but not costing more than 100 gulden) . . . and jewels, chains, rings, gilded belts, and things of lesser quality, in accordance with their custom.

2. StadtAA, Ord. und Dek., K14, Kleider-Ordnung October 11, 1582 (print).

3. The *chape* is the protective metal tip on the scabbard.

Regarding adornments and clothing for those of the Merchants' Room and their wives and children

Those men of the Merchants' Room who were specifically named in the settlement between the Lords' and Merchants' Rooms, which was arrived at on the eleventh day of February in 1581 . . . may wear jerkins lined with marten back fur; the others, however, who were not named in the settlement, may wear jerkins lined with marten underbelly fur, and with woolen cloth on the outside with one or two rows of decorative stitching and no trim, and no better lining. Whosoever violates this will be fined 10 gulden for each offense.

Likewise, those of the Merchants' Room may wear doublets and pants of silk and damask, but without embroidery or edging, and with two rows of decorative stitching. And whoever wants to wear their pants paned[4] and lined may line them with watered silk, double taffeta, or other less valuable silk cloth, but may not use more than fourteen elle[5] of the narrow taffeta width. The penalty for each offense is 4 gulden. As far as outer garments are concerned, they may not be made of silk, damask, watered silk, or taffeta, on pain of the above-noted fine.

On the other hand, velvet Polish bonnets lined with marten as well as velvet hoods and hats are permitted and allowed, as is a silver dagger decorated with ten or twelve loths[6] of silver and a sword with eight loths of silver. . . . Also, a coat or simple jerkin may be lined or edged with one and a half elle of velvet. But it is forbidden to wear a good velvet cap, hose made entirely of silk, velvet scabbards, shoes, and slippers, or gilded hilts, pommels, or chapes on swords, all on pain of 4 gulden. . . .

As regards pearls, clasps, brooches, bracelets and necklaces, golden chains, and other jewels, the honorable members of the Merchants' Room are not authorized to wear these if made either of solid gold or if gilded, on pain of 10 gulden. . . . Wearing gold rings, however, is not prohibited.

The honorable ladies and maidens of the Merchants' Room are not allowed to use watered silk or anything better for their capes, but only double taffeta, or something of lower value, without embroidery. And

---

4. *Paned* refers to the popular men's style of "slit" pants, made of strips of fabric over a puffy lining that was sometimes stuffed to appear wider.

5. A unit of measure that varied from place to place. Reference here appears to be to the Nuremberg elle, about 66 cm. An Augsburg elle was slightly shorter at around 60 cm.

6. A unit of measure equal to 1/32 of a local pound; in Augsburg around 15 grams.

they are allowed no better lining than marten underbelly fur. . . . For the bodice they may use at best silk and damask, with one and a half elle of velvet for trim. But for caps, petticoats, [etc.] only watered silk, taffeta, or that of lower value . . . is permitted and allowed. Wearing velvet shoes and slippers is abolished and forbidden, all on pain of a fine of 3 gulden for each offense. . . .

In the case of counts, knights, and Lords who are currently mayors of this city, as well as doctors and academics, whether they belong to one of the Rooms or not, their estate takes precedence, and they may adorn themselves with solid gold, all kinds of silk clothes, or anything else without restriction. They also may clothe their servants in accordance with custom.

All military captains and officers are free to dress as is their custom.

Regarding craftspeople, their wives and children, and those who do not belong to any [Drinking] Room

Those craftsmen who are members neither of the Lords' nor the Merchants' Rooms should not use any better lining for their jacket than wolf and fox belly or back fur, and for the covering nothing better than arlesian cloth, fustian, satin, machey,[7] grosgrain, or woolen cloth.

In addition, they may trim unlined jackets or coats of the sorts specified above with half an elle of velvet, but without ornamental stitching or embroidery. For doublets, they are allowed to use camlet, double taffeta, fustian, and material of lesser value.

They may also make paned pants from wool cloth or leather, and line them with eight elles of arlesian cloth, fustian, machey, simple taffeta at 24 kreuzer, or grosgrain.

Otherwise, however, they are not authorized to wear rings, pearls, chains, or other such things made of solid or spun gold, or plated with gold. But if one of them has a coat of arms, he may wear a gold ring with his crest or seal on it unimpeded. . . . [Violators will be] fined 4 gulden for each offense.

If a member of the commoners should be elected to the council or the court, he may dress and appear as do the merchants (except for the marten back fur).

Women and maidens of the common estate who are not eligible for either of the Rooms may not use any better lining to line capes and other outerwear than fox (belly or back fur). But they may make their

---

7. *Machey* is a woolen cloth (word origin not clear).

lined and simple capes as well as bodices, caps, skirts, and underskirts from arlesian cloth, fustian, machey, grosgrain, or woolen cloth. . . . The skirt may be trimmed with one elle of velvet, an underskirt with two elles of mock velvet, and the bodice and cap with one woolen cloth or a half elle of plain velvet, but all without decorative stitching or embroidery, all on pain of a 4-gulden fine for each offense.

On the other hand, [women of this estate] are permitted and allowed to wear gold rings of the value established by the wedding ordinance or less; a belt decorated with silver that does not cost more than 8 gulden; a pair of scissors[8] decorated with silver up to 3 gulden in value; silver buttons on the bag or coin purse, also up to 3 gulden; a pearl hair band of approximately 4 gulden in value; and a wool cap, or at the most a double taffeta hood. But otherwise they should no longer wear golden bonnets, strings of pearls . . . nor belts made entirely of silver chains, on pain of 4 gulden for each violation.

Tall, high ruffs are herewith also abolished and forbidden to both men and women. . . .

OF SERVANTS

Servants should not wear any velvet caps, berets, or hats, nor any clothes of silk or anything with pearls, hard or spun gold, or gold or silver plate (aside from a sword decorated with five loths of silver). Rather, they should be satisfied with the clothes they are given by their masters.

But if a servant purchases clothes at his own expense, he may dress in nothing better than London wool, leather, fustian, machey, and that of lesser value. And at most eight elle of fustian, satin, machey, or grosgrain should be used for lining one pair of pants (which should be made without silk). For each violation, a fine of 3 gulden in coin will be paid.

Tall ruffs are also not permitted to them. . . .

Serving girls may have a belt decorated with silver worth no more than 3 or 4 gulden, a head wreath worth no more than 1 gulden, and not more than two edgings on their underskirt, which may be made of nothing better than woolen cloth or an elle of mock velvet . . . and without pearls or decorative stitching. The bodice and skirt may be trimmed with an edging made of an eighth of an elle of velvet, but with no decorative stitching or embroidery. In addition, a fur bonnet, a velvet hair band, and a cape of silk may be worn, but nothing of higher value . . . and they may not wear anything of hard gold, spun gold, or gold plate,

---

8. Wearing a pair of scissors hung on one's belt was a popular fashion for early modern German women.

or any silver or pearls (except the above-noted belt that may be up to 4 gulden in value).

Should any person or persons violate this ordinance as here described, she or they will be fined 2 gulden for each separate violation.

Everyone should also be free to dress and adorn themselves more humbly and simply than allowed here, according to their circumstances.

Concerning mourning clothes

Because abuses in the wearing of mourning clothes have been slipping in for some time now, and servants are often dressed so that one can't tell them from their masters, an Honorable Council hereby orders that henceforth, servants and those of the common estate may not wear a mourning coat longer than approximately one hand width under the knee, on pain of a fine of 3 gulden in coin for each violation.

Because, however, many people may already be supplied with clothes that are somewhat costlier than allowed by this ordinance, and for them it would be rather burdensome to have to get rid of them right away, an Honorable Council herewith allows and permits those people to wear such clothes for one year from today, but not longer, and during that time to wear them out or to sell them.

An Honorable Council also expects all tailors and seamstresses who violate these rules in tailoring clothes and anything else noted above to be fined half of each established fine for each violation without fail . . . all with the additional clarification that where this ordinance makes reference to an elle (in respect to velvet and silk), this should in every case be understood as a Nuremberg elle, unless the Augsburg elle is specifically mentioned.

3.2 Wedding Ordinance, 1599[9]

First, regarding the promise of
marriage and the engagement party

The bride and groom or their parents may invite as many people as they want, men and women, to their promise or engagement.[10] Once the engagement is in force, those who will be holding the wedding at their own expense may invite thirty-two people to their wedding feast,

9. StadtAA, Anschläge und Dekrete 1490–1649, No. 51 (print).

10. *Stulfeste,* i.e., the official engagement ceremony, normally accompanied by a priest or pastor. From that point on, the couple was referred to as bride and groom.

relatives and nonrelatives, among them the bride and groom, but not counting children under twelve years of age. The penalty for those who invite more than the above number is 6 gulden.

However, those who hold the wedding at the cost of the guests[11] are allowed to have either an engagement party or a supper, and must choose one or the other. The bride and groom may invite twenty people, relatives and nonrelatives, and not more. At the engagement party no cooked food may be served, either warm or cold, rather only bread, cheese, fruit, and wine. And if there is a supper, each person may only spend as much as the rate that has been (or may in the future be) set and established by an Honorable Council, and the innkeeper may not be paid anything extra either for drink or for the feast. If anyone exceeds the number of persons established above (which doesn't include the bride and groom), they should pay a fine of 3 gulden for each person.

And if the innkeeper serves anything other than what is noted above at the engagement party, or otherwise serves more than established by an Honorable Council at the supper, or accepts any extra payment, he should pay a 5-gulden fine for each offense.

Regarding engagement parties, weddings, and after parties outside of the city

If any local citizen holds an engagement party, wedding, or after party outside the city at his own expense without obtaining permission from an Honorable Council, he should pay a fine of 50 gulden. If someone asks for permission but doesn't get it, and still holds an engagement party, wedding, or after party outside of the city, he should expect another earnest fine in accordance with his disobedience. But those citizens who hold their wedding at the expense of their guests and plan a wedding, engagement party, or after party feast in the villages around the city should pay 10 gulden, and every guest who attends and is a subject of this city will be fined 4 gulden.

Regarding meals and drinking bouts after the groom's bath

Henceforth the meals and drinking bouts that both wealthy and poor have been having after the groom's bath, or otherwise during the

---

11. In Augsburg, commoners held their wedding parties in public houses, where the guests paid for their own meals. The custom both protected the couple from going into debt and provided a clear boundary between commoners and those wealthy enough to hold private weddings.

preparations for the wedding, should be entirely done away with and forbidden, on pain of 20 gulden for those violators who belong to the Lords' or Merchants' Society. But commoners should be fined 6 gulden for this offense. Those who hold weddings at their own expense, however, are permitted and allowed to invite their wedding summoner[12] to a quiet meal on the day that the invitations are made, along with four or five good friends.

REGARDING THE DAY BEFORE THE WEDDING

All supper parties on the night before the wedding should be done away with, both by those who pay for the wedding themselves and those who hold them at the expense of the guests, in order to avoid excessive costs, unless guests traveling from elsewhere have arrived for the wedding. In that case, for the sake of honor and better hospitality, an Honorable Council will allow enough local persons to be invited to fill a round table. In the case that there are more than six visiting guests, then two round tables may be served.

REGARDING THE WEDDING PROCESSION

No one may be blessed and married in their houses or anywhere else other than a public church without permission. Rather, they should go publicly to church and street, on pain of 50 gulden. Those who carry the expense of the wedding themselves are permitted to invite as many people as they wish [to the wedding procession], relatives and nonrelatives. But those who hold their wedding at the expense of their guests may invite to the procession eighty people or less altogether, married or single, relatives or nonrelatives, men or women, but not more . . . upon pain of 2 gulden for each person over this who is invited.

An Honorable Council herewith decrees that all citizens and residents hold their weddings before Invocabit, that is, the first Sunday in Lent, and no weddings should be held afterward through Easter, or on holidays or Sundays throughout the entire year, on penalty of earnest punishment. . . .

Herewith it is also forbidden on pain of 2 gulden to share any kind of breakfast soup, or sweet wines, brandy, vermouth, or other wine with the wedding guests before the wedding procession, whether in a public house or anywhere else, unless it is inside the houses of those belonging

---

12. A summoner (*Hochzeitlader*) was a person hired to make invitations and organize aspects of the wedding.

to the two Societies. This does not apply to the wine that is carried at the wedding procession, which is allowed in accordance with established tradition.

But insofar as it is an old tradition that those belonging to the Lords' Society send four young men in the early morning to ride around on horseback and invite the women and maidens to the dance in the dance house, [the young men] and their servants may be given a bite of boiled chicken, soup, and meat, along with a suitable amount of drink.

CONCERNING THE ARRANGEMENT OF PERSONS FOR WALKING AND SITTING DURING WEDDING PROCESSIONS, MEALS, AND DANCES

As there has thus far been no evidence of discord or impropriety in the arrangement of the men, rather they have always been placed in accordance with lists prepared by the fathers who arrange the wedding, an Honorable Council will leave that as it is.

As far as the women and maidens go, an agreement was devised and composed in 1581 between the members of the Lords' and the Merchants' Societies, but not all of its contents have been adhered to lately. It is therefore the will and command of an Honorable Council that this will be followed from now on. For the sake of clarity the details are provided below.

During the procession, first and foremost should come the common maidens, followed by the maidens of the Merchants' Room, and after them the maidens of the Lords' Room. Next comes the bride; the two women whom she has asked [to stand up for her], regardless of rank; and then the women of the Lords' Room who wear golden bonnets[13] at the dance. After these come the younger women of the Merchants' Room in bonnets, and then the older women of the Lords' Room who normally wear veils, followed by the old women in veils from the Merchants' Room, and lastly [the women] of the commons.

At the wedding banquet, the bride should be seated first together with her two chosen women, regardless of their rank, and then the oldest women in veils of the Lords' Room, and after them the older women in veils of the Merchants' Room, followed by the women in golden bonnets from the Lords' Room, and after them the younger women in bonnets from the Merchants' Room, and last the old and young women of the commoners. Next the maidens of the Lords should be seated,

---

13. Wearing a bonnet or other head covering indicated that a woman was married.

followed by those of the merchants, and last the common maidens. And at the engagement and also the after party the order should be the same, except that the seating of the bride and bridesmaids should be left as is customary. . . .

Nonresident women and maidens who travel here in honor of the wedding or otherwise do not reside here, as well as baronesses or those belonging to the ancient nobility, are not affected by the above order, rather should be honored in walking and seating as is appropriate and in accordance with tradition.

As far as other women and maidens go, however, those who are not citizens or members of the Societies but are here in service, or live here for another reason, should not be put ahead of the women and maidens of the Lords' Society. They should instead be content to remain either among and beside those of the Lords' or Merchants' Societies, according to age, or among the commoners, in accordance with their own or their husbands' lineage, status, and service.

In order that the above order will be all the more steadfastly adhered to, the wedding summoner is required to arrange the women and maidens, to obtain a list from the fathers who are arranging the wedding, and to follow it [or face a severe penalty].

Each woman and maiden should on her own behave in accordance with her estate and the above ordinance, and not force herself farther forward than she belongs. . . .

[Limits are also included for other aspects of the wedding, including meals and dances, gifts to the bride and groom, the cost of the bride's wreath, sending out food for those who do not attend, fees for musicians and other services, and additional feasts and parties.]

August 7, 1599.

II. Scenes from Life at the Top

3.3 The Lords' Drinking Room Society Is Established in 1412[14]

Although the Lords' Drinking Room appears here to have originated as a kind of exclusive social club, by the sixteenth century, it had become the political as well as the social center of Augsburg's most privileged circles.

14. Markus Welser, *Chronica der weitberühmten Kaiserlichen freien und des H. Reichs Stadt Augsburg in Schwaben* (Frankfurt, 1595, facs., Augsburg, 1984), Part II, 151.

A second society, the Merchants' Room, was established in 1479. While one had to be born to the Lords' Society, membership in the Merchants' Drinking Room could be attained via economic success.

Because the sons of the patricians, when they sought entertainments, merriment, and good cheer, were prone to gather in the Franciscan monastery or in other suspicious corners, their parents and the most distinguished Lords [of this city] had reason to turn to their peer, Peter Riederer, who rented them his house on Perlach Hill in this year [1412] for a certain fee. In this house, gaming and drinking were allowed only to those who were registered as members, to the avoidance of other drinking rooms, as befits the preservation of their station and reputation.

3.4 The Silesian Knight Hans von Schweinichen Describes Elite Hospitality in Augsburg[15]

Hans von Schweinichen (1552–1616), a member of the Silesian nobility, served as chamberlain and later steward to the flamboyant adventurer Duke Henry XI of Liegnitz. Duke Henry is best known for spending much of his life traveling and running up debts, for which he was finally imprisoned in 1581. Schweinichen chronicled his liege's misadventures in a travel memoir, which he kept beginning in 1568. Here, he describes amusements among Augsburg's wealthiest citizens.

1575
[While staying in Augsburg,] I was very often entertained, along with my companions, by wealthy people and patricians. They did me great honor and were well known, and I had good friends among them. There are fine amusements in the [Lords'] Drinking Room there. One finds there gamblers, drinkers, and other knightly games, whatever one wishes. If you invite guests and pay 18 wg[16] per person, you are given food for twenty, and the best Reinfal[17] and Rhine wine that one can get, until you are completely drunk. I invited people to the Drinking Room like this several times. But if you pay a thaler per person, then you are

15. Johann Gustav Büsching (ed.), *Lieben, Lust und Leben der Deutschen des sechzehnten Jahrhunderts in den Begebenheiten des schlesischen Ritters Hans von Schweinichen* (Breslau, 1820, 3 vols.), 1:157–59.

16. White groschen (silver groat). Eighteen white groschen would have been equal to a little less than a gulden.

17. A sweet wine from Rivoli in Italy.

treated like a prince. I wished that I could have spent my life and many years there.

Lord Marcus Fugger once entertained His Princely Grace [Duke Henry] along with a gentleman from Schönberg, who was also staying in the same quarters as His Princely Grace. I have scarcely ever seen such a banquet. One could not have treated the Holy Roman Emperor any better, for it was of abundant splendor. The feast had been prepared in a hall in which there was more gold than any other color. The floor was of marble and so polished that it was like walking on ice. There was a table set up in the shape of a cross that filled the entire hall. It was laid with lots of serving dishes, which, they say, were made of over a ton of gold, and amazingly beautiful Venetian glasses. I was responsible for His Princely Grace's drinks.

Lord Fugger then presented His Princely Grace with a welcome drink in a vessel of the finest Venetian glass, in the shape of a ship, artfully made. After I had taken it from the serving table and was walking across the hall, I slipped, having new shoes on, and fell on my back in the middle of the hall. The wine poured over my neck, and completely ruined my new clothes of red damask. But the pretty ship also broke into many pieces. Although there was then a lot of suppressed laughter from everyone, I was told later that Lord Fugger said he had paid 100 gulden for that ship. But it wasn't my fault, for I had neither eaten nor drunken anything. Once I got drunk, I stood much more firmly and didn't fall down again, even when dancing. It's my opinion that God didn't want me in so much finery, for I had put on new clothes and thought I was the grandest. The Lords and all of us were all very merry over this.

Lord Fugger took His Princely Grace around the house, which was an immensely huge house in which the Holy Roman Emperor and his entire court had stayed during the imperial diets. Lord Fugger brought His Princely Grace into a little tower where he showed him a treasure of chains, jewels, and precious stones, as well as unusual coins and pieces of gold as big as one's head, which Fugger said himself was worth over a million in gold. Afterward he opened a chest that was full to the top with ducats and crowns. He said it was 200,000 gulden that he had loaned to the King of Spain with bills of exchange. Then he took His Princely Grace up the same tower, which from the peak to about halfway down was roofed with good thalers. He said it amounted to about 17,000 imperial thalers. Therewith he showed His Princely Grace a great honor, while at the same time showing him his power and wealth.

It is said that Lord Fugger had so much wealth that he could pay for an empire. He honored me in this instance with a nice groschen of about nine grains[18] because of the fall. His Princely Grace also reckoned with a handsome gift, but on that visit he got nothing but a good tipsiness. His Princely Grace was a guest there several times after that, and was always well treated. I was also invited and Lord Fugger placed himself at my service most assiduously. During this time Fugger promised his daughter to a count, and agreed to provide with her 200,000 thaler in a year and a day, along with jewels. That is some dowry!

III. Providing for the Poor

3.5 A Foundation for the Fuggerei[19]

In the name of the holy indivisible trinity, and the mother of the Almighty and most holy Virgin Mary, and all of God's saints, I, Jacob Fugger, citizen of Augsburg, profess with this deed and charter and give notice to all who see, read, or hear it: My late brothers Ulrich and Georg the Fuggers and I, in praise and thanks to God for the goodness and lucky circumstances that he has thus far shown us in our commerce with worldly goods, built the better part of a chapel for the brothers of Our Dear Lady here in Augsburg. And after the death of my two brothers, I completed the construction together with my brothers' surviving sons. On the seventeenth day of the month of January in the elapsed fifteen hundred and eighteenth year we had it dedicated, in accordance with Christian order, to the honor of the tender Corpus of our Lord Jesus Christ, as well as the Mother of God and Saint Mathew. And further, I and my relatives, in praise and honor of God, and to help poor day-laborers and craftsmen, built a number of houses here in Augsburg, called *In Kappenzipfel,* and have undertaken to complete them in that location. Each and every bit of it [was built with] a part of my and my two brothers' own property, and after their deaths, my brothers' sons' own [property] . . . as well as from the 15,000 gulden that I personally set aside on Friday, St. Valentine's Day of the elapsed year fifteen hundred and eleven, in the accounts of one of my companies. This I [declare] on the sixth day of the month of August in the current year of fifteen hundred and twenty-one.

---

18. A unit of weight measure based on a barleycorn.

19. Hermann Kellenbenz, "Jakob Fuggers Stiftungsbrief von 1521," *Zeitschrift des historischen Vereins für Schwaben* 68 (1974), 95–116.

Being currently in possession of good counsel and well-considered disposition and mind, I have undertaken and established the below ordinance and foundation, and do all of this knowingly, with the power of this document. Thus from this day forward for all time, I myself during my lifetime, and after my death the above-named relatives and their descendents, will maintain the structures of this chapel and the above-noted poor people houses, and also provide the chapel and alter with liturgical vestments, regalia, candles, and other necessary things, and see that the chapel is cleaned every quarter year, and that nothing is built too close to it. We will also see that no one's coat of arms except for ours be allowed in or on it, and that a mass is read every day in the chapel, and otherwise everything is done as is appropriate in accordance with the [orders of the church]. But the organ-maker is granted and permitted at this time, on the basis of his supplication, to place his crest on the organ in order to show that he made it. An organist should also be appointed to the organ for 50 gulden and maintained for all time. . . .

In addition, the Prior, cloister, and their descendents should for all time, each quarter beginning with the next coming quarter and every quarter thereafter, proclaim for my father Jacob Fugger's death, and my mother Barbara Bässingerin's, for Ulrich's, Georg's, and, after my death, mine (Jacob Fugger's), as brothers and their sons; as well as for all of their siblings' and descendants' souls, who have departed from this lineage or who depart from it in the future. This they should do in the evening with a vigil and in the morning with an office for the dead, and also a walk over the grave, as is the custom. . . .

And these poor peoples' houses should be provided to pious poor day-laborers and craftsmen, citizens and residents of this city of Augsburg who are needy and for whom it will do the most good, for the sake of God, and without respect to gifts or remuneration.

In return, each household should pay 1 gulden each year, namely every six months on St. Michael's Day [January 23][20] half a gulden and on St. Jori's Day [July 23] half a gulden for maintenance of the buildings. And each should repair that which he breaks. Also each person, young or old, if he is capable, should say an Our Father, Ave Maria, and a profession of faith each day for aid and solace to the souls of my father, mother, and also Ulrich and Georg Fugger, and all of our siblings' children and our progeny. . . .

In addition, I, my relatives, and our subsequent administrators should have the power and authority to utilize the front building that is located

20. Michaelis eremita.

on St. Jacob Street along with the stables as necessary, or put those who administer the poor people's houses in it, according to our wishes. . . .

And so that the chapel and also the poor people's houses, together with the foundation, buildings, and the rest . . . may be the better and more handsomely maintained and upheld, I hereby provide from my and my brothers' sons' goods and chattel, and also that of the entire company, 10,000 Rhenish gulden.

3.6 Ordinance for the Alms Lords and Administrators of the Needy Poor, 1522[21]

An Honorable Council of this city of Augsburg has previously created and produced many good rules and regulations regarding raising and collecting the holy alms, so that they would be consumed and utilized beneficially, honorably, and in accordance with need. Nonetheless, however, [the council] hears often and daily that . . . many men and women are consuming and wasting these holy alms uselessly, in more ways than one, in spite of an Honorable Council's rules. Thus the other people who are in need have their sustenance taken from them, and are prevented from receiving alms. . . .

First and foremost, four or six men of honorable status and character are to be appointed who will henceforth be called the Alms Lords and Administrators of the needy poor. They will also be given four or six honest subofficials, who are paid a fitting salary. On Sundays and all official holidays, morning and afternoon, these four or six men, together with their appointed subordinates, will visit all parishes and cloisters, and if necessary also go house to house as they deem appropriate, and take up and collect holy alms for the needy poor. These collected donations they will then distribute and give to poor, needy persons as appropriate, and where it will be the most useful. And so that the alms they collect can be utilized and distributed in a way that is most certain to be of good use, these same officials and their subordinates should visit and call at the homes of the poor people once a week, and truly observe and judge what their need, lack, and situation is. Then they should distribute the alms to the poor accordingly, always where it appears to be most needed. . . .

Second (as was also covered in the old ordinance), henceforth no man or woman who is an adult and has reached the age of majority, whether married, widowed, or single, citizen or outsider, may beg in this

21. SuStBA, 4°Aug.10 2. Abt., 1–14, March 27, 1522.

city of Augsburg at any time, day or night, nor publicly seek or collect alms, unless they have been permitted and allowed by the above-noted alms officials. And for this purpose, as a sign and marker, they will be given an alms symbol, which each person who is permitted to take alms should wear openly on their person.

Third . . . if the alms officials should find that anyone who receives alms consumes it wastefully or otherwise uses it in any way that is not appropriate and honorable, or if the officials discover that alms were sought or collected in front of the churches or in other public places without permission (and without wearing the symbol as noted above), the officials will take measures against the person or persons appropriate to the situation. . . .

[And] all men and women who receive permission to seek alms as described above, and await their alms in front of the church, may have with them and sitting by them only their own children, and no one else's. . . . Also no boy or daughter over ten years old who can work and earn their bread will be permitted or allowed to seek or collect alms in front of the church or in any other place. Rather, if the father or mother has knowledge of this, and they are raising their children to do this, they should be banished from the city without mercy. . . .

Each and every beggar in this city, male or female, must stay away from the wine and beer houses and never gamble. And if one or more of them are found therein or caught gambling, he or they will first be put in the Fool's House, and then from there escorted out of the city.

3.7 A New Poor Law, 1541[22]

Although an Honorable Council of this laudable city of Augsburg is most desirous and inclined to offer their benevolent generosity and alms not only to their poor, needy fellow citizens and residents but also to afflicted outsiders and foreigners who come to this city and its environs in great numbers every day, they nonetheless find that God's commandment holds them more accountable to come to the aid of those who have sworn allegiance to them, and who are found within these city walls. For [the local poor] have also reached such numbers that it is nearly impossible to continue to help them as we have up to now, even without tolerating outsiders coming in to collect alms and taking the bread out of the mouths of the locals. . . . Thus an Honorable Council, in good Christian faith and out of unavoidable necessity, has established the

22. StadtAA, Schätze 16, 60v–63r.

following rules and requirements and commanded the appointed Alms Lords to abide by them rigorously. . . .

First, no nonresident or foreign beggar, whether male or female, young or old, under whatever pretense they come here, will be permitted to collect alms or to beg here in the city, but will be put out of the city [and sworn to stay out] by the appointed officials wherever they are found, as has also been the case in the past. And any person who had been put out of the city that should come back in to beg in violation of their pledge will, depending on the circumstances, be placed in the beggar's tower for two or three days on bread and water for the first offense, and afterward be sworn out of the city with an earnest warning that if they come back in, no mercy will be shown, and they will be beaten back out with rods. . . .

And insofar as such a generous amount of alms is provided in this city, and to the extent possible, no one who is in need has thus far been ignored or left destitute, it is also Christian and appropriate that all are satisfied with this. So it is herewith forbidden by an Honorable Council for anyone to go begging among the citizens or residents, either on the open streets or in the houses. And should anyone be found begging here, young or old, male or female, on the streets or in the houses, day or night, they will be given nothing from the poor chest for an entire month, and will be told that if they don't refrain from begging in the future or send their children to beg, they will be put out of the city without mercy. This an Honorable Council also intends to enforce.

In addition, an Honorable Council has taken timely notice of the fact that a great many poor folk in this city, as in other German communities, have thus far been supported from the general poor chest through provision of cash money. However, an apparent defect in this practice has come to light, in that the poor do not all have the adroitness (or in the case of some, the will) to use the money they receive in the most useful and best way for physical nourishment. These people don't always procure for their few pfennigs that which they really need at home—rather, as is so often the case, some are inclined to spend their alms on wine and delicacies, and leave their wives and children empty-handed. In order to address this defect and to change things for the better, an Honorable Council has finally decided that henceforth, no one will be given cash from the common chest without a specific justification. Instead, they will receive bread, lard, and flour, which will be distributed in three locations in the city every week on Saturday, namely in St. Ulrich's Church, at St. Jacob's, and at St. George's. This is in the best interest and in order to better manage almsgiving, so that the wealthy and rich will be more inclined to donate handsomely. The distributions should be conducted in accordance with the opinion of the appointed Alms Lords and the needs of the poor, with as much industry and as honestly as possible, and the giving of cash money should herewith be ceased.

So that these alms will not be used for anything other than physical sustenance and support, it is an Honorable Council's earnest will and judgment that every alms recipient should use alms provisions for himself and his wife and children, and under no circumstances sell them or trade or exchange them for wine or delicacies, on pain of losing all support from the poor chest. Any publican, publican's wife, or anyone else who takes provisions provided as alms and exchanges them for money, wine, or the like, will be earnestly punished. . . .

Those married persons who are in good health and know a trade, and who do not have more than two children, will henceforth not be given anything from the poor chest, rather only those who work faithfully and still do not earn enough to support themselves. . . .

An Honorable Council has also become aware of the sinful, frivolous abuse of people who have no expectation of a livelihood often getting married only in order to collect alms, which is obvious by the fact that after many weddings, the couple applies for alms within a fourth or a half of a year. This is most contemptuous and not to be tolerated. Therefore the council has resolved and concluded that, henceforth, no one will be provided with alms until they have been a citizen here for at least five years. In addition, anyone who enters into such an abominable unchristian marriage shall not have access to alms for at least five years. . . .

Whosoever doesn't wear the alms symbol will henceforth receive no help from the poor chest, unless there is a very good reason for it. For it has become obvious that this generally has been a bad investment.

Another harmful abuse that is practically being treated as a right is that if someone wants their child to learn a craft, they try to obtain the apprentice fee out of the poor chest. This an Honorable Council . . . completely abolishes. . . .

So that no effort will be spared that could increase and improve the poor chest, an Honorable Council has commanded that alms be collected faithfully not only at church services and weddings but also at funerals and burials and that reasons be provided for generous giving, so that it will be seen that an Honorable Council does not forbear to provide what it can for the welfare and well-being of its poor fellow citizens and residents . . . and this ordinance will go into effect and be put in force on Friday, the coming June 17. Proclaimed by an Honorable Council on Saturday, May 7, 1541.

3.8 Visitation of the Fuggerei in 1624[23]

Praise God 1624, in Augsburg on March 11.

Upon the visitation of the Fuggerei graciously ordered by the Most Well-born Lord, Lord Georg Fugger the Elder,[24] Knight of the Order of Calatrava and governor in upper and lower Swabia, etc., administrator of the Common Fugger Foundation, etc., here is how and in what condition we the undersigned [Andreas Spindler and Georg Hanschuecher] found the rooms and persons from [houses] numbers 1 to 52, and first:

No. 1, upstairs and downstairs, where it is customary to put the Lord Fugger's servants when they are ill, lives Leonhard Braun, who is Lord Hans Ernst Fugger's gatekeeper. He keeps [his place] clean and there is nothing needing repairs, except that the well basin is all broken up. His wife has her mother with her, an old woman.

No. 2, downstairs, Georg Schwaiger, carpenter, has four children and otherwise no one else lives with him. He requests boards to fix up his wood shed and the chamber floor.

No. 2, upstairs, Carl Jäger's widow, who is still alone because her husband died only four weeks ago.[25] She has eight children, but only one daughter is still single and living with her. It is a well-made apartment and kept clean.

No. 3, downstairs, Elizabeth Erttiner, widow, who is also still alone, since the widow who lived with her recently died and left four children. Of these, two went to the orphanage, and the other two are still here. One can't really put anyone else with her until these two children are taken care of. At that time, this widow could be placed with Carl [Jäger's widow], who lives upstairs. But since this apartment is in very bad shape, it would be good to consider putting a carpenter in it who could help [fix it up] himself with less cost to the foundation.

No. 3, upstairs, Georg Koler, guard, has three children and a sick wife, and otherwise no one else living with him. There is nothing wrong with the apartment other than that they live rather slovenly.

---

23. Fürstlich und Gräflich Fugger'sches Familien und Stiftungs-Archiv, Dillingen, 5.2.11, 11–23, transcribed in Hans Ropertz, "Kleinbürgerlicher Wohnbau vom 14. bis 17. Jahrhundert in Deutschland und im benachbarten Ausland," Eng.D. diss., Rheinisch-Westfälische Technische Hochschule Aachen, 1976 (typescript).

24. This paragraph actually appears twice, once for Georg Fugger the Elder and once for Georg Fugger the Younger.

25. Widows were normally housed in pairs.

No. 4, downstairs, Silvester Brecheisen, wood measurer, keeps the apartment clean, has done a lot of improvements himself. There are only a wife and husband and a twelve-year-old daughter. There is a new stone bath built onto the oven. In spite of the fact that people started doing this many years ago, it appears that it is damaging to the buildings and ovens because of the condensation and dampness. And because such baths are becoming predominant in many of the apartments (as can be seen in the following list), we await [Your Grace's] orders in this matter.

No. 4, upstairs, Peter Schmach, choir singer at St. Moritz, just him and his wife, old people, keep the apartment fairly clean. There is also a bath built onto the oven. The roof needs work.

No. 5, downstairs, Adam Mülich, widower, guard under Bird Gate with two children, keeps a very slovenly house, but in our opinion the reason is that the children are small and he isn't home much. His apartment is otherwise still in good shape.

No. 5, upstairs, Georg Hauser, border-maker,[26] widower, keeps a clean house, his apartment is in good shape, has two children and has his sustenance for free.[27] And one can immediately see that if someone has a little in the way of provisions, the apartment is kept up and the house is kept clean.

No. 6, downstairs, Tobias Hofherr, weaver, they are old people with two children, but only one with them. Keep house the way poor people do, the apartment is otherwise in pretty good shape.

No. 6, upstairs, Mathias Knöpflin, gate guard, they are only two old, worn-out people living in great poverty, but nonetheless they keep a clean house and there is nothing needing repairs. . . .

No. 8, downstairs, Sebastian Dietz, painter, widower together with a widow, Anna Rait. This is a wide apartment, and is in very bad shape because of their poverty. The best for him would be an institution. The widow was only put in with him so that she could bring what he needs, since he himself can't go out. . . .

No. 9, upstairs, Jacob Fischer, grocer and sack carrier, keeps a clean house, just the two of them, there is nothing to repair. They have only been in the Fuggerei for eight weeks, and were allowed in at the request of Lord Peter Cassian. According to some, there were more needy people at hand. . . .

---

26. Someone who makes decorative borders of braid, lace, etc. on clothing.

27. It is not clear whether this refers to provision of food of some kind, perhaps as a benefice, or a small income that could be from an inheritance.

No. 13, upstairs, Hans Bast, mounted guard, has only one child, and an apartment in good shape. According to what is said, he is supposed to have a good fortune, but they are old, decrepit people, and both were long in service to the Fuggers. . . .

No. 25, upstairs, Adam Niederer, coal shovel–maker, just him and a strong young daughter, with nothing at all in the house. They lie on straw and keep house so badly that we were astonished and saw nothing else like it in any other apartment. He is an old, decrepit man who can't hear.

No. 26, downstairs, Hans Wolf, carpenter, has two children, and according to the neighbors, a bad, dissolute wife, who is always putting up different girls and other strangers. Otherwise they are poor enough, and were taken in by Your Grace two years ago.

No. 26, upstairs, Leonhard Ritter, coachman for St. Ulrich, has two children and keeps a nice house, does improvements on his apartment himself. . . .

No. 32, downstairs, Hans Seitz, gardener, has two children and his sister-in-law with him instead of a maid. She also used to live in the Fuggerei, but was put out for quarreling. She is the sister of the City Fisherman. He otherwise keeps house honorably and well, and takes good care of the apartment.

No. 32, upstairs, Jacob Beichter, locksmith, has one child and a poor income, takes pretty good care of the apartment. But based on his strength and his craft, and the good position and customers he had before, he should have a good fortune. He knows best the reason for his ruin.

Nos. 40, 41, and 42, were three apartments downstairs and three upstairs, but were made into the wood house [i.e., syphilis hospital[28]]. . . .

No. 48, upstairs, Bernhart Elsässer, goldsmith, takes good care of the apartment, just the two people, and according to what is said, what they earn is wasted on beer. . . .

No. 51, upstairs, Veit Gasslin's widow with six children and her husband recently deceased. Therefore she keeps house on her own, and practices the tailor's craft with one journeyman. She has a bath on the oven; otherwise the apartment is in good shape.

No. 52, upstairs, Paul Braun,[29] birdcage-maker, on the arch where it is customary to house the Lord Fugger's servants when they are ill, has

---

28. Thus named because of the use of guaiacum wood to treat syphilis patients.

29. Braun's wife Dorothea was the first woman to be executed as a witch in Augsburg. Her trial took place in 1625, only a year after this entry in the visitation list was made.

a bad oven and two bad window frames. He lodges a schoolboy who attends the Jesuit school and instructs and teaches [Braun's] boys.

Note: There is also a general complaint all over the Fuggerei that some residents who have children or friends in the city let them use the wash kitchen on the pretense that it is their own laundry. Because all residents have to maintain it together, and the kettles are all the sooner ruined, this should be stopped, along with once again putting an end to taking in others' laundry, and using the kettle to boil yarn. . . .

IV. Scenes from Life at the Bottom

3.9 Punishment of Beggars[30]

On the 13th of December 1533, because they were begging here, and the first two have been in the irons and beaten before (Haimlin in particular three times), Leonhard Haimlin from Augsburg; Georg Gall, weaver from Oberhausen; Bartholome Schlagl from Krumbach; and Jacob, who is French, were all put in the irons. As a merciful punishment, they were taken out of the city and told that if they come back in, they will get what they deserve.

July 29, 1540: Hans Rumel of Dinckelsbühl, a beggar who took an oath to stay out of the city before and came back in, was put in irons and beaten with rods.

On [September 16, 1540] Martin Beck, weaver, because he took alms from the poor chest and wasted and consumed it dissolutely in public houses, was put in the Fool's House, and when the council met he was banished from the city and its realm.

3.10 Interrogation of a Beggar Boy in 1558[31]

Thursday, the 25th of February 1558, Simon Schweyer, beggar boy from [Lindau] testified without torture as follows:

1. How long has he been begging here and how often has he been put out of the city? He has been around here with his mother for seven winters or so, and his mother sent him into the city to beg. He's been put out six or seven times.

30. StadtAA, Strafbuch 1533–1539, 17v; Strafbuch 1540–1543, 14r, 17v.

31. StadtAA, Urgicht Simon Schweyer, February 25, 1558; Strafbuch 1554–1562, 84v, February 26, 1558.

2. He has been locked in the Fool's House at least fifteen times, and has taken an oath to stay out no less than five times. He has never been in the Fool's House, but his brother Michael, who is two years older, was in it about three times. [Michael] doesn't come here to beg anymore, and is in Oberhausen with their mother and father.

3. Where is he staying here, or who is giving him shelter? He has very seldom spent the night in the city, and when he has, he stays in a bathhouse on Lech Lane behind the bakers. He doesn't know the bather's name.

4. It is known that his father and mother are staying in Oberhausen, and that what he and his mother have earned begging, they squander out there. With whom are they lodging? They are lodging with the young Schneidt in Oberhausen, whom they give 6 kreuzer a week for rent. His father drinks maybe a measure[32] of wine per month.

5. What do they have to pay for their lodging, and what do they have for income besides begging? In summer, his father sometimes makes hackles[33] and sells them, and also repairs pots. Otherwise they have no trade other than begging.

6. His mother claims to have epilepsy whenever someone doesn't want to give her anything or threatens her under questioning. 7. She also sometimes pretends to have an attack and falls down on the street, but is only faking to move the people to have more sympathy for her so they will give her something. His mother is ill and does not trick people with it.

8. They eat and drink the best in Oberhausen, and support not only themselves by begging here but also their landlords. No, they don't do that.

9. His father also goes begging; what illness or infirmity does he purport to have? His father doesn't beg, but has a bad back.

10. What other beggars are there in Oberhausen who support themselves only from begging, and make enough from it to feed themselves and live in excess? There are a lot of beggars outside the city, but he doesn't know them, and doesn't know what they have to support themselves or how.

11. Where are these beggars staying? He doesn't know the names of the peasants they stay with.

---

32. A serving measure, approximately 1.05 liter.
33. A tool for combing flax to make linen.

12. He and his father and mother also beg on Wertach Bridge;[34] **how long have they been doing it?** They have never sat on the bridge or begged on it, rather sought alms here and there. Requests mercy.

Punishment record:

Simon Schweyer, a boy of sixteen years, was put out of the city seven times for begging, and each time earnestly forbidden to return, but in spite of this he came back in. Therefore he was disciplined in the irons and earnestly warned not to be found here again or face public corporal punishment.

3.11 Questions Put to a Poor Sinner[35]

The case of Susanne Vogelmair is typical in that any woman who was without means automatically came under suspicion of supporting herself with prostitution, just as poor men were typically asked about theft.

On Friday, the 14th of June [15]84, Susanne Vogelmair, questioned under earnest threat, responded to the accompanying questions as follows:

1. What is her name and where is she from? Her name is Susanna Vogelmair; she is from Augsburg.

2. What does she do for a living? She sews, washes, and cleans for pay.

3. How long has she been here, and with whom has she been staying? She has stayed for fourteen days now with Gal Schreiber, layer of cobblestones, and before that she lived with Ulrich Steffan, calf herder, for around four years.

4. Since she is not a citizen, why does she live here? She was born here and has no other homeland, and Karl Höchstetter is her father.[36]

5. One knows that she has long supported herself only through a disorderly life; therefore, she should admit with what married and other men she has fornicated, or it will be brought from her with

---

34. The Wertach Bridge leading to the village of Oberhausen (located just outside the walls) was known to locals as "Beggars' Bridge" (*Bettelbrücke*) because of its popularity as a haunt of the beggars, vagrants, and gypsies who gathered outside the city.

35. StadtAA, Urgicht Susanna Vogelmairin, 14 Juny 1584; Strafbuch 1581–1587, 122r–v.

36. Vogelmair was herself born out of wedlock, thus not eligible for citizenship.

more severity. She has not sinned with any married man, but once with a single fellow, who was a cook at St. Ulrich, and is named Steffan, born in Wasserburg. He promised her marriage and gave her a ring, and also wrote her a letter from Munich around fourteen days ago, saying that he would take her to his homeland and marry her. But before him she had a child with a servant to Hans Magner, baker, which is with Gal Schreiber's wife. Otherwise she hasn't fornicated with anyone else.

6. Has she not been summoned to the Punishment Lords because of her fornication? Answers, she appeared before Lord Burgomaster Ilsing.

7. Why she then denies so fervently that she has sinned with any married man, although it is well known that many married men have come and gone from her? She has not sinned with any married man, but only with the above-noted two people.

8. How many illegitimate children has she had, and with whom, and where are they now? Says as above, only one.

9. Did her landlord have knowledge of her shameful life? Says no.

10. How did she think to get away with her disorderly ways without penalty? Begs for mercy.

[Vogelmair was banished from city and realm on June 16.]

Chapter Four
Marriage, Household, and Sexuality

The institution of marriage was at the center of early modern society, serving at all levels of status as an economic union and as the only legitimate context for sex. As individual workshops, artisan households provided the products that were basic to local economies, while the households of the wealthy engaged in wider ranging trade and investment. As representatives of their local authorities, households provided men and weapons to defend the town and political representatives to govern the city. By producing and nurturing children and training apprentices, journeymen, and servants, households provided future generations of labor and served as a school of religious and communal values. No wonder, then, that civic authorities understood the regulation of household matters as central to their role as governors.

The subject of marriage was a major point of contention between Protestants and Catholics during the Reformation, in a debate that largely centered on the issue of clerical celibacy. While the Catholic Church demanded celibacy of its clerics, convents and monasteries often appeared to the reformers as simply a form of disorderly household, and unmarried priests as an invitation to sin. Between 1523 and 1525, a rash of clerical marriages raised a challenge to ecclesiastical law, which threatened married clergy with loss of their clerical rights, benefits, and property, and even excommunication. As a response to this trend, an imperial mandate issued in 1523 also made secular authorities accountable for enforcing clerical celibacy, meaning that married clergy could face banishment as well. However, these penalties naturally depended on whether local authorities chose to enforce the law. Reform-minded clerics who opposed celibacy rules began by marrying secretly, then increasingly came to see public marriage ceremonies as an effective way to force local governments into taking a stand on reform. What served as an act of protest during this period of transition would before long become the expected norm for Lutheran pastors.

The important place held by marriage in the eyes of both Protestant and Catholic reformers also led to stricter controls on marriage and sexuality. The orderly household so crucial to their vision of a Christian community was an ideal to which reality did not always adhere, for many households were out of order. Drinking, domestic violence, impotence, unfaithfulness, and poverty all tested the institution of marriage.

93

Because a household in ruin was a danger both to the local economy and to Christian discipline, civic leaders were quick to step in with efforts to control areas of life now usually considered personal.

Complaints about marital strife were raised by women more often than men, undoubtedly due in part to power structures in the household, which allowed men more freedom to waste resources on drink and to apply "discipline" in the form of domestic violence. But even when the tables were turned, men were less likely to report marital squabbles on their own, most likely because complaints aired by men only made them appear to have lost control of their household. Women had some power over the behavior of their husbands and could get them locked in a tower for a period of correction, or even gain control over household finances if necessary, but only if they had their own financial means or the backing of an affluent family.[1] The authorities typically banned unruly men from participation in realms and behaviors symbolic of masculinity (social drinking, bearing arms, walking the streets at night). Women they more often simply admonished to go home, obey their husbands, and "house well."

Homosexuality also presented a challenge to the orderly household vision. In early modern Europe, homosexuality was understood as a sin against nature, not a sexual identity or preference. The line between close male friendship and homosexuality was often ambiguous, especially for the privileged. Homosexual relationships were tolerated in some parts of Europe more than others, and also under some circumstances more than others, but none of these circumstances included the Reformation period in Germany. Nonetheless, there is evidence of an underground gay culture. The draconian punishments for sodomy imposed in the fifteenth and sixteenth centuries (which included burning, maiming, and being exposed and left to die) were less likely to be applied by the seventeenth century, which was less because the act was seen as any less heinous than it was because authorities were increasingly concerned with keeping such incidents out of the public eye. The economic problems of the seventeenth century made masterhood and marriage more difficult to attain, so that more journeymen faced celibate lives. Since homosexuality was not understood as an identity specific to certain persons but as a sin that anyone could fall into, authorities feared drawing attention to sexual alternatives to marriage. Thus a conspiracy of silence developed.

The fact that the sources on homosexuality presented here are all concerned with men reflect the even greater silence of the sources on

1. Cf. document 8.13.

lesbian relationships. Women were less likely to be identified and prosecuted for same-sex relationships, largely because sex without penetration defied early modern definitions of sex. Thus lesbian sex (described only as "rubbing" rather than with the biblically damning term "sodomy") rarely came before the courts. Those who did draw the attention of the authorities were more often prosecuted for taking the role of a man, often as a cross-dresser.

I. The Debate over Clerical Marriage

4.1 Description of a Priestly Marriage in 1523[2]

The Act and the Event: That by the will of God, a Christian priest in Augsburg recently turned to marriage, in the face of the suppression of the marital state. By Christof Gerung from Memmingen, 1523.

Christof Gerung of Memmingen wishes that peace, grace, and mercy be granted to all the pious, elect, Christian and Protestant priests by God the Father and our Lord Jesus Christ, who gave himself up in bitter death for our sins and for the sins of the entire world. Glory and honor be upon him in all eternity! Amen.

Those of the elect and most beloved brothers in Christ! Praise be to God that in many places, a most praiseworthy custom long suppressed and buried is back again, namely that the priests [are turning] from their wicked ways and from whoring, which is strictly forbidden in the Scriptures. And now, in order to avoid falling into great and grievous sin, they dare to take wives in holy matrimony. This is given and allowed to them by Scripture.

This godly custom, however, was greatly suppressed here in Augsburg by the papists, and strictly forbidden to the priests. So God in his omnipotence, in order to show that God's power and authority are greater than that of man, fortunately led Jacob Griessbüttel, an honorable priest who is learned in the holy Scripture, to be sent here from Basel in Switzerland. This same priest observed the great suppression

---

2. Christof Gerung, *Der actus und des geschicht: das / neulich zuo Augspurg durch den Willen gots / ain Christenlicher Priester zuo der Ee / gegryffen hat, angesehen der under / druckung des Eelichen standts* (Augsburg, 1523); StadtAA, Strafbuch 1509–1526, 138r.

of the marital state among the priests and, with manliness and courage and in the presence of other pious Christians, he took a pious maiden in marriage.

When other pious lovers of Christ and his holy Word learned of all this, and were informed of it, they advised the bridegroom and his bride to request permission of the mayor to marry in church. But for a number of weighty reasons the mayor refused the request.

Nonetheless, the above-noted pious Christians, of whom there are as many as thirty-two, came to an agreement among themselves without input from the bridegroom. And on Wednesday, the 26th of this last August, they prepared a good breakfast in a public house here in Augsburg, at their own cost and not at the expense of the bride and groom.[3] Now when the time came that all of the guests were sitting at table with the groom, but without the bride, another priest who also lives here in Augsburg with his wife[4] (but who didn't hold his wedding here) stood up from among the thirty-two people and began to speak, saying: "Members of the elect, pious, dear Christians, who are gathered and seated here together! Jacob, the bridegroom here present, requests of you for the sake of God's praise, the defense of his holy godly Word and Gospel, and brotherly love, that you will be so good as to give witness and testimony to the act and event that has taken place here, and that has been concluded between him and his bride. Then, if it is brought before the antichristian suppressors of God's Word, it will have force and validity, and will not be done away with and destroyed."

At about the time that this speech had been completed, the bridegroom stood up at his table and the bride came into the room in her wedding clothes, and stood before the groom's table. Then the groom spoke to the bride in a loud, plain, and clear voice: "Dear Anna! You are well aware that I took you willingly in marriage in front of several good people, and you took me. But unfortunately, as you yourself well know, there is at this time no temple built of wood and stone in which we can marry in public as a testimony to all pious Christians. Yet, so that our cause is not suppressed entirely, rather made manifest, in praise of God and in defiance of those who take it upon themselves to impede the holy Gospel; and as a comfort and an honorable example to others; and in order to demonstrate to every pious Christian that the external pomp and tradition of the churchgoing and ceremonial papist fictions (all of

3. On distinctions in Augsburg between weddings held at the expense of the couple and those held at the expense of the guests, see the wedding ordinance excerpted in document 3.2.

4. Kaspar Aquila, who married in 1516.

which rake in money) are not necessary to this godly institution of holy matrimony, nor based in Scripture; therefore, I ask [for your hand] only for the grace of God, into whose hands we command ourselves. And also so that, if in the future God blesses us with children together, it cannot be said that they are illegitimate priests' bastards, we will take one another once again here in the presence of these pious Christians and honorable people. Thus it will be even more legitimate and public. Therefore, if you are truly willing for the sake of God to take me in holy matrimony again, then offer me your hand and say yes!"

The bride offered him her hand and said, "Yes." And she also said again: "Are you truly willing, in like manner, for the sake of God, to take me in holy matrimony?" The bridegroom also said, "Yes."

Those he had requested to be witnesses said altogether: "The peace of the Lord be with you at all times, and may he grant, give, and bestow good fortune upon you!" After this the bride left again and was not present at the feast. Then they began to eat.

When they had finished dining and the meal had ended, the afore-mentioned priest who held the first speech stood up again, and once again asked the thirty-two persons and witnesses to remember what had happened here. After this, the bridegroom himself thanked the witnesses with great diligence for the goodwill that they had demonstrated, and said that he would duly earn it in the eyes of God through his prayers for them and for all pious Christians. After this, each of them took their leave from the bridegroom and they all returned to their homes.

All of this, I, the aforementioned Christof Gerung, myself observed and heard, and I was also one of the thirty-two people who took part in the feast.

Therefore, elect, pious, Protestant priests, I ask you for the honor of Christ to let this act and event be an admonition and example, and that those of you who are unable to remain celibate also courageously enter into holy matrimony. Thus the Lord God will be praised, if one puts trust and faith in his holy Word, and you will be rewarded by him in eternity. May the Heavenly Father through his godly grace grant us all this eternal reward. This we ask of Jesus Christ. Amen.

Punishment record for the guests at Griessbüttel's wedding

Guests at the priestly wedding
On the twelfth day of September 1523, as a merciful punishment to all of those who [attended] the priest's feast or wedding, an Honorable

Council decreed that each of them should pay double the fine established by the wedding ordinance. And in addition, as the instigator who made the invitation, Melchior Schneider is punished with four weeks in the tower, and is not to come down without the permission of the council. Melchior Schneider should also go to and inform all of those who are not here, so that they can also be fined.

[The fine was officially only for a violation of a wedding ordinance, not specifically because the groom was a cleric. Griessbüttel was not penalized for the marriage.]

4.2 Urbanus Rhegius, a Sermon about Marriage and How It Is Useful, Necessary, Good, and the Right of Everyone, 1525[5]

Beloved in Christ our Lord. . . . There has for a long time been a law in effect against marriage for priests, so that they have had to live without wives in spite of the demonstrated frailty with which they have sufficiently vexed the world. For among other impediments to marriage, ordination has not been the least. Anyone ordained to the priesthood has been ordered to be chaste and the marital state has been forbidden to them.

Although this oath of chastity has not been kept, this human commandment has so severely bound and confused the consciences of the people that one would rather see a priest live a lascivious, objectionable life with loose women than for him to have an honorable housewife in good discipline. In this way, God's Word has been held in contempt. God forbade unchastity or whoremongering on pain of losing eternal life, and has always punished it severely as a serious matter. But he called the state of marriage honest and good. In contrast, the world has held the state of marriage for priests to be wrong and illegitimate, and whoring to be a joke . . . is it not time that we took a lesson from Sodom and Gomorrah? . . .

Paul teaches clearly enough that the state of marriage is free, so that the apostles all had wives, except John. . . . It is also irrelevant to argue that this has been the practice for a long time, and that it has not been the custom for hundreds of years for priests to take wives, so it will cause trouble. What can I do about the fact that they take offense at the Word

---

5. From Urbanus Rhegius, *Ain Sermon vom eelichen stand / wie nutz / not / gut vnd frey er jederman sey* (Augsburg, 1525).

and the work of God? My soul is in great danger without the marital state, and God's Word commands me to take a wife.

II. Controlling Sex and Marriage

4.3 Prostitution before the Reformation[6]

COUNCIL DECREE FROM 1438

On the Saturday before the Feast of the Purification of the Virgin [Feb. 2],[7] the small and old council declared unanimously that from now on, the secret women and daughters who walk the streets here in the city, and are not in the public whorehouses, no longer may wear trains, silk, nor rosaries made of coral, under any circumstances. And on the veils that they wear when outside, each of them must have a green stripe, two fingers wide. . . . And the imperial bailiff and the four city bailiffs are hereupon ordered that if they find one wearing clothing and bonnets not in accordance with what is here written, that they take the clothing and jewelry they are wearing, and keep it.

"THE CHRONICLE OF RECENT EVENTS" BY WILHELM REM[8]

When the women in the whorehouse were first let out to go to the sermon.

In 1520, on the fourth of February, they began here for the first time to allow the women to leave the whorehouse every Sunday during Lent to go to the sermon at St. Moritz. A special gallery was built in the church, onto which they went separately during Lent.

And the keeper of the whorehouse accompanies them to the church and back home with two male servants. And the first day on this date, two women ran away from him while they were at the sermon at the church, and got away.

---

6. StadtAA, Ratsprotokolle 3, 1392–1441, 464; Wilhelm Rem, *Cronica newer geschichten 1512–1527,* 123, in CDS vol. 25 (1896); *Die Chronik von Clemens Sender von den ältesten Zeiten der Stadt bis zum Jahr 1536,* 337, in CDS vol. 23 (1894).

7. Candlemas Day.

8. Wilhelm Rem (1462–1529) was descended from an Augsburg patrician family that, due to the financial difficulties of one of its members, lost its right to participate in local government. Nonetheless, they continued to achieve commercial success and maintained ties to Augsburg's highest circles.

The Chronicle of Clemens Sender[9]

September 4, 1532.
Here in Augsburg the council did away with the two public common whorehouses on the instructions of the Lutheran pastors.

4.4 Control of Sex and Marriage in the Police Ordinance of 1537[10]

Regarding the estate and duty of married people and also matters of marriage

Because holy matrimony is the highest and most necessary bond among humans, upon which the true Christian and honorable origin and sustenance of the human race is based, but much abuse and fault can be seen in it, an Honorable Council, as Christian authority, has decided to look into it properly.

A dangerous abuse has been going on for some time in the matter of marriage promises, namely that it must be considered a marriage when two people promise to marry one another without proper knowledge and assistance [of their guardians], whether they are responsible for themselves or under the authority of their parents or someone else. In order to impede and put a complete stop to this, and so that marriage promises are handled as natural godly and imperial law requires, an Honorable Council herewith orders that no one who still has their father or other living ancestors, or their proper guardians, custodians, or relatives in their stead, should promise or agree to marriage without the advice, knowledge, and wishes of their [parents or guardians]. And if anyone should make a marriage promise under other circumstances, no matter who they are, they should be earnestly punished by the Punishment Lords in accordance with this ordinance, and so should everyone who counseled and helped them to do it. And such marriage promises will be considered invalid and nonbinding (unless the Honorable Court should properly rule otherwise due to particularly important good Christian grounds).

No one should be made to wait an unseemly long time, or be forced into an objectionable, undesirable marriage, or otherwise be burdened in this matter inappropriately, whether by their parents, relatives,

---

9. Clemens Sender was a Catholic monk as well as an Augsburg chronicler.
10. StadtAA, Ordnungen, Zucht- und Policey-Ordnung 1537 (print).

guardians, or custodians. An Honorable Council exhorts and orders all [parents and guardians] to faithfully consider their children, relatives, or young wards when they come of age, or become widowed at a young age, and help them into an appropriate marriage in any way they can that is within their means. But they should not compel or force young people into any marriage that is objectionable or undesirable and abhorrent to them. Rather, they should in all ways truly consider and support the interests and welfare of the young person and their property. . . .

Further, so that no one, in violation of law and common decency, promises marriage or attempts to become engaged to persons who are too closely related, everyone should know and be warned that an Honorable Council will not allow anyone to conclude engagements that are forbidden to them by godly and imperial law. This includes those in direct lineage, ascending and descending as far as the line goes; and in the side lineage, no one should take or have his sister, even if it is only a half sister, likewise his father's, mother's, and grandfather's and grandmother's sisters and nieces or their daughters. And because our Christian forefathers loathed marriage to their cousins to such a degree that they eschewed it, marriage between cousins is also forbidden on pain of permanent banishment, and the marriage will not be recognized as valid.

Likewise, in the case of in-laws, no one should take in marriage or have his son's stepdaughter, mother-in-law, stepmother, grandmother-in-law, step-grandmother of the stepson, brother's wife, wife's sister, or wife's natural daughter, on pain of punishment by permanent banishment from the city. Also no one should marry the foster daughter of himself, his son, his son's son, or any other blood relative without special knowledge or permission of the council.

Because among a Christian people, holy matrimony should be concluded and entered into only with the greatest awe of and devotion to almighty God, an Honorable Council wishes that all those who have made a marriage promise seek and receive the blessing and exhortation of the Word of God in their church before they enter into an actual marriage. . . . And no pastor or vicar should bless anyone unless his marriage with his promised bride has previously been announced publicly from the pulpit three times.

A married couple lives together in awe of God, in great love and unity, even becoming one, so that the man should love the woman as himself, and in turn, the woman should hold the man in awe and esteem as her head. An Honorable Council therefore expects and wills that they should render marital fidelity [to one another] and faithfully demonstrate the highest degree of loyalty and love, aid, and service. For if someone should leave his wife against her will and move out, or should otherwise keep or treat her in an unchristian and improper way; or in turn, if a woman refuses to be subject to her husband with obedience and love, and will not piously help to support her household and raise her children, or leaves her husband or takes any action to harm her husband's person, property, honor, or body, or otherwise behaves improperly or in a blameworthy fashion, the aggrieved partner may rightly bring their grievance and complaint before the three Conciliation Lords, the Punishment Lords, or else to an Honorable Court. There they will receive justice and their right, and also appropriate protection, security, and succor. And the one who is found to be in the wrong will face appropriate punishment.

Because the state of holy matrimony should be indissoluble, and people should not put asunder what God has joined together, an Honorable Council wishes and commands that no married person may separate or divorce from the other on their own volition for any reason, on pain of earnest penalty from an Honorable Council. If, however, someone has a good, Christian, proper, honorable, or legal reason to separate and wishes to do so, he or she should bring the charges and grievances before an Honorable Council, upon which that which is right and appropriate will be discerned and done.

An Honorable Council wishes also that in case the court should allow a divorce, that the divorced spouses will be forbidden to marry again without an Honorable Council's knowledge.

REGARDING THE VICE OF ADULTERY

If someone should so thoroughly forget themselves and, in violation of God's commandment, commit adultery (which leads to God's wrath, many kinds of ruin and trouble, setting a bad example, and great evil), they should without recourse be punished by the appointed Punishment Lords by being locked in a tower for four weeks, under the condition that this penalty should be completed in its entirety without clemency, namely with a minimum of one week[11] in person. Whoever, however, wishes to pay a fine for the other three weeks may do so by paying 3 gulden for each day, and no less.

If someone should commit this offensive vice a second time, he should suffer double the above penalty.

---

11. Lit. "eight days," commonly used to mean one week (i.e., up until the eighth day).

Should someone after such a mild and merciful penalty be so wicked as to pollute himself with this godless evil and turn to it a third time, they should without recourse either be permanently banished from the city or, upon an Honorable Council's deliberation, otherwise be earnestly penalized on their goods, body, or life.

REGARDING RAPE AND VIOLATION
OF MAIDENS AND WOMEN

If anyone should actually rape and violate a maiden or woman, they will be punished by an Honorable Council with their body and life.

But if someone should coerce a maiden or widow into doing his will with words or deeds and dishonor her, he should be punished with four weeks in a tower, a minimum of one of which must be spent in person. And whoever wishes may pay for each of the remaining days at 3 gulden each. But the right of the dishonored woman to appeal to this city's law and court for her lost honor is reserved.

Whosoever should violate this as here described a second time should receive twice the penalty.

If someone violates it a third time, he should be permanently banished from the city, or upon an Honorable Council's deliberation, be punished on his goods, body, or life.

REGARDING EXTRAMARITAL COHABITATION
AND WHOREMONGERING BY SINGLE PERSONS

An Honorable Council also earnestly forbids all extramarital cohabitation, as it is contrary to the commandment of God and is in contempt of the holy state of matrimony. And anyone who is thus polluted should immediately upon publication of this ruling put away his concubine. But if anyone should violate this command and be found in extramarital cohabitation, he should be punished with four days in a tower, and his concubine, as a dishonorable person, be banished from the city, or otherwise be earnestly punished upon deliberation by an Honorable Council.

Anyone discovered guilty of this vice a second time will suffer twice the above penalty.

If, however, against the commandment of God and the authorities, someone is guilty of this vice a third time, he should be punished by an Honorable Council with banishment from the city or in another way.

Aside from extramarital cohabitation, whoever pollutes himself with odious evident public whoremongering and sinful works of the flesh should be punished by the appointed Punishment Lords as they see fit.

IN REGARD TO DAMNABLE
FORBIDDEN INTERCOURSE

Should anyone get into such a state of godless madness that, in violation of nature or imperial law, he engages in damnable intercourse, he should upon deliberation of an Honorable Council be earnestly punished on property, body, or life.

[As is evident in the phrase "in violation of nature," this rather cryptic clause is referring to sex crimes categorized as unnatural, i.e., sodomy and bestiality.]

4.5 Appolonia Hefele,[12] Innkeeper's Wife, Describes the Marriage of Her Parents[13]

The details Appolonia provides about her parents' wedding emphasize the public nature of marriage and its relationship to economic independence, both of which serve to legitimize the match.

1580

On Monday, May 16, Ulrich Stosser, my dear departed ancestor [i.e., grandfather], bought the brewing house and yard on St. Ulrich Church Street next door to Georg Siedler, brewer, and Hans Knöpfle, pastry baker, from Lord N. Schissler, goldsmith, for 1,150 gulden.

1582

On Sunday, January 14, Ulrich Stosser and his wife Apollonia Daigeler, my dear departed ancestors, married their eldest daughter, called Barbara, with their knowledge and permission to the honorable and single fellow Caspar Conanz from Hechingen, who at that time had been a journeyman brewer with the brewer Hans Endriss (otherwise called Gestelin) for five years. And on the evening of this day the engagement promise was celebrated at Hans Beham's, innkeeper on Church Street by St. Ulrich.

Afterward on Tuesday, the 20th of February, this couple who were promised to one another held their wedding day and nuptials, and the

---

12. Appolonia Hefele (1582–1619), wife of brewer Georg Hefele, maintained a household chronicle until shortly before her death in 1619, after which it was continued by her nephew Carl Meuting until 1654.

13. Appolonia Hefele, *Etliche sondere Gedächtnussen, 1554–1654* [Some Special Recollections, 1554–1654]. SuStBA, 4°Cod.S.10, 6v–8r.

wedding procession started in the steadfast Lord Christoph Beckhlin the Elder's house in front of St. Ulrich, and went to church in Protestant St. Ulrich,[14] where it was consecrated by the honorable Father Georg Meckhart, pastor of the church, and they were given together in accordance with Christian convention.

The wedding feast was celebrated at the house of Christoph Breitschädel, innkeeper on Baker Lane. The bride's attendants were Georg Fichtel, rafter's son, and Hans Hefele, pastry baker's son. And these [who married] were my dear departed parents. May the almighty God grant them a joyful resurrection to eternal life on Judgment Day, Amen.

Between then and St. George's Day, this Caspar Conanz, my dear departed father, completed his journeymanship with Lord Hans Endriss. Right afterward, my dear parents moved into my dear departed ancestor Ulrich Stosser's brewery, and immediately began brewing 5-pfennig beer.

4.6 Seventeenth-Century Fines for Fornication by Unmarried People[15]

1643

Leonhard Müller, bathhouse attendant from Stuttgart, admits that he fornicated with Agatha Böck, herb seller, a local married woman, in the following way, and they won't admit to anything else, namely: That they put their bodies together both naked, but did not complete the act itself. Because this act cannot be punished as a complete adultery, but should not go unpunished, and this single fellow [has been fined for fornication before], I fined him 8 gulden this time, of which he should pay 4 this week, and the rest next month in February. January 28.

Agatha, Georg Böck the herb seller's wife, admits that she fornicated with Leonhard Müller as just described, but not otherwise. Because this was not adultery, but not much less (for he rubbed his exposed member back and forth on her naked stomach, but no seed was spilled), and also in view of the fact that she resolutely testified to having committed almost the same kind of fornication with Albrecht Böck, also an herb seller, she was charged a 12-gulden fine.

---

14. The fifteenth-century chapel at the entrance to St. Ulrich and Afra served as a Protestant church from 1526, although the larger minster church ultimately remained Catholic.

15. StadtAA, Strafbücher, Fornicationes 1636–1659, 40, 66.

Magdalena Bäurn of Laugingen, unmarried, for getting pregnant by Dominico Sinwell, local apprentice weaver, is fined 4 [gulden].

Dominico Sinwell, local apprentice weaver and unmarried, admits to causing this pregnancy. His mother guarantees to pay 1 gulden per month for him. 4 [gulden].

1646
Hans Drexel, local journeyman dyer, sinned with his bride Jakobina Sponnagle, dyer's daughter, before their wedding. Both were fined 8 [gulden]. January 31.

4.7 A Secret Promise of Marriage[16]

Daniel Schmid, journeyman diamond cutter, had a long and troubled history of sexual misconduct, wasteful spending, and bad debts by the time he was arrested for breaking a promise of marriage to his former master's illegitimate daughter, Maria Schneider, in 1594. Also interrogated were Maria's parents, whom the council accused of intentionally leaving the young couple alone together and thus encouraging a secret promise of marriage.

Letter to Daniel Schmid, written by Leonhard Schneider in his own hand

First, in willing service, dear Daniel Schmid,

I cannot help but to write you a little letter. Up to now, I have always thought well of you, and I hope that you have also experienced with us all nothing but as much goodwill and friendship as we are capable of offering. We have also always liked you and were happy to see you when you came by. But over the last fourteen days, you've been by three times, and each time I bought wine, which I picked up myself twice, thinking that we wanted to have a nice drink together and be merry with one another. My wife and daughter were also glad to see you. But when I arrived with the wine, you didn't drink a drop of it, and you ran off without even taking leave.

God knows, given how we have implored you, I don't know how we should take this, and we still want to know what you meant by it. My wife and daughter say in plain German that if you don't start acting

---

16. StadtAA, Urgichten Daniel Schmid and Maria Schneider, March 17–23, 1593; Strafbuch 1588–1596, 170v–171r.

differently toward them, and don't abide by the many oaths you have sworn in their presence, you will kill both of them. For they expected of you a different and proper kind of friendship, and still do. And you also certainly know, without meaning to brag, that my daughter is of a pious, upright, and honest temper, which is her best treasure and dowry, for she really wants to keep the promise that she made to you and agreed to. You also should not think that you will find her to be of the sort that you had in the housemaid. Of this you can really be sure. Therefore, it is our most friendly request that you should come by when you haven't yet eaten and drunk and enjoy anything that our house has to offer. You needn't worry that anything untoward will happen to you in my house, as you might think. So I am awaiting a positive and personal answer from you.

A good aspic is waiting for you, which, God willing, we would like to share with you. Come tomorrow and we'll keep the old[17] Shrovetide with one another. God be with us all, written in haste, the 28th day of February

Your willing servant Leonhard Schneider, diamond cutter

INTERROGATION OF MARIA SCHNEIDER, MARCH 17, 1593

On Wednesday, the 17th of March 1593, Maria Schneider of Augsburg testified to the accompanying interrogation and under earnest threat as follows:

1. What is her name and where does she come from? Her name is Maria Schneider; she is from Augsburg and is about twenty years old.

2. Does she not claim to be Leonhard Schneider's daughter? Says yes.

3. Since this Schneider has never had a child with his wife, how can she be his daughter? Her father conceived her with a serving girl, for which he has already paid his penalty.

4. Did Schneider not conceive her outside of his marriage, and with whom? Answers yes. She does not know her mother to this day and has never spoken to her in her life.

5. Was Daniel Schmid not supposed to learn the diamond cutting trade with Leonhard Schneider? Says yes, he did.

---

17. Most likely a reference to the celebration of Shrovetide according to the old (Julian) calendar (cf. Chapter Two).

6. Did she not see what kind of frivolous life this Schmid was leading with his eating and drinking habits? She did see it, but he kept telling her that he was going to quit.

7. Did she not also realize that Schmid got the housemaid pregnant? Answers yes, she did find out about it, but only recently when it became known.

8. Was she not aware that Schmid had spent a long time locked in the tower because of his wasteful living and bad behavior? She is aware of this as well.

9. Is she not aware that Schmid has a guardian, and also still has his mother? 10. Did she not claim before the Lord Burgomaster that Schmid has promised to marry her, and had also robbed her of her honor? Answers yes.

11. Since she was well aware that Schmid was such a frivolous person and that he was also not in charge of his own resources, why did she give in to his promise of marriage? She did express the concern that his mother and his guardian wouldn't allow it, but he kept saying that his mother doesn't matter, and although he would obey his guardian Christoph Schmid in all other things, when it comes to marrying he won't take orders.

12. How did their relationship begin, and where and how often did she fornicate with him? After he got out of the tower, he promised in her father's house to marry her, and they lay together about ten times on her bed while her family was still up and in the parlor. He told her every time that it didn't matter, she was his wife already except that they hadn't held the wedding yet, and he would take care of that in the spring.

13. With what other men has she also fornicated, where, and how often? She has not had anything to do with anyone else.

14. Didn't Leonhard Schneider and his wife coach her to become involved with Schmid? Her father and mother didn't know and never noticed it, let alone encouraging them to do it.

15. Didn't they secretly plan this together? Says no.

16. As she is well aware that secret marriages are not tolerated here, why did she then promise herself to Schmid? She testified above that Schmid promised to marry her many times, and wouldn't leave her alone. He just lay with her today.

17. How did she expect to get away with all of this without penalty? Schmid kept reassuring her that they wouldn't get in trouble with the Lords. Requests mercy.

INTERROGATION OF DANIEL SCHMID, MARCH 23, 1594

On Wednesday the 24th of March, 1593, Daniel Schmid of Augsburg testified to the accompanying questions under earnest threat as follows:

1. What is his name, and where does he come from? His name is Daniel Schmid, and he is a local citizen.

2. What does he do for a living? He is a diamond cutter and learned his trade with Leonhard Schneider, local citizen and diamond cutter.

3. What kind of trouble did he have with Leonhard Schneider's daughter? He slept with her, and promised to marry her, but only on the condition that his mother and guardian approved.

4. Did he not promise to marry her? When and where? Says he promised to marry her as described above, three years ago in her father Leonhard Schneider's house.

5. Did he not fornicate with her? Where and how often? Says yes, he slept with her about nine or ten times, and it happened in her father's house while her father and mother were in the parlor.

6. How did he first become involved with her? He met her for the first time about four years ago, when Spindlmair had some musicians at Leonhard Schneider's, and he was also there. That was also the first time that he slept with her in the chamber, while everyone was still there. He was drunk and she did not resist.

7. Did her father and mother know about it? For his part he doesn't know if they knew about it or not.

8. Is he aware that Maria Schneider was not of legitimate birth? He is aware of it.

9. Does he intend to keep his marriage promise to her? He does not intend to keep it.

10. Do his mother and guardian wish it? They do not wish him to keep her.

11. Did he not tell Maria Schneider that his mother has nothing to say, he won't be told whom he may marry? He doesn't remember saying that to Maria Schneider, and repeats that he promised marriage only on the condition that his mother and guardian agreed to it.

12. Didn't he promise [Maria] Schneider that he would marry her in the spring? He did not say that.

13. Did he not in this way, and with the assertion that she was his wife, bring her to the fall, and rob her of her honor? He did not rob her of her honor with this declaration, rather he was drunk the first time he lay with her and was only fooling around.

14. Did he not also get a maid in Schneider's house pregnant? Says yes.

15. What business did he have that brought him so often to Schneider's house? Schneider invited him over often, and sent him a letter before Shrovetide asking him to come and help him to enjoy an aspic, so he was there regularly to have a drink. Otherwise he had no business there.

16. Has he not spent time in the tower in the past for wasteful living? Says yes.

17. Why then doesn't he stay away from it? He hopes that his guardian doesn't have much to complain about him, other than what happened between him and Maria Schneider. His guardian bought him his own gemstone, and entrusted it to Andreas Schwaiger, gem cutter. This [Schmid] plans to cut himself and therewith complete his masterpiece. Thus he requests that he not be hindered from working on it, for the time he has been given to complete it is already running out.

18. How did he expect to get away with all of this without punishment? He begs an Honorable Council to be merciful, and is willing with the approval of the authorities and the knowledge and compliance of his guardian to reach an agreement [financially] with Maria [Schneider][18] for the loss of her honor.

Punishment record for Daniel Schmid

Daniel Schmid, diamond cutter from Augsburg, fornicated with his former master Leonhard Schneider's illegitimate daughter, and according to her charge, robbed her of her honor and promised her marriage. Therefore he was arrested. But because his mother and guardian petitioned on his behalf, and offered either to come to an agreement [financially] with the Schneiders or to settle it in the appropriate place [i.e., Marriage Court], an Honorable Council has decreed today that he should be released upon his and his guardian's request.

[Schmid's mother and guardian came to a financial settlement with Maria as compensation for the loss of her virginity. Schmid eventually married another and was arrested repeatedly thereafter for debts and wasteful living.]

---

18. Erroneously entered here as "Maria Müller."

III. Households in Disorder

4.8 Establishment of the Marriage Court in 1537[19]

On Thursday, the thirteenth day of the month of September, 1537, an Honorable Council of this city of Augsburg put down in script, decreed, and commanded an orderly legal process in regard to the Marriage Court, and the appointment of eight Marriage Judges to hold court and occupy the bench. . . .

In respect to an Honorable Council's established ordinances concerning all matters of marriage, this council herewith earnestly commands their civic court to hold and sit in Marriage Court twice each week, namely on Monday and Wednesday mornings, just as is done in other matters on other established court days. And in accordance with this, if one or more men or women seek legal process or assistance related to this matter, an Honorable Court should, in accordance with court practice, provide them with a citation or summons as is done in other matters. . . . The Marriage Court should also be held with the door closed, and only when a ruling has been made, it should be read and made public to the parties with the door open. . . .

4.9 Hans Wagner, Married Weaver, Consorts with Prostitutes in 1592[20]

The defendant in this case is accused not only of sex with two prostitutes but also of incest. According to early modern law, incest occurred not only when sexual partners were related to each other but also when one partner slept with two members of the same family, in this case a mother and her daughter. While simple adultery would have been handled with a fine (see document 4.13), the council here apparently wished to make an example of the danger posed by prostitutes. Thus they determined the crime to be "greater than an adultery" and subject to harsher penalty.

INTERROGATION OF HANS WAGNER

1. What is his name and where does he come from? His name is Hans Wagner; he is a local citizen.

---

19. StadtAA, Strafbücher, Ehegerichtsbuch 1537–1546, 4v–6v.

20. StadtAA, Urgicht Hans Wagner, January 20–22, 1592; Strafbuch 1588–1596, 136r.

2. What does he do for a living? He is a weaver and supports himself with his craft.

3. How often has he been arrested here or in other localities, and why, and under what conditions was he released again in each case? He was arrested once because of a fight.

4. With what persons has he fornicated? He did not fornicate with anyone.

5., 6., 7. Where, when, and how often has this occurred? What did he give them for it? Declares his innocence.

8. Did he not also fornicate with Sara Muggensturm? 9. Where, when, and how often has this occurred? Declares his innocence of this also.

10. Did he not sin with Muggensturm at night on the street near Saxon Lane? It was about six weeks ago when he went to get some wine at night on Saxon Lane with Muggensturm. And as they came to the bend, Muggensturm lifted her skirt and exposed herself, and asked him to sin with her. But since he had been drinking and wasn't interested, she took (pardon the expression) his male member out of his pants and held it against her private parts, and really urged him to fornicate with her. But he wasn't able to do anything, because he didn't have any desire, so he didn't sin with her. Adds that he is no man when he is drunk, which his wife can verify.

11. Did the two of them then go to get some wine, while Hans Metzler stayed behind in the house? Says yes, but he is not called Hans, rather his name is Metzler.

12. Did Metzler not also sin with Muggensturm, and with her daughter, just as [Wagner] did? This he doesn't know.

13. Who else fornicated with them? Declares his ignorance. Upon this he was asked specifically if he did not also sin with the daughter, in particular in the kitchen. Then he testified that a daughter named Rosina threw herself upon him in the kitchen, and he doesn't remember if either of them exposed themselves. But what did happen was that this Rosina teased him, saying that he was no man.

14. How did he expect to get away with this without punishment? In that he told the truth, he requests mercy.

January 22, 1592

Hans Wagner should be placed face-to-face with Rosina Mair and Sara Muggensturm, and if they again stick to their testimony, but he will not confess willingly, he should be questioned further under torture.

Note: Muggensturm and Mair should be reminded to tell Wagner where, when, and how often he fornicated with him, with all of the details.

First, Muggensturm was put face-to-face with Wagner and she was told to report where, when, and how often he committed fornication with her. She testified that about six or seven weeks ago, they were walking together on Saxon Lane in order to get some wine, and Wagner tried to get her to fornicate with him. He pulled up her dress in front, although she resisted him somewhat. And he even put his member against her undershirt, but he didn't get anywhere. But when questioned further and threatened [with torture], she testified that he also lifted her undershirt and (pardon the expression) went in a little, but not completely, and still was not able to achieve anything. So in order to excite him she touched him, which didn't help. So they gave up without having done anything.

In response, Wagner answered that it was she, and not he, who incited him to sin by exposing herself and grabbing him. And although he was inclined to do it, he was no man and did not get inside. However, she continued to deny that she had grabbed him and exposed herself, claiming instead that her above testimony is correct. But she verified that he was only against her but (pardon the expression) didn't get inside. Both insisted on this version, differing only in that she said that he lifted her dress, and he said that she did it herself, and also that she grabbed him.

Afterward Muggensturm left [the interrogation chamber] and, instead, her daughter Rosina Mair was placed face-to-face with Wagner and was interrogated just like her mother. She testified that on this evening six or seven weeks ago, Wagner did go with her mother to get wine and then came back to her house. And then he sinned with her [Rosina], standing up in the kitchen, and completed the sinful act. Otherwise they have never fornicated with one another, either before or afterward. But he has tried to get her to do it.

Upon this Wagner responded that he was indeed with [Rosina] in the kitchen at the above-noted time, where she had shut him in. And when they found themselves alone, she lay down on the stove and she pulled him around to her. When he understood what she wanted, he called to God not to let him fall, and he did not sin with her. She is lying about him.

In response [Rosina] stuck to her claim and protested vehemently that it happened as she testified above.

And because [Wagner] insisted on his denial, the questions were put to him repeatedly, to which he first willingly [i.e., without torture] testified as follows:

1. Did he not fornicate with Sara Muggensturm on Saxon Lane?
He did not fornicate with her, and things occurred as he confessed above.

2. How often and where he otherwise sinned with this Muggensturm? Says as above.

3. Did he not also sin with her daughter Rosina Mair, where and how often? No, and Rosina is doing him wrong in saying this.

4. Did he not also sin with Maria Mair,[21] **and how often?** Says he is innocent.

5. How did he expect to get away with such highly punishable, unchristian adultery and incest without penalty? He sinned neither with the mother nor with the daughter, and repeats what he said above.

6. With whom has he otherwise also committed adultery, and where and when? He has never committed adultery.

Since he did not want to admit anything else willingly, he was first raised on the strappado without weights, and then with two weights, and each time left to hang under the torture for a long time. He consistently stuck with his above testimony. But he finally wavered as regards Rosina, and said as much as that he was fooling around with her, but he didn't know if he completed the act with her.

Because he would not admit the truth, four weights were hung on him and he was left to hang for quite a while, under which torture he screamed that if they let him down, he would tell the truth, and he also confessed that he did it. Then he was let down and asked what he did, and he responded that since Rosina says he sinned with her, he will admit it, and it happened in the kitchen, and he completed the act with her. This he repeated several times and confirmed upon further questioning. But he did not admit to completing the act with Muggensturm, because he did not (pardon the expression) get inside, although she held on to him firmly, for at the time he was no man and this is the truth. Otherwise he did not fornicate with Maria Mair or anyone else. Begs for the sake of God for mercy.

Punishment record

January 28, 1592. Hans Wagner, weaver from Augsburg, was accused by Sara Muggensturm and her daughter Rosina of having committed adultery and incest with both of them, for which he was arrested. Because, however, he did not confess completely to this allegation, although he admitted enough about the two of them that his crime can be considered greater than an adultery, an Honorable Council today decreed that he should be permanently banished from the city and the realm.

---

21. Maria Mair was another one of Sara Muggensturm's daughters (Rosina's sister).

4.10 Interrogation of Ulrich Hemerle for Poor Householding, 1592[22]

The accusations made against Hemerle represented here in the council's questions drew directly upon his wife's complaints, recorded in her supplication.

On Thursday, the 3rd of September 1592, Ulrich Hemerle responded to the accompanying interrogation under earnest threat but without torture as follows:

1. What is his name and where does he come from? 2. What does he do for a living? His name is Ulrich Hemerle. He is the civic ropemaker and a local citizen.

3. Weren't taverns and beer houses forbidden to him a year ago, and why? This happened only six or seven weeks ago, because he hit his wife, and never before.

4. Has he abided by this, or why not? He only went the one time to the Lettenwirt[23] [publican], who is a good friend with whom he practices shooting in the Rosenau [shooting grounds], as a personal visit. He gave [Hemerle] a drink of beer, which [Hemerle] didn't pay for.

5. Did he not hit his wife yesterday, who has been in childbed only eight days and had the baby on her arm? And did he swear and threaten to kill her? He didn't do it. He didn't lay a hand on her or the baby.

6. Why does he keep his wife so poorly and threaten her, and why does he blaspheme and swear so abominably? When his wife says two words, hardly one of them is true. He can't break her of this, and her sister eggs her on and turns her against him. Otherwise, it's his wife's nasty talk that drives him to drink, and the fact that she would rather talk to journeymen than with him. She puts him down in front of the least of the servants and apprentices, and she also doesn't perform her marital cohabitation [i.e., sleep] with him as a wife should. This started right at the beginning of his marriage, even before the wedding, insofar as at a party when his sister-in-law's husband saw that [Hemerle] was ashamed to eat or drink anything, he told [Hemerle's sister-in-law] after the meal that she should bring [Hemerle] a drink. And his sister-in-law said to [her husband], "What did you say? Do you want to make a scallywag out of him, too? If he wants to live with my sister, he'll

22. StadtAA, Urgicht Ulrich Hemerle, September 3–10, 1592.

23. Refers to the Golden Lion brewery, known colloquially as *Lettenwirt* (Potter house publican), Frauentorstrasse 49.

have to go through me". . . . etc. All of which he explained in detail in his complaint to Lord Burgomaster Rembold, so that the Lord himself found that his wife treats him improperly at home. So [Lord Rembold] earnestly chastised her, and ordered her to speak civilly to him, and to live with him properly. [Hemerle] further complains that his wife tells other people that he would rather go into a tavern than to church, although he also can't get her to go to the sermon with him. And he has a lot more to complain of, which is too much to tell here. She is doing him wrong in claiming that he beat her. When he got home and lay on the bed with his clothes on, he asked her, "If I have been drinking, will you turn me in?" Whereupon she spoke harshly to him, and said that she could indeed do it. This did make him angry, as he had been drinking, but he didn't do anything to her. Then she started yelling, so that the neighbors came over. And he might well have kept quiet, if it had not occurred to him in his drunkenness that she had often said to her spinning buddies [i.e., female friends], "I've got him now, for they have ordered him never again to go into a public house. So now if he drinks anymore, I'll see to it that he is put out of the city entirely." That's why he asked her if she was going to do it. In sum, under the directions of her sister, his wife has tried every means of dominating him right from the beginning, just as her sister dominated and subdued her husband. Therefore he requests that his wife's sister be made to stay away from her, and then he hopes to live well with his wife. For his part he will do all he can.

7. When he comes into the house at night drunk and foolish, doesn't he move about the house carelessly with the candle and make himself eggs cooked in lard, so that the neighbors have to live in fear of fire? He did cook eggs in lard a few times at night, because his wife didn't want to give him anything to eat, even though she had a good roast in the house. But he handles the fire and candle so carefully that neither his wife nor his neighborhood has anything to fear. If it weren't for his sister-in-law, he would have a good wife, and he wants to live well with her. But his sister-in-law lives very close nearby, and the sisters are together all the time.

8. Did he not threaten the neighbor that he won't quit until he has burned up all of them? This he has truly never said; no matter who says so, it isn't true. He denies it vehemently.

9. Why does he always keep two loaded guns in his house? Whether his guns are loaded or not he doesn't know. He doesn't bear any grudge against anyone. His wife did try recently to cause trouble between him and the neighbors, in that she told him that if he got drunk again, the two coopers would report him. Afterward he asked the neighbors about it and they denied it, and told him to tell his wife to come over to them while they were sitting under the door. But she didn't want to go over to them. She ran into the house instead. Upon that, the neighbors said that they can well see what's going on—just as she doesn't want to live with him, she would also like to cause a rift in the neighborhood, etc., and he should tell her from them that she isn't telling the truth about them. This he told her himself, and she got mad.

10. Since due to his defiant, wicked nature, he very well might carry through on his threats, so that danger and damage are to be feared from him, how can he sufficiently reassure his wife and the neighbors? He did not threaten anyone and no one can truthfully say it of him.

11. Why does he call to the Evil One, saying [the Devil] should have him? This may have happened a time or two when he was drunk, just as it does with his wife also. One difference is that he said, "If she won't house differently with him [the Devil should have him]."

12. How did he intend to get away with such impropriety without penalty? He is sorry that his wife doesn't get along with him better. He would like nothing better than to house well. Requests most devotedly that earnest steps be taken with his wife, and he will house well. Begs to be released upon a promise to reappear, for which he will provide a surety.

Should be presented to Ulrich Hemerle's wife and his neighbors. Decreed in the Senate, September 3, 1592.

[Ulrich Hemerle was released upon a renewal of his oath to house well and stay out of taverns.]

4.11 Records of Discipline for Poor Householding

On the third day of February, 1534, Jacob Holderich, mason, and Appolonia, his wife, who have been living apart, were brought back together and ordered that they had better have and keep one another as married people should, and faithfully live and house together honorably and well. And if any fault should arise, an Honorable Council will act against the guilty party as appropriate.[24]

24. StadtAA, Strafbuch 1533–1529, 19v.

Michel Gigel, tailor, has lived wastefully and as a spendthrift, and pawned his wife's clothing and other things to the Jews. And on top of that he has treated her badly and beaten her cruelly. Therefore he was placed under arrest and informed by an Honorable Council that he will be locked in a tower for fourteen days, and afterward taken to the Punishment Lords, and swords and public houses will be forbidden to him for one year.[25]

Hans Blumenschein, brewer, upon the orders of an Honorable Council, is sentenced out of mercy to six months in a tower for adultery which he committed four times, with the threat of public corporal punishment if he does it again. And in addition he is forbidden to drink wine for one and a half years from this date. However, if necessary, he may have a drink in his own home, but only with his wife, not with guests.[26]

4.12 A Wagon-Maker Takes an Oath to House Well[27]

I, Adam Burkmann, wagon-maker and citizen of Augsburg, profess publicly with this document that I was brought into an Honorable Council's jail and lockup for poor householding, wasteful, spendthrift living, gambling, and ruinous idleness, cursing, blaspheming, and more, by my own fault, and I was kept there several days. But today I am to be released upon the condition that I heretofore refrain from all immoderate drinking of beer and wine, gambling, idleness, and improper treatment of my wife; that I show proper respect for my in-laws; practice my craft and work with diligence; strive to live an honorable, quiet, reclusive life and existence; and behave in every respect as behooves an honorable law-abiding citizen.

4.13 Fines and Punishments from the "Books of Adultery"[28]

These special records of punishment were kept separately from general court records and handled personally by councilmen appointed to the office of a "secret" judge, without the presence even of a scribe. The records are thus written in the personal hand of the judge residing, which explains the unusual first-person form of entry. Adultery fines were high, and the

25. StadtAA, Strafbuch 1571–1580, 53, November 14, 1573.

26. StadtAA, Strafbücher, Zuchtbuch 1567–1571, 242, June 30, 1571.

27. StadtAA, Urgicht Adam Burkmann, February 5, 1600.

28. StadtAA, Ehebrecher Strafbuch 1575–1620.

city certainly profited from this form of discipline. The great variety in
the amount of the fines results partly from the fact that they were levied
in accordance with the status of the delinquent: wealthier adulterers were
fined at a higher rate. Some inflation is also evident between 1578 and
1624.

1578

I fined Anthony Kayser, local cart puller, on October 29, as a married man who admitted to adultery with Anna Stemler, married woman, 4 gulden.

On the last day of October, I fined Hans Thomas, local weaver, as a married man who [committed adultery] with a common harlot in the Rosenau [shooting grounds] 8 gulden.

1580

Jörg Lederer, bathhouse attendant in the New Bath, widower, for admitted adultery for the second time committed with Barbara, Samuel Paulsen the weaver's wife, 10 gulden, 5 to be paid in eight days and then 1 gulden per month. This he swore to on the first of May.

I fined Barbara Paulsen, married woman, for admitted adultery with Jörg Lederer, widower, a bathhouse attendant in the New Bath, 16 gulden for the second offense. Four gulden to be paid in eight days and 1 gulden per month thereafter, to which she swore on the 2nd [of May]. . . .

1611

Caspar Fischer, apothecary, was accused of having committed adultery with Sabina Steinhauser, a local unmarried daughter who was his maid. This neither he nor she completely admitted, in spite of the fact that they were locked up in the vault for twenty-four hours. But they did confess to the extent that they both exposed themselves two or three times and rubbed against each other until he spilled his seed, but *pro vitanda impregnationo* [in order to avoid pregnancy] they did not really commit coitus as it should be. For my part, I cannot see this as adultery, although it is still a great disgrace and sin. But because I am charged by the ordinance only to punish adultery, I sought advice from Lord Mayor Marcus Welser, and on his orders, from Lord Doctor Schiller. And upon this advice and Lord Mayor Welser's orders to fine both of these people with half the ordinary fine, I charged Fischer 42 gulden, half to be paid on St. George and half at Pentecost of this year, which he swore to do on January 7, 1611, which makes 42 gulden.

1624

Mattheis Miller, book trader, admits that he unfortunately sinned while in a drunken state with Regina Klähecklin, and violated his marriage. Therefore, in accordance with the ordinance, out of mercy, I fined him 84 gulden for a first offense. He swore to pay it within fourteen days. June 19.

Sigmund Süssbauer, citizen and publican at the local Smith Guild Hostel, himself admitted that he committed the sinful vice of adultery with a common hag whose name he doesn't know, in a stable in Mering where he went to let water, and he was very drunk. Asks for mercy, and because he admitted it, out of mercy I fined him 15 gulden, which he is to pay in eight days. July 28.

Sigmund Süssbauer paid 15 gulden through Gall Lentz on August 24.

Following is everything that I, Leonhardt Christoph Rehlinger, collected in monetary fines during my time in the office of secret penalties, from February 3 to August 5. . . . [Total of all receipts makes 1,525 gulden.]

4.14 Impotence Leads to a Failed Marriage[29]

Christof Lauginger of Nördlingen was put in the jail because some time ago, having no idea if he were capable as a man,[30] he took the maiden Barbara Axtin in marriage and slept with her. But although he was unable to complete the marital act with her, he did not want to admit this, nor give the aforementioned maiden Barbara the warranted grounds for separation and divorce. And he also swore an oath to the Lord Burgomeister not to leave this city until the matrimonial matter between him and Axtin was handled before the courts, but did not comply with it. Instead, he absented himself from the city, putting off the matter unnecessarily for three fourths of a year so far. Upon intercession and a guaranteed oath,[31] an Honorable Council freed [Lauginger] from jail on the condition that he not leave or absent himself from here until the legal matter between him and the aforementioned Barbara Axtin described above is finally handled and settled.

29. StadtAA, Strafbuch 1543–1553, 37v, October 2, 1544.

30. Lit. "a fit man," i.e., potent enough.

31. I.e., friends and family pled for the defendant and pledged willingness to vouch for him.

IV. Strategies for Suppressing Homosexuality

4.15 Evidence of a Gay Subculture during the Reformation[32]

INTERROGATIONS OF JACOB MILLER,
BATHHOUSE ATTENDANT

April 3, 1532: Jacob Miller, servant at the Upper Bathhouse, testifies willingly: He has had nothing to do with Rummel, nor Rummel with him.

Upon being pressed further, says: He and Rummel kept company with one another, and each has florenced[33] the other about three times and otherwise also fooled around with one another in rubbing the privates.[34] In addition [Miller] also fooled around with Berlin the fruitseller and Berlin with him, and each florenced the other about three times. He believes it was no more often than that.

States that on the eighteenth of April, he did not florence with Berlin, but they rubbed one another's privates. There was another guy called Conz, a servant, who was staying up in the upper room of the baker's house near Holy Cross Church, across on the corner . . . he also florenced with the aforementioned Berlin, and he believes that they are still together, for Berlin has often spent the night in Conz's house. Conz recently took a wife, Hans Schweiglin the merchant's cellar maid, about thirteen days ago. He doesn't know anything else. Requests mercy.

April 4, 1532: Jacob Miller, bathhouse attendant, testifies willingly as before. He played around with Rummel in Middle Bathhouse and in Rummel's house. He fooled around with Berlin on St. Felicitas Day [March 7] three years ago now. They slept together overnight in Schwarz Bathhouse. States that they only florenced with their hands, which they did until nature took its course. In addition he, Miller, spent the night in bed with Berlin in his house near the fountain by Conz

---

32. StadtAA, Urgicht Jacob Miller, April 3–May 6, 1532; Urgicht Bernhart Wagner (Berlin), April 4–June 8, 1532; Urgicht Hans Burkhardt, May 11–June 13, 1532; Urgicht Christoph Schmid, May 1–8, 1532; Urgicht Philip Zeller, May 8–June 11, 1532.

33. "To florence" was a euphemism for committing a homosexual act, either sodomy or, in this case, mutual masturbation. The Italian cities had a reputation for tolerating homosexuality. Compare similar ethnic labeling in the German and English term for syphilis, called "the French disease."

34. Lit. "the shames," euphemism for genitals or the pubic area.

Gerung's house. They also played around with each other, but he was so drunk with wine that night that he unfortunately doesn't exactly know how it went. Berlin was a newcomer to this, and liked it right away. . . . Berlin was doing the thing with Rummel for a long time; it was a long relationship. Rummel convinced Berlin to do it by lending him money. Miller got into this business because of his wife's ten-year-long illness. Begs for mercy.

April 8, 1532: Jacob Miller, bathhouse attendant, testifies willingly: It is true that there was a younger brother where he used to live with whom he played around,[35] as children do, and that was the first time they touched one another on the privates (whether until nature came over them, he doesn't know because it was so long ago). And they didn't do it again. It happened when he was still young, around twenty years ago or more. The younger brother died around twelve years ago. This happened before he came here. . . .

In the afternoon of the same day around one o'clock, [Miller] further testified that he suspects five people with Berlin, namely the schoolmaster at St. Georg's [Philip Zeller]; Father Otmar [Nachtigal],[36] the pastor, and Father Mathies, all three of St. Moritz; and Fingerle, the honey cake baker. Berlin was with these people a lot, but he didn't really know if they were doing anything with one another. He only suspects them because Berlin kept their company a lot, and he has been doing the thing for a long time. . . . He doesn't know anything else, but if he remembers anything he will not hide it. . . .

April 10, 1532: [Jacob] Miller also testifies that Berlin invited him over on Saint Martin's Day and spoke kindly to him, talking him into it, and got him started doing these things. He also set him up with Rummel. Berlin also did it with Rummel often. And while Miller was coming to Rummel and doing it with him, Berlin became angry with Rummel.

They played around with one another's cocks, lay upon each other, and stood in front of one another and pulled on the cock with their hand until nature took its course.

But when he heard from Conz how [Sigmund] Welser[37] had done it with him and harmed him, he and Rummel also tried to florence with one another in the ass, but neither of them could bear it. Neither

35. It is not clear if this was Miller's own brother or (more likely) someone else's.
36. Cf. document 1.9.
37. A member of the patrician Welser family.

of them florenced each other in the ass, but only with their hands, as already stated. Welser did florence Conz in the ass, and did so much damage that [Conz] had to go to a doctor. . . .

May 6, 1532: Jacob Miller, bather, testifies willingly as before with the elucidation: he and Rummel tried three times to N.[38] each other in the ass, but neither could bear it, because a rafting-pole hook once went into Jacob from behind and injured him. So he could not stand it. Rummel had such bad hemorrhoids that he also could not stand it. But they lay on top of one another, beside one another, and stood in front of one another and did it with each other. . . .

Twice [hoisted on the strappado] without weights, twice with the smaller weights.

Testifies as before. And in addition: He, Rummel, Berlin, and the schoolmaster at St. Georg once spent the night locked in together in his bathhouse and drank together. Afterward he and Rummel lay together and had to do with one another, as he said before. Berlin and the schoolmaster were also together at that time overnight in a room at the Schwartz Bath, but what they did, he doesn't know.

Interrogation of Bernhart "Berlin" Wagner, fruitseller

April 4, 1532: Bernhart Wagner (Berlin), former fruitseller from Augsburg, says willingly: He slept one night with the bathhouse attendant, and each florenced the other, they did it on their sides. . . .

April 6, 1532: Without torture . . . adds that he does not do these things anymore with the above-named persons or with anyone else. . . . He heard from Conz in his house, in his chamber on Wednesday night before last Thursday, that Sigmund Welser took this Conz on as a servant from his brother-in-law Ulin, and they made a contract for this purpose. The two of them, Welser and Conz, lay together, and did the above-described things with one another. Welser also gave Conz 2 gulden. Conz also told him, Berlin, that Welser is cheap and doesn't like to spend money. . . .

April 7, 1532: Bernhart Wagner of Augsburg, former fruitseller, verifies the previously recorded testimony. Says also: Fingerle spent the night

---

38. "N." was used by scribes for a name or word that is either missing or should not be recorded, in this case presumably an unspeakable word.

with him in the priest's house in Hainhofen, in the parlor of the manor house, and did not do anything with him. He will not admit anything in respect to the schoolmaster and the three priests. Requests a scribe to record his debts and debtors, so that one can see how his affairs stand.[39]

After this testimony, when the appointed Lords wanted to speak further with Berlin, he became so weak that he passed out, and didn't say anything more. So the Lords were unable to continue the interrogation at this time.

On Monday, the eighth of April, in the morning, lying ill up in the chamber, Berlin further testified without torture that he knows nothing more than he has already admitted, although he did say of the bathhouse attendant some time ago that he [Miller] did these things many years ago with a little brother living on an isolated farm. The bather also went out to see the brother. He doesn't know of anything else to report. . . .

May 6, 1532: Berlin the fruitseller says willingly that he did it twice with Rummel with his hands. And he also did it with the bather, using their hands as above. With Father Christof, the vicar at St. Moritz, he did it four or five times using their hands. With Fingerle, once in Hainhofen, with their hands. With the schoolmaster twice, once in Schwartz Bath and the other time in his house, with their hands. The reason he had nothing further to do with Fingerle was because Fingerle wanted to borrow some money from him, and Berlin didn't want to give it to him. . . . Fingerle also did not give any sign that if [Berlin] lent him money, [Fingerle] would keep doing it with him. Fingerle was also so drunk with wine in Hainhofen that he dirtied the bed. [Berlin] did try it with Fingerle, but at no time was he able to do anything with him.

PUNISHMENT RECORD FOR JACOB MILLER AND BERNHART WAGNER

June 8, 1532: [Bernhart] Wagner, grocer, and Jacob Miller, bathhouse attendant, both of Augsburg, who stand here under arrest and bound, often caused, practiced, and committed the abominable evil and vice against nature, among themselves and also with others. Therefore, an Honorable Council of this city of Augsburg, out of clemency and mercy nonetheless, has determined and lawfully judged and declared that they

---

39. Apparently Wagner is getting his affairs in order in anticipation of a death sentence.

both be executed with the bloody hand[40] and afterward their bodies burnt. All heed this warning.

INTERROGATION OF CHRISTOPH SCHMID, PRIEST

May 1, 1532: Father Christoph Schmid, priest, says willingly: Berlin spent the night in his house on his bed four, five, six, or seven times. [Berlin] said to him [Schmid], "*Ei,* what a cock you will have," and grasped his cock a couple of times, but [Schmid] did not want to let him, and fought him off as well as he could. Berlin asked him to let him do it with him, but the priest did not want to do it.

Hoisted [upon the strappado] once without weights, he testifies as above.

Afterward, Berlin is brought in to him. Speaking freely, Berlin said that what he had testified to is what he did, and he will stand by it. Upon that the priest responded that Berlin was doing him an injustice. But Berlin insisted on it, and the priest did not deny that Berlin fondled him, the priest, on the cock.

Berlin said in the presence of the priest that he had done it to him with his hand three times in his bed, and once afterward in the parlor. Thereupon the priest responded that he let Berlin handle his cock and pull upon it until nature took it course, which happened three or four times. But the priest did not touch Berlin's cock.

May 8, 1532: Father Christoph Schmid, priest, testifies willingly and verifies the above, and doesn't know anything else to report.

Hoisted once without weights, he repeats the above.

Because he did not want to confess at first and then confessed after all under torture, he appeared suspicious. So he should further testify if he did it in the behind. One has good reason to suspect him of this. [Also] if he knows of others who also did such things.

[No further testimony.]

INTERROGATION OF PHILIP ZELLER, SCHOOLMASTER

May 8, 1532: Philip Zeller from Schrobenhausen, schoolmaster at St. Georg's, testifies willingly: He has a wife and lives with her. He does

---

40. I.e., with the sword (beheading).

know Berlin. He visited with him as one good friend to another, and did nothing improper with him.

Upon further questioning without torture, he says, about nine or ten years ago, he was in Berlin's house, and ate and drank with him and with other priests. And he became so drunk that he lay down on the bed in Berlin's chamber during the day. But Berlin, as he was sleeping, came in and took [Zeller's] cock in the hands and pulled it. How long and what Berlin did with him at that time he doesn't know because he was loaded with wine. . . .

[Under torture, Zeller admits to mutual masturbation with Berlin on multiple occasions].

June 11, 1532: Philip Zeller of Schrobenhausen committed the evil and vice against nature in this city . . . therefore an Honorable Council of this city of Augsburg, in response to numerous pleas and out of mercy and compassion, adjudged and declared by lawful conviction that his left hand should be chopped off and taken away, and once he is healed, he should be put out of this city for life and never return to it. All heed this warning.

[Hans Burgkhardt the honey cake baker, called "Fingerle," was also questioned, but released for lack of evidence. There is no surviving record of testimony by patrician Sigmund Welser, the priest at St. Moritz Otmar Nachtigal, or any of the other persons of high status who were implicated by the defendants.]

4.16 Sodomy Accusation in a Journeyman's Hostel[41]

As the economic situation in the German towns declined during the troubled seventeenth century, an increasing number of journeymen were unable to amass sufficient capital to marry and open their own workshops. Since an independent workshop was normally a prerequisite for marriage, such men were condemned to live a single life, often preferring to make a permanent home in a journeyman's hostel rather than sharing the home of the master and his family. It was standard in hostels and inns for unrelated people of the same sex, even strangers, to share beds. The witnesses in this case (whose statements could not be included here due to space limitations) were all sworn to remain silent about it.

41. StadtAA, Urgicht Balthasar Weiss, February 12–16, 1644; Strafbuch 1633–1653, 274.

Testimony of Balthasar Weiss

On Friday, February 12, 1644, Balthasar Weiss, journeyman tailor under arrest, testified willingly under earnest threat to the accompanying questions as follows:

1. What is his name, where does he come from, how old is he, and by what trade does he support himself? His name is Balthasar Weiss, from Hessingen in the county of Oettingen. He is approximately thirty-six years old, and he is a journeyman tailor by trade.

2. Has he ever been arrested before, how often, where, and why in each case was he released? Never an hour in his life, and he has never been called to appear before any authority, and this is too soon for him. But perhaps it will serve him as a warning

3. How did he spend last Shrovetide? In what company did he drink and sleep? On Sunday he attended the sermon twice, and the rest of the time he was dining at his sister's house. And he also spent all of Monday at home. On Tuesday morning he was at prayer, and in the afternoon at the wedding of Master Jacob Schweiger's journeyman. On Wednesday morning he attended the sermon, and spent the afternoon with the tailors' journeymen at their hostel, and at night he slept at the hostel with a journeyman tailor named Johannes from Stuttgart.

4. What kind of frivolous antics have he and others at the tailor's hostel gotten into? And in particular, what kind of highly punishable licentiousness did he commit in bed with another journeyman tailor named Johann Paget at this hostel on the last night of Shrovetide? He should himself describe what happened and what the circumstances were. His fellows say that he was not drunk, but he must honestly admit that he drank so heavily that the next day he couldn't remember a third of what he said and did in his cups. For example, the next day he couldn't find (pardon the expression) his shoes, and no longer knew that he had taken them off in another chamber where he had at first been brought to bed. Admits that he does remember touching his bedfellow's (pardon the expression) genitals and fondling him immodestly, but he is not aware of supposedly having squeezed him so hard. He assumes his bedfellow has made more of this than it was. Note [from the scribe]: the prisoner fell on his knees immediately after this question was posed and said, "I have done wrong, and beg for mercy," etc.

5. Did he not make all kinds of shameless remarks while getting undressed, including talk of sodomy, for which Paget admonished him and warned him away? The maid who brought them both to bed stayed so long in the chamber that the prisoner, as near as he knows, said, "What are you doing standing here so long, you shameless hussy?" And his bedfellow responded by saying that he should settle down, for the maid is probably more pious than the two of them. He doesn't recall having talked of sodomy.

6. Did he not afterward, while in bed, not only disgracefully expose and fondle Paget while he was sleeping but also put [Paget's] (pardon the expression) genitalia between his legs, and squeeze him so hard there and elsewhere on his body that he couldn't cry out, and afterward had to (pardon the expression) throw up? He knows well that he embraced his bedfellow tightly, but he is not aware of supposedly having stuck [Paget's] (pardon the expression) genitals between his legs, and squeezing him. Since his bedfellow is persistent in his claim that this is what he did, he will accept it as so, but he doesn't remember it.

7. What was he doing earlier in the (pardon the expression) stable, so that the innkeeper's maid had to chase him out? He should confess what kind of evil intent and objective he had, and if he were not prevented from it by the maid. He was answering the call of nature, and because the (pardon the expression) privy[42] is right next to the stable, and the maid was just (pardon the expression) milking the cows, he went over to her to pass the time, and asked, "Are the cows giving a lot of milk?" And the maid answered, smiling, "Ten measures." He had no evil intentions, and also didn't go all the way into the stable, rather just stood under the door and talked to the maid. Eventually the maid told the prisoner to leave, and said he had been standing there long enough.

8. Since it is known from the prisoner's own confession, and other reputable witnesses, that he has committed the same kind of frivolous devilry in other places and with other young men, he should himself willingly tell with whom and how far he has taken this. In particular, though, [he should say] if he has ever been involved with (pardon the expression) animals. He should confess truthfully and not give us reason to use harsher measures. When his bedfellow complained to the other fellows that [Weiss] had touched and squeezed him in this way, they answered that [Weiss] had also slept with them, and he had also fondled them, but it was just fooling around. And they also told his bedfellow that he shouldn't take it seriously. One of the two fellows that his bedfellow complained to is called Hans Georg, and is from Wurtzburg and the oldest journeyman in charge here. The other's name is Abraham, and he was born not far from Leipzig, and works for Bachman. [Weiss] has never considered messing around with

42. Lit. "secret [room]."

animals in his life, and it would only be said of him because of an existing animosity toward him.

9. How can he justify this grave misdeed before God and the laudable authorities, and what does he think he has earned as a punishment? He again falls to his knees, begs for mercy, and is willing to bear whatever the laudable authorities demand of him. The prisoner hopes that Dear God will encourage them to be merciful, and not subject him to public scandal.

[Note on back:] Should be presented to Johann Paget. Decreed in the Senate, February 13, 1644.

Response from Johann Paget, February 16, 1544

To an Honorable Most Wise Council: Obedient refutation and supplication by Johann Paget, local journeyman tailor born in Stuttgart, in response to Balthasar Weiss' testimony.

For the fact that [Your Lords] graciously provided me with Balthasar Weiss, journeyman tailor's testimony . . . I am devotedly grateful. And therein, his own confession comes through crystal clear, in that he expressly said in response to the fourth question put before him, "He does remember touching his bedfellow's (meaning me) (pardon the expression) genitals and fondling him immodestly." Likewise, to the sixth, "He embraced his bedfellow tightly." Based on what I have been told, it is the opinion of the law and legal scholars that such a fellow should be punished and condemned by the authorities, if not with the usual death penalty, then at least, and without doubt, with an extraordinary punishment. . . . Therefore Your Gracious [Lords] will want to set an example, and proceed in accordance with the law. For [Weiss'] claim in the fourth question that he was very drunk does not excuse anything, in view of the fact that (1) the reasoning that he gives, namely that the following day he couldn't remember a third of what he said and did, does not specifically and necessarily imply great drunkenness; (2) according to his own testimony, his drinking companions say the opposite; (3) I can also most truthfully confirm the contrary, if necessary under oath; and (4) he himself gives away that he was not as drunk as he claims, because according to the fourth question, he expressly notes that he does well remember, etc. Likewise, according to question six, "He well knows that," etc. Similarly, in the seventh response, he knows well enough to describe everything he said to the maid in the stable and what else he did. Aside from that is the fact that, according to all common law, such drunkenness does not excuse any delinquent from any atrocious crime (such as this certainly is), rather only aggravates it.

The prisoner is also in no way excused by his responses to the oft-noted fourth and sixth questions, in which he says that he is not aware that he (pardon the expression) put my genitals between his legs and squeezed me so that I couldn't cry out, and so that I had to (pardon the expression) throw up, etc. For, Gracious Imperious Lords, this is only an affected ignorance and claim. If he really isn't aware of it, then I am aware of it all the more definitely and certainly, for I unfortunately experienced it in person, which . . . woke me up. And as soon as I could, I ran down to the innkeeper and his wife with my clothes only hastily thrown over my arm to ask them for help and to call the watch.

Aside from all that, I have no doubt at all that, given that the crime of unconsummated sodomy is punishable with the usual death penalty,[43] if [Weiss] should or could be . . . questioned under torture, then he would come out with everything and certainly truthfully confess to what I say, insofar as his conscience is already revealing more than he pretends to know. For to the sixth question, through the power of truth, he added, to wit, "Since his bedfellow is persistent in his claim that this is what he did, he will accept it as so, but he doesn't remember it."

Indeed, if his ignorance were true and his conscience (in which he felt his guilt and still does) were at peace, why would he have needed to fall on his knees right after the fourth question and openly confess, "I have done wrong, and beg for mercy," etc.? Why would he have again repeated this admittance of wrongdoing and begging for mercy when confronted with the last question with the caveat, "He is willing to bear whatever the laudable authorities demand of him, but hopes that they will not subject him to public scandal"?

Finally, it does not excuse the prisoner at all that, in response to the eighth question, he names two journeyman tailors with whom he has also slept in the same bed and committed the same licentiousness, but only in fun, and I should also take it the same way, etc. This claim works directly against him, and by no means in his favor, since it reveals and attests that he is inclined toward the vice of sodomy by nature as well as by custom. In fact, he has already made such a strong habit of it that it would take an awful lot for him to get free of the ropes with which the Devil has thus far kept him bound. In addition, this alleged comparison has not at all been proven, nor can it be proven. And even if

43. Reference to the fact that sodomy was a capital crime according to prevailing law codes, meaning that torture would not be ruled out as a legal interrogation method.

someone or another was a voluntary consort and allied criminal, or like Weiss, thinks such things are fun, it does not follow that I must also do so—rather, I hold fast to my opinion that fun of that sort is not and has never been permitted anywhere but Sodom and Gomorrah. May God the Almighty mercifully preserve me and all pious hearts therefrom.

In accordance with all of that, and with a general objection to everything else, in particular that he doesn't want to remember or admit to the frivolous shameful honor- and God-forsaken things that he said while undressing, and for which I admonished him, I refer again to my above lawfully prepared petition. . . .

Devoted obedient
Johann Paget

Punishment record for Balthasar Weiss, March 1, 1644

Balthasar Weiss, journeyman tailor from Hessingen in the county of Oettingen, around thirty-six years old, drank himself into drunkenness on Shrovetide Day [i.e., Ash Wednesday] at the drinking room in the tailor's hostel with other journeymen tailors, and afterward licentiously exposed and fondled his bedfellow Johann Paget, also a journeyman tailor. Paget harshly accused him, had him arrested, and wanted to make of it a case equivalent to sodomy. But after a thorough inquiry was made and a number of people were questioned under oath, but nothing came to light except that it was a frivolous fondling and billy-goat tailor nonsense,[44] Weiss was earnestly warned against such behavior and released. And the two of them were reunited in friendship [at the order of the council].

V. Dealing with Sexual Deviance

4.17 Arrest of a Pedophile Priest in 1525[45]

Margaret's story

January 30, 1525. Margaret, the late building supervisor Sixt Gartner's daughter, eleven years of age, reported to My Lord Burgomaster

44. "Billy goat tailor" was a phrase used to disparage tailors as proverbially unlucky in love.

45. StadtAA, Literaliensammlung, January 30–February 2, 1525; Wilhelm Rem, 'Cronica newer geschichten' von Wilhelm Rem 1512–1527, 216.

Rehlinger, in the presence of a male and a female cousin of the child, that something improper happened to her recently, as follows:

About ten weeks ago on a Monday, the above-noted little girl ran away from Jorg Strigl, her cousin, who had hit her very hard and pushed her. And on the same day, in the afternoon between four and five o'clock, as it was starting to get dark, she was coming down Perlach Hill, and she sat down on a stone on the corner near Graber's baking house. A man with a lantern in which the light had just been put out came up to the girl and asked her what she was doing there. To this, she answered that she had run away from her cousin. The man then said to her that she should go with him. He took the girl and led her across Perlach Hill, around to the lower slaughterhouse toward St. Anna's Church, and then up to the Herz Inn on the corner near Gögginger Gate.

As they started down Priests' Lane, another man was heading up the street toward the two of them. And as soon as the man who was leading the girl noticed the other man coming toward them, he took her across the street from the corner and behind My Lords' storage hall, and stayed with her there until [the other man] had passed. And while they were standing behind the storage hall, he took a key out of his bag or purse.

As soon as the man had passed them and left the street, [the priest] took the girl on across the street and then a couple steps up to a door, which he opened, and they went inside into a little yard. In front of this yard there was a new wooden wall, and the gate to the yard was the same as the wall. When they got into the yard, he took the girl into the lower chamber and parlor, in which there was no light.

After he brought the girl into the room, he sat her on a bench and said she should sit still, and he would light a light. Outside of the room, he lit a candle and went into the cellar, then brought about a measure of wine back into the room along with the candle. Once inside, he sat the girl behind the table and set before her a plate with good sausage, two rolls, and a piece of cheese, and then set a tall nubbed glass of wine before her. Then he cut the sausage for her along with a piece of bread. And as he was cutting them, he said to the girl that she had to spend this night with his cook. But he didn't have a cook.

When they had finished eating, he kissed her, during which she noticed that he was scratchy but had no beard. And right after kissing her, he led the girl out of the parlor and into a chamber that was located on the other side of the threshing floor, across from the front room. Upon entering the chamber, she saw that there was a large bedstead and a small one in it, and there were clothes on the small bed. The man asked the girl which bed she wanted to lie on, and she answered that she wanted to lie on the small bed. But he answered, "*Ei,* you'll lie with me today. I would have to clear off the other bed first." Then he said she should get undressed and lie down.

Even though the girl refused to lie down on the big bed with him, he still took her clothes off, and gave her a bonnet that buttoned under the chin, which the girl put on. And then she lay down. Once she was lying down, he immediately put out the candle and lay down next to her on the bed she was on. She wanted to go right to sleep, but he turned to her and lay on top of her. And when she screamed, he told her that if she kept screaming he would stab a knife into her, and she had to be still.

As soon as he was lying on top of her, he spread her legs wide apart and put both of his hands on top of one another over her heart, and pressed his breast on them, so that she couldn't move or scream. He then did it with the girl five times after another, somewhat slowly, and each time he did it for a long time, hurting her badly between the legs (as has been established).

When he had gotten off the girl, he kept saying to her that if she screamed again he would throw her over the bedstead, and if she tried to run away he would come for her again.

In the morning at six o'clock, he lit a candle in the chamber and woke her up, and told her to get up right away. He put on a long black robe with a black lining, and belted it. As soon as the girl got up, and as she was getting dressed, he took some rags and wiped off the sheets. The girl saw that the sheets were bloody. And while she dressed he was praying. After all that he brought the girl into the parlor, and went in and out, but she didn't know what he was doing.

The girl raised a candle in the parlor and saw that there was a cupboard behind the oven, and underneath stood a rack with plates and bowls in it, and also a copper pitcher with a copper hand basin beside it. The room did not face toward the street, rather into the yard, down on the ground floor. But the bedchamber he took the girl into and where they both lay faced the street, with high shutters. The parlor windows were of forest glass.[46]

In the morning he didn't give her anything to eat, and also didn't give her any money. He also asked the girl numerous times in the morning not to tell anyone, and comforted her by saying that she could or should come whenever she wanted and he'd give her some money. But she remained silent and didn't give him any answer. He didn't leave

---

46. Greenish glass from the Black Forest. Margaret's detailed description of the cleric's quarters was most likely provided as proof of the truth of her story.

the house at all in the morning. In the ninth hour he said to her that she should leave, and not tell anyone about it. So he went with her out under the gate to the yard and let her go, and closed the gate and also the house door.

When the girl went outside in the morning, as noted above, she looked around and saw that there were little trees in the yard, and also there was a wooden railing in the corner. She had also seen three choir robes the night before when she came into the parlor (but didn't immediately recognize them as such) and some paper lying on the table. And she said, "They are such nice aprons," and he said they were choir robes. The walls of the parlor weren't of masonry but of wood, and there was nothing special about it except what she has already reported.

At night when the girl asked the man if the house belonged to him, he said yes, and he was seldom there, rather he had a room with board. This man . . . was a short, stout, stocky, stubby person, with a wide brow or forehead, and a bald pate over to the back of the head, little hair, and a chubby face. When he came up to her on Perlach Hill, he had a golden cap on, and nothing over it, and a short black linen frock that went over the knee. When the girl asked him as he was taking her to his house if his light had gone out, he answered that he preferred to have no light. And when he got home with the girl he took off the cap, put it in the cupboard, and pushed it into the corner, and put on a biretta that was longer in the back than in the front.

CHRONICLE ENTRY BY WILHELM REM

In 1525, on the first of February, the city caught a priest, who belonged to the chapter at St. Moritz, and who, with another priest who was his colleague, raped a young girl who was eleven years old. But one of the priests fled. And he who was captured was sent by the council on a cart, well guarded with soldiers, to the Bishop in Dillingen on the second of the month. The Bishop locked him in a tower, but didn't do anything to him, and soon afterward let him back out.

[Examiners reported that Margaret suffered permanent damage from the rape, and would have died from injuries to her genitals if she had not received medical attention from midwives. There is no evidence of a second priest involved in the case as reported by Rem—most likely this was only a rumor. Chronicler Clemens Sender identified the rapist as Wolfgang, vicar at St. Moritz, and noted that he was transported to the Bishop in chains.]

4.18 A Day-Laborer Is Burned at the Stake for Bestiality[47]

The normal penalty for theft and manslaughter would have been hanging, or in very grievous cases, perhaps execution by breaking on the wheel.[48] The condemnation in this case to burning at the stake results from the additional charge of bestiality, an offense against nature requiring a greater degree of purification.

Thursday, the 15th of January in the year 1609. Caspar Schefler, a day-laborer from Wendlinging (in the parish of Apfeltrang, two hours above Kaufbeuern), about thirty-three years old, not only committed numerous acts of theft and one act of manslaughter but also fornicated with a number of beasts. Therefore he was arrested, and an Honorable Council decreed that on this day, he should be burned alive until he is dead. But out of mercy, a pouch of gunpowder should first be hung upon him.[49]

47. StadtAA, Strafbuch 1608–1615, 25r–v, January 15, 1609.

48. Breaking on the wheel refers to a form of execution in which condemned persons had all the bones of their extremities broken, either while tied to a wheel or while staked to the ground (in which case the wheel was used to break the bones). The body was then attached to the wheel and raised on a pole for display and to be consumed by birds. Depending on the harshness of the punishment, the neck might be broken either before or after the breaking of the body, or not at all (so that the delinquent would still be alive when raised on the wheel).

49. The unusual measure of hanging a sack of gunpowder on the condemned man was intended to hasten his death and thus reduce his suffering.

Chapter Five
Work and Trade

According to the early modern view, work—a burden placed upon Adam by God as penance for original sin—served those of the lower and middling classes as an antidote for the sin of idleness. Work rhythms were tied both to the calendar, which dictated cycles of work and rest, plenty and want, light and dark, etc., and the life cycle. For commoners, productive labor was a calling and, increasingly as the early modern period progressed, an ethic. A person's trade served as an identity as well as a means of support. This included identity as a member of the civic commune, since for those not of elite status, membership in a craft was a requirement for citizenship.

For urban artisans, work life began with a period of apprenticeship to a craft, normally paid for by the boy's parents. The next stage, as a journeyman, usually included a period of wandering in order to learn the trade from masters in other towns, although masters' sons often learned from their own fathers. The work cycle of women was less clearly articulated. Although women's guilds existed in some cities during the sixteenth century, women increasingly found formal training in a trade closed to them, and the tasks they performed relegated to a position subordinate to that of male labor. Girls typically began their work life either working within their parents' household or as household servants. In this role they often assisted with the household trade as well as more general household tasks, but they did not attain the status of journeyman, and their work identity would ultimately rest with their husbands' craft.

Ideally, marriage was timed to coincide with completion of a masterpiece and establishment of an independent household workshop. Men at this stage became master craftsmen and householders, and women entered into a period of childbearing and shared household authority over children and servants. Naturally, the master was assumed to have the last word. Women's roles in the household workshop included helping with auxiliary tasks related to their husbands' craft (e.g., finishing cloth, selling wares, and purchasing materials), along with managing victuals, washing, mending, and other household tasks. Those of higher status could function as a kind of manager, responsible for overseeing employees as well as domestic responsibilities. In less advantaged households, women often supplemented household income by spinning, sewing, taking in washing, selling herbs or flowers, and other activities considered appropriate to their gender. Some women found a niche as professionals in the health trades, working as midwives, healers, and hospital workers.

As this division of labor makes clear, the household itself was an economic unit whose success depended on effective production. As we have seen in Chapter Four, the early modern view of civic order assumed that an orderly and pious household was a crucial component of an orderly and pious society. A disciplined, productive household supported the civic economy while it encouraged sexual discipline. Both men and women were therefore under pressure to remarry quickly after the death of a spouse in order to ensure that production continued uninterrupted and the family did not end up dependent on alms. Guild rights and citizenship could pass through women as well as men, so that non-resident journeymen could gain citizenship by making the right match with a local daughter or widow. These ideas about the household economy assumed a hierarchy that mirrored that of the society of orders at large. Within the household, this gendered hierarchy was both familial and political: masters ruled over journeymen and apprentices, parents ruled over children and servants, and men ruled over women. Guild ordinances admonished masters to teach their charges in an "honest" manner, while apprentices and journeymen were expected to obey. Master craftsmen, in turn, were subject to the decisions of guild principals, who answered to the city council.

Central to this system was the sense of exclusivity that defined each specific craft. Only those who had been accepted and legitimately trained could practice the trade. Protection of the rights of guild members increasingly depended on layered constructs of guild honor. Membership depended first on being of legitimate and honorable birth, and then on honorable behavior as a member of the craft. First and foremost, this meant obeying the ethics of the trade, including abiding by craft ordinances. Behavior considered criminal could also lead to accusations of dishonor, as could running up bad debts or other questionable financial transactions.

But even more damaging to honor was any connection to members of certain trades designated "dishonorable," who made up a kind of untouchable caste in early modern Germany. Members of this group were not dishonorable due to inappropriate behavior, but attained their dishonorable status at birth by virtue of their fathers' profession. Most dishonorable in this sense were the executioner, whose job it was to apply torture during interrogations and to execute criminals, and the knacker or skinner, who was responsible for skinning animals that died a natural or accidental death and disposing of their carcasses.[1] For those in honorable professions, socializing with the executioner, doing work considered appropriate only for skinners, or other forms of contact with trades and persons labeled dishonorable was defaming. It is for this reason more than any other that punishment or even interrogation under the hand of the executioner could sometimes lead to expulsion from a craft, even where no proof of a crime was established. Because guild honor was collective, if one member of a guild was branded dishonorable, it cast aspersions on the entire craft.

Professional honor also governed economic relations at higher levels of the social scale. Among those of merchant and patrician status, bankruptcy led to humiliation and ritual forms of social exclusion, for example expulsion from the Patricians' or Merchants' Society and loss of the right to wear a sword. Since wealth was assumed to be limited, those who wasted resources, engaged in unfair competition, or made a living by charging excessive interest on loans (called "usury") seemed to threaten the entire community. The period of Reformation is often associated with changes in these attitudes toward wealth. For reformers such as Luther, those whose money came from investments and money lending were simply usurers. Of Augsburg's wealthy merchants he complained, "We must put a bit in the mouth of the Fuggers and similar companies. How is it possible in the lifetime of one man to accumulate such great possessions, worthy of a king, legally and according to God's will?" Jacob Fugger the Rich, of course, had his own view of his success. "A lot of people are against me," he wrote in response to Luther's complaints, "the way it is in the world, and say that I am rich. And I am rich, but by the grace of God and without doing anyone any harm. . . ."[2]

Resources were also assumed to be endangered by the idle poor. Making an honorable living was a mark of good citizenship, thus idleness became a crime. It is this assumption that lies at the basis of the division of the poor into those who were "deserving" of alms and those who were not (discussed in Chapter Three). Eventually, work came to be viewed as the antidote to idleness, providing a context for replacing almshouses with workhouses and forcing orphans into labor. This

1. Other groups occasionally labeled dishonorable in different areas of Germany included barbers, millers, shepherds, bailiffs, gravediggers, linen weavers, and outhouse cleaners.

2. Helmut Gier and Reinhard Schwarz, eds., *Reformation und Reichstadt: Luther in Augsburg* (Augsburg, 1996), 50, 62.

emphasis on industry as a virtue would then provide a basis for labeling the nobility "idle" as well, and has thus been linked to the development of a middle-class or "bourgeois" work ethic that is associated with modern capitalism.

I. Regulation and Self-Regulation of Workers

5.1 Imperial Decree on Journeymen and Apprentices, 1548[3]

His Roman Imperial Majesty [Charles V]'s Ordinance and Reformation of Good Policing, to Promote the Common Good.

Tit. 37. Regarding artisan sons, journeymen, and apprentices

1. In some places it is the custom that linen weavers, barbers, shepherds, millers, and other such craftspeople are not accepted or allowed into guilds that are different from that of their parents. Because it is wrong that those of honorable birth, profession, and character should thus be excluded, it is our wish that this onerous custom or practice herewith be abolished and eradicated. We[4] [hereby] establish, order, and will that linen weavers, barbers, shepherds, millers, tollkeepers, pipers, drummers, bathers, as well as the parents to whom they are born and the children that they keep well and honorably, henceforth will under no circumstances be excluded from guilds, offices, and crafts, rather should be accepted and taken in like other honorable craftspeople. . . .

2. In those cities and towns of the Holy Roman Empire of the German Nation that designate "served" and "unserved" crafts,[5] the idleness, drinking, and feasting of masters' sons, journeymen, and apprentices has caused a lot of disruption, vexation, damage, and harm, not only among themselves but also between their craft masters and others who ought to use their labor. Therefore we wish that [this custom] be

3. Der Römisch-Kayserlichen Majestät Ordnung und Reformation guter Policey, zu Beförderung des gemeinen Nutzens. Reichstag Abschied, Augsburg, June 30, 1548. In Hans Proesler, *Das gesamtdeutsche Handwerk im Spiegel der Reichsgesetzgebung von 1530 bis 1806* (Berlin, 1954), 9–11.

4. "We" in this case refers to the *pluralis majestatis* (royal we), i.e., the Emperor himself.

5. Served and unserved crafts (*Geschenckte und ungeschenckte Handwerck*). This distinction refers to the custom among the larger and more socially and economically elevated crafts of maintaining their own private drinking rooms and entertaining traveling journeymen with feasts and drinking bouts upon their arrival and departure as a symbol of their prestige (cf. document 5.5).

abolished everywhere in the empire. . . . But whenever a nonresident, incoming journeymen arrives in one or more cities or market towns and seeks service or a master, he should report to the guild or guildhall servant for the craft in which he is trained, or if there is no guildhall, to the craft's appointed innkeeper or Craft Father. . . . [And] this same guild or guildhall servant or appointed innkeeper and Father . . . should immediately take the arriving journeyman to find work and seek a master, at any time, with faithful industry and in accordance with local custom, just as the designated journeymen have always done. But no carousing or feasting should be further tolerated at the arrival and departure [of the journeymen], or otherwise in any other way, before or after. Craft masters' sons and journeymen, whether from served or unserved crafts, may not carry out or apply penalties, and none of them should insult the other, nor harass or plague him, nor make him dishonorable. . . . If they do, the one they are vilifying will not be driven out, but left to his craft. And the other journeymen will be bound to work with and beside him [until the matter is settled].

3. And any master's son or journeyman [who doesn't abide by this will lose his right to practice his craft].

4. We wish also that apprentices and journeymen should no longer pressure their masters as to what and how much they give them to eat and drink, but that the masters provide for their apprentices and journeymen in such a way that they have no reason to complain. The authorities should keep an eye on this.

5. Every authority who derives privileges from us and the Holy Roman Empire is free to ignore, reduce, or moderate this ordinance, but under no circumstances to increase its severity or scope.

5.2 Oaths for City Employees[6]

THE OATH FOR PROFESSIONAL GUARDS

You will swear to be obedient and attentive to My Lord Mayors, Burgomasters, and councilmen; appear for and leave guard duty on time, day and night; and guard faithfully, making rounds in the city as is normal and customary. And if during the night after the evening bell, you run into or discover someone who seems suspicious, with or without a weapon, see that you challenge him or them, and don't let anyone off or spare them. And if you discover something inappropriate

6. StadtAA, Schätze 13c, Ordnung des Stadtregiments, August 3, 1548, 85v–86r.

or criminal or someone is defiant, see that you take him or them to the Burgomaster or to the Fool's House. And if you see or smell smoke or fire that appears dangerous, also report it as appropriate, all in good faith and without guile.

You should make peace in each and every sort of quarrel you come upon, day or night, in public houses and on the open streets, and otherwise handle the matter in accordance with your duty. And all such quarrels should be reported to the appointed Burgomaster, with no one being concealed.

You should also always arrive at your post and leave it when the horn blows, and none of you should leave until the fellow replacing you arrives. Anyone who violates this will lose his job, and also anyone who discovers that another [has left his post early] and does not report it and let the Burgomaster know will also lose his job, and not be taken on again.

Every guard should also wear a breastplate, a helmet on his head, and two gauntlets, and have a good halberd . . . [crossed out at some point between 1548 and the eighteenth century because of changes in how guards were armed].

THE MIDWIFE'S OATH

You will swear that you will attend to every woman to whom you are called, whether she is rich or poor, and not leave until she has been given all the care she needs. You will also provide services willingly to both rich and poor, and refuse no one when you are free [i.e., not already attending someone], all in good faith and without guile.

5.3 From the Butcher's Craft Ordinance, 1549[7]

BUTCHER'S OATH

Each and every butcher, as well as the widows who also slaughter or butcher here in Augsburg, should swear a solemn oath to God and the saints[8] that they will faithfully abide by and obey the Meatselling Law and Ordinance established and provided to them by an Honorable Council, without guile.

---

7. SuStBA, 2°Aug.10. 2. Abt. 24.12.1549, 109–36.

8. Reference to the saints is indicative of the fact that this ordinance was issued during the Interim (1548–1555), when Catholicism dominated in the city.

The price of meat follows

One pound of good Hungarian ox meat should be sold for 6 pfennig. Local ox meat should be appraised by the appointed meat inspector and sold based on his decision.

A pound of beef should be sold in accordance with the decision of the meat inspector based on how good or bad it is. . . .

And wether[9] should be slaughtered between St. John's solstice [June 24] and St. Andrew's Day [Nov. 30], and sold according to weight, and not by the piece, without any extras, the pound for 5 pfennig. And a sheep or wether lung with the liver and heart should be sold for 6 pfennigs. . . .

Pork without rind for 5 pfennig, pork with rind for 6 pfennig, bacon for seven pfennig. . . .

Hanging of a price board

Any butcher who wishes to sell ox, cow, bullock,[10] or bull meat must hang a plainly visible board on his stall upon which the price that has been set for the meat slaughtered on that day is clearly written, on pain of half a gulden.

Each and every butcher may also sell no more than one kind of meat on a meat market day. If, however, a butcher has, with permission, slaughtered more than one ox, or more than one cow, bullock, or bull, and one is valued more highly than the other, then he must hang one in the back until the first has all been sold, so that meats of different value are not mixed together or sold for the same amount. . . .

Calves that are under three weeks
old may not be slaughtered

No butcher, male or female, or their representatives may slaughter any calf that is not three weeks old, or sell it, on pain of a half gulden to be paid per calf. And henceforth, if butchers bring slaughtered calves that are too young, the meat should be cut into little pieces and thrown into the river. . . .

Regarding scabby and mangy sheep

An Honorable Council commands that no butcher or anyone else, whether citizen or guest, drive any scabby or mangy sheep or lambs into

9. A castrated ram.
10. A young bull.

the city or its realm, or buy, sell, or slaughter them. Whoever violates this will be banished from the city and its realm for three years, or worse, depending on the seriousness of the violation and degree of guilt. In addition, all afflicted sheep or lambs will be burnt. . . .

5.4 Rules Governing the Brewing Craft, 1568–1648[11]

FROM THE CRAFT ORDINANCE OF SEPTEMBER 1568

Apprentices

Beer sellers who wish to hire apprentices may do so from St. Bartholomew's Day [August 24] up until fourteen days after St. Michael's Day [September 29]. If anyone violates this and takes on an apprentice before or after this specific period, an Honorable Council will not approve the apprentice.

Anyone who takes on an apprentice should teach him for one half year, and notify the appointed Council Lords [who are responsible for the brewing trade] before the apprentice picks up his first scoop, according to old custom. And when the apprentice is brought before the appointed Lords, which should occur as soon as possible, the apprentice is required to pay an Honorable Council 2 gulden without delay.

Every apprentice should also be of honorable and legitimate birth, and provide the three masters [i.e., guild principals] with sufficient testimony and documentation, which the three masters should diligently record.

As long as an apprentice is still learning the trade and has not completed his apprenticeship, he should not practice any other craft nor work as a day-laborer until his apprenticeship is completely done and completed. Afterward his master should again report the completion of the training to the above-noted three masters (who should diligently record it, so that evidence of the apprenticeship can be provided in the future if necessary) on pain of a fine of 4 gulden to be paid to an Honorable Council's treasury.

Any apprentice who leaves before completing his training without an appropriate reason will not be allowed to practice the craft here anymore, unless he starts the apprenticeship over and fully completes his training.

11. SuStBA, 2°Cod.Aug.273, Stadt-Aemter, Bierschenken Articul Buch 1565–1782 (ms.).

And once a master has trained an apprentice and the apprenticeship has been completed, the master must wait two full years before he will be approved to take on another apprentice. As soon as the two years are up, then he may take on another if he wishes.

And in addition, henceforth no widow may take on or train any apprentice.

Journeymen brewers
If any master wishes to take on and employ a journeyman, the journeyman should have already learned the craft of brewing in a specific city in accordance with the regulations and have completed his apprenticeship. Masters who violate this and take on a journeyman [without this training] will be required to pay an Honorable Council 2 gulden, and will not be allowed to keep the journeyman on.

Regarding the craft [i.e., brewing] license
If someone should henceforth attain a license to brew beer by marriage or inherit it, he is required to pay no more than 1 Rhenish gulden to an Honorable Council upon entering the craft. Anyone who thus attains the craft by marriage or inheritance may practice it even if he has not yet learned it, but he must purchase the license within a year.

Do not disdain the principals
Any craftsman who disdains his craft principals, or speaks to them derisively, will be locked in the irons. . . .

ADDITIONS FROM DECEMBER 1596

Dispose of sour beer
As of this date, an Honorable Council has further ordered and established that henceforth, if the appointed beer inspectors find that any beer seller has old, sour beer, they should immediately impress and impose upon him that he should get rid of it and pour it out. Should he fail to comply with this, rather keep the old, sour beer, or mix it in with newly brewed, unfermented beer, he will be fined 10 gulden. And if he is found culpable again, it will be reported to the Burgomaster in Office and action will be taken against him as appropriate for the violation.

Do not refuse anyone beer
An Honorable Council herewith orders and requires both brown and wheat beer brewers to provide beer willingly to the common citizenry here, to take out and bring home, and to anyone else who requests it for

their money. Any beer seller who pulls up his doorbell and refuses any measure of beer to someone (if he has it to sell) will be punished with cessation of his trade for four weeks. And each brewer should provide beer to other brewers at their request, and not hold anything back as long as he has it on hand.

December 7, 1596

ADDITION FROM JULY 1621

For a number of pressing reasons, and above all . . . so that the [brewing] craft does not grow in numbers of masters and become overcrowded, an Honorable Council has decreed that no one other than the local brewers' sons may spend less than two years learning the craft, whether local citizen or nonresident. Also, no one will be admitted as a brewing master unless, during his apprenticeship, he completed a full two years, without missing any of it, and has also sufficiently verified and substantiated it.

ADDITION FROM JUNE 1648

In response to the report from the appointed Lords over the Brewing Ordinance, an Honorable Council [agrees] that anyone who inherits a brewing license, and, having learned the brewing craft, intends to practice it, is required to report to the principals within four weeks of his parent's death if he plans to marry or not. If this isn't done, and he has not married within the next following eight weeks, he will not be allowed to continue to run the brewery as a single person; rather it will be closed down. Brewing is forbidden entirely to other single brewers.

June 30, 1648

5.5 Establishment of a Craft Hostel for the Comb-Maker's Craft in 1597, from the Chronicle of Brewer Georg Siedler[12]

In other towns, the comb-maker's craft, as a served craft, has been keeping and holding stately regimes and ceremonies in their hostels and craft halls, while here in Augsburg, where the comb-makers had only one master, namely Michael Steckh, there was no established treasury and hostel. Now, however, the craft has increased its masters, and the journeymen have also grown in number. And since they had no treasury or

12. StadtAA, Chroniken 20, Chronik von Siedler, 200r–201v.

hostel, in this year of 1597 on the 21st day of the month of September, the honorable Michael Steckh the Elder, and also his son Michael Steckh the Younger, both master comb-makers and citizens here in Augsburg, as well as the honorable journeymen Hans Engelbrunner of Nuremberg, Valentine Kaiser of Leipzig, and Johann Arnoldt of Leipzig, with one unanimous voice, established a treasury and sought a hostel and made me, Georg Siedler, brewer, the Hostel Father. And with my consent, they finally agreed to meet here, and established, instituted, and recognized the following articles.

ORDINANCE AND ARTICLES OF THE COMB-MAKER'S JOURNEYMEN, AS AGREED ON AND APPROVED UPON THE ESTABLISHMENT OF THE CRAFT TREASURY

1. First, the journeymen of the comb-makers craft should gather every four weeks in their appointed and acquired hostel, and hold a general meeting, for which each master is required to put 4 kreuzer in the treasury, and every journeyman 2 kreuzer.

2. Any journeyman who does not appear at the monthly meeting at the appointed time of 12:00 [i.e., arrives late] is required and obliged to pay for a half measure of wine.

3. But if a journeyman does not come to the announced monthly meeting at all, and is absent without permission and without a reasonable excuse, he should be fined 15 kreuzer.

4. Once a month or every four weeks, two treasury journeymen should be elected, one older and one new.

5. When a traveling journeyman arrives here to work, these treasury journeymen should put up 12 kreuzer board money for the fellow. But if he doesn't find any work, then all of the journeymen should provide and honor the outsider with drinking money according to their means, in accordance with craft custom and tradition.

6. And if one of the treasury journeymen should move away before his office is up, or otherwise be unwilling or unable to carry out his duties, he should pass his office on to the senior journeyman in the craft, who may not refuse to take it on, upon a penalty of 3 kreuzer.

7. If the normal monthly meeting is held and a fellow does not or will not attend the gathering and stay there the entire time, he has to pay 5 kreuzer for the table.

8. At the end of their four weeks in office, the two treasury journeymen should make their report at the monthly meeting, and for their trouble be provided with 6 kreuzer to spend. But if they were negligent and didn't execute [their office], they will be liable to pay the 6 kreuzer as a penalty.

9. All journeymen who come to the hostel should conduct themselves honorably, decently, piously, and uprightly. Anyone who behaves otherwise shall, upon an inquiry being made among the company and based on their decision, be earnestly punished.

10. In like wise, the journeymen should be truthful in their words. And if someone agrees to do something or to stop doing something, and doesn't follow through, he shall, upon an inquiry being made among the company and based on their decision, be earnestly punished.

5.6 Clockwork Erected on the Weights and Measures Hall, 1600[13]

Because few people of ordinary status had clocks or watches in their possession, townspeople depended on the sound of night watchmen calling the hours, the blowing of horns by tower guards, and, increasingly, the striking of public clocks to regulate their days. Here brewer Georg Siedler associates the construction of a new clock with good government.

When it comes to houses and buildings, this city of Augsburg's appointed Lords are especially inclined, in the interest of the common people and upon their entreaty, request, and plea, to build and to erect everything with industry and in an orderly way, as can be clearly seen here. For the honorable citizenry and the neighborhood at the weir around the Weights and Measures Hall insisted and petitioned that they are distant from the clocks, and can for the most part not hear them strike because of the rushing water, so that it is empty, gloomy, and very dull there. And [Our Lords] considered and assessed the request of the citizenry and commoners and found it reasonable, and in this year of 1600 had the clock on the Measures Hall at the weir constructed and put it up.

13. StadtAA, Chroniken 20, Chronik von Siedler, 211v.

II. Complaints and Disputes

5.7 Arrests for Complaining about Work[14]

On the 10th day of June 1533, Simon Ment, weaver from Augsburg, used abusive language and tried to get the weaving apprentices to oppose the [weavers'] craft ordinance. For this he was put in a tower for three days and three nights. And when he came down, he was sent to the Punishment Lords [to be fined] because of the swearing.

On September 26, 1534, Agnes Scholhorn, weaver's wife, was put in irons because she spoke evilly and slanderously to the Inspection Masters of the weavers. [Scholhorn] took back what she said to the Inspection Masters, and asked that they forgive and excuse her for what she said against them, for she knows nothing of them other than that they are pious, honorable people. Thereupon she was told to cease and desist from such talk and behavior from now on.

5.8 A Matter of Dishonor among Butchers, 1585: The Case of Jacob Glantz[15]

EXTRACTS FROM PETITIONS PRESENTED
BY THE PRINCIPALS OF THE BUTCHER'S
CRAFT, SEPTEMBER AND OCTOBER 1585

Noble, well-born, steadfast [Lords] Mayor, Burgomaster, and an Honorable Council of this laudable imperial city. . . . We the principals of the butchers have received and read Jacob Glantz's supplication with due attention. In response, we need to point out that we admitted him to the status of a master twenty years ago but discovered that he (pardon the expression) had skinned three sheep that had drowned and threw them in the Brunnen Stream.[16] For this he was put out of the city but subsequently let back in through the grace of His Imperial Majesty [i.e., pardoned by the emperor] and allowed by the honorable craft only to do minor tasks and to chop meat for sausage on the condition that he not keep a stall and refrain from slaughtering, unless he attains his mastership over again. . . .

14. StadtAA, Strafbuch 1533–1539, 2r, 36r-v.

15. StadtAA, Handwerkerakten, Metzger 5, Jacob Glantz, August–November 1585.

16. Brunnenbach—also called Hettenbach. A stream at the border between Augsburg and the former village of Oberhausen (now also part of Augsburg).

Be that as it may, he accosted our elected principal Abraham Burkhart on the street impudently and without provocation, demanding to know how and why he has not been asked to appear [before the Burgomasters] like Bernhard Reischle and Hans Herman.[17] In response, [Burkhart] admonished him with amicable words. But [Glantz] didn't want to leave it alone, so Burkhart told him, "You can take your inappropriate skinner behavior elsewhere. Not with me." Then [Glantz] slandered the entire craft by saying that all those who have worked with and beside him are not honorable, but rogues. . . . It is impossible for our entire craft to accept this, and it would cause all kinds of damage to the city at large if it got around in the countryside.

[And it should be obvious] that he is lying when he says that the principals knew about his skinner's act when they made him a master and allowed him to marry, and knew that he had skinned sheep in the field and thrown them in the Brunnen Stream where people drink, which is certainly not true. For the principals (who knew none of this before they gave him the wedding pass and made him a master, which they can attest to with their oath or whatever is required of them) are honorable enough, and, as is fitting, they know the old rules well enough that they would not have allowed him either one. Nor would the lowest servant or apprentice have allowed it to him.

And although it shouldn't be the case that we can be dishonored by anyone who is himself not honorable and has perpetrated such skinner's business, and we should not tolerate him among and next to us in any way, we must turn to the authorities for help in order to save our honor and that of our children. . . . For it is not true as he claims in [his petition] that he was made a master. . . . We did not admit him to be a master, as the attached document shows, but only allowed him to chop meat for sausage, a right that comes not through him, but through his wife. . . .

We request therefore of [Our Lords] that they declare him unfit for the butcher's trade and also forbid him to chop sausage, and also charge him henceforth to refrain from all defamation and slander. This [we ask in devoted obedience].

RESPONSE FROM THE COUNCILMEN IN CHARGE OF THE BUTCHER'S ORDINANCE, OCTOBER 1585

[Gracious Lords], We have examined what Jacob Glantz and the principals of the butchers here have submitted in response to and counter

---

17. Presumably in order to obtain permission to slaughter as a master butcher.

to one another in the matter of an incident perpetrated by Jacob Glantz about twenty years ago. . . . This particular case is not as bad and dishonorable as the principals are making it, considering that the sheep that the above-noted Glantz skinned (pardon the expression) did not fall over dead on their own, but fell into Brunnen Stream because of a storm, and admittedly drowned therein. Nonetheless, although we did not fail to employ every possible means of reaching an amicable settlement, after a long discussion, we were unable to get anywhere with the principals, or to arrange a settlement between the parties even with all of our efforts.

Insofar as Glantz did not carry out the above-noted deed out of evil intent, or deliberately to commit a dishonorable act, rather only did it because he wanted to serve his master, to whom he also gave the skins, and this incident also occurred a long time ago, and he has already paid the appropriate penalty through his banishment from the city and been invited back by His Imperial Majesty Maximilian II (rest his soul), it is our opinion [that this is only a matter] of bickering and resentment.

It is thus . . . our considered recommendation that, . . . since each butcher can decide for himself whether to use [Glantz's services] or not, Glantz may work and provide his services unhindered . . . without insult and with honor, since for our part we also don't see [his act] as completely dishonorable. [Your obedient servants] the Lords of the Butchers' Ordinance.

[The council decreed that the recommendation of the Lords of the butchers' ordinance be enforced.]

5.9 Hans Krieger, Cabinetmaker, Is Questioned for Insulting his Guild Principals[18]

On Friday, the 3rd of September 1593, Hans Krieger, cabinetmaker, answered the accompanying questions under earnest threat, without torture, as follows:

1. What's his name and where is he from? His name is Hans Krieger; he is a local citizen.

2. What kind of problem does he have with the guild principals and sworn men, so that he ceaselessly maligns them all over the place and so insults their honor? He was speaking guilelessly and said the guild principals and sworn men are always sitting there forever in

18. StadtAA, Urgicht Hans Krieger, September 3, 1593.

the frog puddle, one of them hatching the next one out. Otherwise he has no problem with them.

3. Did he not say loudly enough for everyone to hear that the guild principal has two offices from My Lords, and can't manage one? He said this too. He is sorry.

4. How does he know that [the guild principal] does not keep his offices faithfully? By this he meant that the guild principal has two offices, but he has enough to do with one.

5. Did he compare the principals and sworn men to a frog puddle, in which when one hops out, the other hops back in? He said this for the reason given above.

6. How did he mean this derisive insinuation? It was thoughtless talk, and he is sorry.

7. Doesn't he know that the principals and sworn men are appointed by the authorities? He knows this.

8. Insofar as his insulting tirade could only have referred to changes and replacements in these appointments, why then did he so forget himself and attack the authorities themselves, in violation of his oath and duty? He didn't mean the authorities at all.

9. Did the principals and sworn men not question him about it? Yes, they did.

10. Did he not defiantly respond, "Yes, I said it, and I still say it"? He said what is noted above, namely that one hatches out the other.

11. What did he intend to achieve with his insulting tirade and defiance? He didn't think it would have such serious consequences.

12. Didn't he intend to stir up trouble within the craft? This was not his intent.

13. Who gave him counsel and direction in this? No one gave him any counsel at all.

14. How did he expect to get away with this without penalty? He didn't consider the consequences.

15. Is he also willing to apologize to the principals and sworn men and behave peacefully hereafter? And who can provide surety? He hopes that their honor is not in the least insulted by his thoughtless talk, which was also not his intention. But if an Honorable Council believes he owes them an apology, he will not refuse it and will behave as he should. Otherwise he doesn't think any surety is necessary. Begs for mercy.

Hans Krieger should be released and sent to the Punishment Lords to render an apology. Decreed in the Senate, September 4, 1593.

5.10 Margarete Ammann, Healer, Defends Her Request to Cure Women in "Secret Places"

Margarete Ammann was one of a very small number of women who managed to move from the status of illegal healers to paid members of the medical establishment. While such a status was the norm for midwives, it was unusual for female healers who were not involved in birthing. In part, Ammann's success is owed to her willingness to overcome the protectionist efforts of male members of the medical trade by finding a limited niche in which to work. Ammann's case is also of particular interest because of the supporting testimony that she provided, which came from a variety of women testifying to her skills and her Christian charity, many of them writing in their own hand. Included here are three of the eight such testimonials that have survived and that were penned by women of common status. Ammann's tactics were successful; in 1610, she was awarded an annual salary of 32 gulden from the city budget for her services.

PETITION FROM MARGARETE AMMANN, OCTOBER 26, 1604

Noble, high-born, [and] wise Lord Mayors, Burgomasters, and council of this laudable holy imperial city, Commanding, Gracious, and Auspicious Lords.

A year ago, the appointed principals of the surgeons' and barbers' craft called me before their deputized Lords of Ordinance about the cure I use for sick, damaged women in childbed, and other ailing women, primarily on female hidden places, as well as on the breasts. Through God's blessing, I have helped many with this cure, so that they still render to me eternal praise and gratitude. Because [the principals said] this is in direct violation of their ordinance, they demanded that I give it up and that it be completely forbidden to me. In response to the account and the rejoinder that they demanded from me, the aforementioned Council Lords sent me to appear before [Your Lords]. And in due obedience, I also did submit and present my humble plea on the 6th of September, 1603. Since then, however, I have received neither a decree nor a counterreport, much less was my curing abolished. Only recently, the aforementioned principals, because I continued to practice my cure and to render useful help, have called for me anew, and again commanded me to give up my treatments.

These Lords once again referred me in goodwill to [Your Lords] to request, with humble diligence, gracious permission to practice my cures on these sickly women openly and without fear. [For I have] provided ample reports and clear evidence [of my cures], which have been proven in many ways (with the help of the Highest) on poor, destitute, and infirm women, whom I did not charge, and especially on those that the Lords of Poor Relief have in the Pilgrim's Hospital here (of which they will provide sufficient witness), as well as on quite a number of foreign noblewomen and local sickly women [whom I treated] for a fair and justified compensation. I can produce significant testimony and witness of this.

Illnesses of these kinds, especially on such secret places (of which unfortunately there are many here), cause an honorable woman, out of innate modesty, to prefer to let the illness get out of hand and to perish completely before she lets herself be cured by a man. And aside from that, it seems to me that the most distinguished and best surgeons here don't like to undertake such treatments, and concern themselves all the less about it, insofar as a number of doctors of medicine here themselves refer and send such ill women to me. And if they were to be asked about this, they certainly would not deny it. I have also never before undertaken other cures that violate the Surgeons' Ordinance. It is of more than a little consequence to the city at large that such women are cured and made well again, and in this (to report without self-praise) I have succeeded, praise God, fortunately and well with the cure I use. It's not enough to apply this cure only in one way—it has to be applied in accordance with the form and occasion of the illness, with good faithful diligence.

In merciful regard of these circumstances, but especially in light of the testimony provided by the Lords of Holy Poor Relief, I thus apply to [Your Lords] with my entirely humble and most eager request to graciously allow me to continue these same cures openly, only on women, and on the aforementioned secret places and breasts. This is not in defiance of the barbers and the ordinance on which they raised an objection, because I use medical treatments different from those of the surgeons and above all of the doctors. . . . [Your Lords'] humble obedient fellow citizen.

[Note on back]: Humble request of Margarete, wife of the painter Hans Ammann, to be put before the barbers. Decreed in the Senate, October 26, 1604.

Anna Bilgerim

I, Anna Bilgerim, goldsmith's wife, testify that Margarete Ammann healed me of gangrene, treated me like a mother. I otherwise would have had to perish. This in truthful testimony I give her [in] my own handwriting.

Susanna Fischer

I, Susanna Fischer, tinsmith's wife, testify freely that the honorable Mrs. Margaret Ammann, painter's wife, with God's help, truly and diligently cured me of gangrene, which threatened my life, when I was pregnant and also in my hardest labor. But with God's help, she healed me diligently. And since then I have again had children that, praise God, thus far have no deficiencies. God grant further mercy. This I also give her of my own free will in witness and truthful testimony on November 13, 1604. Susanna Fischer.

Anna Lixen

I, Anna Lixen, testify in my own handwriting that this Margarete Ammann did so much good for my child, like a dear mother. This [child] suffered from a dangerous disease that is assumed incurable, and she protected it with God's help against gangrene and other disorders without taking any money. This I testify on her behalf.

III. Income and Expenses

5.11 Working Conditions for Civic Construction Workers, 1597[19]

Working hours, daily wages, holidays, etc. for city workers in summer and winter, compiled in 1597 by Heinrich Aicheller, copy scribe. . . .

Carpenter and day-laborer daily wages

The carpenters and day-laborers will be credited with 5¾ times the daily wage for an entire week. The carpenters are credited from the Feast of cathedra Petri [Feb. 22] until St. Gallen [October 16] with the summer wage of 9 kreuzer per day, and from St. Gallen to the Feast of cathedra Petri with the winter wage of 8 kreuzer per day. . . .

19. SuStBA, 2°Cod.S.158, Bauamt (ms.).

The day-laborers will be paid the same thing for the entire year, winter as summer, some 8 kreuzer and some 7 kreuzer, depending on the man's strength, or how hard he works, as determined by the Canal Master. The boys get 6 kreuzer a day summer and winter.

Regarding a raise in the carpenters' pay
In 1595 an Honorable Council approved the workers' petition to raise the carpenters' and masons' daily wage by 1 kreuzer. They will be credited and paid 10 kreuzer in summer and 9 kreuzer in winter.

Regarding hourly pay
If it is necessary to work by the hour, the barbers, carpenters, day-laborers, and boys will all be credited with 1 kreuzer per hour. And from Monday morning until Saturday noon (when, in accordance with the general custom, all of My Lords' work ceases), the entire week will be reckoned at eleven hours per day. If it is necessary to work beyond the customary time (early in the morning, at noon, or in the evening), this will also be reckoned and credited by the hour. . . .

Working after hours
If work is performed on Saturday afternoon, during off time, this will be specially credited, based on how long they work, normally up to four o'clock at half a day's pay. But if it is longer, then [the pay will be] according to the decision of a workmaster.

When one should go to and from work
In the summer, when the day begins at 5:00 AM, all workers should arrive at work at that hour, and quitting time is at 6:00 PM. During the rest of the time, when the day breaks later than 5:00 AM, all workers should be at the gate when it opens [i.e., daybreak] and go straight to their place of work. Those who work inside the city should start work as soon as it is daylight. And if it is dark before 6:00 PM, they should quit at dusk.

When the breaks begin and end
On St. Peter's Day, February 22, the breaks begin, and on St. Gallen they cease. This should be understood to mean that starting with St. Peter's Day, all workers take their soup at 7:00 AM, and should all be back at work at 8:00. Likewise, they eat their supper in the afternoon at 3:00, and by 4:00 they start back to work. Anyone, however, who works during these hours, between 7:00 and 8:00 in the morning and then 3:00 to 4:00 in the afternoon, will each be paid for this time.

Regarding quitting time during Shrovetide
On Shrove Tuesday, work ends at 2:00 PM, and on Ash Wednesday at 3:00 PM, and no pay will be docked.

When a worker becomes ill
If a local carpenter, day-laborer, or worker for the city becomes ill, the workmaster should be told. And it is customary to give such sick people two weeks of paid leave. But the workmaster may also give a nonresident worker eight days or up to two weeks, depending on how well he has worked or how long he has been on the job. If a local worker who has been working faithfully for the common city for twenty or thirty years becomes ill, he may be paid the weekly pay for another eight days after the first fourteen days are up, or up to another two or three weeks, but only with the approval of the Lords of Civic Works.

If one has a wedding
A worker who is himself getting married will not be docked pay for his wedding day, and also not for the day after, if he has truly earned his pay and been working for some time; rather, it will be given to him as a wedding gift. When one of My Lord's workers' children marries, the wedding day will be allowed him and will not be docked from his pay. Years ago, those who attended weddings as guests used to get a half day with pay, but this is no longer customary.

Bleeding or medical treatment
If someone needs to be bled or treated by a doctor, he will be allowed one or two days with pay.

Funerals
If someone attends the funeral of a friend or acquaintance, his pay will not be docked.

Those who are taken into the Pox House[20] or poorhouse will not be credited for the fourteen days (as is otherwise customary with the ill).

The sermon on Good Friday
It is also customary that all workers are given time off from the early morning until the end of the sermon, at around 8:00, in order to attend church [on Good Friday], and do not have anything docked for it.

---

20. Syphilis hospital. Augsburg had two such facilities, one located inside the city near Red Gate, and one inside the Fuggerei.

5.12 Typical Expenses for a Well-Ordered Household, 1613[21]

The expenses listed here, taken from a broadsheet with advice for male householders, are appropriate for a relatively well-off craftsman, innkeeper, or officeholder. As is clear from the previous source, artisans at the lower end of the scale earned considerably less than the 175 gulden per year described here as the "minimal" requirement for running a household.[22]

Regarding keeping house. Minimal expenses for one year.

Each week 7 batzen for bread comes to 24 gulden and 4 batzen for a year

Each day 6 kreuzer for wine and beer comes to 36 gulden 7 batzen 7 pfennig for a year

30 gulden and 10 batzen per year for all kinds of meat

30 gulden for lard, butter, and wood

2 gulden 5 batzen for sauerkraut

6 gulden for shoes and repairing all the pairs

Three times a week 2 pfennig for buttermilk comes to 1 gulden 7 batzen 4 pfennig

Each day 1 pfennig for brandy comes to 1 gulden 10 batzen 3 pfennig for a year

3½ gulden for the maid's salary

Every day 2 pfennig for candles comes to 3 gulden 7 batzen 2 pfennig for a year

5 pfennig per week each to bathe comes to 3 gulden for a year

5 gulden 5 batzen for Godfathering

1 gulden for salt

6 kreuzer twice a week for fish comes to 3 gulden 8 batzen for a year

1 gulden 5 batzen for spices

3 gulden for all sorts of side dishes

3 gulden for the women for improving their wardrobe and other necessities

1 gulden 10 pfennig for pots, pans, bowls, and plates

3 pfennig per day for cheese comes to 3 gulden 5 batzen 6 pfennig

8 batzen 4 pfennig for casks, buckets, and brooms and binding

And the rent, repairs, and so on?

Total 175 gulden, 2 batzen, 2 kreuzer, 3 pfennig.

---

21. Martin Wörle, *Für ein jeden Burger oder Hausswirt / hüpsche Spruche / auch was ein Jar auff ein Mann / Weib / vnnd Magd auffs geringst auffgehet / alles kurtz hirinnen begriffen / vnd in Truck verfertigt.* Broadsheet (Augsburg, 1613).

22. For relative values of currency, see the introduction to this volume.

Chapter Six
Sports, Entertainments, and
the Control of Leisure

Some historians have argued that a construct of "leisure time," as distinguished from work time, did not exist before the eighteenth century. It is apparent, however, that people have always found ways to amuse themselves when they were not working, and sometimes when they were. Many early modern forms of play were dictated by the church calendar, as were the work rhythms discussed in the previous chapter. Carnival customs, harvest celebrations, church festivals and processions, and Christmas feasts, for example, provided opportunities for rest and celebration while simultaneously serving as a reminder that both work and play should follow God's plan. Special events such as weddings might also be timed to coincide with the spring slaughter, for lamb and veal were preferable as wedding fare to Lenten fish. But early modern people enjoyed spontaneous social events and entertainments throughout the year as well. Here there is room to introduce only a very small sample of the many ways that early modern folk socialized and amused themselves.

By definition, time that is free exists in opposition to time spent working, and for this reason, leisure could appear suspect to those in control. The period of Reformation, with its new emphasis on moral living, was characterized by a great many rules and ordinances attempting to limit activities seen as frivolous, wasteful, and conducive to disorder. But the standoff between the austere, orderly vision of religious reformers and the more unrestrained and jovial world of carnival and play should not be understood simply as a top-down repression of popular culture by elites. Many urban elites shared in the culture of sociability, and social control could also be exercised from below. Some forms of leisure also contributed to the general welfare and reinforced notions of hierarchy. Thus the interests of the authorities at times came into conflict with their own ordinances, and many morally charged decrees, issued mainly as a public show of piety, were not regularly enforced. Most arrests for activities labeled "frivolous" seem actually to target more serious misbehavior, such as challenging authority, running the household into ruin, disturbing the peace, or perpetrating violence.

Certain leisure activities were overtly encouraged. For men, sports of all kinds represented preparation for war, and this was especially the case with competitive martial sports such as shooting and sword fighting. These examples of what might be termed "political leisure" were financed largely by public coffers. During their heyday in the sixteenth century, shooting matches could be large, elaborate affairs resembling modern folk festivals, complete with drinking, dancing, games, and lotteries. The greatest marksmen and swordsmen enjoyed a regional reputation analogous to modern sports heroes.

Of course, the competitive spirit and emphasis on martial skills fostered by early modern ideals of masculinity could be dangerous as well, spilling out into the streets in the form of spontaneous duels and brawls, which are also recognized by sociologists as important forms of sociability. Fights were most likely to occur during drinking bouts, as alcohol reduced inhibitions and increased aggression among the mostly male company of the early modern public house. But pubs and elite drinking rooms provided space for more than just trouble, and many more benign social activities can be glimpsed behind the scenes as witnesses and participants describe how these fights started.

Elite sociability was more likely to take place in private palaces and closed drinking rooms than in taverns.[1] Certain entertainments staged by the privileged, however, were intentionally public affairs. Tournaments, horse races, sword dances, and displays of fireworks, all of which also had a martial element, were typically organized to accompany weddings and political events as a demonstration of wealth and power.

Most of these activities also provided opportunities for making music. While members of the privileged classes hired court musicians for private performances, commoners employed bagpipers, fife and drum players, and lute players to perform both informally in public houses and on the streets and at formal events such as weddings. More often, however, ordinary folk simply sang, and some artisans made a name for themselves moonlighting as singers. Singing in general was a tradition among craftsmen, as we know from surviving collections of artisans' songs praising the honor of various crafts. Such songs aided in establishing a shared bond and instilling members of the craft with a sense of corporate pride. Those master craftsmen who had a gift for singing competed with one another in the tradition of the Meistersinger, a kind of singers' guild in which artisans honed their skills in creating verse and melodies, usually on religious themes. Journeymen also sang psalms and other religious songs to pass the time while working.

---

1. For a glimpse into elite drinking parties, see document 3.4.

But singing could also be subversive. Singing an insulting serenade under the window of the object of the slander was a standard type of urban charivari,[2] and public singing could provide a common forum for expressions of popular protest. An insult in the form of song accentuated the effect on the honor of the person or institution under attack. Not only was the performance often public, occurring on the streets or in a public house where it drew the attention of spectators, but also the medium of song itself was especially effective as a tool of slander. The rhythm served to attract attention to specific points, and the usually familiar meter and rhyming verses made the message easy to understand and to repeat.

Singing in public during the period of Reformation was strictly a male prerogative. While women were often the subject (or object) of masculine singing, any kind of public performance was considered inappropriate for respectable women. Women joined men in wedding dances and feasts and as spectators at public spectacles, and they appear as participants in more casual drinking bouts on occasion, especially those taking place in private homes. At shooting matches, women participated in accompanying games such as bowls, lotteries, and footraces, but they did not compete with men at shooting. Women also socialized in female groups at spinning bees and during ritual gatherings associated with childbirth, including sitting at childbed and churching. Because so few exclusively female entertainments took place in public, however, they were much less likely to leave traces in the records.

I. The Control of Leisure

6.1 Controlling Leisure during the Reformation[3]

Abolishment of sleigh-riding after nine o'clock at night, and the singing in of the New Year

N.d., between 1531 and 1536: An Honorable Council and the imperial bailiff of this city of Augsburg establish and command that henceforth, no one should ride around the city in sleighs after nine o'clock at night, with the exception of driving directly home from visiting someone (with

---

2. *Charivari* was a French term used to describe noisy public mockery of an object of derision. In German it was called *Rüge,* and in England it was sometimes called "rough music."

3. StadtAA, Schätze 16, 24r–v, 38r–39r.

a lantern). And also no one who is riding in a sleigh, nor anyone else, should throw snowballs or any other objects. Likewise, no one should sing in the New Year, and even less beat drums in the streets by day or night (except at weddings), all on threat of a penalty by the council. All heed this warning.

MUMMERY AND OTHER THINGS FORBIDDEN

January 26, 1539: An Honorable Council recognizes that proper order among the folk allows for honorable merriment and fun, and has nothing against it as long as it is enjoyed without violating proper Christian behavior. However, it is the opinion of an Honorable Council that such merriment and fun among the common citizens here not only is out of proportion but also is so widespread and excessive that it is more like rowdiness and frivolousness than respectable merriment. The result is offensive to an Honorable Council and the city at large, as well as to the holy Gospels, especially in light of the worrisome swift approach of the Turks and other scourges with which God the Almighty might afflict us. To prevent this, and for the establishment and maintenance of civic order and good morals as well as the avoidance of offense and bad example, an Honorable Council here admonishes each and every one of the citizens and residents of this city, for the sake of discipline, honor, and fear of God, that everyone refrain entirely from wearing masks, deceptive costumes, and other disguises by which they are made unrecognizable and, in general, to refrain from all unusual costumes and mummery, day or night. And also, all pulling of plows, hauling in a water trough,[4] and all accompanying drumming and piping in the streets, whether by day or night, should be done away with entirely. . . . And so that modesty is maintained here during the day, there will be no taking walks or sleigh-riding in this city on Saturday during the evening sermon or on Sunday during the morning sermon. Anyone who violates this order in any of its points will be earnestly punished by an Honorable Council. All heed this warning.

GAMBLING FORBIDDEN

May 25, 1539: . . . An Honorable Council herewith earnestly commands and wills that no one in this city or its realm as far as it reaches may

---

4. Playful carnival practices meant as satire. In the case of plow pulling, plows, which symbolized fertility, were pulled through the streets by unmarried women in order to tease them for not taking husbands.

gamble in any way during holiday sermons, in any open squares inside or outside the city, whether for a little or a lot. But if someone wishes to gamble in public streets and squares on holidays after the morning sermon and between the other sermons, he may not play for more than 1 pfennig per any game that takes place in public, inside or outside of the city. On workdays, however, all gambling in public squares or streets is completely forbidden and abolished throughout an Honorable Council's jurisdiction.

6.2 Wartime Decree against Frivolity, 1631[5]

DECREE REGARDING PLAYING MUSIC, DANCING, DRINKING LATE INTO THE NIGHT, AND SLEIGH-RIDING

Everyone is aware of the dangers that are right before our eyes and the horrors of war now seen in every corner of the empire. God's wrath at our sins is obvious. All Christians therefore have more than enough reason to plead ardently with God to spare us from his discipline, and to reconcile with him by abstaining from sins, bettering their lives, doing good, and forbearing normal merriments, entertainments, and frivolities.

Thus an Honorable Council has deemed it proper first of all to encourage their dear citizens to fervent, ardent prayer and a reserved, Christian, virtuous lifestyle. In addition, all musical entertainment and dancing in houses and on the streets is herewith earnestly abolished on pain of certain punishment (for both the musicians and those who retain them), and is only allowed at weddings for the customary music during the meal, and also for an honorable dance after the noon meal on both wedding days. But this should last no later than 7:00 PM for those paying for the guests, and until 6:00 PM for the others.

It is also more than a little scandalous that drinking, gambling, and all kinds of loud yelling and shouting is going on in the beer and wine houses, at times until late in the night, which has already been forbidden. An Honorable Council herewith repeats the earnest command that no beer or wine publican shall tolerate any guest in his place after the nine o'clock bell has sounded, much less bring him wine or beer [after nine], upon pain of a 2-gulden fine for each person, half to be paid by the innkeeper and half by the guest. But those guests who are lodging

5. StadtAA, Schätze 16, 370–72.

at the inn, and may have invited someone else [to drink with them], are excepted. . . . Decreed on November 13, 1631.

6.3 Punishments for Frivolous Behavior[6]

On January 27, 1534, Ulrich Hunold and Jeromius Welser[7] were both given the following punishment because they were sleigh-riding and behaving drunkenly, and also spoke insolently to the guards: for one half year, they are not to enter the streets at night between the evening and morning horn blows, and are not to enter any public house or questionable place by day or by night. Instead, if they can't refrain from it, they are to spend their money only at the Lords' or Merchants' Rooms, and bear no weapon longer than the Lords' measure.[8] And each is to pay for 3,000 stones for the city wall, and henceforth to treat the guards properly.

And for the same reason, Melchior Manlich, Christoph Jenisch,[9] and the journeyman baker Otmar Dannenbair, who was driving, and all of whom were also singing indecent songs, were all three put in the irons and punished as follows: Manlich and Jenisch are to drink no wine in a public house or questionable place, and to stay off of the streets at night between the horn blows, for one half year. And each is to pay for 1,000 stones for the city wall. And the journeyman baker is to stay out of public houses for one year, and to refrain entirely from singing bawdy songs. But Manlich and Jenisch may well spend their money in the [Merchants'] Room.

Weavers who were locked in the irons for gambling

On November 3, 1534, the following persons were locked in the irons and referred to the council because they housed poorly, kept company in their houses, and gambled and allowed gambling with cards and dice, often staying up all night and leaving their wives and children alone. We therefore impose the merciful punishment that each and every one of them, for one entire year, may drink wine only by themselves, and in no public house or meadseller's house or questionable place. And they

6. StadtAA, Strafbuch 1533–1539, 18v–19r, 38v–39r, 97v–98r, 100v, 105v.

7. Hunold and Welser were both members of powerful patrician families.

8. "City measure" and "Lords' measure" refer to a limit on the length of swords and daggers that the defendant may carry, which differed by status. City measures were often marked on the walls of public buildings; in Augsburg this was the courthouse.

9. Manlich and Jenisch belonged to wealthy merchant families.

also may have no company in their houses, and under no circumstances gamble or allow gambling in their houses, rather avoid it entirely. They may not enter the public streets at night between the evening and the morning horn blows; and they may carry no other weapon than the city measure. By all of this they pledged to abide. [The names of seven weavers follow.]

On September 13, 1537, Bartholme Tagwercker, weaver, was given a good talking to because he gambled away his clothes, and he was forbidden to visit public houses or gamble, as well as to enter the streets at night between the horn blows, etc.

On February 9, 1538, Matheis Buck from Ulm, Matheus Hauswirt from Grossaitingen, and Michael Schwab from Merner Zell, all three journeymen millers, were locked in the irons for sword fighting at Berkenmair's [public house] and not wanting to keep peace. And as a merciful punishment, they were released on the condition that they make a legal settlement with Stichsen, who was injured by them, for his injuries, and that they appear before the Punishment Lords [to pay a fine for fighting] and pay the innkeeper for the bill.

January 15, 1602: Johann Daniel, weaver and local citizen, sang [slanderous] songs he had written himself in a public house, for which he was arrested. But because he begged for forgiveness, an Honorable Council today decreed that he should be released with an earnest warning not to be brought in again for the same offense.[10]

II. Martial Sports

6.4 An Invitation to a Shooting Match, 1567[11]

Shooting invitations such as this one arrived regularly in towns and cities throughout the empire, especially during the sixteenth century, which was the high point of martial sports competitions. Hosting a match provided the town with an opportunity to demonstrate hospitality as well as martial skill. Because winning a shooting match brought honor to the shooter's hometown, marksmen who traveled to distant matches could often count on a stipend from their local government to help cover expenses. The most

10. StadtAA, Strafbücher 1581–1587, 83v, 85r; 1588–1596, 182r; 1596–1605, 160r; 1615–1632, 81.

11. StadtAA, Schützen-Akten 1, 1567 (print).

elaborate shooting matches lasted for days and included a great variety
of entertainments, including lotteries, dances, feasts, bowling, footraces,
sword-fighting lessons, and other amusements.

We the councilors of the city of Augsburg invite our _____ and give notice to _____[12] that, in the interest of friendship and good neighborliness, we have arranged and prepared for a crossbow shooting match on the Monday of St. Michael's Day, which is the sixth of October,[13] of this year. Each person who wishes to attend and participate in the match should arrive at the inn on the evening of the day before, Sunday the fifth of October, and appear at the shooting hut at the shooting grounds by seven o'clock on Monday morning in order to elect the Nine [shooting officials]. Of these, four will be chosen from among our local shooters, and the constellation of the rest will depend upon the number of shooters who show up. In accordance with shooting law and tradition, those elected will have the power to make all decisions in regard to the match.

The selection [of the shooting sequence] by lots will begin immediately, after which as many shots will be shot as possible, the rest being shot on the following day, until [each marksman] has fired twenty-four shots at a target the size of which is drawn below on this invitation.[14] And no one may shoot any bolt unless it fits through the hole that has been cut at the bottom of this letter.[15] And in support of this shooting match, a special clock will be hung at the shooting grounds, and if any marksman shoots and scores a hit after the clock has struck, this will not be counted. Also no bolt may be shot unless it has been approved by the scribe and properly marked and recorded, or the shot will be forfeited. The range of this shooting match is 276 official Augsburg feet, the length of which is also provided here.[16] And whoever hits the target

12. Most likely, the first blank was for "fellow councilmen" and the second blank was for "the citizens of [city name]."

13. Octava Michaelis archangeli.

14. A target with a diameter of between 6 and 7 inches and a small bull's-eye is drawn on the bottom of the invitation. Visual aids were included with shooting match invitations so that shooters would know at what distance to practice shooting ahead of the match, since standard units of measure were lacking.

15. Also glued to the letter is a piece of parchment, with a hole about the width of a finger through it and the paper.

16. Lit. "workshoes," a unit of measure that varied from town to town. The length of this unit was provided at the bottom of this invitation in the form of a printed line; some shooting match invitations were also affixed with a length of string for

will be ascribed one shot. Each marksman should fire with his arms free of any support and without any unfair advantage.

As a prize for the winner of this shooting match, we are providing a gilded silver cup worth 100 gulden in coin, which will remain the top prize. The winner is free to choose this cup or to take the 100 gulden. In addition, each participant must stake 2 gulden as an entrance fee, out of which the main prizes will be established in accordance with the direction and decisions of the Nine.

Any shooter found using an unfair advantage will have forfeited his equipment and also be subject to a penalty imposed by the officially elected Nine. And since plain steel crossbows can cause harm when they break, no bow will be allowed in the match unless it is wrapped and secured with a wire or braid or otherwise sheathed. Further, if a shooter's crossbow happens to become disjointed, or the stock snaps or breaks at the nut rest, in the middle, or elsewhere, the shooter should be given two shots out of turn; but if the binding, nut, or catch should break, no more than one shot. All of these defects should be inspected by the Nine and a decision made based on their opinion. A broken windlass, bowstring, or arrow, however, doesn't count.

And whichever shooter scores the most hits out of twenty-four shots will be given the first-place prize in its entirety together with a pennant. If there should be a tie, the two shooters must come to an agreement between themselves or have a shoot-off.

All of this information we extend to _____ with our goodwill and our diligent request to come and help us enjoy a merry shooting match.

July 29, 1567.

6.5 Two Shooters from Ingolstadt Defend Their Honor as Marksmen, 1554[17]

Petition from Hans Geler and Wentzl Winckler to the city council in Ingolstadt, 1554.

We apply to [Your Lords] with [our] humble request. . . . On Monday following last Saints Simon and Jude (October 28) in this current year of [15]54, a gun shooting match was held in Augsburg, and as is

---

the same purpose. Official local units of measure were marked on the exterior walls of the courthouse for reference (see also document 6.3). The Augsburg workshoe was just less than 30 cm.

17. StadtAA, Schützen-Akten 1, 1554.

traditional and proper, invitations were sent here [to Ingoldstat] and to other nearby towns. In response, as lovers of this chivalric art, we also showed up there to participate in the match and to keep honest company with other gentlemen and marksmen there, as did the other assembled marksmen. . . . And in the course of this chivalric entertainment we won two pennants, honorably and honestly according to the rules of the art, and took them with us. We still have them and, if God wills, will honorably defend them for the rest of our lives.

However . . . we have been accused—unjustly, inappropriately, falsely, and with particular injury to our honor and good name—of not having won these pennants at the shooting match, but of having bought them with cash, out of our own particular vanity and deceit. In support of this charge, we have been shown a document that published the results of this shooting match, supposedly printed and distributed in Augsburg. In this piece of fiction, although the names of the other people who won shooting pennants are listed and reported, ours were overlooked, and no report of us was made.

[Your Lords], we place little value on unnecessary glory or displaying our pennants in public shooting matches or otherwise. Nonetheless, however, it is impossible for us, as men of honor, to put up with this unfair burden, for we are being offended unjustly as a result of it. We face great ignominy and reproach and great damage to our honor, as if we had not only acted dishonorably but also have deceived [Your Lords]. And for this we have already been expelled from the shooting society here. As a result, we not only have to put up with mistrust, insult, shame, and reproach from all honorable people but also [face] the complete ruin of our honor and our fortunes.

Thus we apply to [Your Lords] with our devoted petition to write favorably on our behalf to the [wise] mayors and council in Augsburg, for the sake of our honor, and to inform them of our justifiable grievance, so that the Lords in Augsburg can immediately investigate the facts of this and provide us with the truth. [This we ask] for the sake of our honor and good names, which we have kept well thus far, and with the help of God hope to keep by all who love honor for the rest of our lives. . . .

Hans Geler and Wentzl Winckler of Ingolstadt, 1554

[The Ingolstadt council subsequently wrote to Augsburg for clarification of this matter; there is no record of the response. It is very likely that this misunderstanding resulted from an error in the printed results of the match.]

6.6 Entertainments at a Shooting Match (Illustration)

Spectators at a shooting match, Augsburg 1570–1577. The picture is intended to depict a shooting match that took place a century before (in 1470). Note the women running footraces in the background. University Erlangen-Nürnberg, Library, Ms. B 213, fol. 176v–77r. By permission.

6.7 Accidental Death at a Fencing Match, 1595[18]

The fencing "school" referenced here was actually a temporary event that combined competitive fencing, public demonstrations of skill, and sword-fighting lessons, not a permanent school. Fencing schools were usually organized by traveling sword-fighting masters who moved from town to town teaching their art. Sword fighting with the long sword was a dangerous military sport and should not be confused with modern foil fencing.

Interrogation of Samuel Probst

On Monday, the 4th of December 1595, Samuel Probst, in the jail, testified under earnest threat to the accompanying questions as follows:

18. StadtAA, Urgicht Samuel Probst, December 5, 1595; Strafbuch 1588–1596, 258v.

1. What is his name and where does he come from? His name is Samuel Probst; he is a local citizen.

2. What does he do for a living? He is a furrier by trade.

3. How often has he been arrested here or in other places, and under what conditions he was released in each case? He has never spent an hour under arrest.

4. Did he not participate in a long-sword fencing match yesterday, during the fencing school held at the dance house, with a journeyman printer who was from out of town? Says yes.

5. Who was this journeyman printer, and what was his name? He had seen this journeyman printer here once three years ago, but had never spoken a word to him. This time they fenced with one another. He doesn't know his name.

6. Did he not know him beforehand, and what was the nature of their relationship? He has never had any relationship with him.

7. Did he not, immediately in the second round, strike him so grievously on the temple that he died the same night? Answers yes, he gave him a blow to the head. This was not out of any rancor; rather he fought with him in accordance with sword-fighting custom. [His opponent] was attacking him, so he also had to watch out for his advantage.

8. What kind of grudge or rancor he held against him that caused him to strike him so defiantly and in violation of the rules of fencing? He has never in his life had any grudge against him, and he also did not violate the rules of fencing.

9. Isn't he aware that an Honorable Council had closed down the fencing schools for a long time because of inappropriate sword fighting? He did not do anything inappropriate. It happened in the course of practicing his art.

10. Doesn't he also know that an Honorable Council only allowed the fencing schools to resume eight days ago on the promise that the sword fighting would be conducted modestly? He does know this.

11. Why then he turned such rage upon the printer, in violation of an Honorable Council's command and the promise of the fencing masters? Says again that he fought in accordance with sword-fighting custom and not out of rage.

12. Who incited or goaded him into doing it? No one at all.

13. How did he expect to get away with this without punishment? He hopes that he will be mercifully released, since he was fighting according to the rules of the art.

PETITION FROM THE FENCING SCHOOL MASTERS

Obedient Report and Truthful Testimony of the Official Proprietors of the fencing school, in response to the interrogation of the accused Samuel Probst, furrier and fellow citizen.

December 7, 1595.

Noble, well-born [and wise] Lords Mayor, Burgomaster, and an Honorable Council of this city, Gracious Imperious and Auspicious Lords: [Your Lords] have provided us with the accused Samuel Probst's record of questioning and his testimony, which we have received with due reverence, and the contents of which we have read. We are thus compelled to respond to [Your Lords'] request. We can only conclude from this request that what is required of us is a truthful account of what happened between the accused Probst and the journeyman printer who was killed during their fencing match at the recently held fencing school.

First, it is true that this Probst was the fencing master's starting fencer, and that before the call, the late printer came forward to challenge [Probst] in the long sword, and requested a match with him. But it cannot be said of us, the fencers, or the spectators that we knew of any kind of anger, grudge, or hatred between the two of them. Rather, Probst fought with him in accordance with the tradition of the sword and according to the rules, and did not attack with the point or pommel, or with an onrush, or use any other dishonorable move that is forbidden to sword fighting. This we can assert with a clear and intact conscience. For in addition to our own observations, we have gathered reports from the other fencers present, and all the spectators. These leave no doubt that [Your Lords] could obtain many truthful testimonies upon request to support the fact that Probst did not behave inappropriately, but conducted himself toward his opponent as is proper in a fencing match. We have no idea, however, what the circumstances were that caused [the printer] to end up dead of the wound he received. That is best known to the Lord God. For from the standpoint of human reason, it is surprising that he died of the wound, although we have been told that this was largely due to the fact that he was a heavy bleeder, which would also have had a significant impact.

Because, then, the situation occurred as noted above (and common sense indicates that Probst was not at fault, rather it occurred as a result of a blow he delivered in the course of his art) . . . it is our devoted and most diligent request to [Your Lords] to show mercy to the above-noted Probst, and not understand this incident as a crime, intentional act, or some kind of contract from someone else. For we did not notice, perceive, or observe any impropriety on his part. And we request in addition that he be shown mercy and be released from jail upon sufficient surety and a promise to reappear, and that this incident not be held against other fencers, rather that they mercifully be allowed to further practice their art. [At Your Lords'] favor,

Most devotedly obediently . . . the two official proprietors of the fencing school

Punishment record, December 7, 1595

Samuel Probst, furrier and local citizen, struck a nonresident journeyman a wound in the temple while they were sword fighting with long swords in a public sword-fighting school. Because the journeyman printer died the same night, Probst was arrested. But because he asserted that he struck the journeyman in the course of the free art of fencing, and not out of any ill will, an Honorable Council today decreed that he should be released upon a surety to reappear if necessary.

6.8 Chronicler Georg Siedler Describes Martial Entertainments, 1600[19]

Sword and horse dance held here in Augsburg, 1600

It has been the case in the past, and still is, that all kinds of public entertainments are common during Shrovetide and are allowed to continue unhindered. So, too, in this year of 1600, around the time of Shrove Sunday on February 3/13,[20] . . . Simon Eycklen of Schongau, now a resident and tenant in Lechausen, staged a sword dance. This hasn't been done here in Augsburg for forty or fifty years. It was held by day, and then there was also a horse dance at night that was even more amusing because of the fact that each rider had a light. This was done with the permission of an Honorable Council here in Augsburg, who also gave Eycklen 24 gulden for the cost and expense.

19. StadtAA, Chroniken 20, Chronik von Siedler, 1055–1619, 251v.

20. The inclusion of dual dates in Siedler's entries is a reference to the ongoing controversy over the introduction of the Gregorian calendar (see Chapter Two). The calendar was not accepted in some parts of the empire until the seventeenth century. Siedler's stubborn inclusion of dates according to the old calendar as late as 1600 provides evidence of his virulent Protestantism.

III. The Dangers of Male Sociability: Fights and Tavern Comportment

6.9 A Swordfight in the Street, 1591[21]

Fights and brawls over drinks were a daily affair in early modern cities. Records of fines collected for fighting in Augsburg during the late sixteenth century record around a thousand fights per year, 80 percent of them involving only men and about 10 percent of those with blades, mostly swords. Most likely there were many more that went unnoticed by the authorities. Fights such as this one, which turned deadly, were more unusual, with less than one per year resulting in a killing. But because deadly fights were more likely to provoke a major investigation, they provide us with greater detail than do the less serious incidents. And even though the deadly outcome was not typical, witnesses and participants in such incidents often provide rich descriptions of the ordinary tavern comportment that led up to the fight and of the expectations of the company for adhering to social norms.

WITNESSES IN REGARD TO THE SLAIN CASPAR RAUNER, CALLED PASTRY BAKER[22]

Note: These witnesses were not sworn in, rather only brought into the chambers by the Lord Burgomaster for information and preparation of the interrogation questions.

Tuesday, August 13, 1591
Eve Rüepin from Dillingen, serving girl to Sophia Keppeler and around fifteen years old, says that yesterday at about six in the evening, she went into Caspar Hefele the Younger's public house[23] to sell bouquets of carnations. Afterward she heard the slain pastry baker Caspar Rauner and Caspar Aufschlager arguing with each other, and the pastry baker took two bouquets from her for which he didn't pay her. Then he challenged Aufschlager to fight, and called him (pardon the expression) a dog's

---

21. StadtAA, Urgicht Caspar Aufschlager, August 16, 1591; Strafbuch 1588–1596, 119r–v.

22. *Küchelbacher,* lit. "little ball baker," maker of dough fritters, Shrovetide cakes, and other sweets.

23. Hefele was a publican at the brewery Potted Flower (*Blumenstock*) on Karrengässchen.

cunt.[24] After that he went into the baking hut and called for his sword. His wife wanted him to stay there, but he threatened her with his fist, as if he was going to hit her. The maid gave him the sword and what happened after that she doesn't know, except that the baker headed with the sword toward the public house where Aufschlager had remained.[25]

Lucas Krüg, lacemaker and local citizen, says he was drinking at Caspar Hefele's yesterday. When he came in, he saw the pastry baker Caspar Rauner and Caspar Aufschlager playing cards, over which they had a disagreement. So the pastry baker called Aufschlager (pardon the expression) a dog's cunt, and called him out. Aufschlager responded that he would meet him in the morning at the soldier's quarters. Then they both went out of the public room together, and what happened outside he doesn't know, but Aufschlager came back in. And then a youth who was also with them in the room started up, "If someone called me a dog's cunt, I would slap him up the side of the head." In about a quarter hour the pastry baker came back, and was wearing a sword, but he didn't come inside. And someone else started saying, "The pastry baker is back." Aufschlager got right up from the table and went out. The witness stayed inside, only looking out the window, so couldn't know who drew first. But Aufschlager stabbed at the pastry baker after about the second strike.

Jacob Hetenberg, gunstock-maker; Hans Schuldhaiss the Younger, mold-maker; Hieremias Gimpel, illuminator; and Leonhard Mösch, shoemaker, all four local citizens, testify that the four of them were standing on the street when the pastry baker Caspar Rauner came up from the baking hut with the sword, and they saw Caspar Aufschlager come out of Caspar Hefele's place. When the two of them saw each other, they approached one another. Aufschlager drew first, and then the pastry baker right afterward. Aufschlager made the first strike, which the pastry baker deflected, and then Aufschlager made another strike at him and then immediately a jab, injuring the pastry baker under the left armpit. The pastry baker was still able to deflect a few blows from Aufschlager, until he dropped his sword, and the blade on Aufschlager's sword broke, leaving him with only the hilt in his hand. Although there was a call to Aufschlager to keep the peace, he picked up the pastry baker's sword anyway and struck at him, and also gave him a stab in the shoulder and a strike. And on top of that, in his haste, he struck Rauner

---

24. Obscene insult implying a sniveling coward.

25. Presumably Eve Rüepin followed Rauner home in order to collect the money he owed her.

a large wound. The pastry baker's maid fell upon Aufschlager and held him back. Hans Schuldhaiss took the pastry baker to the barber-surgeon Georg Schiger, where he perished in about a half hour.

Interrogation of Caspar Aufschlager

On Friday, August 16, 1591, Caspar Aufschlager answered the accompanying questions willingly under earnest threat as follows:

1. What is his name and where does he come from? His name is Caspar Aufschlager, a loden weaver by trade and a citizen of Nördlingen. Since the imperial diet he has been a member of the guard here.

2. Was he not drinking at the publican Caspar Hefele's place last Monday? Answers yes.

3. Who was drinking with him? Says, Caspar Rele of the local guard, who is also from Nördlingen; two carpenters whose names he doesn't know, but who are currently working in Lord Marcus Fugger's house on Hafenberg; plus Christoph, who used to be a sutler in the soldiers' quarters; and Michael Seidler, David Hauser, Hans Widenman from Munich, and Caspar Rauner, and others whom he doesn't know. These were sitting at his table, and otherwise there were a lot of other people in the public room at the time, but at other tables.

4. What kind of disagreement did he start with Caspar Rauner, the pastry baker? Answers that some of them at his table were gambling for beer, but he was just watching. Then it happened that Caspar Rauner was losing, and thus became surly, and also began to quarrel. So he told [Rauner] to settle down, in response to which [Rauner] called him a freeloader and (pardon the expression) a dog's cunt, thus giving him reason to defend himself verbally and to say he is nothing of the kind, rather an honorable soldier. Thus they came to words, so that he would have been justified in hitting [Rauner] in the public room. Finally Caspar Rauner left and got a sword, and when he returned he challenged him by saying that if he is an honorable soldier, he will step outside. So he could not do less than to face him. As soon as he came out of Caspar Hefele's house and met Rauner in the street, they both drew their rapiers. Then he attacked Rauner in accordance with sword-fighting custom, that is, for his part, jabbing once and otherwise only striking with the flat of the sword. But Rauner fought only with strikes. He also says that after he had struck at Rauner two or three times, his sword fell apart, and he was left with only the hilt in his hand. And as he saw at that moment that Rauner's sword was lying on the ground, he picked it up, but gave him neither a stab nor a strike with it, as far as he knows, given that he was drunk. Once he got his sword again, he put down Rauner's, and the people standing around brought him back into Hefele's pub. Finally there was a cry that Rauner was dying and he should flee. So he went out the back door of Hefele's and toward Jacob's Gate. But because there were a lot of people there, he turned back and headed for the Bird Gate in order to get out [of town]. But he was caught. He knows nothing else to say of this matter and the incident. . . . He has never in his life had any animosity toward Rauner, other than what happened between them described here, and Rauner has always been his good fellow. . . .

He is sorry from the heart that such a thing and misfortune should occur, and begs for the sake of God for mercy. Notes also that he had assumed up until now that Rauner was only injured and still alive, until he learned otherwise only in the course of this interrogation.

SUPPLICATION FROM THE GUARD CAPTAIN TO THE CATHEDRAL CHAPTER, REQUESTING INTERCESSION FOR AUFSCHLAGER

To a Most Venerable Cathedral Chapter of Our Dear Lady in Augsburg Devoted appeal of the Captain, commander, and the entire common guard:

Venerable, well-born, noble, and learned, Gracious Lords. Last Monday, Caspar Aufschlager, citizen and our comrade-in-arms in the Augsburg guard, became involved in a disagreement with Caspar Rauner, also our late comrade-in-arms, over a very minor, insignificant matter while drinking beer together. In the course of this Rauner not only greatly injured Aufschlager's honor but also among other things accused Aufschlager of not having the manhood and honor to fight. Aufschlager said to Rauner that he [Rauner] well knows that fighting with each other is strictly forbidden, but since [Rauner] is so eager to have him, [Aufschlager] was willing to face him at a specific approved spot, or to settle the fight amicably in front of me, their Captain. But none of this helped. [Rauner] was thus earning an Honorable Council's pay dishonorably. Robbed of his senses, Rauner then went home and got his sword, and challenged Augschlager with more immodest words to come out of the public house, so that Aufschlager had to step out in defense of his honor, which is held equal to life. And after they had crossed swords a few times and the pommel of Aufschlager's rapier broke so that he was only able to defend himself with jabs, one (unfortunately) went badly, so that the provocateur was struck through the shoulder to such an extent that soon afterward, as he was being bound by the barber-surgeon, he ended his life. After this, Aufschlager was arrested at the city gate as he tried to betake himself into safety.

Now, we are comforted by our confidence that once an Honorable Council has collected the witness statements (which are readily at hand in this case), [the council] will, on its own, mitigate the severity of [Aufschlager's] punishment . . . especially since he has thus far led an honorable, reserved, peaceful life, of which we can provide good and truthful witness. Still, we are entirely of the opinion that if Your Graces appeal to an Honorable Council with your intercession and plea, the mitigation of the penalty could come to fruition all the sooner. We therefore present to Your Graces our devoted, most diligent request, in light of the justification described above, and especially for the sake of the prisoner's wife and two children, to provide your gracious intercession. This we are eager to earn, together and individually, by laying down our lives, goods, and blood to the extent of our responsibility to an Honorable Council at any time.
In devotion to Your Graces,
The entire Augsburg guard

[in another hand]
Should be presented to the Burgomaster in Office, and therewith reported that a venerable cathedral chapter here wishes to intercede with an Honorable Council on behalf of this Caspar Aufschlager. We hereby offer neighborly intercession for a pardon. Decreed in the Chapter Office on August 16, [15]91

Punishment record

Caspar Aufschlager, loden weaver, citizen of Nördlingen and a soldier in the local guard, got into a sword fight with Caspar Rauner, local citizen and soldier, and thereby stabbed and killed Rauner, for which he was arrested. However, after an examination of witnesses revealed that Rauner had provoked Aufschlager with defamatory words, an Honorable Council has decreed today that Aufschlager should be released, but be put out of the city and realm for five years.

6.10 A Fight at a Wedding, 1600[26]

These statements describing a sword fight at a wedding are excerpted from a very lengthy collection of charges and countercharges exchanged by the

26. StadtAA, Urgicht Hans Vogel, February 4–March 11, 1600; Strafbücher, Protokolle der Zucht- und Strafherren, March 27, 1600.

two parties, probably resulting from the victim's expectation of a cash
settlement for his injuries more than as an accusation of criminal conduct.
The participants in the fight were both members of the local guard, but
neither made his living by the sword, one being a military piper and
the other a military scribe. The case provides a glimpse of the standard
entertainments at a commoner's wedding as well as representations of the
demands of masculine honor.

Selections from the first interrogation of Hans Vogel, February 4, 1600

What is his name, where is he from, and how old is he? What does he do for a living? Hans Vogel, from Ellwang, approximately forty-five or forty-six years old, a piper in the local guard unit.

How often he has been arrested here or elsewhere? He has never been arrested other than being locked in the military stockade two or three times for drinking too much, and because he missed his watch as a result.

Did he not on last Monday, at a wedding at Beham's public house on Baker Lane, badly stab and injure Georg Siber, soldier in the local barracks, with a dangerous and potentially deadly wound to the chest, and also in the left hand? It's true, he did injure Georg Siber, for the following reason: namely, because Siber was very drunk at the wedding, and after the wedding feast he danced for a short while. Afterward [Siber] came up to him and his drummer, who were hired for the dance and were playing, and suddenly expected them to give him his coat. And he went after them very fiercely about this coat, as if they had stolen it, until he was finally got out the door. After all that, he got his coat from a woman who brought it over from a spot near where the bride was sitting. A little while later Siber came back to the dance, and challenged him with defiant words. And then finally, although he was being repeatedly begged for the sake of God to leave it alone, Siber said, "If he (the piper) is a rogue and a thief, then he should stay seated. But if he's an upright fellow then he'll come down and fight." After such impertinance, in order to save his honor, he couldn't do less than to get right up from the table where they were sitting and playing for the dance, and they crossed swords on the dance floor. Before they had exchanged three or four blows he injured [Siber], as is known. And based on what his drummer boy told him, Siber was supposedly injured on the fingers of his left hand, and afterward received a stab wound on the breast near the armpit.

What caused him to do this? And what did he have against Siber? He has never had any ill will toward Siber in his life, rather this all happened because of his defiant challenge, as above.

Is it honorable and soldierly to stab his comrade like that? He had to defend his life and honor. If his strike went badly, he is truly sorry about it. But one can still see by looking at his weapon that Siber also did not spare any blows against him.

Was Georg Siber not very drunk at the time? Says yes, he was very drunk.

Why he then stabbed such a drunken man so dangerously? He was patient for a long time, yet Siber went after him so harshly and so attacked him that he had to defend himself.

Petition from Vogel's wife Maria, February 5, 1600

Last Monday, my dear husband Hans Vogel, piper, and his fellow Peter Krumper, drummer, both of whom are in the local guard, were hired to play at a wedding at Beham's [public house] on Baker Lane. There, a conflict occurred between my husband and Georg Siber from Munich, also in the guard, during the dance. Although [Vogel] asked him repeatedly to let it be, Siber spoke to my husband (as can be proven) so ignominiously, challenged him so vehemently, and went after him so dreadfully, that he had to cross swords with him to rescue his manly honor and [prevent] defamation by other soldiers. Therefore my husband was arrested and put into jail. . . .

Georg Siber's statments in response to Vogel, February 10 and 17, 1600

On Monday, the last of January, I was invited along with a number of other people to a wedding at Hans Beham's. After eating and drinking, I merrily joined the dance along with others. Near some musicians, I took off my coat. Then I wanted to go home peacefully and without any trouble. At this time one of the men attending the bride honored me with a request to lead the next dance. Even though I didn't really feel much like doing it, I could not refuse this honor, rather accepted it, and lay my coat back down beside the musicians where it had been before and where I had just picked it up. But after the dance had ended, I couldn't find it anymore. I couldn't afford to leave it behind, so asked around for it in general, and not at all specifically from these frivolous persons, Vogel the piper and his fellow, the drummer. And no one else took it personally at all. Once the coat was found again, and brought to me by a woman, this Vogel, as is his way, was heard to assail me brazenly with unbeseeming words and to call me a scalawag. This I could not and would not ignore because of the unavoidable requirement of honor. Upon that he said I was no fighter but only a scribe and a bootblack, to which I responded that he should step outside of the inn with me, and I would show him if I'm a fighter or not. . . .

I never in my life had in mind accusing him of stealing my or any other coat, or anything else, as he claims. . . . If his goal was peace and not going after me life and limb, then he should have attended to the playing and piping for which he was paid, and left me alone, as I was an invited guest and, as he himself points out, I was very drunk, and he was sober. . . .

Discipline Lord protocol

Hans Vogel and Georg Siber, both in the guard, for a bloody fight in which Vogel seriously wounded and injured Siber, were both fined 2 gulden, but under the condition that [they both retain the right to pursue their legal charges against each other, and if one is shown to be in the right, the other has to pay him back his 2 gulden].

IV. Music and Other Entertainments

6.11 Dancing and Piping among the Poor, 1593[27]

Interrogation of Hans Gross, piper

On Saturday the 8th of May, 1593, [Hans Gross] testified to the accompanying questions under earnest questioning as follows:

1. What is his name, where is he from, and how old is he? His name is Hans Gross, he's from Unterstotzingen, and he is around eighteen years old.

2. What does he do for a living? He is a piper.

3. How often he has been arrested here or elsewhere? Why and under what conditions he was released in each case? He has never been arrested here or in any other place, and has never been here before he arrived yesterday.

27. StadtAA, Urgicht Hans Gross, Maria Reitenbeurin, May 8, 1593; Strafbuch 1588–1596, May 8, 1593.

4. Did he not play for two common women to dance? Says yes, there were two of them. They gave him and his fellow half a batzen to play while they danced, and one of them danced with a beggar girl.

5. What did they give him for it? That he reported above.

6. How did he come to meet them, and what kind of relationship does he have with them? He and his fellow, Hans Winkel from Uhlstetten, wanted to go from [outside the Gögginger Gate] to Pfersee over the Pfersee bridge. But they ran into two women in front of the bridge who asked him and his fellow to play for them. So they did. He and his fellow had never seen the two women before and didn't know them.

7. Is he married? Says no.

8. Did he not fornicate with them, and how often, and with which of them? He did not fornicate with them.

9. Since he travels about in idleness and does not work, where does he get his support? He supports himself by piping, and his parents were on the dole.

10. With whom does he go about, and what misdeeds have they committed? He has no other fellows but Hans Winkel. But he did not commit any misdeeds with him.

11. Has he not committed theft, or does he know of others who have? Professes his innocence, and knows of nothing else to report.

12. How did he expect to get away with this without punishment? Begs for mercy, he didn't consider the consequences.

Interrogation of Maria Reitenbeurin, beggar

On Saturday, May 8, 1593, [Maria Reitenbeurin] testified to the accompanying questions under earnest questioning as follows:

1. What is her name, where is she from, and how old is she? Her name is Maria Reitenbeurin, and she is from Lauingen.

2. What does she do for a living? She lives by begging.

3. How often has she been arrested here or elsewhere? Why? And under what conditions was she released each time? She has never been arrested. This is the first time.

4. What is she doing here, and how long has she been staying here? She has been living around the city and seeking alms since a year ago with six others, namely with Anna [Weiblingerin], and Barbara Reitenbeurin, and the others died. She does it so that she and her mother, who is ill and staying in Oberhausen, can get by.

5. With what married and single persons has she fornicated? She has never fornicated in her life.

6. What crimes has she committed, or does she know about? She has committed no crimes, and knows of nothing to report.

7. Was she not dancing in the Rosenau? Who played for the dance, and who danced with her? As she was coming from Gögginger with a beggar girl and arrived in the Rosenau, she ran into two pipers there that she doesn't know, along with Catherina Steger. She wanted to ask them for alms. Then Steger said she should dance with her first, and she would give her a pfennig. Upon that the pipers began to play, and she danced with Steger, and they were caught during the dance. Otherwise there were two fellows standing there while they were dancing, who were also brought in with the others.

[Gross, Winkel, Reitenbeurin, and Weiblingerin were all banished as idlers.]

6.12 Selections from "A New Song," Made by Christof Halbritter, Tailor and Singer, 1594[28]

This song is typical of satirical songs used to slander the object of one's scorn in early modern German towns, in this case a girl named Euphrosyna Bair who, the author believed, had insulted the tailor's craft by suggesting they weren't good enough for her. Young men occasionally sang such songs in pairs or groups under a young woman's window in a parody of courtship rituals; those who could not sing themselves engaged more gifted craftsman singers to perform for them. Halbritter composed and wrote this song himself, using less offensive printed songs as a basis and changing the text to suit his needs. This English translation does not reflect the meter and rhyme of the original.

Just because I'm in the mood for it,
I must sing a song
about a greengrocer's good daughter.
She always puts on airs,
coarsely disparaging the tailors.
Because none of them is good enough for her,
She forced me
to make this song about her.

---

28. StadtAA, Urgicht Christof Halbritter, June 28, 1594.

She thinks herself lovely and fine
and wants to be a sweetheart.
And as soon as she gets a beau
Then she fills him full of lies.
If it's a beau that mayn't come upstairs,
then she comes down and talks to him in the doorway,
flirts with him for half the night,
Then laughs at him afterward.

No fellow can go along his way
Without her hanging on him like a cocklebur.
He is then branded with mockery;
The first is too short, the next too tall,
The third, he doesn't walk right at all
The fourth is just too ordinary
The fifth she doesn't like for some other reason.

Just see what she recently did,
she went to one of her best girlfriends,
She said, "You must braid my hair
For I want to go to a dance.
So braid all my hair up pretty
So that I will please my lover in front of the young tailor.
He will be there too,
And will take me for a drink."

Then her friend said to her,
"My dear, but when will you take a husband?
I heard just now as the truth
That it's getting serious with the tailor."
She said, "I think you're drunk!
I would be crazy.
Do you really want to tell me
That I should have a tailor?"

"Don't you think I'd be ashamed
If I took a mere tailor?
Especially one as he is.
With him I'd have a fine household.
You have always known
That my true sweetheart is no tailor-boy!

So I say to you right now,
Forget about the tailor."

And now I say to you, look,
you're not even good enough for a tailor.
You'll have some time to wait
Before anyone wants to have you.
You see me as just the type
to be enchanted by you at first sight—
right, like a hedgehog as an ass wipe
I'm telling you that right now.

So now I sing to you
What my real motive is
For singing this song
And directing it at her.
For we heard, from certain quarters,
That she was spreading rumors about me.
So I made this song for her,
And send it her way to say,
good night.

End.

[Halbritter was arrested for singing in the streets and sent to the Punishment Lords, presumably to pay a fine and/or make a public apology to Euphrosyna.]

6.13 An Elephant Visits Augsburg[29]

The elephant described here received considerable attention from chroniclers and engravers during its trip in 1629 from Amsterdam through Frankfurt, Nuremberg, Strasbourg, Regensburg, Augsburg, Memmingen, and other German towns before touring Austria and Italy. Most likely, it was the same animal first brought to Paris in 1626 by Mijnheer Sevender (of the Netherlands), believed to be the first elephant to be displayed in Europe for commercial purposes.

In 1629 during the month of July, for St. Ulrich's Kermis, a live elephant was here, which could be seen at the dance house for 5 kreuzer.

29. StadtAA, Chroniken 32, Ludwig Hainzelmann der Elter.

It was able to do tricks. First, the man who was performing with it held up three glasses of wine, and it took them with its trunk and put them into its mouth. Afterward, [the man] put a bread roll on the ground and another on his head, which [the elephant] took one after the other with its trunk and gobbled up in a moment. This happened twice. Afterward the man asked if it was good, and it made itself understood with its rough voice as if to say, "yes" and reached out with its right front foot to say thank you. Afterward the man sat on its neck, for which the animal even helped lift him up. Afterward he also sat on its trunk and then on its ear, which everyone could see. The man spoke to it only in French. The animal is ten years old and was ten feet tall.

And right afterward in August, the Reformation in religion took place[30]. . . .

30. See Chapter Ten.

Chapter Seven
Ethnicity

When exploring relations between Christian Europeans and persons belonging to other ethnic groups in early modern Europe, historians often speak in terms of "center and periphery" or the European definition of "self and other" rather than in terms of race. Under these categories, people living or traveling in Europe who belonged to nondominant ethnic groups are regularly grouped together with marginal elements, including poor and vagrant populations, religious dissidents such as Anabaptists, and even imaginary enemies in the form of witches. This approach is not due to insensitivity to minority identities. Rather, it is the result of historians attempting to understand early modern mentalities on their own terms instead of applying our definitions to their social relationships. Ethnicity and race were not recognized categories in early modern Germany. Instead, Europeans during this period identified other ethnic groups in terms of what they understood as wrong religions, moral failings, and physical features associated with minorities, also often presumed to represent flaws of character.

Although the questions posed to such persons in cases of arrest suggested that these wrong religions and character flaws were a matter of choice, ethnic identity was in fact not fluid. In the case of arrivals in the city whose religion was supposedly the defining factor that made them suspicious, such as Jews and Turks, conversion to Christianity hardly eradicated the boundaries of identity. In fact, Jews asserting conversion to Christianity could appear particularly suspicious to their Christian hosts, who assumed that those claiming to be converts might only be pretending to seek salvation in order to infiltrate the community and cause damage from within.

Rules of inclusion and exclusion in the early modern view were influenced by definitions of citizenship and membership in the civic commune. Locals were assumed to have a stake in defending their homes and neighborhoods, whereas one could never be sure about the interests of noncitizens and other outsiders. Especially during periods of tension, which in the early modern city often grew out of religious differences, civic authorities believed that they needed to be certain of the loyalties of those who walked their streets. Ethnic minorities were suspect even in towns where they resided permanently. In Frankfurt, which maintained a Jewish quarter throughout the early modern period, Jews did not share in local defense duties like other town residents; instead, local laws required them to submit to the protection of the Christian community and forbade them to refer to themselves as "citizens."

With few exceptions, ethnic minorities were present in Reformation Augsburg only as visitors. Jews were expelled from Augsburg during the fifteenth century, as they were from most German cities. They remained as significant settlements only in Frankfurt and Worms. Some Jews emigrated after the expulsion, many to Poland or northern Italy; others eventually established Jewish settlements in the German countryside. Nonetheless, Jews and Christians remained economically integrated. Jewish communities existed around Augsburg in a number of the Swabian villages and smaller towns east of the Lech River, and their residents were regular visitors to the city. In order to enter town to conduct business, however, Jews were required to pay for an armed escort to accompany them wherever they went, and had to leave town before the city gates closed for the night, normally around 8:00 or 9:00 at night. Being escorted under arms was humiliating and reminiscent of captured criminals, implying a state of dishonor, which underscored the value judgment inherent in the system. Nonetheless, escort passes that have survived from the late sixteenth and early seventeenth centuries allow a rough estimate of at least 100 to 300 visits to the city per year by Jews who came to shop and engage in trade and other unspecified business, often with members of the local elite. Jews also received special dispensations during imperial diets to prepare meals and serve wine, most likely in order to provide kosher meals for the so-called court Jews, who worked as bankers and factors for members of the nobility. Other Jews who entered the city without the required escort were subject to arrest, and depending on their means, could be charged exorbitant fines for their release. Augsburg residents regularly visited Jewish settlements as well in order to pawn clothing and household goods and negotiate other loans, activities that were theoretically illegal, but were generally tolerated by Christian authorities. Recent research suggests that Jews residing in communities that enjoyed close connections to imperial cities achieved a higher socioeconomic status than those with less regular contact.

Appearing even more suspicious to local authorities than Jews were bands of gypsies (*Zigeuner*), often identified in the records as "Little Egyptians" due to confusion about their origins.[1] Gypsies were a mat-

---

1. "Egyptian" is the basis for the English word "gypsy." The terms *Zigeuner* and "gypsy" in modern German and English have maintained negative connotations from earlier centuries, leading many members of this group to self-identify themselves by the names of particular tribes, such as Roma or Sinti. As neither the

ter of concern because of both their obvious ethnic difference and their mobile lifestyle. All wandering folk carried a taint of suspicion in early modern Germany, including not only gypsies but also traveling musicians and entertainers, peddlers, discharged soldiers, and others who were forced to travel to seek their living. Many of these drifters turned to theft or trickery in order to combat poverty. Gypsies in particular were subject to accusations of thievery as well as sorcery and espionage, even as they were sought out for their assumed skills at fortune-telling and healing and for providing entertainment in the form of music and sleight-of-hand feats. Discrimination against these wanderers was stepped up by imperial decrees issued in 1530 and 1551 ordering all gypsies to leave the empire, making their presence officially illegal wherever they went. Later ordinances aimed at controlling the poor often lumped gypsies together with vagrants and beggars.

Not only gypsies and Jews but also anyone of foreign origin could appear suspect to local authorities. Compared to the other categories included in this volume, however, sources on ethnic minorities are scarce. Those that exist tend to be heavily influenced by the attitudes of those in power and provide only the briefest glimpse into the internal structures of minority culture. The nature of available records also constrains the range of groups represented. Images of more distant non-Europeans who rarely if ever passed through the city, including Africans, Asians, and Native Americans, depended largely on received stereotypes, sensational descriptions from travel reports, and local imagination. Faraway places with unfamiliar populations perceived as "wild" presented the Europeans with opportunities for both economic exploitation and religious conversion. As Germans worked to make sense of new information coming from travelers and conquerors and to subject it to their prevailing worldview, some also recognized the sales potential of sensational news reports that exaggerated ethnic stereotypes.

A fairly typical description of the untamed "periphery" is provided in a report to Count Philip Eduard Fugger of Augsburg in 1590 by a factor traveling with the Portuguese Armada, in which Africans in Kenya are described as particularly voracious consumers of human flesh:

> Those of the Armada relate that the Simbas are well equipped with sharp arrows and eat all the men they can lay their hands on, and their wives they lead away with them alive.

---

origins nor the tribal connections of the persons treated here can be identified, however, it is most accurate to refer to them in accordance with early modern sources.

> But they do not suffer a sick person among them. As soon
> as one falls sick, they kill and eat him. . . . Once they reach
> a place they do not leave it as long as they can find a man to
> eat, after which they depart.[2]

Lurid descriptions of supposed cannibalism,[3] like assumptions about
indiscriminate sex practices, provided presumed evidence of the lack of
a moral imperative among non-Europeans and thus demonstrated the
need to convert them to Christianity.

Because published travel reports are plentiful, emphasis in this chapter is on visitors to the city rather than reports from afar. But not only
those in faraway places were viewed as cannibals. Both Jews and gypsies
were occasionally subjected to accusations of consuming Christian flesh
or blood, as were those accused of witchcraft. Assigning immoral or
even satanic activities to those who were different provided Christian
Europeans with a powerful means of clarifying boundaries of identity
between themselves and those they viewed as outsiders, and also shored
up local assumptions about ethnic and religious superiority.

I. Imperial Law

7.1 Imperial Recess regarding Jews and Gypsies, 1530

Charles V's Ordinance and Reformation of Good Policing in the Holy Roman Empire, established in 1530 in Augsburg

Concerning clothing of Jews
The Jews are to wear a yellow ring on their frock or cap in plain sight,
everywhere they go.

Concerning Gypsies
Regarding those who call themselves gypsies and travel about in the
lands: We earnestly wish and command all electors, princes, and estates,
in keeping with their duty, which binds them to the empire, that henceforth, these gypsies, having been credibly identified as spies, traitors,

---

2. Victor von Klarwill, ed., Pauline de Chary, trans., *The Fugger News-Letters: Being
a Selection of Unpublished Letters from the Correspondents of the House of Fugger during the Years 1568–1605* (London, 1924), 144.

3. For cannibalism in another context, see document 10.10.

and scouts who pass information about the Christian lands to the Turks and other enemies of Christianity, not be allowed to pass through their lands or conduct business there, nor be provided with security or safe passage for that purpose. It is our will and our wish as well that the gypsies vacate the lands of the German Nation within three months of this order, and no longer be found therein. If they enter here thereafter, and anyone should take physical measures against them, the perpetrator will not have committed a crime or done wrong.

II. Jews

7.2 Mandates Governing Contact between Jews and Christians

MANDATE IN THE COUNTRYSIDE, THAT OUR SUBJECTS SHOULD NOT PAWN ANYTHING TO THE JEWS NOR BORROW FROM THEM. DECEMBER 16, 1538[4]

We the Burgomasters and councilmen of the city of Augsburg offer our greetings to each and every one of our almshouse, hospital, and cloister tenants, peasants, and other subjects in the countryside, no matter where they live. We have credible reports that a number of you have allowed yourselves to borrow money and valuables from the Jews at usurious rates and under other inappropriate circumstances in return for securities or collateral. This not only brings one into ruin and poverty oneself but also reduces the value of the farmyards, estates, and rents. As ruling directors of said hospitals, poorhouses, and cloisters, we will under no circumstances tolerate or stand for this. Therefore, we earnestly order and command each and every one of you herewith that none among you, under any circumstances, borrow anything on surety, collateral, or security from any Jew, no matter who they are, from near or far, nor have anyone do so on your behalf. If anyone should violate this, and do business of this sort with the Jews on a small or large scale, he or they will be removed from their farm, homestead, and property and will under no circumstances be tolerated there. And anyone who is at this time liable and obligated to the Jews for loans, pawns, or debts, should free themselves of this within one year's time, or face a particular

4. SuStBA, 4°Aug.1021 4 Band 1 Abt., Nr. 3.

penalty from an Honorable Council. All thus know to heed this warning. . . . December 16, 1538.

INSTRUCTIONS FOR THE CITY BURGOMASTERS REGARDING PASSAGE FOR JEWS, 1584[5]

Permission for the Jews to enter the city should not be given lightly. When they want to buy something here from a local citizen and the citizen puts in the request, then permission may be the more likely granted, but only for this purpose. And right afterward, before nightfall, the Jews must leave the city. The guards are to be earnestly instructed that they should escort the Jews to the given place, and immediately afterward, back out of the city.

When a Jew requests safe passage, he should give the guard at the gate a note for the Burgomaster on which is written where he requests to go in the city, which the Burgomaster signs, "Approved on day, year, etc." The guard takes this note with him, and should not go with the Jew to any place not written on it, and under no circumstances allow the Jews that they are escorting to stay overnight. Rather, they should take them back out through the gate before it closes, and immediately bring the signed escort pass back to the Burgomaster.

7.3 Requests to the City of Augsburg from Jews for Safe Passage[6]

Gietlin, Jewess from Steppach, requests safe conduct
to several doctors and several barber-surgeons,
and to shop,
and to visit the sick child.[7]
   [Approval missing]
   Undated, 1577

Seckel, Jew von Schnaitheim
requests safe conduct
to shop
and to see some things, he has never been inside.
   Safe passage granted

5. SuStBA, 2°Cod.Aug.244, Burgermaister-Instruktion 1584, 110 (ms.).

6. StadtAA, Reichsstadtakten 812, 813.

7. A Jewish child apparently being treated in the city.

on April 21, 1586
    Michel Mair
    Burgomaster

Lichmann, Jew in Pfersee, requests
safe conduct
to Kreuz,
to Lord Doctor Fridl,
to Joachim Gretel,
to Lord Doctor Jeckel,
and in addition to shop.
    Safe passage granted
    on April 1, 1587
        Michel Mair
        Burgomaster

Joseph, Jew in Steppach, requests safe conduct
to the noble and principled young Lord Christoph
Wilhelm von Knöringen,
to Doctor Hohlmeier,
to Doctor Stenglin,
and in addition to several doctors
to the Lord Secretary of Hospital,
to several goldsmiths,
to the young Schwyker, Notary,
to Jacob Münch, leatherer,
[to] Otmar Zimmermann.
    Safe passage granted
    on April 2, 1587
        Michel Mair
        Burgomaster

7.4 The Case of Andreas Salomon: Converted Jew and Medical Practitioner, 1566

Andreas Salomon had resided in Augsburg briefly before being arrested in 1564 and accused of malpractice. He claimed at the time to have earned a medical doctorate in Bologna, but to have left both his medical credentials and his conversion papers behind in Frankfurt. According to Salomon's son Jonas, interrogated in an unrelated matter, Andreas Salomon was married to a Christian pastor's daughter from Maastricht in the Netherlands.

Testimony of Chaim the Jew[8]

On October 14, 1566, [Chaim the Jew] testified to the accompanying questions as follows:

1. First, what is his name and where does he currently reside? His name is Chaim, Jew from Aurbach.

2. Doesn't he know that he and other Jews should not enter this city and its realm without permission and an escort? He does know this.

3. Since he was also arrested for this a few days ago, why didn't he take this as a warning, instead coming right back to the [realm] without an escort yesterday? Because he has a poor child afflicted with dropsy, and didn't know how to help her, other than to seek counsel from the Jew in Lechhausen [Andreas Salomon]. He was going from Leitershofen to Lechhausen to see the Jew (who presented himself as such), and wanted to show him his daughter's urine. But he didn't really know how far My Lords' territory or realm reached, and as he was going over Wertach Bridge, he was immediately arrested.

4. What was he planning to do here, and whom he wanted to see? He did not want to come into the city, rather only to go to Lechhausen.

5. How did he plan to get away with his mischief without notice or penalty? He didn't think that this was anything wrong. Pleads for mercy.

On October 16, 1566, Chaim the Jew once more testified as follows:

1. Because he recently testified that [Salomon], the Jew in Lechhausen, was passing himself off as a Jew, one wishes to learn from him under what circumstances and to whom he presented himself as a Jew? He should tell the truth, and not give cause for more severity. This Jew in Lechhausen presented himself openly to him and other Jews as a Jew, in particular at a wedding in Leitershofen. But Moses the Jew from Altenbrun told him that he had heard from the priest in Lechhausen that he is supposedly a baptized Jew [i.e., a convert], and calls himself Andreas Salomon. Otherwise he called himself Marchia in Jewish.

2. Did he not hear from [Salomon] that his claim that he had been baptized was merely a pretense, and he was never really baptized? Doesn't know anything about it.

---

8. StadtAA, Urgicht Haim Jud, October 14–16, 1566.

3. Has he not seen written documents belonging to this Jew with which he wishes to prove to Christians that he has been baptized? Of this he also knows nothing.

4. Are these documents not forgeries, and who wrote them, and how did he manage to get them? This he should reveal to them and hide nothing, or he'll be taught to talk in another way [i.e., under torture]. For it is easy to surmise that, since this Jew has presented himself to him and to others as a Jew, he would have told them why he passes among the Christians as baptized. Claims his ignorance.

5. What have he and others heard or been told about this? He has never heard anything else about him other than that he presents himself to him and to other Jews, as a Jew. Pleads for mercy.

PETITION FROM ANDREAS SALOMON[9]

[My] Lords, I beseech you in humble devotion to listen with favor to my grievance and necessary request, [My Lords]: On Saturday, the last day of this August just past, my two sons and I went into the palisades near Wertach Bridge in order to answer the call of nature (pardoning [Your Lords] for the expression), meaning insult to no one, sticking straight to our path and without bothering a soul. As we were making our way back to the road from Wertach Bridge to Lechhausen and headed toward Lechhausen, in the light of day between eight and nine o'clock, a gate guard criminally and maliciously attacked us without warning with a halberd or pike, brutally and for absolutely no reason, in violation of God and all justice, with such willful action that my children and I feared for our lives. Not satisfied with this unnecessary, unlawful attack, the gate guard then wretchedly forced off my clothes and unjustly took them, and also struck me several times with the halberd or pike, so that if I had not escaped I might have been left dead in my tracks.

If such behavior is fitting to an honorable man, or if he had orders to do this from [Your Lords], I would be pleased to hear the reason for it, so that I would know how to answer for it to [Your Lords], and especially to the gate guard for his misdeed. I am also prepared to make a stand against this. Although I am aware that I have been highly and greatly maligned before Your [Lords] by some ill-wishers, still I have not until now heard from Your [Lords] that my response (to whomever has brought charges against me) is to be heard, in spite of the fact that every form of law provides that, if a complaint is brought by someone, justice demands also hearing the responder, and not only one side. I have not

9. StadtAA, Urgicht Andreas Salomon, 1566.

yet had any success [in my attempt to be heard], but have been denied, which is most burdensome to me. I once again plead with Your [Lords] in humble devotion, . . . in the first instance, to deliver and turn over to me unharmed the clothes that were taken from me.

In the second instance, [My Lords], I am compelled to note that it has been credibly reported to me that Your [Lords] regard me as a Jew, and supposedly I lend money usuriously, and engage in business with other Jews. This is, God knows, an insult to my honor and to justice. Whoever made this claim to Your [Lords] made it falsely and without regard to the truth, and there is no person who can honestly deduce nor prove that I have made loans to anyone for frivolous profit or usuriously. I am prepared to answer to this, for as a Christian, I can provide certified documentation.

In the third instance, I have been told that I supposedly attended a Jewish wedding in Leitershofen, which again does me wrong and is a lie, for . . . it can be proven that I was called to the innkeeper herself (who was very ill) as a doctor, to do my professional duty. Numerous honorable people and citizens in Augsburg who were there might be questioned about this.

And I am very much of the most humble devoted hope that Your [Lords] will examine my documentation showing how I comported myself in Frankfurt and other towns, which I can detail if necessary, and take into account that I suffered great losses in Frankfurt where nearly 1,400 gulden was stolen from me by a servant. . . . Despite great travel expenses trying to recover it, I was not able to regain my losses. Therefore I humbly request, as before, to get my clothes back and graciously have them returned to me. This I plead in devoted service. . . .

Andreas Salomon, Doctor of Medicine in Lechhausen (n.d.)

7.5 Jews Arrested for Passing by the City in 1566[10]

On September 9 of the year 1566 the following Jews and Jewess testified without torture to the accompanying questions as follows:
Chaim, Jew from Aurbach

1. What is each of their names, and do they know that they should not enter here without the exceptional grace and permission of the authorities? Says in response to the first, he does know that he may not come into the city without escort, but did not know that it is

10. StadtAA, Urgichten Chaim Jud, Mossy Jud, Hanna Jüdin, September 9–12, 1566.

forbidden to him to pass by from one village to another. And he did not come up to the city, but was arrested outside along the Lech near the hospital.

2. Why, then, did they, in violation of this, enter the city and realm without escort? He didn't know that passing by was forbidden.

3. What did they intend to do here? He didn't want to come here, rather to Lechhausen.

4. Did they not sell wine at the house of a sack-making woman named Freisinger during the last imperial diet, and afterward still owe a crown in excise taxes on it? 5. Why did they sneak out of the city secretly before paying, and wish to deprive the public weal of its taxes? Yes, he stayed here during the imperial diet with the Freisinger woman, and sold wine and beer, and also paid his taxes on it and owes nothing. There was another Jew called Isaac the cook, who had traveled abroad and also sold wine and beer at the same time. [Chaim] doesn't know if [Isaac] left owing anything. In addition, it just occurs him, in the Freisinger woman's house, above the pig stall, there was another Jew [also] named Isaac who had some trouble with the tax office because of a keg of wine. One could ask him. But as he said, he [Chaim] owes nothing for taxes.

Hanna, Chaim the Jew's wife, says [in response to the same questions]:

1. First, she didn't know that they were forbidden to pass by on the Lech.

2. She does know that they should not enter the city, but thought that passing was allowed.

3. She had no business here but wanted to go to Lechhausen.

4. Her husband served wine at the young Freisinger woman's and does not owe any taxes on it.

5. She doesn't think that he owes anything; he paid his taxes honestly.

ACCUSATION AGAINST THE JEWS
FROM A LOCAL TOWNSMAN

On Tuesday, September 10, 1566, Sebastian Braun testified how last Friday, his little son and two other boys were hanging around the Newmill and were approached by a Jew, who told them that they shouldn't go back into the city. For, he said, there was a war there and people were strangling each other. So they should go down by the mill instead. His little boy, who fled in panic, told him this. But the Jew got hold of one little boy and wanted to take him away. Matheus Cramer, the son of a local citizen, then came upon them, and heard the Jew telling the story to the boys to get them away from the city. Cramer did not want to allow this, so he took the boys from [the Jew] and reported it to the Lords. Afterward, they caught him at the moat near the bleaching area[11] and confronted him, but the Jew denied it, and didn't want to admit anything. This Jew had a short, black, thin doublet, a faded black slit[12] shirt and a black coat on, and also a tall black hat, with a black and white lacing. And [the Jew] first asked him for help taking the boys away.

The two Jews in the jail should be questioned each alone and separately under earnest threat.

On September 12, 1566, the two Jews testified to the accompanying questions as follows:

1. Was he not near the city at one of the bleaching fields last Friday, and what business did he have there? Chaim the Jew from Aurbach, to the first: He is not aware that he came to that spot on Friday, but he was going from Leitershofen to Lechhausen last week on Thursday, and if his memory serves him, he certainly did not come to that spot on Friday.

2. Why did he get into a disagreement with a citizen's son and draw a dagger against him? No, he knows nothing of this.

3. What did he have in mind when he told three boys that he ran into there that they should go down along the mill, and not go back into the city, because there was a war in the city and people were strangling each other? 4. What did he plan to do with the poor children if he had gotten them down by the mill? 5. It is reasonable to assume that he wanted to steal the boys and take them away, as he had already gotten hold of one and took him, but the aforementioned citizen's son took him back. And that's why [the defendant] drew his dagger against [the citizen]. 6. Where did he want to take the poor boys, and who put him up to it, and what had he been promised or given, and by whom? 7. How many other boys has he abducted, where did he abduct them, and where did he take them? To 3, 4, 5, 6, and 7 he declares his innocence adamantly, and that is what they will find even if they do their worst to him.

---

11. Fields outside the city where linen cloth was hung to whiten in the sun.

12. It is not clear whether this means that the shirt was paned (i.e., the sleeves were made of panes with slits in between in the style popular during the sixteenth century) or simply that it was ripped.

8. What have he and other Jews done to the poor innocent children? This is only a fiction created against the Jews, and they can find out what reason there is for it among the baptized Jews.[13]

Moses Jew from Lautterbrünnen [in response to the same questions]:

1. No, he did not arrive at this city or that spot last Friday.

2. No, he had no fight with anyone. But on last Friday there was a journeyman goldsmith, who works here with Abbt, and on the way to Oberhausen he approached an Italian Jew, whose name is Leo, and insulted them, saying that they were all rogues, they cheated him and his boss, etc. So the Italian got into a fight with him. But he didn't see that anyone pulled a dagger, or that the goldsmith drew a weapon. He saw this but didn't get involved.

To the third, fourth, fifth, sixth, and seventh, he insists vehemently that he is innocent. To the eighth he knows nothing of such things and doesn't believe a word of it.

7.6 Simon, Court Jew from Vienna, 1585[14]

INTERROGATION OF SIMON

Monday the 9th of September 1585, [Simon] Wendel the Jew, in response to the accompanying interrogation, responded without torture as follows:

1. What is his name and where is he from? His name is Simon the Jew. He is from Vienna and after his father is called Simon Wendel, court Jew.

2. Since he owes [the goldsmith] Tobias Zainer 54 gulden for goods he purchased, why has he not yet paid him? Admits that he owed Zainer 54 gulden, and that he also gave him a handwritten IOU for it. But Zainer sent this document down to Vienna to Zainer's brother, in order for him to collect the 54 gulden. However, since Simon and his father do a lot of business with this same Zainer [i.e., the brother] in Vienna, he didn't want to make this request to them himself, so he gave the document to Zainer's sister, also in Vienna. She demanded payment of the debt and received the money from his father. This his father wrote to him while he [Simon] was in Prague. His father is in possession of the

---

13. Reference is to the myth that Jews ritually murdered Christian boys and consumed their blood.

14. StadtAA, Urgicht Wendel Jud, September 9, 1585; Strafbuch 1581–1587, 170r.

documentation showing he is no longer in debt to Zainer. But if Zainer can produce his [Simon's] note, then he would pay him again.

3. Is he prepared to pay Zainer right away? His father paid Zainer's sister for him. Therefore he is willing to produce the promissory note he gave to Zainer within four weeks after his release, in order to prove that it has been paid. And meanwhile, he will leave here as surety the promissory note for 758 gulden 10 kreuzer that he has from Philipp Zwitzel of Augsburg.

4. When did he arrive here, and where has he been staying? He arrived here on Tuesday, eight days ago, and spent the first night at the Lily on Baker Lane; then one night in front of Wertach Bridge Gate, with a publican who he believes is a Saxon, and has a stair going up from the street; and afterward one night at Schnapper; then two nights at Lindenmair;[15] and the rest of the time with the imperial bailiff [i.e., in jail].

5. Who gave him escort and permission to stay here? No one provided him with an escort, but that is because he had business with the Count of Schwartzenburg, who did not wish to subject him to being escorted.

6. Has he been passing as a Christian? He was never asked if he were a Jew or a Christian, and did not present himself as a Christian in any way other than that he did not volunteer that he was a Jew.

7. How did he expect to get away with this without punishment? He only came here because of the Count of Schwartzenburg, who did not wish to subject him to accepting escort.

8. Has he settled with the Lord Imperial Bailiff for this, or is he is prepared to do so? As far as he knows, the imperial bailiff is satisfied in this matter, for the Count of Schwartzenburg paid [the bailiff] 100 gulden on his behalf for the fine and 26 gulden for expenses. Requests mercy.

[According to a petition from Simon's mother, the court Jewess Regina, Zainer had tricked Simon into a shady deal for a gold-plated necklace and two rings during the recent imperial diet in Augsburg (1582), and a settlement had already been arranged through an intermediary.]

---

15. Schnapper and Lindenmair were names of local publicans.

Notice of settlement from Zainer

September 24, 1585
Noble [Lords] Mayors, Burgomaster, and an Honorable Council, I should, in devotion and obedience, not withhold that I have settled my claim with Simon Wendel the Jew and therefore do not wish that he be detained any longer.
Your . . . devoted obedient citizen
Tobias Zainer, goldsmith

Record of punishment

September 24, 1585
Simon Wendel, Jew from Vienna, came into the city without escort and under the pretense that he was a Christian, for which he was arrested. Although he reached a settlement for this offense with the imperial bailiff, the goldsmith Tobias Zainer then brought further charges against him because of a debt, so that he remained in jail longer. Because he settled with Zainer, an Honorable Council has today decreed that he be released upon a written oath [of peace]. Note: This Jew gave the bailiff a special oath.[16]

7.7 Expulsions of Suspicious Jews[17]

October 30, 1533: Abraham the Jew, unmarried, entered here without reporting to and informing the Lord Mayor and getting permission, thus without escort, and was going around here for some time buying bad old coins. For this he was locked in the irons. And because he had nothing, rather was poor, but there was reason to punish him, he was put out of the city and the city was forbidden to him, and he was informed that if he came back in, he would be subject to corporal punishment.

April 26, 1572: Salomon Ricco from Modena appeared and behaved suspiciously in a variety of ways, and among other things was heard

16. Special formulations existed for Jews taking oaths before Christian authorities, which included swearing by God and Old Testament figures. Simon had to take an oath that his detention was due to his own fault and he would not seek vengeance.
17. StadtAA, Strafbuch 1533–1599, October 30, 1533; Strafbuch 1571–1580, 21r; Strafbuch 1588–1596, 69v; Strafbuch 1596–1605, 134.

to say that he was born a Jew but wants to convert to Christianity and be baptized. But he didn't stay away from the Jews, rather kept company with them everywhere. Therefore he was taken into custody, but released again and told to spend his dime elsewhere. [Note: Salomon Ricco's case includes both an Italian transcript of his interrogations and a German translation. During the first round of questioning, Ricco identified himself as a peddler from Venice, and was forced to fend off accusations that he was actually of the Muslim faith rather than a Jew or Christian.]

May 17, 1590: Seligman the Jew, from Frankfurt, fornicated with a Christian woman, for which an Honorable Council decreed that he should be beaten with rods and banished from the city and the realm.

May 19, 1599: Samuel the Jew from Memmelsdorf near Bamberg came into the city without an escort, and was arrested. Although he then claimed that he was planning to be baptized [as a Christian], he was nonetheless banished from the city and its territories today as a suspicious person.

III. Gypsies and Other Travelers

7.8 Gypsy Women before the Courts

CATHARINA, 1593[18]

Interrogation of Catharina
On Tuesday, March 9, 1593, Catharina the Little Egyptian, gypsy, under arrest, testified to the accompanying questions under earnest threat as follows:

    1. What is her name, where is she from, and how old is she? Her name is Catharina the Little Egyptian and she is from Little Egypt, and doesn't know her age.

    2. What does she do for a living? She doesn't do anything except to beg for God's sake and to tell fortunes.

    3. Where and how often has she been arrested before, why, and under what circumstances she was released each time? She has never been arrested in her life until now.

---

18. StadtAA, Urgicht Catharina Zigeunerin, March 9, 1593; Strafbuch 1588–1596, 168v.

4. Is she married, and to whom? She is married. Her husband's name is Stoffel, she doesn't know his last name.

5. How long has she been a gypsy, and where and under what conditions she came to them? She has been a gypsy her entire life from her mother and father, for her parents were also gypsies.

6. Where all has she been staying since then? She spent the entire winter near Güntzberg and around Weissenhorn.

7. Because it is known that she has committed many acts of theft, she should describe these in detail, or it will be gotten out of her through torture. A man came up to her in front of Wertach Bridge Gate who had a bad thigh, which she healed, and therefore the man brought a coat, two sheets, and other things, which he gave to her. She doesn't know who he was. But a woman asked to see these things, and when she realized that they had been stolen out of her house, she took the coat and what else the man had given her, and hit and pushed her.

8. What all has she pilfered and stolen here? She didn't steal anything from anyone.

9. Did she not steal five sheets, several shirts, and a coat from a dyer in front of Wertach Bridge Gate last Saturday? They were the things that the man gave her, as she testified above. She did not steal them herself.

10. Did she not break into a garden in front of Wertach Bridge Gate with another gypsy woman and steal from the garden maid twenty-four bundles of flax,[19] **4 gulden in cash, two bodices, and a wedding ring?** She did not break into any garden or steal anything out of it.

11. What did she do with these stolen things? Says she is innocent. She did not steal anything, rather has supported herself up to now with begging for God's sake and fortune-telling.

12. Because she didn't start with this, she should confess what else she has stolen here and there? 13. Who helped her in each case? 14. In what cases has she broken and entered to commit robbery? Claims her innocence.

15. Because she does not work and only travels about idly, how does she make her living? This she testified to above. Her husband also supports himself with horse trading, and they also teach people healing, for which they are given something.

16. Why did she join up with the gypsies? She has been a gypsy from childhood.

---

19. The exact term is *Schläge*, semantically multivalent in this context.

17. What have those who belong to her band stolen here and there? In front of the gate there are about twenty gypsies, old and young. She doesn't know what they may have stolen here and there. One is called Pasha; he is her father. The second is called Hans, the third Georg, the fourth Michael. They have wives, and she doesn't know all their names, but they are called Madlen, Rosina, and Margretha. She doesn't know the names of the children.

18. What other misdeeds have she and her band committed? She has not committed any misdeeds.

19. Because they are well equipped with weapons and guns and are only idlers, have they committed violence against the people in the countryside? They have not committed any violence, just traveled around and begged.

20. Because it is known that not only thieves but also murderers are among them, she should testify where and what murders and robberies they have committed. There are no thieves or murderers among them. They have never harmed anyone.

21. At what murders and robberies was she herself present? Says she is innocent.

22. Who are those in her band, what are their names and what are their crafts, where did they join up, and how long have they been together? This she testified above. The gypsies don't know any crafts. They gathered together in Elsass, and stayed near Strasbourg. They have been together one or two [years].

23. What are her intentions? Does she plan to roam about her whole life, and why? She can't be anything else, she has to remain a gypsy. Begs for mercy.

Petition from the gypsy captain

Humble supplication to an Honorable and Wise Council of the laudable imperial city of Augsburg, March 9 1593: We poor gypsies first of all wish [Your Lords] much joy and good fortune, in this world and the next. We have discovered, [honorable Lords], in our homeless and impoverished travels in this wretched temporal life, that a poor woman or gypsy who is beset with the terrible falling sickness[20] has been taken into custody by Your Judiciousness, as the rulers of the laudable imperial city of Augsburg, etc., and her many poor little children are calling for her. Thus we poor Egyptians or gypsies request [that she be released to care for her children].

---

20. Epilepsy.

Requested by me, Junker[21] Martin Wechsler of the gypsies, a Captain over a band of gypsies.

Record of punishment

Catharina, a gypsy, had a number of stolen articles with her, and thus fell under suspicion of having stolen them. Therefore she was arrested. Because, however, she returned the items upon the assurance that there would be no further consequences for her, an Honorable Council declared on this date that she should be released, but banished from the city and its domain.

ANNA DOROTHEA, 1642[22]

Interrogation of Anna Dorothea

On Thursday, October 9, 1542, Anna Dorothea the gypsy in the jail testified without torture to the accompanying questions under earnest threat as follows:

1. What is her name, where does she come from, and how old is she, and also what does she do for a living? Her name is Anna Dorothea, and she is a gypsy, baptized in Lauchringen in the county of Stühlingen. She doesn't know how old she is. She has already had eight children, and a second husband. She was not over fourteen years old when she took her first husband, with whom she had three children, and already has five with the second. She doesn't know where her husband is at this time. She supports herself with begging and fortune-telling, and also with bartering.

2. Has she often been arrested? Where and under what circumstances was she released each time? She has never been under arrest for a single hour in her life.

3. When and at which city gate did she enter this city, and where has she been staying day and night? She came into the city by the gate where one comes in from Friedberg, and didn't stay anywhere here. She spent the night in Haunstetten in an empty house right next to the manor.

4. Since she didn't come in wearing gypsy clothing, rather dressed as a peasant woman, who gave these clothes to her, or in what village she stole them? And did she know herself that gypsies weren't allowed in this city, or who told her? She got the peasant

---

21. *Junker* normally refers to a member of the German nobility, presumably used here to indicate the elevated status of the captain among the gypsies.

22. StadtAA, Urgicht Anna Dorothea Zigeunerin, October 9–November 4, 1642.

woman's clothes by fortune-telling in Württemberg at Inningen, in a village not far from Esslingen. She did know that as a gypsy, she wouldn't be allowed to beg here.

5. How often has she been in this city before, and what did she steal each time? She has never been here before, and has also not stolen anything here.

6. How long and by whom is she pregnant? Where is her band staying, and how many of them are there? Are they all thieving scalawags like she is? Her husband's name is Hans Caspar and she is pregnant by him. She doesn't know where her band is staying. They are all fortune-tellers; they barter, buy, and sell, and are very good at handling fire. If they make a fire in the middle of a stable, there is no danger of it spreading.

7. What does she do with the large sack? And since she was caught in the act of stealing in the Lords' Drinking Room by the Drinking Room landlord Simon Zacharias, to whom was she planning to take the stolen things? In the sack she was planning to put the things she gets by begging and fortune-telling. She only wanted to check in the Drinking Room if she could collect some alms, and did not try to steal the least thing from the landlord.

8. Just last Monday she stole a doublet and cap in a house on the hill near St. Anthony's almshouse, together with a green woman's skirt and bodice. Where did she take these stolen items, and to whom did she sell them? She was not here on Monday, and even less so in a house near St. Anthony's almshouse. She hasn't stolen the least thing. They are doing her wrong.

9. Because a strong pry- or crowbar was found in her stocking, she should confess how often she has broken in to steal in this city or elsewhere. She doesn't use the pry- or crowbar to steal, but just to shoe horses and repair saddles.

10. How can she be so impudent as to steal the woolen cloak out of her very jail cell? Did she think that they would let her right back out and allow her to get away with her theft? Can she then leave no place without stealing from it, not even the jail? She didn't intend to steal the cloak. She only pulled it around her because it was so cold.

[11–14. further questioned about specific thefts] [Note from scribe:] She makes a lot of chatter, speaks only of the name of Jesus, the suffering of Christ, and Mother Mary, and admits nothing, attesting to her innocence.

15. What was her intention with the unsheathed knife that was found in her sack? Has she harmed anyone with it or attacked

anyone? **She should herself admit what kinds of thievery and evil deeds she has committed all over the place, and how long she has been living this evil and thievish life.** She has always carried the knife in her sack, and has harmed no one with it. She has no sheath for it, and she uses it to eat bread. Begs that they should just release her to go to her children. She does not wish to revenge herself on anyone, rather to be good to everyone. She will also raise her children to do the same.

Note: The beadles report that she can well speak Swabian, but during the questioning she spoke foreign and gypsy-like, so that we could hardly understand a tenth of it. She talked constantly during the questions, and among other things requested of the Lord Burgomaster, and also those of us who went to her in the irons, that we be Godfathers. She looks like an evil, devious woman who is full of bad deeds.

Petition from Augsburg's subjects outside the city

Noble, intrepid, most well-born [Lords] Mayors, Burgomasters, and council of this laudable holy imperial city, [Your Lords]: . . . We poor subjects are compelled to point out the extent to which we are being burdened and reduced to extreme poverty during this ongoing, most difficult time of war—not only from continuous summer and winter quartering, the passing through of troops, and the wartime taxes but also on top of this, from roving gypsies. . . . Now, we are dutifully willing to accept all of the deserved penalties that come from the hand of God, and to continue to bear them with patience, as long as it is God's will and within our capacity. . . .

But in particular, two large companies of these gypsies are currently roving about here, and are likely to be staying here somewhat longer because one of their womenfolk has been arrested by [Your Lords] for her misdeeds. We don't know for our part what her crime is . . . but we can easily guess that this woman was arrested only for theft. Since this is the real profession of these people and their cart and plow, as we in the countryside experience on a daily basis, the deserved punishment for it will do little to help the situation, and nothing to help us poor people in the countryside. Rather, it is more to be feared that these people will revenge this arrest and any resulting punishment against us [and our villages] with fire or other damage.

In addition, the prisoner has an innocent child that was just born in the jail and six other young, naked, impoverished orphans who cannot be brought away without their mother . . . it is therefore our devoted entreaty to [Your Lords to show] fatherly clemency to this imprisoned woman . . . and to let her go.

The devoted, obedient surrounding villages and poor subjects of the common city of Augsburg and its endowments and citizenry.
October 30, 1642

Response of the Council Lords
Anna Dorothea the gypsy should be released from imprisonment upon a sworn oath [of peace] in response to the received supplication. Decreed in the Senate, November 4, 1642.

7.9 Petrus Phocas[23] from Constantinople and His Entourage Visit an Augsburg Inn, 1593[24]

INTERROGATION OF PETRUS PHOCAS

On Monday the 12th of July, 1593, Petrus Phocas, in jail, testified to the accompanying points of interrogation, under earnest threat, as follows:

1. What is his name, and where does he come from? His name is Petrus Phocas; he is from Constantinople.

2. What does he do for a living? He spent two years with His Royal Lordship in Poland Archduke Maximilian,[25] currently residing in Neustadt. But because his father's brothers, Andreas and Johannes, the Phoca of Capha, are lying in prison, he left His Royal Lordship to come here in order to raise a sum of money to free his relatives from their captivity [i.e., by paying a ransom]. He has petitioned to an Honorable Council here about this.

3. Where and how long has he been staying here? He has stayed with Stophel[26] Schmid, the brewer by the steps, for eight days now.

4. What kind of company does he have with him here, and what do they do? In Bamberg he met a Junker named Hans Georg von Rabeneck, who had been imprisoned by the Turks.[27] He had a servant with him, and they traveled together to Nuremberg. There, Hans Georg von Rabeneck picked up a maiden, who is supposed to have been

---

23. Petrus Phocas was presumably ethnically Greek.

24. StadtAA, Urgicht Petrus Phocas et al., July 12, 1593; Strafbuch 1588–1596, 178v.

25. Maximillian III, Archduke of Austria.

26. Nickname for Christoph.

27. Rabeneck, in a separate interrogation, claimed to be raising money to pay off the ransom he owed as a condition of his release from Turkish prison. High-ranking prisoners sometimes arranged for release via a bailsman or ransom dealer, who then held the rights to the ransom owed, normally including interest.

born in Bamberg, and promised her that he would marry her here in Augsburg. Thereupon he, Phocas, together with his servant (whom he hired in Prague) came to Augsburg with said von Rabeneck, Rabeneck's servant, and the maiden.

5. Did he not present himself as a Turkish prisoner, and request a contribution from an Honorable Council? For his part he did not present himself as a prisoner, rather petitioned for a contribution for his two captured relatives.

6. In addition to the honorarium that he collected from an Honorable Council, did he not go about here and there soliciting without permission? Says yes, he did solicit among the merchants as well, but didn't think it would do any harm.

7. Who are the people with him, where are they from, and of what status? He has a woman with him, and her name is Christina Riger. She is from Königgrätz and he has her from Holnitz in the land of Moravia. He is married to her, for which he can provide documentation.

8. Why did he and his company ask that their presence in the inn be hidden, and keep their door locked? Answers, he has never had anyone deny his presence, and did not lock anyone out of his room, and no one can claim otherwise.

9. What were they doing in there the whole time, and how long did they intend to stay? They spent very little time in the inn, rather they were inquiring about among the merchants and the cathedral chapter and raising money. And they did not plan to stay longer than it took to get a contribution for his captive relatives from the two Lords Fugger and the cathedral chapter.

10. Weren't they making soap balls, and why, since they are claiming to be nobles and Turkish prisoners? Says yes, they made them in order to present them as gifts to the merchants and nobles.

11. Were they not inquiring about cart pullers, and why? Answers, von Rabeneck found a man to whom he promised a half thaler if he would show them to a few merchant houses here. This was so that they could solicit contributions in a place that was unknown to them.

12. Did one not come to see them, and what did they want to know from him? Says yes, a cart puller visited them yesterday. They only wanted him to show them to a few rich merchant houses, which the cart puller offered to do for the promised half thaler.

13. Didn't they ask him if he knew where all the merchant houses were, and also where and with what they trade in German or Italian lands? Answers, von Rabeneck, not he, spoke with the cart puller, and asked him where the merchants here live, especially the rich ones, and in what lands they trade that they become so wealthy. To this the cart puller replied that the merchants do their business in German and Italian lands.

14. Did they not also say that they wanted to send a servant with him to note down the persons, houses, and streets? Says yes, it is true.

15. Didn't they lock the door of the room behind the cart puller? He can't answer that. While the cart puller was with von Rabeneck, he was in the other chamber.

16. Didn't they promise to give the cart puller 9 batzer for his trouble? Answers, von Rabeneck promised to give the cart puller that much money.

17. Didn't the cart puller have to shake hands with one among them on his word to come on Sunday morning, and to keep quiet about it? Says yes, von Rabeneck asked the cart puller to show them the merchant houses on Saturday, but the cart puller didn't want to because of his work. He shook hands with Rabeneck on his word that he would come back on Sunday morning, and go around with the servants. But for his part he doesn't know if the cart puller was supposed to remain quiet about it, or if this was pressed upon him, for although he was in the room where von Rabeneck's servant and the cart puller were talking with each other part of the time, he didn't understand everything, since he doesn't have much experience yet with the German language.

18. Did they not inquire specifically about the merchants who trade on a large scale, and not those who were shopkeepers, or ordinary citizens dealing in trifles or practicing itinerant trades? Von Rabeneck and the others may have talked about it, but he can't say.

19. Why did they inquire about these merchants, and what were their intentions? Says for his part that he inquired about the merchants' houses only so that he could raise money.

20. Did they not want to collect information about their goods [crossed out: ~~in order to attack while they were in transport~~]?[28] This he never had in mind, may God forbid. He has conducted himself uprightly and honorably the entire time, for he had honorable, well-bred parents, who were in service to His Royal Highness Archduke Maximilian, and died in this capacity. Lord Jacob Kurtz knows well of the life he and his parents lead.

---

28. Likely eliminated from the list of questions in deference to the prisoners' noble status. A direct accusation of armed robbery would have been dishonoring and could have led to legal repercussions.

21. How are they able to have so many servants and other dependents, since they say they are poor prisoners from Turkey and are gathering ransom? He has only one servant, whom he keeps with him because he doesn't speak much German. He personally studied in Rome under Pope Gregory XIII in the Roman Seminary, where he received a Christian and Catholic education.

22. Since there must be something else behind this, he should tell the truth about what they are up to, and not provide a reason for something else [i.e., to apply torture]. God deliver him from this, he has never had anything wicked in mind in his life.

23. How did he meet von Rabeneck and how long has he known him? He met up with him a year ago in Cologne, and two years before in Vienna, which is where he got to know him, for he presented himself as a member of the nobility.

24. How many servants does he have, and what does he pay them, and what does he need them for? He has only one servant, to whom he gives each year a thaler, a suit of clothes, and food and drink as he has it. He mainly needs him to help carry his things over land and to be his interpreter. Requests mercy.

JOB SPIEGEL, PETRUS PHOCAS' SERVANT

On Monday, July 12, 1593, [Job Spiegel] testified in the jail under earnest threat as follows:

1. What is his name, how old, and where does he come from? His name is Job Spiegel, he was born in the Bishopric Paderborn, and he is around twenty-one years old.

2. What does he do for a living? He has been in service with Lord Petrus Phocas for ten or eleven weeks, and he joined him in Prague.

3. How long has he been with these Lords, and what has he done for them? How long he has been with him he has already testified, and otherwise he has been working as his interpreter, for [Phocas] is not very experienced with the German language.

4. What is the business of these Lords, where has he traveled with them, and what kind of company do they have with them? [Phocas] began to travel because of his relatives who are imprisoned among the Turks, and now he is planning to go to Neustadt to His Royal Lordship Archduke Maximilian, to get a new letter. For his part he joined his master in Prague, and went with him from there to Nuremberg, then from Nuremberg to Bamberg, and afterward to here, and his master also has a wife and child with him.

5. Have they not presented themselves as nobles and Turkish prisoners, and traveled about soliciting contributions? [Phocas] and another, Georg von Rabeneck, say they are nobles. His Lord, however, as far as he knows, has not claimed to be a Turkish prisoner, rather is only raising money for his relatives. But Lord Hans Georg von Rabeneck was imprisoned among the Turks. He doesn't know exactly how or under what conditions, for he hasn't read his petitions.

6. How does he know that this is true? From his master's letters, he knows that he was born to the imperial line of Phoca. He has not read von Rabeneck's documents.

7. Were they not peddling soap and similar things, and what was the reason for it? Says yes, they made soap in order to present it as gifts. He knows of no other reason to report.

8. Did they not make a lot of soap balls here? Last Saturday evening they made several of them, but that was all.

[9–14. questions about the locked door and the cart puller with responses similar to those of Phocas]

15. How long do they want to stay here, and where do they plan to go from here? This he wouldn't know. His Lord wants to wait to see if the cathedral chapter will give them something. Where he plans to go next he has already testified. Where von Rabeneck plans to go he doesn't know.

16. What is he paid, and where does it come from? He has no other pay than his keep, and only came to work for [Phocas] so that he could experience something. While in Prague he gave his master 8 Reichsthaler and a gulden to keep for him, so that if he should become ill or something, he would be cared for.

17. Have Phocas and von Rabeneck been traveling together long, and where did they first meet? As far as he knows they met in Bamberg.

18. Since it is obvious that whatever they are up to is not aboveboard, he should tell the whole truth about what misdeeds they have committed. He knows of no dishonorable deeds perpetrated by his master in the time he has been with him.

INTERROGATION OF THE INNKEEPER

On Monday, the 12th of July, 1593, Christoph Schmid testified to the accompanying questions as follows:

1. What is his name, and where is he from? 2. What does he do for a living? His name is Christoph Schmid; he is a local citizen and a brewer.

3. Has he been lodging the people that have been arrested, and for how long? Says yes, they have been his guests for eight days.

4. Insofar as these persons have been here for several days, did he report their presence to the Burgomaster? Admittedly he did not. He didn't think it would be a problem.

5. Doesn't he know that numerous ordinances and decrees have been issued forbidding innkeepers from lodging strangers for more than one night without permission? He did know this, but he wasn't worried that it would lead to any harm.

6. Why, then, did he put up these people for so long without registering them? He wasn't thinking.

7. Did he not provide them with their own room, which they have constantly kept locked? He gave them one heated room and two chambers, which were open all day.

8. Why did his servants deny having these people there when they were asked? This did not happen.

9. How much have these people spent, and have they paid him? Says they owe him 19 batzen, which they haven't paid. Otherwise they have been decent, moderate, quiet, and peaceful during their stay.

10. What did these people want here, and what were they doing? He assumed them to be military folk and never knew anything about their activities.

11. Were they making soap balls? Says yes.

12. Who did they claim to be? They said they were soldiers, and he got the idea from the servant that they were of noble status.

13. Who came and went from their quarters? He's not aware of anyone.

14. Didn't they make all kinds of inquiries to him about the merchants? He doesn't know anything about that either.

15. Didn't he notice that these people were frivolous riffraff, and why did he keep them for so long? He can't say that they have behaved inappropriately, for as he has already noted, they have been gentle and modest in eating, drinking, coming, and going.

16. Since he has done the same thing before, he should testify what other worthless rabble he has lodged for more than one night without registering them? He admits to putting up the occasional guest for more than one night, but they were not frivolous persons, which is why he assumed it wouldn't do any harm. Not having reported these occasional guests, however, he wouldn't know who they were or be able to name them by name.

17. What suspicious things has he noticed about these people during their stay? He did not notice anything improper about them.

18. How did he expect to get away with all this without punishment? Begs for mercy.

RECORDS OF PUNISHMENT

Petrus Phocas from Constantinople and Hans Georg von Rabeneck lodged here for a long time, and sought information about the wealthy merchants' houses from a cart puller, and also collected a lot of money here without the permission of the authorities. They also recorded false entries in their [collection] books. And they also had two women traveling with them, the one Christina Riger from Königgrätz in Bohemia, who is Petrus Phocas' wife, but the other, Anna Bernhard from Bamberg, was Rabeneck's mistress. They therefore came under suspicion of being involved in criminal activities. For this reason they and their two servants, named Job Spiegel from the Bishopric Paderborn, and Georg Timling from Weida, as well as a musician, Andreas Schall of Gravern in Württemberg (all of whom were staying with them) were brought into the jail. However, since both Petrus Phocas and von Rabeneck had convincing documentation with them, an Honorable Council today decreed that they be released, but told to seek their living elsewhere.

Christoph Schmid, brewer and local citizen, lodged the above-noted seven strangers for a long time and did not register them with the Lord Burgomaster in Office, as required by My Lords' decree. Therefore he was brought into the jail, and today released with a warning to stay out of trouble.

IV. Far-away Populations

7.10 A Description of Natives from the New World, 1505[29]

This description is from a broadsheet that circulated in Augsburg and elsewhere during the early sixteenth century.

The people are naked and comely, brown and well-formed in body, with the heads, necks, arms, pubic area, and feet of both women and men covered a little bit with feathers. The men also have a lot of precious

---

29. Gisele Ecker, *Einblattdrucke von den Anfängen bis 1555: Untersuchungen zu einer Publikationsform literarischer Texte* (Göppingen, 1981), vol. 1, 162–63, Nr. 217 (Augsburg, 1505).

stones on their faces and breasts. No one owns anything, rather every-thing is held in common. And the men take the women as it pleases them, whether it's their mother, sister, or relative; they make no distinc-tion. They also fight wars with one another. They also eat one another, those that are killed, and they smoke the meat. They live to be 150 years old. And they have no government.

7.11 Natives of India with Camel and Elephant, 1508 (Illustration)

Hans Burgkmair, *Natives of India with Camel and Elephant,* 1508. Kupferstichkabinett, Staaliche Museen, Berlin, Inv. 1000–2.

Chapter Eight
Ritual and Ceremony

Ritual, deriving from the word "rite," is often defined as a formal act performed in observance of some ceremony, usually religious in nature. But the term is also more broadly applied to any custom or practice habitually repeated in an established context. The study of ritual has been informed by the methods associated with anthropology, which has taught us to think in terms of symbols and "rites of passage" that give meaning to social or communal relationships. Early modern rituals and celebrations associated with the stages of life, the religious calendar, political events, or even day-to-day social and professional transactions forged bonds of identity among the participants and reinforced common ways of looking at the world.

In reinforcing identities, ritual could underscore difference as well as unity. Thus rituals and ceremonies also provided a means of constructing and demonstrating distinctions of gender, social standing, confessional identity, and political power. Social and gender boundaries were reinforced by formal ceremonies such as churching and oaths of citizenship, as well as in less formal occasions involving ceremonial drinking bouts, ritual forms of insult and reconciliation, celebratory noisemaking, and rites of social violence. Rituals associated with religious life were undergoing a shift during the early modern period, as reformers questioned matters of clerical privilege and the rituals of the official church. Church rituals (baptism, Eucharist, marriage, etc.) were all a central focus of negotiation during the German Reformation. Bitter disputes took place over the administration of the Eucharist and what it meant, and Protestant reformers likened veneration of the saints and their images to idolatry. "Praying and honoring graven images and likenesses has led to all kinds of uncertain, Godless superstition," Augsburg's reformed church ordinance of 1537 charged, leading to the destruction of many works of church art in acts of zealous iconoclasm.

In certain circumstances, profane rituals could also carry sacred weight, as the participants drew natural associations between, for example, carnival celebrations and the religious calendar, or between drinking to seal a commercial contract and the sacred power of communion wine. Ritual also served as a way for authorities to demonstrate power and model social hierarchy. Here, sacred imagery was regularly recalled as a means of legitimating authority, as oaths to God enforced homage

214

to secular governors, rulers portrayed themselves as God's representatives on earth, and capital punishment was characterized as divine judgment. Rituals at these events provided easily identifiable symbols for witnesses, participants, and those who read about them afterward, leaving no doubt as to their meaning or gravity.

I. Negotiating Religious Ritual

8.1 Artisans Protest Catholic Ritual in 1524[1]

As is the case with most earlier testimonies, the questions asked of the defendant in this case have not survived.

On Sunday, May 8, 1524, Bartholomew Nussfelder, glazier from Augsburg, testified without torture:

[First], they hear in the sermon every day that the holy water doesn't take away sin and is useless, and that they should put their hope in God alone, and not in the water. So a group of women, namely Ulrich Rischner's wife and others as well, along with some men whom he can't name, yelled warnings to several monks at the Franciscan Church that they should forget the holy water and salt. But the monks didn't want to. Seeing that, he went up to one of the Franciscan monks who was getting ready to bless the water and salt and said, "My dear sir, bless the water in German, so that we can understand it too." To that the monk answered that he didn't want to do it, and that Nussfelder should leave him alone and let him bless the water and salt. Nussfelder then said to the monk, "What do you want to bless? Loan me the book[2] and get out of here, for you are turning us away from the Gospel truth that they preach to us every day. You're keeping us from it." The monk then handed him the book and left, and he took the book and threw it into the font. Franz Laminit, the purse-maker on Smithy Lane, then took the book out and tried to tear it, but he couldn't because it was made of parchment. So he threw it back into the holy water. Nussfelder then took it back out and cut it up, saying that he was doing it "so they can't turn us away from the Gospel anymore with their folly, and so they don't need to preach in vain, because the preacher says one thing and then they do the opposite." With these words he left to go to church in St. Moritz. . . .

1. StadtAA, Urgicht Bartholomew Nussfelder, May 8, 1524; Strafbuch 1508–1526, 145, 160.
2. I.e., the breviary or other book from which the monk was reading the blessing.

Eight days ago today after the sermon, the preacher at the Franciscan Church [Johann Schilling][3] joined Nussfelder, another monk of the Franciscan order who came from elsewhere, Ulrich Richsner the weaver, a guy named Peter who is a weaver on the Breu Bridge, and Hans Has, mason on Lautterlech, for drinks at Has' house. And among other things they were talking about the holy water, and Nussfelder said, "I'd like to take the book from the monk blessing the water and throw it in the holy water." Then another of them said, "Somebody had that in mind a couple of weeks ago," but didn't name him. He doesn't know which one said it, because they had all been drinking a lot. To that Nussfelder said he would take the book from the monk this Sunday and throw it in the water, and the preacher said he'd have nothing against it, because they won't leave it alone otherwise. Then they went their separate ways. So this Sunday he did as described above. It was only for the sake of God's word, and for no other reason, that he spoke with the monk and treated him like that. No one else helped him and no one told him to do it, neither the persons named above nor anyone else.

[In response to further questions, he says,] his fellows with whom he was drinking and talking he has already named above, but it was the purse-maker Franz Laminit who was present when the thing over the holy water with the monk happened. He took the book out of the font and wanted to rip it up, but he couldn't, rather threw it back in, as he has already explained. Otherwise Laminit didn't do anything. Peter, a weaver who was drinking with him and the others at Has the mason's place, as noted above, was also present and was saying something, but he doesn't know what because the women were talking and yelling so loudly that he couldn't hear it. The weaver Hans Ballinger was also standing nearby as Nussfelder spoke with the monk, and he also asked the monk to bless the water in German so they could understand it and better themselves. He isn't aware of doing anything else. Otherwise there were a lot of people standing around talking, but he doesn't know what they said because he couldn't catch all of it. He heard that some women were yelling that someone should throw the monk in the holy water, too. They included Ulrich Richsner the weaver's wife, a candle-maker at Gaugerin's, and an old woman, along with some others. . . .

He had not plotted with anyone to do anything other than what he has already reported, [and] he didn't say or hear from anyone else that if the monks in the Franciscan Church didn't read the mass in German, they would be chased from the altar. . . . Pleads for mercy.

---

3. See Chapter One for more on the Protestant-leaning Schilling and others mentioned in this incident.

[Nussfelder was banished from the city for life, then pardoned about ten months later on the condition that he wear no sword and stay out of public houses for a year.]

8.2 An Incident during the Lord's Supper at the Church of St. George, 1527[4]

WITNESSES, JUNE 1527

Tuesday after St. John the Baptist Day [June 24], 1527, witness statements taken in regard to the case of the Lord's Supper at St. George:

Jorg Meuting, weaver, says: As they were conducting the Lord's Supper at St. George, people who had been fighting with one another for years approached each other and, with tears in their eyes, asked one another in God's name to forgive them for what they had done to each other. And everyone was behaving piously. Then he and the other elders were told that the Provost of St. George's maid, the Auxiliary Bishop's maid, and the wife of the schoolmaster at St. George's had come into the church and were behaving most indecently. So he and others went up to the altar where the Eucharist was being received. He only saw that the Auxiliary Bishop's maid snapped up a particle [of bread] with her mouth as it was being offered to someone else and said some words, for which she was scolded and told she should leave, as she could see that they were conducting the Lord's Supper. At this the Auxiliary Bishop's maid turned and said to them, "*Ei*, you cursed Lord's Supper, choke it down alone, and you can shit it out alone." With these words she left. And he was afraid the young people would do something to her, for they were very enraged about these three people. But the preacher prevented it with gentle words.

Lucas Zottman, bell caster, says almost the same thing as Meuting, and adds in particular that the Auxiliary Bishop's maid was standing not far from the preacher who was administering the Eucharist, and as he offered someone the bread, she said, "*Ei* Lord's Supper, *ei* Lord's Supper, what a nice Lord's Supper," etc., and all kinds of inappropriate talk. And when they corrected her by saying that if she didn't like it, she should get out and leave the people in peace, she replied that he should get out himself. Finally, when she got down from the steps [to the altar], she said to them, "*Ei* Lord's Supper, you choke it down alone, and you can vomit it up alone." He saw that the Provost's maid was with her, but

---

4. StadtAA, Literaliensammlung, Katharina Vöglin, June–September 1527.

didn't hear anything from her. Renhart said to the Auxiliary Bishop's maid, "If you don't want to leave, then someone can toss you out by the hair," to which she said, "If he feels like it he should go ahead and do it, since they are so fond of fool's work and trifles."

Anna Zimmerman says, she heard the St. George schoolmaster's wife say as they were administering the Lord's Supper, "It might be right, but I don't believe it. But if it involved pretty women [i.e., prostitutes], then I would believe it was all right."

Anna Weber says that as she was going up to take the Eucharist, the Auxiliary Bishop's maid was coming toward her, and said, "I hope everyone who ate the Lord's Supper swallowed death with it."

Appolonia Wencher testifies as did Anna Weber, adding that as the Lord's Supper was being administered, several bits [of bread] fell down, and the Auxiliary Bishop's maid, who was standing not far off, said (pardon the expression), "I shit in the Lord's Supper."

PETITION FROM KATHARINA VÖGLIN, AUXILIARY BISHOP'S MAID, SEPTEMBER 1527

[Vöglin's petition is addressed to the Auxiliary Bishop, requesting intervention with the Augsburg council.]

Gracious Lord Your Grace, I beg of you to give me, a poor daughter, your gracious ear. When a Lutheran preacher at St. George's in Augsburg announced to his Lutheran flock after Easter that he planned to administer the Lord's Supper to them, I, as a simple maiden, and because My Lord was not at home at the time, also went into the church and wanted to see how such a Lord's Supper was done. Several men and women knew me, however, and knew I was not Lutheran. They asked me what I was doing there, and said I should get out or they would drag me out by the hair, along with many other such insults.

I answered that I wanted to see how they conduct their Lord's Supper, and see if I would also be enlightened, and take it, too. They said I should get out, and that I should be pilloried, and so on. So I said as I was leaving, "If that is your Lord's Supper, then eat it until you die." Afterward, Gracious Lords, a number of the Lutherans reported to the mayors and an Honorable Council in Augsburg that I wanted to start a tumult, and that I blasphemed God, and disgraced their Eucharist, etc. And they did so falsely represent me that the council interrogated these same witnesses, without asking me for my side. I was also not asked to appear for this, or to face them, or to provide articles for questioning.

And based on the testimony and account of these witnesses (who are my adversaries and are biased), I was banished from Augsburg, to stay away from the city forever.

Therefore, it is my humble plea to Your Grace that Your Grace will intervene with the mayors and council of Augsburg on my behalf to allow me back into the city, so that I, a poor daughter, can serve pious, honorable people there as I did before, and earn my daily keep. For the matter was not so grievous, but only because of some talk, and was done to me because of a grudge. Henceforth I will stay away from their Eucharist and other Lutheran matters. This I want to earn with lifelong devotion to Your Grace and an Honorable Council in Augsburg and to God. Your. . . . poor servant Katharina Vöglin from Oberkainlach near Mindelheim.

[Vöglin was ordered to remain outside the city. A separate petition indicates that her fiancé broke his marriage promise to her as a result of the dishonor brought upon her by this incident, after which she petitioned again for clemency, apparently without success.]

8.3 Suppressing Catholic Church Ritual during the Reformation[5]

EXCERPTS FROM THE MINUTES OF THE CITY COUNCIL, 1537

On the 27th of March, 1537, an Honorable Council proclaimed and ordered that close attention should be paid at the city gates for evidence of people leaving the city, whether few or many, citizens or subjects, men or women, on horseback, on foot, or by wagon, for the purpose of attending mass, worshipping images, or taking part in other such ceremonies and abuses outside of town. If this appears to be the case, those appointed to the gates should pay close attention, and send someone to follow them or otherwise find out if it's so, and where they are going outside of Augsburg, and report [them] to the Burgomaster. . . .

On the same date, it is proclaimed that midwives should earnestly be warned and forbidden to baptize any baby unless it is an emergency. Instead, the babies should be carried [to the church] for baptism, and the midwives should under no circumstances get in the way.

5. StadtAA, Schätze 16, 39v–40r, May 25, 1539; Ratsbuch 1529–1542, 122r–123v; Strafbuch 1533–1539, 152v.

On April 7, 1537, the council presented the group who left the city to hear mass in Lechhausen, Oberhausen, and Friedberg with the following instruction:

As you and everyone else know from the council's published edict, an Honorable Council has, for honest reasons, undertaken a Christian Reformation of the mass, image worship, and other ceremonies. This change should eventually be supported and established in a free, general, Christian, and neutral council or national assembly on the basis of Scripture. The council has credible information that, in violation of this, you have taken it upon yourselves to attend the mass, worship images, and take part in ceremonies elsewhere that have been done away with here, as if the council is in error, and did not act properly. In the case of some, the council understands it as simplemindedness; but among others, it shows defiance and contempt, about which the council is more than a little perturbed. Thus they are warning you this once, out of confidence that you will abstain from such things in the future, and show yourselves to be no different from other citizens. For whoever persists in attending mass, worshipping images, or taking part in ceremonies in violation of the council's Reformation will be punished for disobedience. This the council wanted you to know as a preventive warning.

The above was read word for word to those who were called in. Then they were told that anyone clever enough to believe that the council is in error should identify himself, and his name will be provided to the council, and the council will listen to what he has to say.

PUNISHMENT RECORDS, 1539

[The following incident occurred less than a month after the council issued a new ordinance forbidding the attendance of "alien teachings and ceremonies in the countryside," which, city leaders charged, occurred "more out of contempt for the authorities than out of Christian devotion."]

On June 17, 1539, the honorable Lady N. [Meuting],[6] widow of the late Laux Meuting (rest his soul), had her daughter [Sibilla] Schrenckin's baby taken from Augsburg to Lechhausen to be baptized in violation of

6. Helena, born Adlerin, wife of Lucas Meuting. The Meutings were a powerful merchant family in Augsburg with connections through marriage to high-ranking patricians, and the baby's mother, Sibilla Schrenckin, was married to a member of the nobility. There is no record of questioning or punishment of the baby's parents.

the council's decree; and this occurred on [Lady Meuting's] orders and instructions. For this she was punished with three weeks in a tower, or 3 gulden for each day of this sentence to be paid to the city poor chest. She agreed to pay 3 gulden for each day and was thereupon released from the tower penalty.

On the same day, Ännli, Schrenckin's lying-in maid, because she went with them and carried the baby to the baptism, was sentenced to and punished with three days in the tower, which she accepted willingly and obediently.

8.4 Two Conflicting Versions of an Exorcism in 1568[7]

According to the Protestant who assembled this account, the first of these two descriptions is excerpted from a news report circulated by the Jesuits, and the second is a true eyewitness account.

News from Augsburg of the conjuring and exorcism of the Devil, as from time to time is spewed out by the Jesuits.

In 1568, on the 25th day of June, in the Dominican Church in Augsburg, Doctor Wendel, a Jesuit, exorcised a maiden who was in service to Georg Fugger. With the grace and aid of the Almighty, he thus freed her of an evil spirit. It was the eighth time that she had been possessed by the evil spirit, and she had been exorcised before by Doctor Simon Scheibenhardt.[8]

And it happened like this: This possessed maiden was brought into the church and taken straight to the tabernacle,[9] which greatly horrified her, for she did not want to approach it. The Jesuit then began to conjure up the Evil One, who refused to answer him for a long time.

But finally, when [the Evil One] could no longer resist, the Jesuit exhorted him so strongly by the power of the Almighty that he confessed that this maiden had first committed adultery with a married man, and then was also guilty of the death of a baby. The maiden was thus so plagued and pained in her heart that she fell into despair, and she couldn't bear it, saying, "If God won't help, then the Devil should help her." And at that, one of his demons entered her. . . .

---

7. StadtAA, Evangelisches Wesensarchiv, Akt 632.

8. A canon in St. Moritz.

9. The ornamented receptacle in which the consecrated host was stored.

And when the Jesuit, Doctor Wendel, further exhorted him to leave, the Evil One answered, "Jesuit, don't fail to understand me. If you fail, I won't fail to get you." The Jesuit did not want to stop, and pressured him hard to leave. In front of the tabernacle the Evil One said, "Where must I go?" and the Jesuit said, "Do you want to go into the tabernacle?" He answered with a horrible bellow, "No, I don't want to go in; I don't want to have anything to do with him, who was crucified. . . ."

[Upon further exhortation, the Evil One then said that] there was someone in the church who didn't believe that he and his kind can possess people. The Jesuit should allow him first to enter that person, so that [the unbeliever] will also understand his power, and then let him leave by the door. Then he asked to leave by a window above Lord Fugger. This the Jesuit did not want to allow, but showed him a pane, and exhorted him to go through it into the depths of hell and back to that place where God has damned him. [The Evil One] went through the pane with a great cry, and the pane clattered and fell into the church. The maiden was thus released, and fainted. When she finally came to herself, she was asked about and accused of what the Evil One said of her, and she confessed that it was unfortunately true, and she had turned to the Devil. Mayor Fugger, a Burgomaster, and as many as 200 honest people were present at this exorcism. There was also a [Protestant] pastor there, who went right up to Georg Fugger's wife and told her that he had a daughter who was possessed, and was confined to the hospital, and he asked her to convince the Jesuit to help his daughter . . . and Lady Fugger said, "My dear sir, you claim to be the heirs of the apostles, why don't you exorcise her yourselves?" And he answered, "Maybe we don't have the grace of God. I see that the grace of God is with this Jesuit. . . ."

TRUE RESPONSE AND COUNTERREPORT TO THE ABOVE-NOTED JESUIT NEWS REPORT . . . IN THE YEAR 1568

[At the request of Lady Fugger, the unnamed pastor who is the source for this story joined others gathered at her house.] A number of respectable gentlemen and ladies were present in Lady Fugger's house at that time, among them Lord Hans Fugger, along with the pastor. And all of them saw and heard for themselves what happened.

First, before the pastor arrived (as he was told later by another) they read a mass, in the hope that their plan would proceed all the more fortunately and would be successful. After the mass, the poor maiden, who

was brought to the Fuggers from the hospital, was taken into a wide hall
and laid on a bedstead. The Jesuit stood to her right along with his servants, holding a manuscript book in front of him, and to her left stood
Lord Georg Fugger's wife. . . .

The Jesuit stood very close over the poor maiden, constantly holding
a silver crucifix before her with his right hand. In his left hand he held
a stole that they had placed around her neck, with which, once he had
sprinkled her with holy water, he perhaps thought he could chase out
the Devil all the more quickly. He immediately began his rite, which
lasted until nearly three o'clock. He read all of the Gospels about the
possessed, as well as the Epistles and hymns, along with the Gospel of
John (which he repeated over and over, together with the exorcism text).
And he tried so hard and so plagued the poor girl that, if she hadn't been
sick already, it would be no wonder if this would have made her so. . . .

When the rite was completed and the Jesuit had not been able to
achieve anything . . . [he] held the crucifix in front of her mouth and
asked her to kiss it, which she refused to do. And although he pushed
her very hard, she gently pushed it away from her with her hand three
times. And in all of this there was nothing out of the ordinary that
would lead one to say that she displayed any sign or behaved in any
manner or spoke any word that suggested any lack of reason or sign of
possession. After this, the Jesuits recited the Articles of Faith to the girl
in German in a loud voice, for the rest of it was all done in Latin. The
girl repeated the Articles and professed to them with mouth and heart,
and also with tears and sighs.

Upon this the pastor couldn't restrain himself and keep silent anymore, so he stood up and addressed the Jesuits in a friendly manner,
saying, "Brother Wendel, this girl is in no way possessed. . . ." At that
the poor girl spoke to the pastor with these words, "My Lord, I beg of
you for the sake of God to advise me and help me to get free of this and
get out of here, for I have done wrong in coming here and allowing this."

8.5 Controlling Catholic Rituals in the Countryside: Excerpts from the Bavarian Police Ordinance of 1616[10]

Regarding baptism feasts and funeral rites

It is also our will that all baptism and birthing feasts are done away with
and forbidden to the extent that, if a woman wants to have one, she does

10. Der Fürstlicher Bayrischer Landts- vnd Policey Ordnung (Munich, 1616),
568, 575–82.

not invite to it more than four women. And it may consist of no more than one meal, the amount of wine and food for which should be limited to that established for weddings. But the women who are invited are forbidden to make special donations or gifts to the new mother.

And in light of the fact that great feasts are also regularly held at funerals, we order and will that henceforth, funeral ceremonies will only be conducted with an appropriate church service, but should no longer be accompanied by feasts, parties, or social gatherings. . . .

REGARDING THE FEES THAT ONE PROVIDES FOR RECEIVING COMMUNION FOR THE SICK OR EXTREME UNCTION.

If a priest administers the Holy Communion or the Extreme Unction to a sick person, and the person is well off, [the priest] should be given 12 kreuzer, and get 6 kreuzer from the commoners. Those who carry the canopy should get 1 kreuzer each; the schoolboys who carry the lanterns and storm lights 1 kreuzer each; and either the custodian or the sacristan (or both) who accompanies them 2 kreuzer from the commoners, 4 from those who are well off, and 6 kreuzer from the rich. But nothing should be expected of the very poor.

If in one place or another it is customary for a confraternity or church to pay these expenses for common people, then nothing should be requested or demanded of the sick, rather they should be told that they are not required to pay anything. If they provide something anyway, it should be given to the brotherhood or church in that place from which these costs are paid, and then the priest and church attendants should be given their fees from there.

If a priest has to go out a quarter or half mile into the countryside, he should be given 20 kreuzer from the wealthy, and the sacristan should be given 10 kreuzer. But the commoners should give the priest 12 kreuzer and the sacristan 6 kreuzer. And from the very poor, nothing should be requested or accepted.

[Additional fees are described in a similar manner for the nuns who watch over the dying; the sacristan and custodian in the case of setting gravestones and singing masses; delivery of candleholders by confraternities; the cantor and schoolboys for singing Psalters; pallbearers for carrying the dead and gravediggers for burying them; various persons who take part in the funeral processions, including bearers of black flags, lanterns, torches, and the censer, as well as choir singers, the priest, and other church officials; the ringing of bells during the procession; and postfuneral processions and masses held on the seventh and thirtieth day after the burial and the one-year anniversary.]

It also happens that some priests in the countryside want to set requirements as to what the people should donate, such as flour, lard, eggs, and the like. This is to be done away with, and donations should be made in accordance with each person's goodwill.

II. Rites of Power

8.6 The Citizens Swear an Oath to the New City Council, 1548[11]

As a condition for leaving the city with his occupying troops, Emperor Charles V required in August of 1548 that all citizens of Augsburg swear a traditional oath of homage to the newly constituted council, and that the remaining Protestant preachers also swear an oath to uphold the terms of the Augsburg Interim. The citizens gathered in three separate groups on different squares of the city to swear the oath collectively, as they did every year after council elections. The form of the oath of citizenship is presented here.

You will swear a prescribed oath to God,[12] with raised fingers, that you of this city of Augsburg will be true, law abiding, and obedient to the Lord Mayors, named Lord Leo Ravensburger and Lord Heinrich Rehlinger, and also to the Lord Burgomasters who are in office at any time here present, and to their representatives, and to an Honorable Council as it was elected on the third of August of this year, and that you will always obediently comply with and obey each and every one of their orders, bans, laws, statutes, and ordinances, now and in the future, and that you will not oppose them with words or deeds, secretly nor openly . . . upon threat of loss of citizenship.

Upon that the first Lord Mayor will tell them to raise their fingers, and repeat after him: "This as it was read to me, I will willingly and faithfully comply with and obey, so help me God the Almighty."[13]

11. StadtAA, Schätze 13c, Ordnung des Stadtregiments, August 3, 1548, 3r.

12. Later added, "the Almighty and the saints"; the phrase "and the saints" was subsequently crossed out again, presumably after the Peace of Augsburg legalized Lutheranism in the city.

13. Similarly, "and all the saints" was crossed out.

8.7 The Citizens Pay Homage to Emperor Ferdinand I, 1559[14]

Emperor Charles V abdicated his crown in favor of his brother Ferdinand in 1556, and Ferdinand was officially elected Emperor in 1558. Charles died soon afterward in September of that year. Here the traditional rite of paying homage to the new ruler is described by Augsburg chronicler and council apparitor Paul Hector Mair.[15] Not included for reasons of space are lengthy descriptions of the elaborate damask canopy erected to welcome the Emperor, the expensive banquets held in the Fuggers' palace in his honor, and other details of the great pomp accompanying this event.

How the arrival of the [newly] elected Holy Roman Emperor Ferdinand in Augsburg was celebrated, and also in what way His Imperial Majesty was honored by the people of the city, and how they rendered homage and swore an oath to His Imperial Majesty, in 1559:

[It was His Majesty's wish] that My Lords . . . ride out to meet him with a large contingent of riders. But the citizens should be told to wait in two lines along the streets where His Majesty would be coming into the city, bearing their arms and armor. . . . The council summoned the quarter captains, and ordered them to tell their lane captains that the citizens and residents under their command should be ordered to appear with their breastplates and pole arms when the alarm sounds, in due obedience and honor to His Imperial Majesty, who wished to arrive here on New Year's Eve. And when their people were assembled, the lane captains were to lead them to the appointed gathering place of their quarter captain, and await his orders and do as he tells them. . . .

In addition, the members of the supplemental guard, about 300 in number, of whom forty or fifty were hook gunners,[16] stood lined up next

---

14. *Paul Hector Mairs 1. Chronik von 1547–1565,* Beilage VI, 475–81. In CDS vol. 32 (1917).

15. Paul Hector Mair (1517–1579) was a lover of books, collector of rarities, and martial arts enthusiast whose addiction to his hobbies ultimately cost him his life. Mair used his position as civic apparitor and cashier to the Office of Provisions in Augsburg not only to collect information for his city chronicles but also to embezzle the funds he needed to support his collections. He was discovered and executed in 1579 after having misappropriated around 40,000 gulden in municipal funds over the course of thirty years in office.

16. The hook gun (*Hackenbüchse*) had a long barrel that had to be stabilized on a stand by means of a hook in order to aim and fire.

to each other from beneath the Red Gate to the gate at the toll house with their armor, pole arms, and guns.

In the meantime, the [Lord Mayors, Burgomasters, and other dignitaries] all gathered on horseback in front of Gögginger Gate. And all of the Lords were dressed in black coats and mourning hats,[17] but the servants were in black riding coats. And when they had all assembled, they rode in order of rank to meet His Imperial Majesty at the Lech Bridge, where My Lords' district and jurisdiction comes to an end. There His Majesty was welcomed by Lord Mayor Heinrich Rehlinger.

When Lord Mayor Rehlinger had finished his speech, three ranks of the Council Lords' mounted escorts rode ahead. And although they were told that they weren't supposed to be in front, rather the Bavarians should be, they didn't let this bother them, but answered that they were only riding ahead in order to show those coming behind them which streets to use. After these three ranks of escorts came the Bavarians; after the Bavarians, the Bishop of Augsburg's horsemen; then the Duke of Bavaria; the two heralds; and the imperial marshall, who held His Imperial Majesty's exposed sword before him. His Imperial Majesty came next. After His Majesty came the guards; after the guards . . . the captain of the mounted escorts; . . . all My Lords' Provisioners; . . . the two Lord Mayors; . . . [and] last came My Lords' mounted escorts and riders. . . .

My Lords also arranged for several large artillery guns to be placed on some earthworks, which were fired when His Majesty came into the city through the Red Gate. . . .

How an Honorable Council and the people of this city paid homage and swore allegiance to the Emperor:

After a few days, His Most Gracious Royal Majesty sent word that an Honorable Council and the common people should pay homage and swear allegiance to His Majesty as the Holy Roman Emperor, and also provide His Majesty with a written account of how this ceremony had previously been performed for his imperial forbearers, praise their memories. Thereupon an Honorable Council provided His Majesty with the requested account, which can be found recorded in the old council book on folios 25 and 26. In addition, he requested [that all the citizens], upon their oath and duty of citizenship, appear with their sons

---

17. A show of respect for the new Emperor's recently deceased brother, Emperor Charles V.

at Perlach[18] on Thursday, the fifth of January, between seven and eight o'clock in the morning, and swear allegiance to His Majesty. They were also told to impress upon and order their wives, daughters, and maids that they should stay home during this time and not enter the streets.

On the above-noted Thursday, the fifth of January, once an Honorable Council had gathered in the council room at their normal time and taken care of some of the business matters before them, the Lord Mayors sent for word about when and at what time His Imperial Majesty would ride from the [Fugger] palace to the council house. The council was informed that His Majesty was planning to be ready at nine o'clock. The two Lord Mayors and the two appointed Lord Burgomasters went at that hour to meet His Majesty, and then rode ahead of him from the palace to the council house. The Lord Mayors and Burgomasters immediately hurried up the steps at Iron Hill[19] to the council house, so that they would be there ahead of His Imperial Majesty, and could take their place together with all of the Lords of the Privy Council and all of the councilmen on the stairs that go from the council room up to the hall. His Imperial Majesty then came up to the council house by the other stairs (near the fountain), and arrived at the stairs, where an Honorable Council was waiting. At that point, the council had Lord Doctor Bemler, city secretary, ask of His Majesty, with the greatest devotion, to allow an Honorable Council and the civic commune, in accordance with ancient custom, to keep their good traditions, customs, freedoms, dispensations, confirmations, and privileges that have been granted them by the Holy Roman Emperors and Kings, and to continue to command and protect them, and also to be their Most Gracious ruler.

Thereupon His Imperial Majesty responded, through the Lord Vice Chancellor Lord Doctor Georg Sigmund Seld, that as soon as the council and the people of the city of Augsburg took their oath of allegiance, His Imperial Majesty would demonstrate his grace to them and the city of Augsburg.

After this request, His Imperial Majesty went into the oriel with those electors and princes who were present at the time. But the councilmen went down the stairs in front of the oriel. And the vice chancellor made the announcement approximately as follows: The late Emperor Charles V, praise his memory, having abdicated, resigned, and passed on the administration and stewardship of the Holy Roman Empire

18. The square in front of the council house.
19. Iron Hill (*Eisenberg*) was the hill next to the council house on which the irons were located.

last year, in 1558, for pressing and appropriate reasons, in particular because of his age and increasing weakness. . . . His Imperial Majesty [Ferdinand] accepted this cession and capitulation upon the request and plea of the electors, and took upon himself the burden of the administration and stewardship of the empire, along with the accompanying dignities, authority, government, titles, scepter, and crown of the Holy Roman Empire, in the name of the Almighty, and with comforting and certain faith that His Godly Majesty [would provide His Imperial Majesty with the necessary strength and wisdom]. And as it is an old, laudable tradition and custom that, when the Holy Roman Emperor visits the imperial cities, they pay him homage and swear allegiance to him as the highest ruler and their authority, the council and the people should pay heed to the oath that will be read to them, and abide by it.

Thereupon the oath was read by the Lord Vice Chancellor, to wit: We the mayors, Burgomasters, council, and all of the people of the city of Augsburg promise allegiance and swear to you, the most illustrious Prince and Lord, Lord Ferdinando, Holy Roman Emperor, our Most Gracious, proper ruler, to be true and obedient, to promote what is useful and best for Your Imperial Grace and to protect you from harm, and to do everything that faithful and obedient subjects are bound and beholden to Your Imperial Grace as their Most Gracious, proper ruler to do, faithfully and loyally and without guile, so help us God and the holy Gospel.

After the oath, His Imperial Majesty provided the council and the people with the following response: His Holy Roman Imperial Majesty, our Most Gracious Lord, has graciously seen and heard the allegiance and oath of you of Augsburg, subjects of His Majesty and of the Holy Empire, and will take you under his gracious command. And he herewith verifies and confirms that your old customs, good traditions, practices, and freedoms, which have been granted to you and repeatedly confirmed, will remain in force, and that he will command, defend, and protect you, and be your Most Gracious proper ruler.

Upon that Lord Mayor Heinrich Rehlinger devotedly thanked His Imperial [Majesty], and then His Majesty rode from the council house back to the palace, accompanied by the two Lord Mayors and Burgomasters.

Note: During the oath all of the city gates were closed and locked down.

8.8 Witness Oath for Swearing In at Court[20]

WITNESS OATH

Two raised fingers
That I will tell the truth in the matter for which I have been called, without prejudice to anyone, faithfully and impartially, so help me God the Almighty.

THE WOMEN'S PLEDGE

When a woman takes a pledge in an important matter, this has no force in law. Therefore in important matters, a woman should take a corporal oath[21] in the presence of two men, after being reminded about perjury, and then it will have force in law, and no one will have an excuse. Note: The woman's oath [is taken] with two fingers of the right hand placed on the left breast.

8.9 Rituals of Execution[22]

Executions of criminals were public affairs and sometimes took elaborate and symbolic forms. This broadsheet, which circulated in Augsburg after 1606 and describes both gruesome crimes (presumably confessed to under torture) and equally horrific acts of justice, is typical of sensational reports meant both to titillate and to serve as a warning to their readers.

New Tidings. Unheard-of, abominable, and unnatural acts and misdeeds perpetrated by a group of gravediggers in the Principality of Silesia, and also how they were executed for their misdeeds in this year of 1606 on the 20th of September.

[The world is full of so many evils that God must be horrified.] For in Frankenstein in Silesia,[23] eight gravediggers were arrested, six of whom were men and two women, who confessed under torture that they had prepared a poison powder and spread it around in the houses of Frankenstein, smearing and spreading it on the thresholds,

---

20. SuStBA, 2ºCod.Aug.244, Burgermeisteramt-Instruktion, 1584 (ms.).

21. I.e., with ritual action such as raising the fingers toward God or placing them over one's heart.

22. SuStBA, S Einblattdr. nach 1500, Nr. 29 (Augsburg, c. 1606).

23. Now Zabkowice, in present-day Poland.

doorknockers, and door handles. From this many people were poisoned and died miserably.

In addition, they stole a lot of money from the houses, robbing from the dead. They took their frocks and overcoats, and they even cut open the pregnant women and removed the fruit of their wombs, and ate the hearts of the babies raw. They stole the altar cloths from the churches there, and took two clocks or hourglasses from the pulpit and pulverized them and used them in their sorcery. A new gravedigger from Strigau fornicated with a dead maiden in the church. And they committed other unheard-of and horrible acts as well.

For these misdeeds, they were executed on the 20th of September in the following way: First, they were all driven around in the city and torn with red-hot pincers, and the thumbs were pinched off of their hands. The older gravedigger, and also another old man of eighty-seven years whom they used as their assistant, had their right hands cut off. Next, these two were chained onto a pillar and a fire was set a distance away, so that they were roasted. The new gravedigger from Strigau had his male member pinched off with red-hot pincers, and afterward was also chained to a pillar along with another one, and they were likewise smoldered and roasted. But the other four people were burned at the stake . . . it is estimated that around 1,500 people, young and old, died from this poison powder. . . . The Lord God protect us from such evil, devilish hearts, and root them out of our midst, as these were. . . . Amen. Printed in Augsburg at Georg Kress, illuminator and artist in Jacob's Suburb.

III. Rituals of Socialization and Celebration

8.10 Bans on the Celebratory Firing of Guns[24]

Firing so-called peace shots or joy shots into the air during celebrations was a well-established ritual by the sixteenth century and was repeatedly forbidden by the authorities throughout the early modern period.

Joy shots during the Festival of Peace, 1650
An Honorable Council is aware that during the current anniversary celebrations,[25] in this time of general peace in the empire, praise God,

---

24. SuStBA, 4°Aug.1021 Band 4 Abt. 1, Nr. 69.

25. Reference is to the annual celebration of the conclusion of the Peace of Westphalia, still observed in Augsburg as the Festival of Peace (*Friedensfest*, August 8). The first such celebration took place in 1650.

everyone is first and foremost allowed to demonstrate his happiness in a seemly manner. This tends to occur by means of joy shots. However, [the council] can under no circumstances allow shooting to be abused in this way and to continue to occur in the city at will, for it can easily lead to disaster and harm. Aside from that, no citizen or resident has the right to fire guns in the city at his own pleasure, which has been strictly forbidden by numerous decrees . . . [thus no firing of any kind of gun is permitted within the city] on threat of punishment by fine, in the tower, in the irons, or worse. . . . August 11, 1650

8.11 A Celebratory Gunshot during Carnival Goes Awry, 1587[26]

INTERROGATION OF BERNHARD KLEBER

1. What is his name, where is he from, and what does he do for a living? His name is Bernhard Kleber; he is from Augsburg and is a journeyman locksmith.

2. Has he not been staying outside of the city since last Shrove Tuesday, and why is that? Says yes, and it's because he fired his gun from his attic while the salt sellers were riding by [for their annual Carnival procession], and afterward a serving girl accused him of shooting her with a piece of shot, and she wanted to charge him. So he left town.

3. Did he not fire a shot from his father's house on last Shrovetide while the salt sellers were holding their parade? He says yes.

4. Did he not hit a serving girl named Catharina Holtzmann in the breast with a piece of iron shot? She did accuse him of it. He doesn't know if he did it. He was shooting with brass shot.

5. Why did he so shamefully seek to kill this maiden, and was this his intention? He did not shoot at the girl, rather did so randomly, and he believed that shooting on this day was allowed. And the reason he fired from the attic was so he wouldn't do anyone any harm.

6. Does he not know that it is forbidden to fire a gun in the city? He does know it, but he thought this day was exempt from the rule.

7. Why he then acted in violation of this ban? Says he believed it was allowed for everyone on this day.

8. Was this not the reason that he fled and has been residing outside the city? Answers yes.

26. StadtAA, Urgicht Bernhard Kleber, September 2, 1587; Strafbuch 1581–1587, 232v.

9. Is he willing to settle with Holtzmann for the injury she received, her pain, and her medical costs? And who can provide a surety? He would be glad to settle with her, and his father and Melchior Lacher will pledge a guarantee.

10. How did he think he would get away with his mischief without penalty? He begs for mercy and forgiveness.

[Kleber's father agreed to pay 4 gulden over two months' time for injury to Catharina Holtzmann.]

Punishment record

September 3, 1587: Bernhart Kleber, journeyman locksmith from Augsburg, fired a shot out of his father's house on last Shrove Tuesday as the salt sellers were holding their parade and hit a serving girl with a piece of shot, injuring her. Then he fled from the city . . . but because he then settled with the girl, an Honorable Council today decreed that he should remain locked up for eight days, and then be let go.

8.12 Expressing and Settling Political Differences, 1584[27]

This chronicle description of events following the riot over the introduction of the Gregorian calendar in 1584 illustrates both ritual forms of slander and the rituals of friendship employed by the council in order to settle the matter and restore honor to the slandered parties. At issue are the actions of Endres Zölling, a supporter of the new calendar. Zölling had earlier been anonymously accused of reporting the secret deliberations of the citizens' committee to the Fuggers.

Copy of that which was hung on Endres Zölling's house on September 3, 1584 new style, with a picture of a gallows on it,[28] which said:

> Endres Zölling is my name
> That is what my father called me.
> I have not behaved in good faith
> My brother-in-law Doctor Dickh misled me.
> And I became a public traitor

27. SuStBA, 2°Cod.S.41, Kölderer Chronic, 3. Buch, 57r–v, 79r–v.

28. Hanging or drawing a picture of a gallows on someone's house or in connection with a person's name was defaming, suggesting that the object of scorn was fit to be hanged and thus to be dishonored by the executioner. Also, a standard form of defamation was to post a person's name on the gallows.

In the course of which the Devil possessed me.
I wrote false letters and broke seals
And for this, a rogue they called me.
Which I must remain forever
The Devil come and take me
And all my fellows, that is my wish.
Amen.
That will soon come true.

This was what the note said, and this is the same Zölling [who had been accused before]. He immediately showed [the note] to Mayor Rehlinger, [and Rehlinger] ordered that the delegation of twenty-four commoners[29] should be called to the Weavers' Hall the next day, where the carpenters should be asked if they have a complaint against said Zölling. Among them was a carpenter who had insulted [Zölling] as a rogue because he opened the delegation's letter. This he had so far not been able to deny. And he now could not take [the insult] back, since the note with the above-recorded contents had been hung publicly on the house. . . .

Now, when they had gathered in the morning at the usual time at the Weavers' Hall, the matter was put before them. And it finally happened that the two parties had to shake hands and settle the matter, and take back what they had said. So the carpenter, whose name was Caspar Hag, offered Zölling his hand five times . . . and they became good friends again, so that neither party should suffer any prejudice or detriment to his honor. So this Hag . . . took everything back, and upon that the two of them went with their witnesses to Clement [the publican] at Franciscan Square (Zölling having first requested of the mayor that he might have something to eat prepared) to have a good drink to confirm the matter, and to tie one on, which was then done, and they thus again became good fellows. The next day Zölling rode off to Nuremberg to take care of his business there and beyond. Thus once again a storm was avoided.

8.13 Exceptions to Tavern Bans for Ritual Drinks

As demonstrated in Chapter Four, a temporary ban on tavern drinking was a common penalty imposed upon irresponsible householders. Here we see that the authorities often allowed exceptions to the ban for

---

29. The citizens' committee discussed in Chapter Two. Zölling was also a member of the delegation.

certain situations in which drinking took ritual forms. Sales contracts,
employment agreements, marriage arrangements, and other legal
settlements became binding only when sealed with a drink.

JONAS SCHMID, BATHER AND LOCAL CITIZEN, 1593[30]

Excerpt from interrogation
Was he not previously arrested for poor householding and wasteful
living, kept for a time in the tower, and forbidden to visit taverns
by the Lord Burgomaster in Office? It is true that at a previous time,
when his wife refused him wine and he became angry with her, he was
put in a tower in response to her charges and those of her father, and
visiting taverns was also forbidden to him. But afterward, his father-
in-law himself allowed him to drink a measure of wine when he had a
contract to drink to or something else to settle, and his wife herself gave
him money to drink a measure of wine from time to time.

Excerpt from the response from Schmid's father-in-law and wife:
First, regarding the fourth question, that he would like to sugarcoat his
actions as if I, Hans Raydel [Schmid's father-in-law] myself had allowed
him to drink a measure of wine when he had something to settle, this
was so that on such occasions as he was honored with an invitation, such
as to a wedding or a contract drink, he should not be impeded. It was
not permission to sit in taverns constantly on a daily basis, as he did.
And in saying that I, his wife, am supposed to have myself given him
money to drink a measure of wine, he is not telling the truth. He did
do this when I gave him money to pay a wood seller, running with it
directly into a tavern. . . .

PUNISHMENT RECORDS[31]

November 14, 1541: Hans Schacher, cart puller, because of his daily
drunkenness, was enjoined to drink no wine outside his house for one
year starting now, unless a respectable man who employs him offers him
a drink. In addition, Hans Ausshalm asked the above-noted Schacher's
wife to forgive him for calling her a whore, adding that it occurred
in anger and he knows nothing of her other than that she is a pious,

30. StadtAA, Urgicht Jonas Schmid, March 17, 1593.
31. StadtAA, Strafbuch 1509–1526, 45; Strafbücher, Zuchtbuch 1540–1542, 88,
132; Zuchtbuch 1542–1543, 83.

honorable woman. Thereupon he was enjoined not to invite any company to his house other than his family.

June 14, 1542: Hans Miller, called Cartier, on the one hand, and Hans Klauber, weaver, and Barbara Jägerin, on the other hand, pledged to keep the peace with one another in words and deeds. And Miller in particular, upon the earnest command of My Lords, pledged to keep his wife as one should keep a pious, honorable woman; to attend to his work assiduously; and to drink no wine outside of his house, unless he were called to his guildhall or to a wedding or otherwise an invitation for the sake of honor, or at the Rosenau [shooting grounds] for shooting matches, but then in a seemly fashion.

June 20, 1543: Hans Lechbeck, playing-card-maker, and his wife pledged to keep the peace with one another in word and deed. And Lechbeck had previously been forbidden to visit public houses inside the city or up to two miles outside of it, to which he also took a pledge, but did not abide by his oath, rather kept getting drunk outside the city and behaving inappropriately. Therefore My Lords decreed out of mercy, and especially at the request of his wife, that he, Lechbeck, should stay inside his home for the next half year and not leave the house other than on Sundays for the sermon, and at appropriate times to bathe. But then he should come straight home and not go anywhere else. He should also not consume wine excessively in his house or keep company there. And his wife should also get rid of her surplus of dogs and not keep them anymore. Both parties agreed and pledged to abide by all of that.

On June 30, Lechbeck appeared again and complained that if he follows My Lords' command, it will bring him to ruin, so he requested and appealed for mitigation of the penalty. Thereupon My Lords, in consideration of Lechbeck's sustenance and out of great mercy, allowed and permitted that he might well go out to taverns on Thursdays and Fridays to seek his sustenance and to drink moderate contract drinks with the people. But he is to engage in no drinking bout on his own or at anyone else's expense, much less get drunk or behave in violation of the merciful order here described. If he is found liable in any way in this regard he will be punished without mercy. All of this he pledged to obey.

Chapter Nine
Magic and Popular Religion

During the sixteenth and seventeenth centuries, both Catholic and Protestant reformers launched campaigns against popular practices they labeled "superstitious" or "pagan." While Protestants included some accepted Catholic beliefs and practices in the category of superstition, both religions sought to clarify the boundaries between what theologians understood as legitimate religious beliefs and popular ideas they deemed illegitimate. However, since church doctrine accepted the idea that God could interfere at will in the physical world, the distinction for many people remained unclear. Early modern folk persisted in their conviction that the material world could be manipulated through prayer, magic, or the invocation of spirits partly because it provided them with a sense of power over their environment. Belief in magic could help one deal with misfortune and regain a sense of control over a world that often appeared arbitrary.

Historical explanations for the early modern attack on magical practice are many and varied, and are the topic of considerable scholarly debate. Most useful for understanding the sources presented here are the links historians have established between the campaign against popular magic, and the process of confessionalization discussed in Chapter Two. Prior to the Reformation, people often employed sacred objects blessed by a priest (holy water, candles, salt, etc.), sometimes even removed from the church surreptitiously, as protection against negative forces. The use of such objects for physical and worldly ends was never part of official church practice, but it was often tolerated by holders of official religious power because it represented a form of piety, however imperfect. Once the Reformation had taken hold, however, the climate of religious repression created by confessional competition increased pressure to persecute those who did not conform to religious norms. No matter what their method or motive, all those who sought to harness supernatural powers on their own terms were redefined as religious deviants. The exercise of magic was thus linked to the power of Satan, gradually leading to an atmosphere of fear that spread along with news of sensational witch trials. As fear of demonic magic grew among the populace, accusations of witchcraft increased, especially once the magical counterspells formerly used to defend people against witches were also demonized. With no spells to protect them, the populace was left vulnerable to attacks by "malicious people" (documents 9.4 and 9.5).

Unlike some other German towns, Augsburg did not experience a major witch hunt. This does not mean, however, that its citizens were not concerned about the use of magic. Trials for witchcraft in Augsburg occurred in tandem with major concentrations of witch trials elsewhere, with especially high numbers of accusations during the early 1590s, just as the surrounding countryside was emerging from the region's first major spike in witch accusations. Beginning during the agrarian crisis of 1586–1587, witches were identified in terrifying numbers throughout the Catholic territories of the Prince-Bishop of Augsburg, which included a number of villages around the city. The town of Schwabmünchen became the major hub for the trials. Forty-five suspected witches were imprisoned there between 1589 and 1591 and twenty-seven were eventually burned at the stake. Large numbers of additional trials were going on in neighboring Bavaria as well.

In Augsburg, none of the late sixteenth-century trials resulted in a witch burning. The only sixteenth-century execution thus far identified in Augsburg that involved a witchcraft accusation was that of the notorious robber and murderer Michael Schwartzkopf, who confessed under torture in 1568 to supporting his thieving arts through sorcery. The rest of those accused, generally charged only with spell casting, treasure hunting, and crystal gazing, were either sent home with a warning or banished as hucksters. Their responses under questioning reveal a very fluid boundary between the popular view of religious practice and official definitions of magic and superstition: When did a prayer become a spell, when was an herbal remedy a magic potion, how did the manipulation of religious symbols move from sacred to blasphemous, or even satanic? The overlapping character of these cases explains the organization of this chapter, which is arranged chronologically rather than attempting to distinguish between different categories of sources.

The first witch to be burnt at the stake in Augsburg was Dorothea Braun, whose trial took place during the first decade of the Thirty Years' War in 1625. A second witch, this time male (Hans Hellinger) followed Braun to the stake in 1643. The rest of the executions, about seventeen in all (depending on how one chooses to define a "witch"),[1] occurred

---

1. Wolfgang Behringer ("Augsburg") gives the number of executions after Braun's as sixteen, all of them female, apparently discounting the cases of male witches Hans Hellinger (1643) and Veit Karg (1680), both of whom confessed to concluding a pact with the devil. According to chronicles, a male sorcerer was also executed

during the later seventeenth century. This pattern is more consistent with Protestant cities (including Salem, Massachusetts) than with the Catholic territories noted above, whose witch trials tended to occur sooner.

Individual trials in Augsburg also included elements familiar in other areas. The vast majority of those executed were women, and many of the accusations revolved around fantasies of perverted motherhood and antifertility: causing hailstorms that destroyed crops, drying up milk in nursing mothers and cows, contaminating food, causing women to become barren and men impotent, and, most frightening of all, killing and cannibalizing babies. Witches thus represented the inversion of the female ideal of bearing and nourishing children, becoming murderers and consumers of them instead. Because such trials are very long and similar cases are available in English elsewhere, the concentration here is on less dramatic cases that did not lead to execution.

Not all of these cases involved actual attempts to use magic or sacred power. The function served by magical beliefs as an approach to problem solving also opened the door to deception. Some common folk knew how to capitalize on beliefs in miracles, magic, and spells, exploiting not only their peers but also the faith of civic elites. Claims of miraculous martyrdom and magical power were common forms of fraud. Such cases illuminate both the popular beliefs exploited by hucksters and the real threat of a witchcraft accusation—as the period of witch hunting heated up, a confession of fraud became preferable to facing a trial for witchcraft. This phenomenon also illustrates the fact that popular belief systems that included magic and witchcraft were hardly limited to those at the lower end of the social hierarchy.

9.1 Anna Laminit, Spiritual Huckster[2]

Anna Laminit was one of a number of women who sought sainthood by claiming to live for long periods of time without physical nourishment, depending instead only on the spiritual food of the Eucharist. Her public persona was so successful that she gained an international reputation and drew the attention of numerous dignitaries, including Martin Luther, who

---

by the Swedes during the Swedish Occupation in 1633 (Georg Magoldt), although court records for the case do not seem to have survived in Augsburg.

2. Friedrich Roth, "Die geistliche Betrügerin Anna Laminit von Augsburg (c. 1480–1518)," *Zeitschrift für Kirchengeschichte* 43 (1924), 355–417, Anhang II, 415–17.

visited her while in Augsburg in 1511. The account here is taken from a family chronicle commissioned by Hans Jacob Fugger.

In 1503, little crosses fell down from the sky through a fog on all the people, rich and poor, here and elsewhere, and especially on those women who were dressed in white linen. They also fell on the bakeries, on cloths that were hanging out to bleach, and on grocery shops where linen and fustian were laid out. The little crosses were red, flesh colored, and (mostly) black, and such a thing had been completely unheard of in the city of Augsburg. . . . But when the cloths were washed, they came out again, although the black crosses only came out in the third or fourth washing. The nobles and others were very shocked by these crosses.

There was a supposed virgin in the parish of the Holy Cross Church, who, by behaving very spiritually, got the people to believe stalwartly that she had not taken any physical nourishment in many years. Her name was Anna Laminit, and several years before, she had been exposed on the pillory. She gave the Holy Roman Emperor [Maximilian I] to understand that she had seen a vision, in which the Heavenly Father was angered at the confederalists because of the blood money, and also at the world because of the blasphemy and horrible pledging of healths.[3] And Jesus Christ and his dear mother Mary, the pure Virgin, had fallen on their knees before God the Heavenly Father and pled with the holy Almighty that he send to the people on earth a sign of the cross as a warning to repent. And the Heavenly Father heard this prayer from his dear son and the holy Virgin Mary, and sent these little crosses as an admonishment to Christian penance. Therefore [Laminit] requested that everyone, poor and rich, hold a procession, and beg God the Almighty in great devotion for forgiveness for their sins.

This advice was followed, and such a procession was organized by the Bishop and the city council of Augsburg. . . . [They gathered at the Cathedral of Our Lady] and went to St. Ulrich, and the men walked at the front. The women followed separately. The Empress was also among them, and processed along with her ladies and courtesans dressed in black mourning clothes. Leading them was Count Adolf from Nassau. And guards were ordered to walk between the men and the women with their poles, so that no man could mix in with the women. Looking

---

3. Pledging of healths, i.e., social toasting, meaning excessive drunkenness among the upper classes. "Blood money" may refer to the Swiss Confederation's much maligned practice of exporting mercenary soldiers.

down from Perlach Tower they estimated that there were 10,000 men and around 15,000 women. . . .

This woman [Laminit] lived in the city of Augsburg for more than sixteen years, and claimed that she could not consume or digest any natural food. Many citizens also put her to the test. With this, her false claim, she deceived the Emperor himself, along with many princes and all of the nobles. Every Sunday she received the Holy Sacrament, wherefrom she became very frightened and very weak, thinking that she wouldn't be able to digest it. But finally, in 1516, the Emperor's sister Princess [Kunigunde] of Bavaria, who had gone to live out her life in a cloister of the Third Order of the Franciscans after her husband's death, sent for this woman. She lodged her in a special room that had hidden holes drilled into it in several places, so that one could see everything she did. In this room [Laminit] was alone, and no one was allowed to come and go there.

When she had been in the room for five days, having to eat the food she had sewn secretly into her clothes only at night, she began to complain that she couldn't stand being locked up like that, and needed to have some air, or she would die. So the laudable and earnest princess ordered that all of her windows be opened, which was done. Then at night [Laminit] threw her own excrement out of the windows into the garden. So the princess had a light put into the room that should burn day and night. It was then clear to see through the holes that [Laminit] was eating. The princess herself went to her and accused her of trickery, showing her that which she had thrown into the garden, and also took out her food and drink and held it in front of her. . . . And she wrote to her brother, the Emperor, in Innsbruck to tell him what happened. When the Emperor found out about it, he decided not to apply the full weight of the law, rather wrote to the council in Augsburg telling them to banish this Laminit from the city along with her goods and chattel (for she had taken in several hundred gulden with her scam), and this was done. . . . When she was banished, a good fellow took pity on her and married her.[4] So they moved together to Switzerland. What she did there I don't know, but she was drowned there.[5]

---

4. A crossbow-maker from Kaufbeuern named Hans Schnitzer.

5. Laminit was arrested for fraud in Switzerland and executed by drowning after confessing to a series of crimes, including her offenses in Augsburg.

9.2 A Case of Treasure Hunting, 1544[6]

INTERROGATION OF REGINA KOCH

On Tuesday, the 27th of May 1544, Regina Koch, whom they also call Mauerin,[7] from Augsburg, testified willingly to the accompanying questions as follows:

1. On what day did two women from Nuremberg come here to her house? The two women from Nuremberg came to her house last Wednesday.

2. Did she know either or both of them before? The one woman, called [Otilia] Wolkenstainer, is the daughter of the deceased innkeeper Mechart. She has known her for a long time, but she doesn't know the other woman.

3. Who sent these women to lodge with her, and did she know ahead of time that they had come here? No one asked her to lodge these two women, and she didn't know they were coming.

4. Why did these women come here? On last Good Friday, the above-named Wolkenstainer came to her house and asked where she could find Mrs. Greiff, who had lived in the house before. She answered that this old woman Mrs. Greiff had died. Wolkenstainer then said, "Dear woman, there is a treasure in your house, which Mrs. Greiff gave to me eighteen years ago. If you have no objection, I know a woman who could dig it up." But [the witness] declined and asked why she should have anything to do with such foolishness, for she knows of no treasure and doesn't believe in such things. Then Wolkenstainer said she only knows that there was a whole pot full of money there, and she would like to bring a woman who can find it. But she, Koch, did not allow it, saying instead, "Dear woman, it is all the same if you bring her or don't bring her, I don't believe any of it." Then Wolkenstainer left again, and didn't come back until this Wednesday. Otherwise she doesn't know why the women came here, or what they were after.

5. Were any noises, such as a spirit or something, heard or seen in her house, and when? She knows of no spirit or other unnatural thing that was heard in her house. She also didn't see anything.

6. On whose orders or request was a hole dug in her garden yesterday morning? As she said above, the two aforementioned women

6. StadtAA, Urgicht Regina Koch et al., May 27–31, 1544; Strafbuch 1543–1553, 29r.

7. Mauerin may be Regina Koch's married name, or it may refer to her husband's trade (i.e., "the mason's wife/widow").

came to her house on Wednesday. Wolkenstainer put pressure on her, saying that there really was a treasure buried there, and she knew how to find it. And if Koch wanted to dig it up, she would find people to dig. If they found anything, whether much or little, Wolkenstainer said that they would divide it in four parts: the first for the infirmary, the second for other poor people, the third for those who do the digging, and the fourth should go to [Koch] because it was her house. Then if [Koch] wished to honor the two women by giving them something from her part, they would take it thankfully, and would not keep it, but give it to the poor. So she allowed them to dig. But she didn't put any store in it, and was not at all afraid or concerned that they were doing anything wrong, since it was on her property.

7. **What were they looking for or hoping to find there?** Wolkenstainer said there was a pot of money there, and that's what they were looking for.

8. **Were she and the two women from Nuremberg there while they were digging?** The tall woman from Nuremberg [Sophia Voit] was present at the digging, but Wolkenstainer and Koch stayed in the parlor. They occasionally looked out the window, but they didn't go out where they were digging.

9. **Who was the priest or man who was there in the garden while they were digging?** She doesn't know the priest or man who was there, and also doesn't know if a priest was there at all. More than one man was there and she doesn't know them. She only heard them call one of them Meichsner, and one Nessle.

10. **Who called for this priest for this business, and where did he come from? 11. Did she not have burning wax or candles there? 12. Were these candles blessed, or were they just simple candles? And who provided them? 13. Did the priest and one of the women read out of a book in the hole, and make a cross, as well as say a blessing or a magic spell? 14. What was in the little pitcher that the woman had in the hole, and then gave back to the maid? 15. Was it holy water, and where did they get it?** To questions 10, 11, 12, 13, 14, and 15 she says she doesn't know anything about these things.

16. **What single and married men came in and out of her house with these two women? She should name them by name. 17. What did these people have to do with these women, and especially with the one? 18. Who arranged for them to come there?** To 16, 17, and 18 she says there were neither single nor married men with these women in her house or going in and out. . . .

19. What men bathed in her house with them? No one took a bath with the two women in her house. . . .

20. The fact is that these women, and especially the tall one, committed disrespectable, sinful acts in her house. She should say with whom this occurred. Neither of these women, either the tall one or the other one, did anything disrespectable or sinned in her house, and she did not allow it. . . .

[Tortured with thumbscrews, Koch admits nothing more.]

Statement by Koch's neighbor Walburga Thennin, butcher's wife

On Monday morning at 4:00 AM, she saw the women that she didn't know come out of the shed. One of them had a book in her hands and read from it. Then the village priest also came and read from a book. The strange woman's servant made a circle with a drawn sword, in which the woman sprinkled water with a little aspergillum, just as if it were holy water, and afterward made four lines in the circle with a hoe. More than two hours later, a man with a yellow beard brought a little girl out of the house, and said something in her ear. The girl said something back to him, and then walked with him around the garden. . . . She doesn't know anything else to say in response to the other questions, except that she heard that the priest is from Täfertingen.

Interrogation of Hans Meichsner, cabinetmaker

On Saturday the last of May, 1544, [Hans Meichsner] was interrogated with the accompanying questions, and testified as follows:

1. What were they doing at Regina Koch's house the other day? 2. Who called them there, and why? 1., 2. Wolkenstainer, his sister-in-law, told him twenty years ago that there was a treasure in this house where Koch now lives. She came to him last week with another woman, who was here for that reason, and asked if he would help them dig for it, and if he knew anyone else who would also help. He said he would help dig, and that he has a good friend who would also help, Jorg Nessle. So they went to Koch's house and started digging.

3. What were the women from Nuremberg, in particular the tall one, doing in the garden there? He doesn't know what the two women did, but he, Meichsner, and those who were digging with him first said an Our Father, a Confession of Faith, and some psalms. And afterward they didn't need to talk anymore, but just dug. Wolkenstainer didn't come out to where they were digging, but stayed in the parlor. But the tall woman was in the circle.

4. Who was the priest with them at the digging, and what did he do? The priest from Täfertingen, whose name was Hans, was there. He had a censer with glowing coals and spread smoke, and occasionally read out of a little book. He doesn't know what it was.

5. Who else was there at the digging and the related goings-on? Jorg Nessle, shoemaker; Claus Schmid, a weaver; Koch's landlord; a peasant who was named Pangratz; and Hansel Koch were digging.

6. What and how much did they receive as compensation or pay for this digging? He didn't get paid anything for it, but if they had found anything, he would have turned down his part.

7. Who else, male or female, comes and goes from Koch's house for disreputable reasons? He doesn't know of any disreputable behavior in Koch's house. He neither saw nor heard of any.

PUNISHMENT RECORDS

May 29, 1544: Sophia Voit and Otilia Wolkenstainer of Nuremberg brought a village priest, a young girl, and several men to Regina Koch Mauerin's house, and Sophia Voit made a circle or ring, went around it with candles, then took a naked sword from a young man and marked a spot with it where they should dig. Afterward, she sat in the circle, stuck a cross or crucifix in the grass and lay a little cloth over it, and read out of a little book. The above-noted village priest also sat there and read from a little book, and both made crosses and magic signs. In sum, they were digging for treasure, and in perpetrating this superstitious act they seriously abused the name and word of God. Therefore they were called before an Honorable Council and told to leave the city immediately upon this oral order, and never to come back without the permission of an Honorable Council. Two bailiffs were also sent with them to the place where they were lodging, and waited until they got on [the cart] and left.

Regina Koch housed Sophia Voit and Otilia Wolkenstainer from Nuremberg without reporting them, in violation of an Honorable Council's statute and command. She also allowed them to dig for treasure in her garden without the knowledge of the authorities, and thereby to practice all kinds of devilish spookery and superstitious works. Therefore she was put in an Honorable Council's jail, but was released upon a plea, and was given a good talking to in the presence of the council.

And because Hans Meichsner; Jorg Nessler, shoemaker; Claus Schmidt, weaver; and Jorg Weber, otherwise known as Little Jorg, all helped with this devilish spookery and treasure hunting, Hans Meichsner (as the one who encouraged and incited the others to dig) was mercifully punished with eight days and nights in a tower, and the others with four days. This they pledged before the council to fulfill, and they also pledged to request a representative to take them up and down from the tower.

9.3 A Case of Possession from the Chronicle of Paul Hector Mair, 1563[8]

A possessed woman, whom the Evil One led out through the window.

The tailor [Michael] Kacheloffen's wife [Katharina] had for some time been regularly assailed by the Evil One. This she did not report to anyone, keeping it secretly all to herself, until she was finally completely possessed and severely tormented, and was brought into despair. And on Wednesday, the 7th of April, during the night, her husband and also her mother were with her, and were watching over her in the parlor. But when the little child who was lying in the cradle in the bedchamber began to cry, the mother left the parlor to attend to the child. When she returned to the parlor, her daughter was not on the bed. They searched for her all over the house and couldn't find her anywhere. Then they found an upper window open in the parlor, and they saw that she was lying below on the street, for the Evil One had led her out of the window. When they got down to her, she was covered in blood, and her mouth was also wide open and the tongue pulled far out of it, but she wasn't yet dead. Then she raised her hand up toward heaven. There are different versions of this story.

9.4 The Case of Thomas Trummer, Amateur Sorcerer, 1577[9]

First interrogation

On Friday, the 8th of February, 1577, Thomas Trummer, [cloth-shearer], testified willingly and under threat to the accompanying interrogation as follows:

---

8. *Das Diarium Paul Hector Mairs von 1560–1563*, 208–9. In CDS vol. 33 (1928).

9. StadtAA, Urgicht Thomas Trummer, February 8–11, 1577.

1. Was he not in Regensburg last summer, and when? To the first question he responds, he was in Regensburg around St. Bartholomew's Day.

2. What business did he have there, and where else did he travel to, and who with him? He went from Straubing to Regensburg, where he spent a day or two. And otherwise, a person who called himself Leonhard Endorffer from Moosburg, and who told him that he had injured his sister-in-law, traveled with him from Straubing to Ingolstadt. Outside of Regensburg, a boy who called himself Lang from Dinkelsbühl joined them on the road, and went with them.

3. Does he know someone called Leonhard Seier, who is from Moosburg? That would be the above-named Endorffer, who also claimed to be the cousin of Lord Endorffer here.[10]

4. What kinds of deeds did he perpetrate with this Leonhard? He didn't do anything untoward with [Leonhard]. He only wrote letters for him at his request, to [Leonhard's] wife and to the city of Moosburg.

5. Since he bragged to him and to others about all kinds of arts [i.e., spells, charms], he should testify what kind of arts these are, where he practiced them, and what he achieved through them. They are all kinds of arts that he collected and wrote down, to help someone who is bewitched by malicious people, or otherwise is robbed of his manhood. And his wife threw some of these books into the fire when he got home.

6. Was he not in Passau around St. Bartholomew's Day, and what business he had there? Around Easter time he was with a nobleman called Heinrich Gotsberger down in Passau, who had a son with one ear that was rather defective, and he helped him get somewhat better. He stayed with them there for about a month.

7. It is known that he took all kinds of parts from [an executed criminal] who was on the wheel at the place of execution. So he should describe these in detail, and explain what he used them for, or it will be brought out of him by the executioner. During the night he took a finger from the person on the wheel and the rope with which he was tied. There was one other person with him, who called himself Erhart N. and was a linen weaver by trade, at Hals near Passau. Erhart knocked out two chips from the wheel and one or two from the gallows, and gave him one of them. He didn't do anything with them. He only heard that these things are good for gambling and shooting and such.

---

10. A member of an important local patrician family in Augsburg.

8. He should describe in detail what all is in the little green box that was found in his house. He doesn't know of any little green box; he can't remember.

9. Where did he get the hair and other objects? Testifies that some hair was cut from his child a while back, which was somewhat curly, and was kept in a little box in his wife's trunk. He doesn't know of anything else. Otherwise there were also some umbilical cords from babies that his wife also saved.

10. What kind of sorcery did he practice with these and other objects? He has not practiced any sorcery.

11. In his little book one finds spells for conjuring evil spirits and other magical arts, thus one wants to know when and where he has practiced this, and what he perpetrated by this means. He did not practice these arts, he was just having fun writing them down and reading them.

12. Because he well knows that such sorcery is not only inappropriate for a Christian but also forbidden on pain of punishment on life and limb, how did he expect to get away with this without being caught and punished? He has not harmed or hurt anyone with his arts. Begs for mercy.

Second interrogation

On Monday, the 11th of February, 1577, Thomas Trummer, [cloth-shearer], testified as follows in response to the accompanying questions, and being presented with a little box:

1. Does this little box not belong to him? Upon presentation of the little green box, he testifies that it belongs to him.

2. What is all of that which lies inside? He should describe it individually, piece by piece. No. 1 is, as far as he knows, a white hellebore. No. 2 are chicory roots, which are used in place of a wound blessing.[11] No. 3 is myrrh. No. 4 is a piece of the wheel or gallows, along with a needle with which a dead person was sewn up in a shroud. No. 5 is a wound blessing, and this he wrote himself. No. 6 are umbilical cords and cauls from newborn children.[12] No. 7 is hair that his wife cut from his newborn child, about which he already spoke. The other hair that is

---

11. A blessing or spell used to cure wounds.

12. Babies' cauls (i.e., the amnion or inner membrane enclosing the fetus when it remains on the baby's head at birth, resembling a cap) were traditionally understood as a good omen and were also associated with magical spells.

in the box he assumes is from his deceased mother, and his wife could presumably explain about that.

3. What did he use these things for, in particular so many different kinds of hair? He would do better to provide the reason without torture than with. He has never used it for wrongdoing.

4. For what did he use the finger and the piece of rope that he took from the man exposed upon the wheel in Passau? 5. Where did he put this finger and piece of rope, and also the splinters from the wheel and the gallows? He wanted to use them for gambling, but afterward lost them while drunk.

6. It is known that he has long practiced such magical arts, therefore he should say where, when, and how, and what all he has achieved with them? He did nothing evil with it.

7. What did he perpetrate with Leonhard of Moosburg and Lang from Dinkelsbühl? He did not perpetrate anything with them.

8. Has he not been involved in treasure hunting, and where and when? The district officer of Osterhofen summoned him because of a treasure, and while he was there, [the district officer] took him to Siebeneichen and said that there was a trunk with money in a forest. And when he had taken a look, he advised [the district officer] that there was nothing there.

9. Whom he has harmed or cheated with his arts and sorcery, how and by what means? No one, and nobody would be able to complain of him for this.

[There is no record of punishment for this case.]

9.5 Catharina Bretzler, Herbalist and Seller of Charms, 1590[13]

On Monday, the 2nd of July, 1590, Catharina Bretzler, earnestly threatened, responded without torture to the accompanying interrogation as follows:

1. What is her name, from where, and how old is she? Her [maiden] name is Catharina Pausinger, born in Rangendingen. She traveled around in the countryside with her parents, who were peddlers. Now she is the wife of Ulrich Bretzler, soldier and local citizen. In the Peasants' War she was ten years old [i.e., she is about seventy-six], and

---

13. StadtAA, Urgicht Catharina Bretzelerin, July 2, 1590; Strafbuch 1588–1596, 78v.

she has had a household for forty-seven years, namely in the beginning with Besti Ruep, lute-maker from Mundingen near Ehingen, for ten years; with Hans Schwartz, armament-maker from the Rhine Valley, for sixteen years; with Caspar Asperger, soldier, for several years; with Jacob Rinninger from Burlafingen for twenty-two years; and now with Ulrich Bretzler for around sixteen years. This however exceeds the first number she gave. Upon being questioned about this, she testified that she may be wrong, but she knows her age and that she has had a household for forty-seven years.

2. What does she do for a living? She supports herself with spinning, because her husband has been sent to Innsbruck. But where he is now, she doesn't know.

3. Has she not taken it upon herself to cure people, and to help them with their illnesses? Says yes.

4. What people has she taken on for treatment, and what kind of illnesses they were? The wife of Urban Moll, the civic guard, brought a gunsmith from Smithy Lane to her about three or four weeks ago. He was a single fellow who looked about twenty-seven or twenty-eight years old. He told her that he was so weak in his limbs that he couldn't walk, and said that a crystal gazer told him that it had been done to him by malicious people. If this were true (she said to him), then she would (pardon the expression) bathe him with herbs.

She treated a little boy of seven three years ago, the son of the potter at the Hofstatt, because he had great pain in his limbs, which she held for the cold flux.

About four years ago she treated the daughter of the head mason on the Lech in Lechhausen (she doesn't know whom he works for). [This daughter] was pregnant and was gleaning grain in the field, and according to what she said, she crossed evil footprints, which caused such a swelling on her body that other people thought her kidneys were hanging out of her body. But as soon as [Bretzler] saw it, she knew better. Based on the sick person's description, she held it instead for something caused by bewitchment.

About a half year ago she healed the innkeeper Huldenreich's daughter, named Christina, on the hand from something one could not see, but only caused her great pain. This she took to be caused by bewitchment, as other people supposedly told her. Otherwise she has also healed animals here and there. She doesn't remember any other sick people, but if any more occur to her she will gladly report it.

5. What ingredients has she used for her cures and medicines? She has used only herbs, namely nightshade, greater chicory, ribwort chicory, chamomile, red beech, willow shoots, oak leaves, pine cones, pine chips, haircap, and birch and poplar and alderberry wood. She boiled them and put them in a tub, and then heated up flint stones like blacksmiths use, which she added to the boiled herbs so that the tub was warmed and made a sweat bath (pardon the expression). Otherwise she has used no salves, powders, or anything else in the world, and also never provided anything to ingest or said any blessings, as truly as God made her.

6. Did she not recently tell Daniel Endris that he should let her help him, or it would cost him his life, claiming that his affliction comes from malicious people? She did not do this. He was the one who came to her and said that he didn't know what was going on with him; he is so weak in his limbs that he can't work. And he said that he once had an injury on his loins and is afraid that it hasn't gone away. So she answered, "Some people may not have been happy to see him and his wife get together at first." He said, "Indeed, they didn't like it." And she said, "God protect us, the Devil can do a lot. If you have an evil suspicion, or are afraid of something, then I will give you a pouch of herbs that you can hang around the neck or sew into a doublet, whichever you prefer, and the vermin will have to leave you in peace." Endris asked what it would cost, and she said it would cost a gulden. He said he would ask his wife. Then he came back, and she loaned him 11 gulden to buy linen yarn, and he again brought up the subject of the above-noted herbs. She then said that if he doesn't believe in it, or doesn't have faith in her and in God in heaven, he should stay away from it, for she doesn't like it when she advises someone and it doesn't help. Thereupon he asked her for the herbs, which she gave him, and he paid for them with 1 gulden.

7. Did she not offer to help Endris for money? He is doing her wrong. She didn't do this, which she denies vehemently.

8. Because she said among other things that two women who live on his street did this to him, she should say who these women are, and what they are called, and how she knows this? This she also denies.

9. Did she not also tell Endris' wife that malicious people had also killed her previous husband, Martin Schlichting? 10. Did she not also say that if Endris doesn't go along, then his wife will come to a sixth husband? 11. How does she know all of this? She claims innocence throughout; this is not true and she's being wronged.

12. Did she not then put a cross-shaped key into a book and say some words over it, and cause the key and the book to move around? This she did, she admits it.

13. How did this happen, and what did she use and say to do it? She should describe it in detail and truthfully. After the incident explained above, Endris came back and wanted a second pouch with herbs, for he had thrown the first one away. She wasn't happy about this, and said that if it didn't help, he should have brought it back to her, and she would have given him his money back. For once the vermin have settled on a person, they won't let up if one doesn't take the cure, and throws it away. This will only make them stronger. So she didn't want to give him another one. He said his wife and lad[14] talked him into throwing it away. Then she offered to lay out the herbs for them, so they could see what they were. The wife and lad thus asked to see it for themselves. But the lad said to Endris (according to what Endris said), "If you go out to her, she'll just gaze into her crystal," although she doesn't have one, and doesn't know what it is. Upon that she showed him a book that was given her by a soldier named Peter Heberle, who had been the comrade of the current Lord Bailiff when they were in the Netherlands. According to Heberle, it's supposed to be the Old Testament, although she herself can't read or write. She laid a cross-shaped key in it, and didn't say anything but "In the name of God the Father God the Son and the Holy Spirit," and didn't use anything else. And upon these words, the book and the key moved around.

14. Did she not wish to give the impression that Endris' illness came from malicious people? Yes, and one is supposed to be able to tell by this book whether illness comes from malicious people or not, and if the malicious people will yield or let a person go or not. She laid the key on the place in the book where there is a picture of a monk, which is supposed to be St. John the Evangelist. And if the book moves around, then it's a sign that it is the result of malicious people, and that they won't let go of him. But if it doesn't move around, then it's not malicious people, or they leave him. That's what the above-noted Heberle told her.

15. Didn't she give Endris two pouches to hang around his neck, for which he had to pay 2 gulden? Says as above. She gave Endris only one but also gave one to his wife, each for 1 gulden.

16. What was in these pouches? She should report everything. The following herbs were in them, namely nightshade; St. John's Wort; pine cones; two sedge roots, male and female; haircap; greater chicory; ribwort chicory; alderberry wood; and a little bread, and a little salt, as much as one can pinch between two fingers, as one does for food.

---

14. Someone who works for Endris (*Knecht*); it is not clear if this is a servant, apprentice, or journeyman.

17. Did she not at the same time advise Endris to sell his bed-stead, or if he didn't want to do so, she would put some herbs in it? Says yes.

18. Because she claimed among other things that if she were to help Endris, she would have to unlock a lot of doors, and it would shock a lot of people, she should say what she meant by this, and what she was planning to do? She honestly didn't say that. This is not true and she is being wronged. . . .

19. What was the letter that she showed to Endris, with which she wanted to show him how long his affliction would have lasted if he hadn't thrown away the pouch that he got from her? That's not how it happened; rather, she had a calendar with the signs of the zodiac lying on her trunk. And when Endris saw it, he asked what kind of letter it was, and she answered that it is a calendar on which are the twelve signs, from which one can find out what planet a baby is born under.

20. Did she not then say that if she holds this letter against the sun, morning and evening, she can see right away what kind of good and bad fortune a person has? He is lying (pardon the expression) like a desperate rogue, thief, and villain, and is doing her injury and wrong. An Honorable Council can see and judge by this what kind of frivolous person this Endris is, in whom one cannot put much faith. She can upon the loss of her blessed soul affirm and prove that when Endris once wanted to leave his wife and children, but she warned him against it, reminding him of the oath that he swore to his wife in the church when they were blessed, he said that an oath is no more important than a pretzel stick. . . .

24. Did she not . . . claim that she has a fumewort,[15] and who gave it to her? Says yes, she bought it for half a gulden in the house of a clockmaker on Saxon Lane who is supposed to be called Marquart. She purchased it from a saleswoman who was selling the household goods, along with several babies' cauls, which were all in a box together.[16] She also bought a book on herbs there for 1 gulden . . . for she had heard all her life that cauls are lucky. . . .

[Bretzler was interrogated three more times and tortured both on the rack and the strappado. She consistently denied using witchcraft, consorting with the Devil, or knowingly using magical arts, and also denied

15. A plant commonly used in magical spells, including treasure hunting.

16. The clockmaker's widow Maria Marquart had been banished only the year before for activities similar to Bretzler's. Apparently the tools of her forbidden trade were sold off by an intermediary along with the rest of her property.

knowing anyone else who practiced witchcraft to cause harm. During the interrogations she also described obtaining information about her patients from a crystal gazer, reiterated her belief in the positive energy of cauls, noted that bad luck can be brought to a house by burying a skull in it, and explained that she had learned to make her herbal mixtures by observing the medical practice of Master Veit, the executioner, when he was treating her for pain that she believed to be the result of "malicious people." Although she insisted on her own belief in the effectiveness of her cures, her motivation for applying them, she ultimately admitted, was money.]

Punishment record

August 21, 1590: Catharina Pausinger or Bretzler, wife of Ulrich Bretzler, soldier and local citizen, came into the jail on suspicion of witchcraft and magic. Although she in no way admitted to practicing magic, nonetheless her statement reveals that she has shamefully cheated many people out of their property under the pretense of all kinds of [forbidden] arts. Therefore, an Honorable Council decided on this date that, after she returns the money to those whom she has aggrieved, she should be released, but forever banished from the city and its territories, and also escorted out of town.

9.6 A Love Potion Leads to Adultery, 1590[17]

September 1, 1590: Anna Rhemin or Mozart, wife of Leonhardt Mozart the baker and local citizen, on the advice of [Maria Dorenerin], placed a pouch under the straw mattress of her servant, Leonhard Federle from Binswangen, with the intent of winning his love. Thus the two also committed adultery numerous times, and Federle complained that he lost his manhood with other women. Both were therefore arrested. And on this date, an Honorable Council decreed that (Anna) Mozart should be released upon a pledge that she will appear again if requested. But Federle should be notified that he should seek his fortune elsewhere.

[Leonhard Federle was pardoned and let back into the city on February 6, 1592.]

May 2, 1591: Maria Dorenerin from Augsburg, wife of carpenter and local citizen Veit Obermaier, has for a long time been crystal gazing in

17. StadtAA, Strafbuch 1588–1596, 80r, 109v.

order to recover lost things. She also gave a baker's wife some herbs with instructions to slip them under [the mattress of] her servant, and she would win his love, which resulted in the servant and the baker's wife committing fornication and adultery several times. She was therefore arrested, and on this date banished forever from the city and its realm.

9.7 Elisabeth Rormoser, Seamstress and Finder of Lost Things, 1592[18]

On Monday, December 14, 1592, Elisabeth Rormoser responded to the accompanying questions under earnest threat as follows:

What is her name, and where is she from? Her name is Elisabeth Rormoser; she is a local citizen.

What does she do for a living? She is a seamstress and that is how she supports herself.

Did she not claim to be a fortune-teller, and take money from people to give them information about stolen things? She did not claim to be a fortune-teller, although it is true that she purports to be able to help people retrieve stolen things. This she does only by praying, which happens like this: She kneels on a grave, and prays, "All Christian souls, I exhort you by the power and the authority of the Almighty that you allow the thief neither peace nor rest until he returns to the people that which he has taken from them, in the name of God the Father, God the Son, and God the Holy Spirit." Then she prays again, "Jesus was lost, Jesus was found again. God and his five holy wounds help me find the things again." Then she prays three Our Fathers, three Creeds, and three Ave Marias. When this is done, she doesn't do anything else, and a lot of them were helped by it.

For whom has she told fortunes, and what was she given for it each time? She used the above prayer for Jeremias Zolling's son-in-law in Jacob's Suburb, but because he didn't get back what was stolen from him, he charged her before the Punishment Lords and she was arrested. Otherwise, for praying at the churchyard in Lechhausen three mornings in a row, Zolling's son-in-law gave her 15 kreuzer the first time, 3 batzen the second time, again 3 batzen the third time, and the last time 6 kreuzer.

Doesn't she know that this sort of fortune-telling is forbidden? Why then does she not refrain from doing it? She does know that

---

18. StadtAA, Urgicht Elisabeth Rormoser, December 14, 1592; Strafbuch 1588–1596, 161r.

telling fortunes is forbidden, but she is no fortune-teller. She also didn't think that she would be suspected of being one due to the above-noted prayers.

How did she intend to get away with this without penalty? What she did was out of ignorance. Requests mercy.

[Rormoser was banished from the city, then pardoned three months later upon her family's guarantee that they would support her.]

Chapter Ten
Dealing with War and Catastrophe

For many Europeans who lived during and after the Reformation, God's vengeance must have appeared very real indeed. The sixteenth and seventeenth centuries were beset with a series of natural and man-made circumstances that challenged the faith and the problem-solving capacity of Europe's populace. An attack of plague, a poor harvest, or the changing fortunes of war could send an entire city into chaos and mourning. Coinciding as they did with the social, religious, and psychic turmoil of this period of transition, such catastrophes, whether natural or manmade, often appeared to the people of Europe as evidence that the final Day of Judgment was at hand. After all, they already seemed to be facing daily the four horsemen of the Apocalypse, who were prophesied in the biblical book of Revelation as harbingers of war, famine, disease, and death.

Early modern folk did not consider themselves helpless in the face of such uncertainty, however. Preparing their souls for Judgment Day was only one of the ways in which they dealt with crisis. Whether by storing grain in anticipation of bad harvests, by calling for increased shows of collective piety, by making improvements in defensive weaponry and tactics, by casting spells or saying prayers, or by annihilating those they viewed as the enemies of God, early modern rulers and their people drew upon all of the weapons they had at hand to solve the problems of disease, hunger, war, and bad weather.

Outbreaks of contagious disease had always been a problem, one that would not be solved during the early modern period. Considerable advances were made, however, in the realm of public health. New attitudes toward treating disease came about largely in response to new diseases, beginning with the so-called Black Death (bubonic plague), which swept through Europe for the first time in the mid-fourteenth century. After two centuries of dealing with periodic outbreaks of this virulent killer, another new disease appeared on the European scene toward the end of the fifteenth century that was particularly well suited for a moral response. Syphilis, in Germany called the "evil pox" or the "French disease," appears to have entered Germany at the end of the fifteenth century with French troops returning from war in Italy. By now accustomed to isolating plague victims and lepers, cities moved quickly to establish "pox houses" to house and treat victims of syphi-lis, a measure that combined protection of the general populace with charitable provision for the sick. Europeans quickly understood that the pox resulted from sex, which naturally increased the tendency to view it as punishment from God for the sins of the flesh. Yet syphilis was not unique in being interpreted in this way. Early modern theorists under-stood all epidemics as moral and spiritual problems, so that responses to outbreaks of plague, smallpox, tuberculosis, influenza, and other deadly contagions invariably included appeals for general shows of piety as well as medical treatments.

Periods of famine and inflation also led to calls for penance to turn away God's wrath. In an economy that produced little excess, one poor harvest or an unstable political situation could lead to spiraling infla-tion, and two bad years in a row could plunge a region into famine. The early modern world was particularly vulnerable to crop failure because of the unstable weather conditions associated with the so-called Little Ice Age of the later sixteenth century and the seventeenth century, dur-ing which temperatures were lower than average and storms more fre-quent. The combination of darker skies and periods of famine provided theologians with additional evidence of God's anger. At the same time, because hunger led to instability, the more pragmatic civic governments also took more worldly measures to protect their citizens from hunger, including storing grain for distribution during difficult times. The price controls and attacks on usury covered in previous chapters were also aimed at controlling inflation.

The problems of disease and famine could be exacerbated by war. War also brought death in more direct forms through military attacks, which, like the plague, could appear to choose victims randomly, as a result of either the whim of fate or the hand of God. Many admo-nitions to clean living cited military losses to the Turks, understood as the enemy of Christendom and God's ultimate scourge. Along with prayer, military weapons were naturally also employed to defend against attacks, and while most towns hired professional guards to protect the gates and walls, primary responsibility for local defense rested on the citizenry. The civic oath taken by every male citizen thus included not only a pledge of obedience to authority but also expressions of loyalty to the town and its other residents and a promise specifically to protect the community from harm. In order to fulfill requirements for collec-tive defense, all male citizens were bound by their oath of citizenship to maintain appropriate weapons and armor, to provide men for the night watch, and to respond armed and ready in any emergency.

The fact that defense duties were shared between civilian guards and professional soldiers could lead to tension, even during periods of relative peace. As we have seen in Chapters One and Two, local citizens often viewed decisions by the authorities to increase local troop strength by hiring noncitizens as threatening. Things could go from bad to worse in wartime, when larger numbers of troops were garrisoned in the city. During the sixteenth and seventeenth centuries, soldiers typically supported themselves by exacting food, shelter, and contributions (i.e., special wartime taxes) from the local populace, or by resorting to plunder. In order to prevent the latter, early modern people periodically faced having soldiers forcibly quartered in their homes. Normally, the households in which soldiers were quartered had to provide provisions, usually in the form of food and supplies, but sometimes also as cash contributions. Officers typically chose the comfort of a public house rather than a private home, in which case the publican might hope to obtain some compensation for the visit from the military man's regiment, usually also financed by extracting contributions from the populace. Either way, the presence of soldiers in the city was always a burden to the local population.

During the cruelest phases of the Thirty Years' War, many cities and villages of Germany faced all of these scourges at once. No wonder, then, that the height of the witch persecutions occurred during this period, as both populace and authority sought an explanation and a solution for the problem at hand. Whether the difficulties of the seventeenth century were the result of God's wrath or the work of Satan's minions, many believed that destroying enemies of Christianity could only have a positive effect. The result was not only an increase in fear of witches and other invisible enemies but also increased confessional division, as each faith blamed the other for the wrongs of the world.

Only after thirty years of violence and bitter confessional repression did the war-weary empire establish a diplomatic peace with the Treaty of Westphalia in 1648, which brought few changes to the map but ushered in a new and more stable political order. Catholics, Lutherans, and Calvinists were granted the right to worship, with state religions again being determined by local sovereigns under the principle of *cuius regio, eius religio* (first established by the Peace of Augsburg in 1555).[1] Other religious confessions remained illegal. Augsburg's system of enforced religious parity within all government offices ensured that in the future, neither of the city's dominant religions would suffer oppression at the

---

1. See Chapter Two.

hand of the other. For Augsburg and the other cities of the empire, the age of religious war was at an end.

I. Weather and Inflation

10.1 The Effects of Inflation from the Perspective of Brewer Georg Siedler[2]

1520
This year barley cost 8, 9, or 10 gulden, so that one had to sell the small measure [of beer], which was around two or three quarts,[3] for 1 heller. And the price of yeast was negotiated at 14 pfennig in the summer, and 12 pfennig in winter.

1523
In this year, because barley kept going up in price, the summer price for yeast was 16 pfennig and the winter price 12 pfennig. And the large measure of beer was again sold for 1 pfennig.

1524
Because in this year barley was selling for 5, 6, or 7 gulden, but hops were very expensive, the small measure of beer was again sold for 1 heller, and the yeast priced at 14 pfennig in summer and 12 in winter. And because there was such a great shortage and inflation in the price of hops this year, the [brewing] craft bought 106 schaff of hops for 2 gulden 7 kreuzer 1 pfennig per schaff, and distributed it for 3 gulden per schaff to those in the craft who requested it.[4]

1528
Storm on St. Peter's Day and inflation: On St. Peter and Paul's Day [June 29] there was such a terrible storm that it completely destroyed all

---

2. StadtAA, Chroniken 20, Chronik von Siedler, 1055–1619, 3Cr–v, 212r, 283v; Kümin and Tlusty, *Public Drinking in the Early Modern World* 2 (London, 2011): 473–74.

3. The amount comprising a "measure" of beer or wine varied considerably from place to place and from time to time. In Augsburg during the sixteenth century, a measure was probably around 1.05 liters, and thus a small measure (as described here) between half and three quarters of a liter.

4. This was standard practice, and Siedler recorded similar distributions on several other occasions during the sixteenth century. A schaff is a unit of measure consisting of around 161 kilos or 214 liters, with some variation.

of the fruits of the field in a wide area. This was followed by a period
of great inflation. Then the next year, in 1529, there was again such a
monstrous storm on St. Peter's Day that it destroyed everything on the
road up to Weringen, and tore the trees out of the ground by their roots.
So there was no relief from the inflation.

1531
In this year the small measure [of beer] was again done away with, and
one had to sell the large measure for 1 pfennig. And an Honorable
Council established the summer price [of yeast] at 18 pfennig and the
winter price at 11 pfennig. This the brewers did not want to accept,
claiming that they could not do it without losing money, for barley was
constantly going up in price, so they would rather be idle than brew.
A number of members of the council were appointed to settle the matter, but they didn't really want to get on with it, so it took some time.
And the Lords insisted that the brewers keep brewing, which they were
forced to do without any relief. In the following year of 1532 nothing
changed, and [the brewers] were put off with only a promise of relief.
This went on for a long time. And in all this time the only thing they
did was to decree on July 13 that all of the yeast should be brought
to one cellar to be measured by people appointed by the council. And
four brewers, namely the elder and younger Michael Ried, Leonhardt
Stimber, and Ambrose Schmid, were locked in the irons because they
complained somewhat harshly to the guild master Claus Mair that this
was too hard for them.

1598. Inflation falls upon Augsburg
Because of sin, as set forth in the Scripture, humans are subject to all
kinds of misery, want, and danger, as well as, finally, to death. So in
this current year of 1598, along with many other different kinds of well-
deserved punishments and plagues, God visited upon us his chastisement in the form of crushing inflation, and especially grains (which
because of the storm varied extremely in price one from another) rose so
much in price that the best spelt cost 9 to 10 gulden, and the rest 5 to
6 gulden; wheat was 5, 6, and up to 8 gulden; rye, 6, 7, and 8 gulden;
barley, 5 to 6 gulden; oats, 2½ to 3 gulden.

1602. Wine inflation
That God punishes harshly the abuse of his gifts, we can see by the
example in this year of 1602. For wine not only rose in price here in
Augsburg from 10 to 17 and 18 kreuzer, but it got so expensive in all

parts of the German Nation, even in the wine-growing country, that it didn't just go up in price by half again, rather went up four or five times.

10.2 Inflation (Augsburg, c. 1621) (Illustration)

Inflation (*A New Riddle*), Augsburg, c. 1621. The answer to the riddle posed in this broadsheet is money, which is without voice or feeling, yet travels throughout the world in great honor; which cannot walk or move, but is always climbing upward; and which is in great demand although its only power is to dirty the hands of those who desire it. In the image, the greedy financier at the bottom of the ladder sends his "children" soaring ever higher, enriching his own treasury at the expense of the peasant, craftsman, and merchant in the foreground. By permission of the Herzog August Bibliothek, Wolfenbüttel: (IE 187).

10.3 Satan Causes a Storm, 1586 (Illustration)

News from Ghent (storm attributed to Satan), Augsburg, 1586. SuStBA, S Einblattdr. nach 1500, Nr. 2. By permission of the Staats- und Stadtbibliothek Augsburg.

II. Plague

10.4 Andreas Osiander: A Sermon Based on the Ninety-First Psalm, c. 1534: How and to Where a Christian Should Flee the Terrible Scourge of the Plague[5]

Because the almighty God is afflicting and chastising this region with the terrible, dreadful scourge of plague, and as a result many people are so unduly horrified that . . . all works of love that Christians are bound to show to one another, no less than to Christ himself, are being dangerously ignored. . . . I find it useful and necessary under these circumstances to share with you, dear ones, a brief instruction and solace from the holy Scriptures, [namely] the Ninety-First Psalm, which says:

5. Andreas Osiander, *Ain Predig auss dem 91. Psalm / Wie / vnnd wohin / ain Christ / von der grausamen plag der Pestilentz fliehen soll* ([Augsburg], c. 1534).

He that dwelleth in the secret place of the Most High shall abide under the shadow of the Almighty. I will say of Jehovah, He is my refuge and my fortress; My God, in whom I trust. For he will deliver thee from the snare of the fowler, And from the deadly pestilence. . . . Thou shalt not be afraid for the terror by night, Nor for the arrow that flieth by day; For the pestilence that walketh in darkness, Nor for the destruction that wasteth at noonday.

Before, then, we try to understand these comforting words, dear ones, you should first know that it is not my intention to advise anyone in these terrible times against fleeing, or getting medical help, or avoiding dangerous places and ill people, as long as it is not in violation of one's faith or God's commandments, nor of one's vocation, nor contrary to neighborly love. For although some claim that this plague hits only those that God orders it to, for which there are several examples in the holy Scripture . . . one can also respond, "My dear, even if that's the way it happened in those times and those places, who can assure us that this is always the case in all other deadly scourges?" Therefore, I will leave that alone for now, along with all other natural things that we are capable of understanding and over which we are commanded to govern, and won't interfere [with medical opinion]. At the same time, however, I am eager to offer to those Christians who are unable to flee because of their office, their poverty, or for other honorable reasons, the best and greatest comfort there is.

Likewise, I do not wish to engage in a dispute with those who speak of this in natural terms, and say that such plagues may come from the influence of the stars, from the effect of comets, from unusual weather conditions and changes in the atmosphere, from south winds, from stinking water, or from noxious vapors out of the earth. For we do not wish to spurn their wisdom or fight against it; rather, as Christians, we want to abide by the word of God, [in whose wisdom] we will find much greater and more certain advice: To wit, that this terrible scourge of the plague is the result of God's wrath at our contempt and violation of his holy commandments. . . . For even if the above-noted natural causes also have something to do with it, it is certain and without doubt that these causes are also the result of God's wrath at our sins and ingratitude. . . .

So we can find the true cause of this terrible pestilence in the word of God, namely, that our sins of lack of faith, disobedience, and ingratitude are at fault. If we want to be protected and saved from this horrible plague, then, it is necessary above all that we turn away from these sins, repent, and improve our lives. . . . [For] then he will also turn away from his wrath, and mercifully spare us from this terrible chastisement, along with the other heavy burdens from which we now suffer, such as war and inflation. For as St. Paul says, 1 Cor. 11: "For if we would judge ourselves, we should not be judged. But when we are judged, we are chastened by the Lord, that we should not be condemned with the world."

And from all of this, my dears, you can well imagine how unwise and unchristian those people are who greatly sin against God's commandment, out of irreverent fear of this plague, and leave their calling and office or refuse to show their neighbor the love, help, and loyalty that God's commandment requires of them. This is certain only to incite all the more anger from God, so that he will attack them more vehemently and do away with them. For one keeps hearing that some people are not only afraid of the sick and flee from them but also flee from those who are well. Even more ridiculous, they are afraid of bowls and pitchers from other peoples' houses, as if they contained certain death. And out of such misguided, childish fear, people not only leave sick people to die without any care, help, and comfort but also leave pregnant women alone in childbirth, or don't come to them in the first place. One even hears that children leave their parents, and one spouse abandons the other, and doesn't show them the love that one would like to see oneself if lying in the same misery. . . .

It is also worth noting that [God] calls it a horrible plague not because it brings death, for all other deadly diseases do that as well (and death for the faithful is no loss, but a gain, as Paul says in Philippians 1[6]); rather, it is horrible because it takes the people very quickly, unexpectedly, and without preparation. . . .

Therefore, my dearly beloved, take this instruction and comfort to heart, and follow it. Flee with righteous sincerity, through true contrition and penance, from the sins that have brought this horrible plague upon the world; and flee through an honest, upright faith to the word of God, in which is the fountain of life and the only light of mankind; and you will recover and be safe from this and other plagues. And live in honor of God and in service to your neighbor until the time comes that God the Father, in the death of Christ in which we are baptized, calls us from this miserable life to his eternal kingdom. God grant this to all of us. Amen.

---

6. Phil. 1:21, "For to me to live is Christ, and to die is gain."

10.5 A Plague Year in Augsburg, 1563[7]

The description of events in the Plague House in 1563 that is excerpted here was written by Plague House director and city councilman Michael Reischner, who was a belt-maker by trade. Augsburg chronicler and council apparitor Paul Hector Mair then included it in his first chronicle. The Plague House was located just outside the city gate at Wertach Bridge.

As God the Almighty afflicted us in this year with the grievous sickness of plague, and much effort and work grew out of the fact that there was no record of how it has been handled in the past, I decided to record some of the details of what was done and how things went in this plague year, so that one would know better [what to do] should it happen again, sooner or later (may God in his grace deliver us). By Michael Reischlin, director of the Plague House and the Pox House.[8]

First, it happened that in March, a few people were sporadically hit with plague. It would have been desirable to keep this quiet, but it was impossible to hide, because a maid became ill that they did not want to keep in the house. She was thus placed in the hut in the upper cemetery by Doctor Schludy, and we, the directors of the Pox House, were ordered to provide her with food and other necessities.

On the orders of the Steadfast Lord Burgomaster Hainzle (whom we had informed), the directors sent for the gravedigger and his wife. They were paid 1 gulden 30 kreuzer per week for watching [over the sick] and for food. In less than a week, five people had arrived. We provided food from the Pox House (meat and bread, but no rolls, wine, or side dishes, which the gravedigger had to buy and then settle up every Saturday). We needed a barber-surgeon right away, and we had to pay him 2 gulden per week. This we reported to the mayors, who were Mathias Rehlinger and Lord Bartholomeus Mai; they thought it was too much, and that a gulden would be enough, but the barber-surgeon wouldn't take it, so we gave him a crown.[9]

Afterward, we had bed stands made for ten or twelve people. Right after the first week, on the 17th of April, four more people arrived. These we cared for as we had the first, and there were more and more of them as time went on. That made ten people for whom we had to provide caretakers. We reported to the mayors, and also to the Burgomasters, that we could no longer house up there, and asked if we shouldn't open

---

7. *Paul Hector Mairs 1. Chronik von 1547–1565*, Beilage VIII, 485–94.

8. For those afflicted with syphilis.

9. Ninety-three kreuzer, i.e., a little more than 1½ gulden in Augsburg currency.

the Plague House. [The Plague House was then opened, and the sick moved into it.]

When we had housed for several weeks in the outer Plague House, we, the directors, ordered that all of the food (such as meat, bread, lard, flour, and seasonings), bedclothes, sheets, sackcloth, linen for binding and bandages, and other things as needed be brought in, all of which was managed by the Pox Father. Only with the wine, we bought one barrel, and when that was empty, the Pox Father presented an account and another was purchased. We also took on a chaplain named Johannes Meer, who comforted the people and instructed them in the Christian faith, and who was sent by the pastors. We directors also had two gilded vessels made for administering the Lord's Supper, which cost 16 gulden including the case.

We also had two physicians, named Doctor Schludy and Doctor Trincklin, one of whom was in the Plague House in the evening, and the other in the morning, and there was a lot of discord between them. What the one wanted to have, the other didn't want to have; what one wanted to do, the other didn't; [so one was eventually removed]. We directors also employed eight women to care for the plague victims by lifting them, bedding them down, and whatever was needed, and also to sew up the dead [in their shrouds]. They were also needed when the parents of a child died, in which case one of them was sent to the children, or the children were put in the women's quarters, so that each had three children. The Alms Lords provided the food for them. We paid the caregivers for four weeks, and afterward the Alms Lords provided for them. Those of means, however, had to support themselves or receive support from relatives. . . . And we also had a midwife to come to the Plague House. We paid her ½ gulden per week, and another 15 kreuzer whenever she had to make a visit to the Plague House. . . .

At one point the Plague Father and Mother also were struck with the sickness, so that they lay very ill. There were a lot of complaints that things were very disorderly. . . . It wasn't long before the Plague Mother was better and could walk about again. She was very quarrelsome with the servants, who complained bitterly. So we went back out and questioned both her and the servants. The sick also complained that their food arrived completely cold, and that otherwise there was no order being kept. We hired a man who had to be present during the preparation of meals and to go around into all of the rooms when the sick were eating, and see what was wrong, then report it to us so we could take care of it. He also had to care for the sick and do whatever else was needed. In addition, he was assigned to take care of all of the refreshments, such as strength-giving biscuits and all invigorators, for the servants had been taking care of this previously, and they carried off more than they gave to the sick who needed it.

Then the [chaplain] became ill, so that we thought he would die. So the pastors sent another, whose name was Hans Bader, also a weaver, and a very young man. He was in the Plague House for a while and was not badly versed in doctrine. But we had a servant, a married man, and they became good friends. They went into a room where they had no business, one behaving as impertinently as the other; for the [servant] laid himself down with a woman on her bed, and the chaplain lay on the other bed, which belonged to the woman who was watching over the sick that night. After midnight, she came back and also lay down with him on the bed, and they lay together until two or four o'clock. I will leave aside the question of whether they both kept their innocence.

When we heard about this, we called them to appear before us. . . . The two could not deny it, but they made it out to sound as harmless as they could. We suspended both of them. This greatly insulted the chaplain, who said he would seek counsel elsewhere.

It was also reported to us that two maids out there were most impudently drinking with young men at night, and that they saved up their rations of wine and drank it with the fellows, and otherwise behaved badly. So we went right out [to the Plague House] and suspended them both. And as we also heard of fornication and lust among servants and the sick, we were forced to enforce order. So we posted a list of rules, as follows:

> God, the Almighty, in his great mercy, visits us daily with the onerous sickness of plague, in order to move us to penance and to turn us from our evil ways. But few wish to better themselves, so that God may be moved to punish us more severely. And our Lords, an Honorable Council, have at great expense set up a house in which the poor who are burdened with this sickness can be cared for. But there are those who do not appreciate this good deed, and some among the employees and those lying ill show themselves to be most impudent, completely shameless and quarrelsome, and otherwise disobedient, and practically no one will listen when they are corrected. This has often been reported to the directors. Because of this they are most disturbed, and have therefore created this ordinance in order to counter and put a stop to it.

The Plague House Rules

First, when a sick person is brought into the house, he should be laid immediately upon a clean bed and be given a sweating-draft, and afterward he should be treated in accordance with the doctors' orders. And there should be several beds with freshly washed linens available at all times in both the men's and the women's quarters so that no ill person has to wait. Grace should be said before each meal in all of the rooms, which may be rotated so that everyone says grace once. And when someone is in danger of death, the healthy should say a common prayer in good faith that God will redeem the dying. But if there is shameful behavior or impudence among the employees or the sick, whether in the form of words, deeds, or blasphemy, the offender should be duly punished for each violation along with those who instigate quarrels, whether it is an employee of the house or a sick person, as follows: First, they will receive no wine on the day of the incident; and if the offense is great, then they should also be given no meat. If the incident is really bad, they should be put out of the house on the spot. If it is a sick person, they should be put out of the house and city, and not be allowed back in for a month. The doctor, the chaplain, and the Plague Father should have the power to impose such punishments. And if it happens that the Plague Father and Mother also behave improperly, one or more of the other employees of the house may report this to the directors, and they will know how to handle it properly. The Father at the Plague House should report such cases to the Father at the Pox House, and the Pox Father in turn to the directors, so that one knows how things are being handled and where the complaint about the Father or Mother should be made. House employees or others should make such complaints without fear of retribution. No one is to malign one another, upon pain of the penalties described above. This ordinance should be read in all rooms in the presence of the employees every week. August 14, 1563.

To take things up where we left them: After the chaplain and the other employees were let go, the old chaplain . . . recovered, and we returned him to his post so that he could comfort the sick as before.

Around the same time, the Plague Father became very ill, and could not get up. Then complaints arose about how improperly the wine was being handled. [The cellar master was reckoning] an *Eimer*[10] more than was in the barrel, and a complaint came from the sick that the wine was

10. An *Eimer* (bucket) was a standard wholesale measure for wine that varied from place to place (a little more than 75 liters in Augsburg).

so watery. So we called in the cellar master together with the servants and the Plague Father (who by now was well again), and fired the cellar master and turned the key over to the Plague Father. But we let [the cellar master] stay as a servant, and paid him 30 kreuzer per week.

On the 18th of December, the plague began to let up, so we let three litter-bearers go, but with the understanding that if we needed them again we would hire them back.

On the 15th of January [1564], we laid off the eight women who were caregivers, but on the condition that if we needed them again and sent them back to work at an institution, we would pay them ½ gulden per week. . . .

On the 4th of March, we summoned the four gravediggers to the Plague House along with a servant and two maids. And in the early morning when the city gates were opened, we ordered that the wood and all the things be brought down as soon as we directors arrived, and everything be burnt, except for a few good beds. This included all of the clothes, about a wagon full. There was a huge commotion and labor and a great fire, until we had burned everything.

And in this year, from the time the pestilence began on the 10th of April [1563] until the 4th of March [1564], altogether 954 people died of the plague, of which 446 died in the Plague House.

I have provided this description not to serve or to harm anyone, rather so that if this should happen again, be it sooner or later (may the Lord God in his mercy protect us from it), everything can the better be faced and coped with.

10.6 Augsburg Physician Achilles Gasser's *Short Instruction on the Plague*, 1564[11]

Achilles Pirmineus Gasser (1505–1577) was a prominent Protestant physician, historian, and humanist with wide-ranging interests. Aside from his medicinal works, he produced chronicles, histories, and works on astrology, and dabbled in astronomy and geography.

Because all illnesses result from our disorderly and evil lives and our ungratefulness to God the Lord Christ, and death is the wages of sin, nothing would be better or more helpful to the people for maintaining health and staying alive during these difficult times than proper

11. From Achilles Pirmineus Gasser, *Kurtzer Unterricht wider die Pestilentz* (Augsburg, 1564).

atonement and true faith. One should pray to God for his blessing, and defend himself against the plague by the following means.

Because no one can live without air, it is first most necessary that the air be kept pure and clean. Therefore all excrement, filth, and stinking, nasty things should be cleared out of the houses and yards and also from the streets. And as far as possible, people should not live near dung heaps, cesspools, outhouses, or other unclean and bad-smelling waters or such things, or by pigsties. In addition, every morning and in the evening when the sun goes down, the rooms, chambers, and parlors, in fact the entire house, should be incensed with juniper twigs, wood, or berries, or with rosemary or sage . . . or with incense and fragrant preparations from the apothecary. Common folk can do this with savin juniper, oak leaves, or pine wood. . . . And if one wishes to go out among the people in church or at other gatherings, he should keep in his mouth at all times zedoary, angelica, astrantia, lovage, or laurel, and carry a pomander in his hands to smell of it frequently. . . .

Further, since one cannot exist without physical sustenance, one should be orderly in drinking and eating. Avoid that which is beginning to spoil, is very fatty, raw, or of fruit, or that which is difficult to digest. Flee all excess and gluttony. In sum, eat moderately and suitably, as if preparing for being bled.

Being regular on a daily basis in the elimination of stool, urine, and other unclean things; not going to sleep right after eating; not taking sweat baths; and avoiding anger, fear, resentment, and that which lays heavy on the heart are all most useful and good for preventing this and other illnesses. Above all, however, it is good to keep sheets, shirts, and all clothing clean, and to stay away from people and houses where there is plague.

As further preventative for plague, no one should neglect or skip their yearly purgations and bloodletting.

But if in spite of such measures, almighty and righteous God should afflict someone with his well-deserved rod, they should pray for mercy, and quickly send for a doctor, the sooner the better, so that as much help and counsel can be given as possible. . . . If one discovers a bubo, recurring abscess, or black pustule, no matter where it is on the body, the closest vein away from the body should be bled. And soon after such a sign appears, knead together well a piece of yeast or sour dough the size of two walnuts, two egg yolks, a spoonful of salt, and a quent of tiriak[12]; or cook a large onion and mash together with half as much tiriak into

---

12. An antipoison medicine; an alexipharmic.

a paste; or if there is none of that available, boil pigeon droppings with vinegar and make a plaster with honey and flour, and apply it. And as soon as it dries, replace it. And when that has drawn it out somewhat, on the third day or before, open it with a cut as deep as necessary, for which a hot iron is best, and drain the wound well, then keep it clean in the normal way.

On top of all of that, one should keep good order in eating and drinking during this illness, but drink no wine for three weeks, rather barley water. . . . In addition it is important to use everything that strengthens the heart, cools the body, and drives out poisons, some of which is noted above. And the juice of the sour lemon, or also the lime, is in particular most valuable. These remedies one should take every evening and morning until, with God's help, one reaches the ninth day . . . God in heaven grant us mercy through Jesus Christ his son and our only savior, that this and all else serves to praise his name and for our betterment. Amen.

Achilles Pirmineus Gasser, Doctor of Medicine in Augsburg

III. War and Peace

10.7 Preparing for the Worst: Guard Ordinance for the Common Citizenry, 1540[13]

This ordinance calling for an auxiliary civilian night watch represented an increase in the standard militia duties expected of all men.

Due to the alarming threat of murderous arson and for other compelling reasons, an Honorable Council of the city of Augsburg, in the interest of the common citizenry and to protect them from harm, has ordered and established an additional special night watch of general citizens in addition to the normal watch, tower guards, and the guards on the city walls. This [additional watch] should be continued as long as is deemed necessary and reasonable to an Honorable Council, as follows.

First, all four of the quarter captains should order their lieutenants[14] to visit each of their ten appointed houses and make a record of them, counting each married couple as one person, and also counting as one person each widower or widow, or each single fellow who is keeping his own house, with no exceptions. This they should present in writing to

13. StadtAA, Schätze 16, 56–58.
14. I.e., their lane captains; see Chapter Two, note 9.

the quarter captains so the captains know how many people are available in each lieutenant's sector.

Then the quarter captains should inform their lieutenants, on the orders of an Honorable Council, that sixteen men are to stand guard in each quarter every night. The orders for this watch should originate from the quarter captain and be passed on by the lieutenant, and should be conducted by sixteen people from the quarter (assuming the lieutenant has this many). The first sixteen should stand guard as described below on the first night, and then another sixteen the next night, continuing until all of the people for whom the officer is responsible have stood guard. If he finds on a given night that he is unable to provide all sixteen people, then the next officer should make up the difference. But the officer in charge should report any such shortage to his neighboring officer one day ahead of time so that a substitution can be arranged. . . . And when the entire round of watch has been completed, they should start again from the beginning.

Any citizen or resident unable or unwilling to stand watch should appoint and send another citizen, or a mature male appointee who has taken an oath to an Honorable Council. He should not send young boys or others who are not suitable.

The sixteen people who are to stand guard in each quarter should be informed by their officer a day ahead of time that it is their turn to watch, so they don't seek an excuse to get out of it, rather guard as required. These sixteen people should appear to their officer at a quarter to eight in the evening, and he should provide proper orders on how far and where they should go on their hourly rounds, and tell them to start their rounds at eight o'clock sharp in wintertime and at nine o'clock in summertime. The guards may leave in the morning when the tower guard has blown his horn.

The persons appointed to this night watch, whether they are in the streets or in their houses, should avoid entirely all drinking, gambling, and anything else on the night of their watch that could interfere with giving it their assiduous attention, anywhere and everywhere, on pain of an Honorable Council's earnest punishment.

Because, however, the night is now long and the cold is to be feared, the Lord quarter captains should each seek out an appropriate heated room in their quarter in which the sixteen guards can gather, and then half of them, that is eight people, should guard for an entire hour, namely four in one direction and four in the other (but spread out and not all together). They should make their rounds quietly and unassumingly, and they should decide among themselves at the start how and where they will cover their rounds, so that no spot in their quarter remains unseen or unobserved. And at the end of the hour, they should gather again in the house from which they started, and the other eight who had spent the hour in the heated room should go out in their place, and make rounds as the first group had, so that there are always eight people on guard and eight in the room, trading off guarding every hour until the tower guard blows the horn in the morning and it is time to go home.

And so that there will be absolute equality here and to avoid resentment, each and every citizen and resident should be included in this watch duty—those in servitude and those of free status, those of the nobility, officers, doctors, servants of the clergy, and widows,[15] without prejudice—with the single exception of those who are receiving alms and are also ill or bedridden. But any young and healthy man is duty bound to stand watch, even if he wears the alms sign.[16] In the case of widows who receive alms and are healthy, two of them should be considered as one person and provide one guard between them.

The quarter captains should also duly inform their lieutenants of the duties of these sixteen people from each quarter. These are that they begin their watch at eight o'clock, as noted above, and that they keep an eye out most attentively for anything troubling or dangerous, especially dangerous, dubious persons, whether local or outsiders, and observe whether they have concealed or forbidden weapons or otherwise appear suspicious. They should take such persons into custody and send for the nearest permanent guard and tell them to handle them in accordance with their orders. If they should smell or see smoke or fire, they should immediately inform the residents of the house where the fire is located as well as the neighbors and wake them up, and also let their officer know without delay. The officer should then swiftly report it to the sworn Lord Mayors.

And when the alarm bell is rung, these guards should appear at the spot to which they are normally ordered, each with his armor and weapon, without regard to the fact that they are currently on watch.

The officers should also order and require the watch that, when they pass by the city gates, towers, and walls at night, they should yell up to the guards on the towers and walls, and find out if they are awake or

15. Women did not participate directly as guards, but widows had to pay for a man to stand watch.

16. I.e., the symbol worn by those receiving alms to identify them as "deserving poor" (see Chapter Three).

asleep. If they find [anyone asleep] they should report it in the morning to the Lord Mayors.

It should be noted that it is unnecessary for these sixteen guards from each quarter to wear armor, rather they should be equipped only with their sword and halberd.

Finally, the regular appointed permanent guards should continue on their duty and office regardless of all of this, and faithfully keep their watch, subject to the authority of an Honorable Council. December 6, 1540.

10.8 Emperor Charles V Occupies Augsburg, 1547[17]

Thus far, an Honorable Council has in every way governed and behaved in as Christian, faithful, and fatherly a means as God allowed, for the welfare of its dear citizenry, so that it is entirely to be expected that all people, young and old, should be friendly, obedient, and satisfied with the council. And it is the laudable custom of this Christian free and imperial city not to hide anything from the worthy community. Therefore, all should know that the small and large councils, for unavoidable reasons, have most dutifully capitulated to His Imperial Majesty, and this has also graciously been accepted. For this reason His Majesty has decided, in accordance with his custom, to station a colonel and a small number of troops in this city for a short while. In addition, they will take over the opening and closing of some gates, along with an Honorable Council's appointed guards. This could give pause and lead to suspicion among some pious and honest men, and also provide cause for those who lack judgment or are restless to cause a disturbance or insurrection.

However, this request and intent from His Imperial Majesty [to occupy the city] applies not only here [in Augsburg], but has also been devotedly accepted and allowed in other cities with whom he has reached an agreement. And it is also not being done as a show of force or a threat, but only to increase the honor and reputation of His Imperial Majesty, and will soon be done away with. Therefore, an Honorable Council could not avoid giving in to this, in order to avoid the much worse and more burdensome treatment, large penalties, and changes to the government and the worthy guilds that would follow if we resisted. An Honorable Council thus makes the fatherly and friendly request that no one see this as a burden or annoyance, rather in God's name accept it patiently for this short time. Then almighty God will all the sooner

17. StadtAA, Anschläge und Dekrete 1490–1649, Nr. 23, February 21, 1547.

provide his grace for the preservation of the holy Gospels and the freedom of this city. . . . Should anyone, however, violate this with words or deeds, creating any trouble or insurrection, as a result of which this city must certainly drown in blood and fall to ruin, either from within, or due to outside forces, then an Honorable Council must take steps to punish him or them . . . on life and limb, without mercy. . . . Monday, the 21st of February, 1547.

10.9 Complaints about Quartering of Troops in Private Homes, 1551[18]

BARTOLME LOTTER, KNIFESMITH

Noble, steadfast, farsighted, honorable, and wise Lord Mayors, Burgomaster, and an Honorable Council. . . . A soldier has been billeted in my chamber in Anthoin Nusshart's house, called the stone house. Now I have one small heated room and a little bedchamber, and I have three journeymen, who all have to lie together on one bed. And the four of us have to work in the little room, so that I can't have a table in there. I also have a maid and four little children, one of which is still in the cradle. Thus it is not possible to take on a soldier. There are nine other rooms in the building, each of which could take in a soldier, but none of them have been given any. I request devotedly that if [Your Lords] will examine my little apartment, it will be found that I can't take in a soldier. And if it is found that I can, then I'll take three of them. . . . [in humble devotion]
Bartolme Lotter, knifesmith

RADIGUNDIS EGGENBERGER, WIDOW

Noble, steadfast, farsighted, honorable, and wise Lords Mayors, Burgomasters, and an Honorable Council of this laudable city of Augsburg. . . . Normally, all widows belonging to the two Societies[19] and those among the commoners as well, who do not have married sons or sons-in-law in their houses, are freed of quartering. But six soldiers have nonetheless been billeted in my house, which is not fair, and more than a little difficult for me, since I don't have any married son or son-in-law in my house, and my unmarried sons live mainly in Aichstetten. Thus I appeal

18. StadtAA, Militaria Nr. 55, Landquartierwesen Contributionsamt, 1518–1638.
19. I.e., the Patricians' and Merchants' Societies (the petitioner in the case is a member of the patriciate).

to [Your Lords] to treat me the same as other widows, and with your favor, remove these soldiers. . . .

[in devoted obedience]

Radigundis Eggenberger, the late Erasmus Herwart's widow

10.10 The Fortunes and Misfortunes of War: The Chronicle of Protestant Schoolmaster Ludwig Hainzelmann[20]

In the year 1629 on August 7, St. Afra's Day, an Honorable Council had it proclaimed and commanded at all squares that on the following day, that is the 8th, everybody, young and old, male and female, should stay inside his home after the morning sermon on threat of corporal punishment. That same night, 600 of the Bishop's musketeers were let into the city. [The day after that, the Protestant preachers were all removed from their posts and it was announced that all children should be baptized Catholic.] After that, on August 9, a gallows was erected in the Fish Market with two ladders leaning on it, so that if anyone started anything, he could be hung on it. . . .

On April 2, [1632]. . . . The soldiers were spread about the city to stand guard, and the city guards also rode through all the streets fully armed, in case the citizens should prove to be rebellious. Then they took from the Protestant citizens their swords, guns, and armor. There were a number of different squadrons that did it, and with each squadron was a Burgomaster or a councilman, along with many musketeers, so that they came up to the houses thirty or forty strong to demand the armaments. One could immediately see where things were headed.

During the night on April 7, 1632, around 11:00, five companies of mostly Protestant cavalry came into the city and were quartered with the innkeepers around the Wine Market. At this time the papist council had around 200 wooden maces with long iron spikes made for defense against the King of Sweden [Gustavus Adolphus]. . . .

On April 9, which was Good Friday, another eleven patrols of infantry came in, most of whom were garrisoned in the uptown area, and they stationed artillery at all of the watch points. The Good Friday procession was cancelled. . . .

20. StadtAA, Chroniken 32, Ludwig Hainzelmann der Elter.

On the morning of April 18, a Sunday, it was openly proclaimed that if the citizens should hear the alarm bells, they should all go home and stay in their houses. . . . [And] the city mayors sent Philip Hainhofer to ask the members of the two Societies [of patricians and merchants], who were gathered together, whether they would resist or not if the enemy came into the city. Hainhofer received the pretty sharp reply that their weapons had been confiscated along with those of the entire [Protestant] community, so they couldn't resist. No one ever asked them about anything, and their offices were taken away, all of which was done without them. So this [the Catholics] can also do on their own. They would not resist, and that is that. Meanwhile, the King of Sweden took Friedberg, a mile from here.

On [April] 20th . . . Praise God, the King of Sweden took this city without the spilling of any blood, under four conditions: First, that in matters of religion and everything else, things should return to the status in force during the time of Emperor Charles [V] [i.e., the terms of the Peace of Augsburg]; second, the Protestants should be given their churches back, and on the sites where they had been torn down, they should build new ones as they wished; third, His Royal Highness [King Gustavus Adolphus] was to be paid three tons of gold, for which the citizens should make a settlement with the clerics; and fourth, 6,000 troops were to be garrisoned here.

During this time the papist citizens who held government offices formerly held by Protestants were removed from their positions. Now only Protestants are given offices. Thus [the Catholics] are treated as they had previously treated us.

On Tuesday of Pentecost in the same year, His Royal Majesty [Gustavus Adolphus] and Duke Bernhart, Duke Augustus, and other princes and Lords who were here played a game of pallone[21] with a number of patricians' sons in the cathedral yard, and that night held a royal banquet followed by a nice dance in the Fuggers' palace on the Wine Market. . . .

On June 16, a lot of armaments, including swords, guns, armor, and halberds were found among the papists and priests as well as the cloisters. Also on this day, ten large and sixteen small cannons were brought from Donauwörth, along with seven baggage wagons, nineteen wagons

---

21. An Italian game similar to tennis, played by striking a large ball with a wooden guard worn over the hand and wrist.

of ammunition, four wagons with materials for building earth fortifications, and seven carts of powder.

On the evening of November 26, a very sad report came in that our pious king [Gustavus Adolphus] had been shot at Lützen. On the 28th, the first Sunday of Advent, our pastor at St. Anna also reported the king's death right at the beginning of the sermon, which not only moved the people to anger but also caused them to shed many tears.

In 1634, my servant Mossi died at the age of fifty-five.

On April 6, [1634], the authorities here erected a wooden donkey in the Fish Market for the purpose of punishing bakers, butchers, and brewers by making them sit on it when the bread is too small, the meat too expensive, and the beer too wretchedly brewed.

On the 12th [of May 1634], seven soldiers [serving under the Swedes] were taken to the gallows at St. Jacob's between 10:00 and 11:00 in the morning under a strong guard, from among which the three highest-ranking were selected, and they had to gamble with one another. A Protestant one lost the game and was hung, and the two papists were released. Their crime was that they attacked the escort guards and injured them, and also took bread from a peasant and seriously wounded him.

[In October of 1634, shortly after the Swedes lost the decisive Battle of Nördlingen, Catholic forces surrounded and blockaded the city of Augsburg.] On December 17, a Sunday, it was proclaimed from the oriel [on the council house] that bulk sales and excesses in foodstuffs should be ceased, and one should not buy more than one needs. Also drinking bouts in beer, wine, and mead houses should be avoided, and excess in drinks and foods should not be ordered to take home, on pain of unavoidable punishment.

Toward the end of this month [December 1634] the authorities here set the price of bread so that a loaf that previously went for 4 batzen now cost 5 batzen, a Metze[22] of grain could be bought in the grain hall for 4 gulden, a Metze of wheat for 4¼ gulden. All types of foodstuffs are getting more expensive by the day, and there is almost nothing to be had, so that a pound of pork costs 30 kreuzer. . . .

---

22. *Metze* was a measure used for grain, about 56 liters.

On January 24, [1635], a common craftsman's wife left her children for two hours to seek bread to still the children's hunger, but when she came home, one of the children, out of great hunger, had begun to chew on his hand, and tried to eat his fingers. Only when this was discovered did anyone help, and the child was bound by the barber-surgeon. The want here is so great that one not only turns to eating dogs, cats, mice, horses, donkeys, leather, and even dead people, but some are found who don't have even this, and who become weak and die of hunger. For the peasants can't bring anything in, because it has been forbidden to them on threat of their life. . . . When bread was again distributed at the end of this month, they mixed spelt, rye, barley, and oats all together, and nonetheless charged 4 batzen for a loaf. And since the bread is provided every fourteen days, My Lords must always have 500 schaff of grain to provide everyone with bread, and each person only gets one loaf. . . .

The want becomes greater with each day, for not only is everyone being driven into poverty and ruin because of the many taxes and heavy tributes they have to pay, but many are dying of hunger. Horse flesh is being sold for 6, 7, 8, 9, and 10 kreuzer. The people eat bread baked of straw with a little rye mixed in, and bread is also being baked from bran or from nothing but rapeseed. A Metze of good flour costs 8 gulden, if only it were to be had. When something is brought into town by the peasants in their sacks, which hardly ever happens, whether it is bread, flour, cabbage, beets, chaff, oats, meat, oatmeal, or pea meal, my God, the peasants are practically ripped apart for it, and still such high prices must be paid for it . . . for the enemy stops everything from being brought into the city.

[In February], that which was wasted last year during Shrovetide of 1634 in wine, beer, meat, and other foodstuffs by celebrating carnival, one has all the less of in February of 1635, so that many people can't even get bread for eight days, fourteen days, even three or four weeks . . . even if a person has the money in their hands and is ready to pay for something to eat, there is still nothing to be had, so that many people and children weaken and die of hunger, sometimes on the streets. Even the little children . . . must die, and the living in their hunger take their dead and begin to eat them, all of which is caused by the blockade, because the enemy will not let anything in.

It is being said that when the Swedish King came here three years ago, and the people of the city were rich, that there was at that time a total of around 70,000 or 80,000 souls here, rich and poor, young and old. But now, because of the great losses due to the reign of the plague[23] and the people who died of hunger, it is estimated that there are not more than 18,000 souls altogether. Thus 62,000 people passed away in these three years from plague, war, and hunger, so that there are entire houses, even entire lanes full of houses standing empty with no one in them. The houses here are thus worthless, and one can get a house right now for a pittance. But the Swedish soldiers have laid waste to many houses, and practically torn them down, taking the wood, windows, ironwork, and other materials to sell, and causing great damage to the citizens by robbing and stealing. Not even the stray dogs are safe, for if they see a dog on the street, no matter how he growls, they shoot it and eat it. And as much as we welcomed their arrival with the king, rest his soul, three years ago, we would now equally welcome seeing them pull out. . . .

During this month, there was a craftsman in the lower city, two of whose children died, and he ate them both out of great hunger. Thus their father's stomach became their grave. Afterward a widow on Kappeneck whose child died also ate it out of hunger.

At this time a pound of pork, which one could get from the butcher before for 4 kreuzer, now costs 36 kreuzer.

[On March 22, 1635, Augsburg surrendered to the Bavarians and the Swedish troops left.]

10.11 Architect Elias Holl Requests Relief from Excessive Quartering, 1635[24]

The well-known architect Elias Holl (1573–1646) was the designer and master builder of Augsburg's showpiece city hall, as well as more than 100 other city buildings, many of architectural or technical significance. Holl served as the city's master builder from 1602 until 1629, when, like many other civil servants, he was removed from office for refusing to convert to Catholicism. Holl regained his position briefly during the Swedish phase of the war, only to have it revoked again when the Catholics regained power in 1635. These excerpts from his complaint to the council and the response from the Quartermasters reflect the tendency of both religions to use troop quartering as a form of confessional harassment.

23. Augsburg suffered a plague year during 1627–1628.
24. StadtAA, Militaria 55, Landquartierwesen und Contributionsamt in der Stadt betr., 1518–1638.

The petition from Elias Holl, July 21, 1635

[Your noble] Lord Mayors, Burgomasters, and council of this laudable imperial city of Augsburg. . . . It is in the greatest of need that I present [Your Lords] with this dutiful complaint about the fact that I have been much more hard hit and heavily encumbered with quartered soldiers than others of my rank since the very beginning of this garrison, for I am loaded down with four officers' orderlies, who cost me 2 gulden 24 kreuzer a day. Under this unbearable burden I have faced near collapse of body and life, goods and property, especially since I have no income here, and don't earn anything anywhere else; I have an expensive household with many children; and I am also overburdened with the extraordinary [war] contributions.

I hope that I have not earned being stuck with such heavy quartering, since nothing more is asked of a civil servant than that he is loyal and hardworking, and this I have honestly proven to be in respect to all my employers. I have spared no care and effort, and made no difference between the religions, as I elegantly improved this city above all others in Germany with useful and beautiful buildings, and made it famous. These works give witness and speak for themselves on my behalf, not to mention the service I have rendered to neighboring electors, princes, and Lords, who undoubtedly would have gracious sympathy for me because of my imminent ruin.

In sum, one can say of me that I used myself up in service. Now I am old, and sickened by the great challenges, and increasingly faint of heart, for I hoped through my assiduous and tireless service to have earned mercy and peace in my old age. But I will not let my confidence in God and [Your Lords] dwindle away.

I therefore [request that] you take to heart my hard service, great works, advanced years, weakened body, the heavy burden of quartering that I have borne so far, and the decline I have endured as a result, and do whatever is necessary to exonerate me and assign the quarters more tolerably in accordance with my capacities.

Devoted citizen and former civil servant of thirty-four years
Elias Holl

Response from Chief Quartermasters, July 28, 1635

[My Lords] Mayors, Burgomasters, and council . . . Elias Holl, former non-Catholic city builder, in his partly hypocritical lament and partly ostentatious production, which is provided here, starts right out with an obvious untruth, namely that he has been much more hard hit than others of his rank right from the beginning of this garrison. For it is known to everyone that the former Quartermasters only spared him from quartering, along with many others of status belonging to his religion, along with all the civil servants and city workers. In contrast, they burdened the Catholics excessively and quartered many soldiers with them. . . .

The officers' orderlies described by the supplicant were only in his house until the Lombard Regiment pulled out on the [blank space] of May, and the quartering was changed. Then Holl was given one field surgeon, who was entitled to two rations per day. After this, we quartered an orderly under Captain Mattia della Cerva with him, whom he also had for some weeks, until we got the order that, for certain reasons, the orderly should be removed, and a stronger contingent of Catholic soldiers should be placed with [Holl] in order to keep a general eye on his activities.

This entire billet that Holl has endured since we came into office may have come to around 100 gulden altogether. . . . In contrast, it is possible to show with countless examples that the common citizens and craftsmen who don't have a fourth of his fortune have born heavy quartering the entire time as a result of the large numbers of troops, and therefore had much greater expenses.

As far as his much vaunted industry, loyalty, and honor is concerned, and his claim that he made "no difference between the religions as [he] elegantly improved this city above all others in Germany with useful and beautiful buildings and made it famous, . . ." we respond to him by saying that . . . during the time of the Swedish trouble, he inflicted upon and demonstrated to the already extremely beleaguered Catholics so much vicious ill will, terror, defiance, derision, mockery, and prejudice that it is beyond description. And it is obvious that these earlier deeds give sufficient evidence of his highly punishable malice and unforgiving hatred of us Catholics, which not only obliterates and wipes out all of that which he has bragged of with his exceptional vanity but also makes him more than a little culpable. . . .

[And it is also well known that] he and his family constantly advocated and urged the former Quartermasters to heavily burden us Catholics with quartering, to which his entire neighborhood can testify. In addition, his two sons, who also terrorized us Catholics with gunshots and other actions, afterward left with the Swedish garrison, and no doubt are still to be found among the enemy. Thus we cannot see how his request can be approved and he can be relieved, nor do we consider it advisable. . . . Rather we are more of the opinion (without

meaning to impose an injunction) that because of his abuses and those of his sons, he should be earnestly questioned. . . .
Obediently
The Appointed Senior Quartermasters

[On the basis of this recommendation, the council decreed that the soldiers quartered in Holl's home should remain there.]

10.12 Religious Parity Is Established in Augsburg[25]

From: Detailed report on the implementation of rules regarding ecclesiastical and worldly matters, established in the imperial city of Augsburg in 1649 through the Imperial Subdelegation of Lord Commissioners, in accordance with the Osnabrück Peace Treaty [i.e., the Treaty of Westphalia of 1648]. Augsburg, 1652.

Oath that is to be rendered by every pastor of the Augsburg Confession to all of the city mayors of both religions:
I, (name), pledge . . . that I will be obedient, loyal, and vigilant to both Lord Mayors and an Honorable Most Wise Council of this laudable imperial city, properly adhere to and obey their decrees and bans in political and worldly matters, promote that which is honorable, good, and useful for an Honorable Council and the common city, and protect it from harm, to the best of my ability. In addition, I will pay taxes on my real property within the city's jurisdiction, as do other citizens; pay the standard excise tax on wine, beer, and mead for myself and those of my household; submit, along with the members of my household, to the Honorable Council and the appointed court in all political and worldly matters and actions, as do other citizens and residents here; and in general do and abide by all that is fitting and proper for an honorable citizen (resident). I will also assiduously keep the Decree of Peace, to which I am bound and as I pledged to the Lord Mayors of the Augsburg Confession, truly and faithfully.

How the imperial subdelegate commission of this imperial city of Augsburg distributed the public offices of the Senate and the other offices between the two religions:
First, the small council.

25. Extracted from StadtAA, Anschläge und Dekrete 1490–1649, Nr. 80 (print).

	Catholic	Augsburg Confession
Lord Mayors	One	One
Lord Privy Councillers	Three	Two
Patricians	Twelve	Twelve
Mehrer[26]	Two	Two
Merchants	One	Two
Commoners	Four	Three

First, as regards the Lord Mayors: For now, Lord David Welser the Elder should have precedence as the Catholic, but in the future, in case of death or abdication, this should alternate. As far as the other Catholic mayor, Lord Hans Caspar Rembold, is concerned . . . this office should alternate every three years between the two Catholics who have been mayors up to now. Thus Lord Mayor Welser remains in office for the first three years, and after these three years pass, or immediately upon his death, Lord Rembold should take over the office. And the two should thus continue alternating every three years as long as God grants them life.

The three Lord Collectors[27]

The first Lord Collector should be Catholic, the second should be of the Augsburg Confession, and both should be members of the Privy Council. The third should be a Catholic from the patriciate, who alternates yearly with the second Lord of Public Works.

Three Lords of Public Works

The first of these should be a Catholic patrician, the second a patrician of the Augsburg Confession who alternates yearly with the third Lord Collector, and the third a member of the Augsburg Confession belonging to the Council of the Fourteen.

Four Tax Lords

The first Catholic, the second and third patricians of the Augsburg Confession, the fourth Catholic from the Council of the Fourteen.

26. *Mehrer* were members of the Patricians' Society who did not have patrician status; they normally married in.

27. Collectors (*Einnehmer*) were officials responsible for civic income and expenses (treasurers).

Three War Lords
The first Catholic, the second Augsburg Confession, the third a Catholic from the patriciate, and the third should alternate yearly with the third Lord of Provisions.

Three Lords of Provisions
The first Augsburg Confession, the second Catholic, the third a patrician from the Augsburg Confession, and the third should alternate with the third War Lord.

Six Burgomasters
The first a Catholic patrician, the second a Catholic from the *Mehrer,* the third a patrician of the Augsburg Confession, the fourth a merchant of the Augsburg Confession, the fifth a Catholic patrician, the sixth a commoner of the Augsburg Confession. . . .

Passel and Tower guards
Forty passel guards, of which twenty-one are Catholic and nineteen Augsburg Confession. These should be allowed to die off on both sides until the number is reduced to thirty, observing parity as it goes.
Four field guards, two and two.
Twenty-eight tower guards, equally divided between the religions.
Fourteen Lech canal guards,[28] done likewise.
Four Wertach Bridge Gate guards, same. . . .

[Etc.—detailed rules for enforcing parity are provided for all civic offices and employees.]

---

28. Water for the city was provided by a network of canals diverted from the Lech River.

Timeline of Events: 1517–1650

1517 Martin Luther presented his *Ninety-Five Theses* against indulgences, originally in Latin and intended to stimulate debate among theologians. Within a month, the *Theses* were translated into German, printed, and circulated throughout Germany, creating a storm of controversy.

1518 Martin Luther defended his critique of the church before the papal legate Thomas de Vio de Gaeta, called Cajetan, in the house of Jakob Fugger on the Wine Market in Augsburg. Luther was ordered to recant and refused, fleeing the city soon afterward.

1519 Charles V succeeded Maximilian I as Holy Roman Emperor.

1519 Disputation at Leipzig between Andreas von Carlstadt, Martin Luther, and Johann Eck. Soon afterward, Luther began to question the church's teaching on the sacraments and other issues.

1521 Luther was excommunicated for heresy by papal bull. Charles V issued the Edict of Worms, placing Luther under an imperial ban and ordering his works burned.

1522 Luther's translation of the New Testament appeared in German.

1523 Ulrich Zwingli presented *Sixty-Seven Theses* at the Zurich Disputation. Among them were his case for clerical marriage and an attack on the Catholic view that the mass was a reenactment of the sacrifice of Christ.

1524–1525 Peasants' revolts throughout Germany (the German Peasants' War).

1524 Uprising in Augsburg over the removal of Franciscan friar Johann Schilling from his post in Augsburg.

1526 William Tyndale's English-language New Testament was published in Worms and subsequently smuggled into England (where it remained illegal) and distributed.

1526 Zwingli published his rebuke of belief in transubstantiation (the physical transformation of the Eucharist bread and wine into the body and blood of Christ, in substance if not in form), arguing instead that the transformation was symbolic.

1527 The Schleitheim Confession was concluded in Schleitheim, Switzerland, summarizing the tenets of the Swiss and south German Anabaptist faith.

1529 Colloquy of Marburg, at which Luther, Zwingli, Philip Melanchthon, Johann Oecolampadius, and Martin Bucer debated the nature of the presence of Christ in the bread and wine of the Eucharist. The colloquy was called by landgrave Philip of Hesse in an attempt to settle the controversy on transubstantiation in order to unite the Protestants in opposition to Catholicism. No final accord was reached on the issue.

1530 Diet of Augsburg, at which the Augsburg Confession was completed under the guidance of Philip Melanchthon. The new faith was rejected by Emperor Charles V, but the document survived to become the doctrinal standard for the Lutheran faith.

1530 Emperor Charles V's Imperial Recess banned gypsies from the empire and required that Jews identify themselves with a yellow ring on their clothing.

1530–1531 Establishment of the Schmalkaldic League. At a meeting set up by princes Philip of Hesse and John of Saxony, eight princes and eleven cities adopted the Augsburg Confession.

1532 Appearance of Charles V's law code, the Carolina, which provided rules for the application of torture and instituted capital punishment for the practice of black magic.

1533 Henry VIII of England declared his first marriage to Catharine of Aragon invalid, in defiance of the Pope, and married Anne Boleyn.

1534 The First Act of Supremacy declared Henry VIII of England the supreme head of the Church of England.

1534 Anabaptists assumed political power in the city of Münster. Under the leadership of Jan Matthys, opponents of Anabaptism were expelled from the city and their property seized. Declaring Münster to be the New Jerusalem, Matthys instituted policies of communal ownership of property and polygamy.

1535 Münster was besieged and taken by forces of the Prince-Bishop of Münster and other German princes, and its ringleaders were executed.

1536 John Calvin arrived in Geneva and was appointed as a preacher, from which position he influenced religious reform on a model of strict moral discipline.

1536 Rules requiring armed escorts for all Jews entering the city were established in Augsburg.

1537 Zwinglian-style reformation introduced in Augsburg, including publication of a church ordinance outlawing Catholic practice (produced in close cooperation with Martin Bucer and on the Strasbourg model).

1540 The Society of Jesus (Jesuits), founded by Ignatius of Loyola, was recognized by the Pope as an order.

1545–1563 The Council of Trent met periodically, instituting reforms to the Catholic Church.

1546 Death of Luther.

1546 At the Diet of Regensburg, Charles V attempted unsuccessfully to force the Lutherans to abide by the decisions of the Council of Trent.

1546–1547 Schmalkaldic War between the Protestant Schmalkaldic League and the Emperor's forces. Charles V was victorious.

1548 Charles V occupied Augsburg with imperial troops in the so-called armored Imperial Diet.

1548–1555 The Augsburg Interim, during which most Protestant practices were forbidden.

1553 Mary Tudor restored Catholic doctrine in England, revoking the Act of Supremacy a year later.

1555 The Religious Peace of Augsburg recognized both Catholicism and Lutheranism and established the principle of *cuius regio, eius religio* (whose realm, his religion), giving rulers throughout the Holy Roman Empire the right to determine which faith their subjects should practice. Some cities remained biconfessional, and Calvinism, Anabaptism, and all other new faiths were still forbidden.

1558 Elizabeth I succeeded Mary Tudor to the throne of England and, one year later, reinstated the Act of Supremacy, declaring herself Supreme Governor of the Church of England.

1558 Ferdinand I was elected Holy Roman Emperor, succeeding his brother Charles V, who abdicated in 1556. Charles died soon after Ferdinand's election. The Pope did not recognize Ferdinand's title until 1560.

1564 Maximilian II succeeded his father Ferdinand I as Holy Roman Emperor and pursued a more liberal religious policy that sought compromise between Catholics and Protestants.

1564 Death of Calvin.

1572 The St. Bartholomew's Day Massacre: As part of the French Wars of Religion, a series of assassinations of French Calvinists (called Huguenots) in Paris was followed by a wave of violence that left thousands of French Protestants dead. Tales of the massacre inflamed anti-Catholic sentiment among Protestants throughout Europe.

1576 The mentally unstable Rudolf II (1552–1612) succeeded his father Maximilian II as Holy Roman Emperor.

1580s A surge in witch trials throughout much of Europe, including the Catholic territories surrounding Augsburg.

1582 The new Gregorian calendar was decreed into force by Pope Gregory XIII, for whom it was named, and made law by the Emperor a year later. The calendar replaced the flawed Julian calendar, which was ten days out of synch with the astronomical calendar.

1584–1591 Continued protests and complaints about the new calendar (the "Calendar Fight") and about procedures for appointing local preachers in Augsburg.

1589 Assassination of Henry III in France.

1598 Henry IV of France granted religious freedoms to Protestants under the Edict of Nantes.

1610 Assassination of Henry IV in France.

1611 James I, King of England since the death of Elizabeth I in 1603, authorized publication of the King James Version of the English Bible.

1612 Matthias (1557–1619) succeeded his elder brother Rudolf II as Holy Roman Emperor and, reversing the policy of his father, Maximilian II, led a Catholic revival in the Habsburg lands.

1618 The Defenestration of Prague: During negotiations between a local Protestant assembly in Prague and a group of Catholic Regents over Matthias' unpopular, anti-Protestant policies in Bohemia, the Protestant delegates threw two Catholic Regents and a secretary out of a third-story window. The "defenestrated" delegates (from the Latin *fenestra,* "window") landed on a pile of manure and survived. This event is usually credited as the start of the Thirty Years' War.

1618–1648 The Thirty Years' War.

1619 Ferdinand II was elected Holy Roman Emperor and became a strong force for Catholicism in the Empire. The Bohemians rejected his rule and elected the Protestant Frederick of the Palatinate to be their king, escalating tensions in the Empire.

1629 Ferdinand II issued his Edict of Restitution, which forced Protestants to return to the Catholics all church property seized since 1552. The Augsburg Bishop Heinrich von Knöringen, hoping to make Augsburg a model of Catholic revival, provided support for the Emperor's efforts.

1629 Augsburg was occupied by Catholic troops and the city forced into Catholicism. Protestant pastors had to leave the city, Protestant churches were closed, and all civic offices were given to Catholics.

1630 The Swedish King Gustavus Adolphus, a champion of Lutheranism, invaded Germany.

1632–1635 The Swedish occupation of Augsburg, during which Protestantism was reinstated and Catholics were in turn repressed.

1632 Gustavus Adolphus was killed in the Battle of Lützen.

1634 Catholic victory at the Battle of Nördlingen, after which Augsburg was surrounded and blockaded by Catholic troops, cutting off food supplies to the city.

1635 Augsburg again fell to the Catholics. Under the terms of the Leonberg Accord, so named because it was signed at Imperial General Matthias Gallas' headquarters at Leonberg Castle, most of the terms of the Edict of Restitution were reinstated. Protestants were allowed to exercise their faith but were not provided with a church. Protestant worship continued in the yard behind the Church of St. Anna.

1637 Emperor Ferdinand II died and was succeeded by his son Ferdinand III.

1648 The Peace of Westphalia ended the Thirty Years' War and reinstated the principle of *cuius regio, eius religio* (first established by the Peace of Augsburg in 1555). Calvinism was recognized as a religion. In Augsburg, religious parity was instituted in the holding of all civic offices.

1650 The Augsburg Festival of Peace (*Friedensfest*) was celebrated for the first time on August 8 to commemorate the religious peace. The holiday, historically celebrated primarily by Protestants as a symbol of their liberation, is observed only in the city of Augsburg. It remains a legal holiday to this day.

Bibliography of English-Language Works Consulted and Suggested Reading

Chapter One. Popular Responses to Reform, 1520–1554

Abray, Lorna Jane. *The People's Reformation: Magistrates, Clergy, and Commons in Strasbourg, 1500–1598*. Ithaca, NY: Cornell University Press, 1985.

Broadhead, Philip J. "Guildsmen, Religious Reform and the Search for the Common Good: The Role of the Guilds in the Early Reformation in Augsburg." *The Historical Journal* 39, no. 3 (1996): 577–97.

Dixon, C. Scott. *The Reformation in Germany*. Oxford, UK: Blackwell, 2002.

Hanson, Michele Zelinsky. *Religious Identity in an Early Reformation Community: Augsburg, 1517 to 1555*. Studies in Central European Histories, vol. 45. Boston: Brill, 2009.

Karant-Nunn, Susan C. "What Was Preached in German Cities in the Early Years of the Reformation?: Wildwuchs versus Lutheran Unity." In *The Process of Change in Early Modern Europe: Essays in Honor of Miriam Usher Chrisman*, edited by Sherrin Marshall and Phillip Bebb, 81–96. Athens: Ohio University Press, 1988. Reprinted in *The Reformation: Critical Concepts in Historical Studies*. 4 vols., edited by Andrew Pettegree, 1:41–54. London: Routledge, 2004.

Moeller, Bernd. "What Was Preached in German Towns in the Early Reformation?" In *The German Reformation: The Essential Readings*, edited by C. Scott Dixon, 33–52. Oxford: Blackwell, 1999.

Rublack, Hans-Christoph. "Martin Luther and the Urban Social Experience." In *The Reformation: Critical Concepts in Historical Studies*. 4 vols., edited by Andrew Pettegree, 1:54–70. London: Routledge, 2004.

Scribner, Robert W. *For the Sake of Simple Folk: Popular Propaganda for the German Reformation*. Cambridge: Cambridge University Press, 1981.

Sea, Thomas. "Imperial Cities and the Peasants' War in Germany." In *The Reformation: Critical Concepts in Historical Studies*. 4 vols., edited by Andrew Pettegree, 1:106–34. London: Routledge, 2004.

Walsby, Malcolm and Graeme Kemp, eds. *The Book Triumphant: Print in Transition in the Sixteenth and Seventeenth Centuries*. Leiden: Brill, 2011.

Chapter Two. Enforcing the Peace of Augsburg

Creasman, Allyson F. *Censorship and Civic Order in Reformation Germany, 1517–1648: "Printed Poison & Evil Talk."* St Andrews Studies in Reformation History. Farnham, UK: Ashgate, 2012.

Dixon, C. Scott. "Urban Order and Religious Coexistence in the German Imperial City: Augsburg and Donauwörth, 1548–1608." *Central European History* 40, no. 1 (2007): 1–33.

Friedrichs, Christopher R. *The Early Modern City 1450–1750.* A History of Urban Society in Europe. London: Longman, 1995.

Headley, John J., Hans J. Hillerbrand, and Anthony J. Papalas, eds. *Confessionalization in Europe, 1555–1750.* Farnham, UK: Ashgate, 2004.

Hendrix, Scott H. "Luther's Impact on the Sixteenth Century." *Sixteenth Century Journal* 16, no. 1 (1985): 3–14.

Hsia, Ronnie Po-chia. *Social Discipline in the Reformation: Central Europe, 1550–1750.* London: Routledge, 1989.

Oettinger, Rebecca Wagner. "Thomas Murner, Michael Stifel, and Songs as Polemic in the Early Reformation." *Journal of Musicological Research* 25, nos. 1–2 (2003): 45–101.

Pettegree, Andrew. *Reformation and the Culture of Persuasion.* Cambridge: Cambridge University Press, 2005.

Reinhard, Wolfgang. "Pressures towards Confessionalization? Prolegomena to a Theory of the Confessional Age." In *The German Reformation: The Essential Readings,* edited by C. Scott Dixon, 169–92. Oxford: Blackwell, 1999.

Scribner, Robert W. "Oral Culture and the Diffusion of Reformation Ideas." *History of European Ideas* 5, no. 3 (1984): 237–56.

Scribner, Robert W. "The Reformer as Prophet and Saint: 16th Century Images of Luther." *History Today* 33, no. 11 (1983): 17–21.

Tlusty, B. Ann. "Rumor, Fear, and Male Civic Duty during a Confessional Crisis." In *Masculinity in Reformation Europe,* edited by Scott Hendrix and Susan Karant-Nunn, 140–63. Kirksville, MO: Truman State University Press, 2008.

Chapter Three. A Society of Orders

Friedrichs, Christopher R. "Poverty and Marginality in the Early Modern City." In *The Social Dimension of Western Civilization,* vol. 2, *Readings from the Sixteenth Century to the Present,* edited by Richard M. Golden, 132–43. New York: Bedford/St. Martin's, 1999.

Groebner, Valentin. "Inside Out: Clothes, Dissimulation, and the Arts of Accounting in the Autobiography of Matthäus Schwarz, 1496–1574," *Representations* 66 (Spring, 1999), 100–121.

Jütte, Robert. *Poverty and Deviance in Early Modern Europe.* Cambridge: Cambridge University Press, 1994.

Rublack, Ulinka. *Dressing Up: Cultural Identity in Renaissance Europe.* Oxford: Oxford University Press, 2011.

Safley, Thomas Max. *Charity and Economy in the Orphanages of Early Modern Augsburg.* Studies in Central European Histories. Atlantic Highlands, NJ: Brill, Humanities Press International, 1997.

Scott, Tom. *Society and Economy in Germany, 1300–1600.* Houndmills, UK: Palgrave Macmillan, 2002.

Tillyard, E. M. W. *The Elizabethan World Picture: A Study of the Idea of Order in the Age of Shakespeare, Donne and Milton.* London: Chatto & Windus, 1943. Reprinted Harmondsworth, UK: Penguin Books, 1963, 1978, 1990 and Piscataway, NJ: Transaction Publishers, 2011.

Chapter Four. Household, Marriage, and Sexuality

Kingdon, Robert M. *Adultery and Divorce in Calvin's Geneva.* Harvard Historical Studies. Cambridge, MA: Harvard University Press, 1995.

Myers, William David. *Death and a Maiden: Infanticide and the Tragic History of Grethe Schmidt.* DeKalb: Northern Illinois University Press, 2011.

Ozment, Steven. *The Burgermeister's Daughter: Scandal in a Sixteenth-Century German Town.* New York: Harper Collins, 1997.

Plummer, Marjorie Elizabeth. *From Priest's Whore to Pastor's Wife: Clerical Marriage and the Process of Reform in the Early German Reformation.* St Andrews Studies in Reformation History. Farnham, UK: Ashgate, 2012.

Puff, Helmut. *Sodomy in Reformation Germany and Switzerland, 1400–1600.* Chicago Series on Sexuality, History, and Society. Chicago: University of Chicago Press, 2003.

Roper, Lyndal. *Oedipus and the Devil: Witchcraft, Sexuality, and Religion in Early Modern Europe.* London: Routledge, 1994.

Roper, Lyndal. *The Holy Household: Women and Morals in Reformation Augsburg.* Oxford Studies in Social History. Oxford: Oxford University Press, 1992.

Rublack, Ulinka. *The Crimes of Women in Early Modern Germany.* Oxford: Oxford University Press, 1999.

Safley, Thomas Max. *Let No Man Put Asunder: The Control of Marriage in the German Southwest; A Comparative Study, 1550–1600.* Sixteenth Century Essays and Studies. Kirksville, MO: Sixteenth Century Journal Publishers, Truman State University Press, 1984.

Chapter Five. Work and Trade

Farr, James R. *Artisans in Europe, 1300–1914.* New Approaches to European History. Cambridge: Cambridge University Press, 2000.

Häberlein, Mark. *The Fuggers of Augsburg: Pursuing Wealth and Honor in Renaissance Germany.* Studies in Early Modern German History. Charlottesville: University Press of Virginia, 2012.

Stuart, Kathy. *Defiled Trades and Social Outcasts: Honor and Ritual Pollution in Early Modern Germany.* Cambridge: Cambridge University Press, 1999.

Wiesner, Merry E. *Working Women in Renaissance Germany.* The Douglass Series on Women's Lives and the Meaning of Gender. New Brunswick, NJ: Rutgers University Press, 1986.

Chapter Six. Sports, Entertainment, and the Control of Leisure

Behringer, Wolfgang. "Arena and Pall Mall: Sport in the Early Modern Period." *German History* 27, no. 3 (2009): 331–57.

Burke, Peter. "Viewpoint: The Invention of Leisure in Early Modern Europe." *Past and Present* 146, no. 1 (1995): 136–50.

Kümin, Beat. *Drinking Matters: Public Houses and Social Exchange in Early Modern Central Europe.* Early Modern History: Society and Culture. Basingstoke, UK: Palgrave Macmillan, 2007.

Tlusty, B. Ann. "Martial Sports and the Technological Challenge." In *The Martial Ethic in Early Modern Germany: Civic Duty and the Right of Arms,* 189–222. Early Modern History: Society and Culture. Houndmills, UK: Palgrave Macmillan, 2011.

Tlusty, B. Ann. *Bacchus and Civic Order: The Culture of Drink in Early Modern Germany.* Studies in Early Modern German History. Charlottesville: University Press of Virginia, 2001.

Chapter Seven. Ethnicity

Bell, Dean Phillip. "Jewish Communities in Central Europe in the Sixteenth Century." In *Defining Community in Early Modern Europe,* edited by Michael J. Halvorson and Karen E. Spierling, 141–62. St Andrews Studies in Reformation History. Hampshire, UK: Ashgate, 2008.

Hillerbrand, Hans J. "The 'Other' in the Age of the Reformation: Reflections on Social Control and Deviance in the Sixteenth Century." In *Infinite Boundaries: Order, Disorder, and Reorder in Early Modern German Culture,* edited by Max Reinhart, 245–69. Sixteenth Century Essays and Studies. Kirksville, MO: Truman State University Press, 1998.

Hsia, R. Po-chia, and Hartmut Lehmann, eds. *In and Out of the Ghetto: Jewish-Gentile Relations in Late Medieval and Early Modern Germany.* Cambridge: German Historical Institute and Cambridge University Press, 1995. Reprinted Cambridge University Press, 2002.

Hsia, R. Po-chia. *The Myth of Ritual Murder: Jews and Magic in Reformation Germany.* New Haven, CT: Yale University Press, 1988.

Johnson, Carina L. *Cultural Hierarchy in Sixteenth-Century Europe: The Ottomans and Mexicans.* New York: Cambridge University Press, 2011.

Ruderman, David B. *Early Modern Jewry: A New Cultural History.* Princeton, NJ: Princeton University Press, 2010.

Ullmann, Sabine. "Poor Jewish Families in Early Modern Rural Swabia." In *Household Strategies for Survival, 1600–2000: Fission, Faction and Cooperation,* edited by Laurence Fontaine and Jürgen Schlombohm, 93–113. International Review of Social History Supplements. Cambridge: Cambridge University Press, 2000.

Chapter Eight. Ritual and Ceremony

Forster, Marc R. *Catholic Revival in the Age of the Baroque: Religious Identity in Southwest Germany 1550–1750.* Cambridge: Cambridge University Press, 2001.

Karant-Nunn, Susan C. *The Reformation of Ritual: An Interpretation of Early Modern Germany.* Christianity and Society in the Modern World. London: Routledge, 1997. Reprinted London: Routledge, 2007.

Koslofsky, Craig M. *The Reformation of the Dead: Death and Ritual in Early Modern Germany, 1450–1700.* Early Modern History: Society and Culture. Houndmills, UK: Palgrave Macmillan, 2000.

Luebke, David. "Churchyard and Confession: Grave Desecration, Burial Practice and Social Order during the Confessional Age." In *Leben bei den Toten: Der Kirchhof in der ländlichen Gesellschaft der Vormoderne,* edited by Jan Brademann and Werner Freitag, 193–211. Münster: Rhema, 2007.

Muir, Edward. *Ritual in Early Modern Europe.* New Approaches to European History. 2nd ed. Cambridge: Cambridge University Press, 2005.

Myers, William David. *"Poor, Sinning Folk": Confession and the Making of Consciences in Counter-Reformation Germany.* Ithaca: Cornell University Press, 1996.

Spohnholz, Jesse A. "Multiconfessional Celebration of the Eucharist in Sixteenth-Century Wesel." *Sixteenth Century Journal* 39, no. 3 (2008): 705–29.

Wandel, Lee Palmer. *The Eucharist in the Reformation: Incarnation and Liturgy.* Cambridge: Cambridge University Press, 2006.

Chapter Nine. Magic and Popular Religion

Ankarloo, Bengt, Stuart Clark, and E. William Monter. *Witchcraft and Magic in Europe,* vol. 4, *The Period of the Witch Trials.* Philadelphia: University of Pennsylvania Press, 2002.

Behringer, Wolfgang. "Augsburg, Imperial Free City of." In *Encyclopedia of Witchcraft: The Western Tradition,* edited by Richard M. Golden, 1:65–67. Santa Barbara, CA: ABC-CLIO, 2006.

Behringer, Wolfgang. *Shaman of Oberstdorf: Chonrad Stoeckhlin and the Phantoms of the Night.* Translated by H. C. Erik Midelfort. Charlottesville: University Press of Virginia, 1998.

Behringer, Wolfgang. *Witches and Witch-Hunts: A Global History.* Malden, MA: Polity Press, 2004.

Briggs, Robin. *Witches and Neighbors: The Social and Cultural Context of European Witchcraft.* New York: Penguin Books, 1996.

Cameron, Euan. *Enchanted Europe: Superstition, Reason, and Religion 1250–1750.* Oxford: Oxford University Press, 2011.

Dillinger, Johannes. *Evil People: A Comparative Study of Witch Hunts in Swabian Austria and the Electorate of Trier.* Charlottesville: University Press of Virginia, 2009.

Dillinger, Johannes. *Magical Treasure Hunting in Europe and North America: A History.* Palgrave Historical Studies in Witchcraft and Magic. Basingstroke, UK: Palgrave Macmillan, 2011.

Gordon, Bruce, and Peter Marshall, eds. *The Place of the Dead: Death and Remembrance in Late Medieval and Early Modern Europe.* Cambridge: Cambridge University Press, 2000.

Levack, Brian P. *The Witch-Hunt in Early Modern Europe.* 2nd ed. London: Longman, 1995.

Parish, Helen, and William G. Naphy, eds. *Religion and Superstition in Reformation Europe.* Manchester, UK: Manchester University Press, 2002.

Parish, Helen. "'Lying Histories Fayning False Miracles': Magic, Miracles and Mediaeval History in Reformation Polemic." *Reformation & Renaissance Review,* 4, no. 2 (2002): 230–40.

Roper, Jonathan, ed., *Charms and Charming in Europe.* Houndmills, UK: Palgrave Macmillan, 2004.

Roper, Lyndal. *Witch Craze: Terror and Fantasy in Baroque Germany.* New Haven, CT: Yale University Press, 2004.

Rowlands, Alison. "'Superstition', Magic, and Clerical Polemic in Seventeenth-Century Germany." In *The Religion of Fools? Superstition Past and Present,* edited by S. A. Smith and Alan Knight, 157–77. Oxford: Oxford Journals, 2008.

Schutte, Anne Jacobson. *Aspiring Saints: Pretense of Holiness, Inquisition, and Gender in the Republic of Venice, 1618–1750.* Baltimore, MD: Johns Hopkins University Press, 2001.

Scribner, Robert W. "The Reformation, Popular Magic and the 'Disenchantment of the World,'" *Journal of Interdisciplinary History* 23, no. 3 (1993): 475–94.

Scribner, Robert W. *Popular Culture and Popular Movements in Reformation Germany.* London: Hambledon, 1987.

Thomas, Keith. *Religion and the Decline of Magic: Studies in Popular Beliefs in Sixteenth and Seventeenth Century England.* London: Weidenfeld & Nicolson, 1971; New York: Scribners, 1971. Reprinted New York: Penguin Group, 2003, 2012.

Chapter Ten. Dealing with War and Catastrophe

Asch, Ronald G. *The Thirty Years' War: The Holy Roman Empire and Europe, 1618–1648.* New York: St Martin's Press, 1997.

Cunningham, Andrew, and Ole Peter Grell. *The Four Horsemen of the Apocalypse: Religion, War, Famine and Death in Reformation Europe.* Cambridge: Cambridge University Press, 2000.

Hammond, Mitchell Love. "The Origins of Civic Health Care in Early Modern Germany." PhD diss., University of Virginia, 2000.

Naphy, William G. *Plagues, Poisons, and Potions: Plague-Spreading Conspiracies in the Western Alps, c. 1530–1640.* Manchester, UK: Manchester University Press, 2002.

Parker, Geoffrey, and Simon Adams. *The Thirty Years' War.* London: Routledge, 1997.

Stein, Claudia. *Negotiating the French Pox in Early Modern Germany.* History of Medicine in Context. Farnham, UK: Ashgate, 2009.

Walter, John, Roger Schofield, and Andrew B. Appleby. *Famine, Disease, and the Social Order in Early Modern Society.* Cambridge: Cambridge University Press, 1989.

Select Bibliography of Additional Primary Sources Available in English

Baylor, Michael G. *The German Reformation and the Peasants' War: A Brief History with Documents.* Bedford Series in History and Culture. Basingstoke, UK: Bedford/St Martin's, 2012.

Baylor, Michael G., ed. *The Radical Reformation.* Cambridge: Cambridge University Press, 1991.

Brennan, Thomas Edward, Beat A. Kümin, B. Ann Tlusty, David Hancock, and Michelle Craig McDonald. *Public Drinking in the Early Modern World: Voices from the Tavern, 1500–1800.* London: Pickering & Chatto, 2011.

Burr, George Lincoln. *The Witch-Persecutions.* Philadelphia: Department of History, University of Pennsylvania, 1897. Reprinted Philadelphia: University of Pennsylvania Press, 1907, 1971.

Calvin, Jean. *John Calvin: Institutes of the Christian Religion* [excerpts]. Translated by Henry Beveridge. Grand Rapids, MI: William B. Eerdmans, 1966. Reprinted Peabody, MA: Hendrickson, 2009.

Calvin, Jean. *Calvin: Commentaries.* Translated and edited by Joseph Haroutunian, in collaboration with Louise Pettibone Smith. Library of Christian Classics, vol. 23. Philadelphia: Westminster Press, 1958.

Calvin, Jean. *Calvin: Theological Treatises.* Translated with introductions and notes by J. K. S. Reid. Philadelphia: Westminster Press, 1954.

Calvin, Jean. *John Calvin: Writings on Pastoral Piety.* Translated and edited by Elsie Anne McKee. Preface by B. A. Gerrish. Mahwah, NJ: Paulist Press, 2001.

Calvin, Jean. *Letters of John Calvin.* Edited by Jules Bonnet. Translated by M. R. Gilchrist. 4 vols. 1858. Reprint. New York: Burt Franklin, 1972–73.

Chojnacka, Monica, and Merry E. Wiesner-Hanks. *Ages of Woman, Ages of Man: Sources in European Social History, 1400–1750.* London: Longman, 2002.

German Historical Institute. *German History in Documents and Images.* Washington, DC. http://germanhistorydocs.ghi-dc.org/Index.cfm?language=english. Accessed April 2012.

Gibson, Marion. *Early Modern Witches: Witchcraft Cases in Contemporary Writing.* London: Routledge, 2000.

Helfferich, Tryntje, ed. and trans. *The Thirty Years War: A Documentary History.* Indianapolis, IN: Hackett Publishing, 2009.

Jussie, Jeanne de. *The Short Chronicle: A Poor Clare's Account of the Reformation of Geneva.* Translated and edited by and Carrie F. Klaus. Chicago: University of Chicago Press, 2006.

Karant-Nunn, Susan C., and Merry E. Wiesner-Hanks, eds. and trans. *Luther on Women: A Sourcebook.* Cambridge: Cambridge University Press, 2003.

Klarwill, Victor von, and Lionel Stanley Rice Byrne. *The Fugger News-Letter (Second Series): Being a Further Selection from the Fugger Papers Specially Referring to Queen Elizabeth and Matters Relating to England during the years 1568–1605, Here Published for the First Time.* Edited by Victor von Klarwill. London: John Lane, 1926.

Klarwill, Victor von, ed. *The Fugger News-Letters: Being a Selection of Unpublished Letters from the Correspondents of the House of Fugger during the years 1568–1605.* London: Bodley Head, 1924.

Kors, Alan Charles, and Edward Peters, eds. *Witchcraft in Europe, 1100–1700: A Documentary History.* Philadelphia: University of Pennsylvania Press, 1972.

Levack, Brian P., ed. *The Witchcraft Sourcebook.* London: Routledge, 2004.

Liechty, Daniel, ed. and trans. *Early Anabaptist Spirituality: Selected Writings.* Preface by Hans J. Hillerbrand. Mahwah, NJ: Paulist, 1994.

Lindberg, Carter. *The European Reformations Sourcebook.* Oxford: Blackwell Publishing, 2000.

Luther, Martin. *Luther: Letters of Spiritual Counsel.* Translated and edited by Theodore G. Tappert. Library of Christian Classics, vol. 18. Philadelphia: Westminster Press, 1955.

Luther, Martin. *Luther's Works.* Translated and edited by Jaroslav Pelikan, Hilton C. Oswald, and Helmut T. Lehmann. 55 vols. Saint Louis, MO: Concordia; Philadelphia: Fortress Press, 1955–86.

Maxwell-Stuart, P. G., ed. and trans. *The Occult in Early Modern Europe: A Documentary History.* New York: St. Martin's Press, 1999.

Melanchthon, Philipp. *Melanchthon on Christian Doctrine: Loci Communes, 1555.* Translated and edited by Clyde Leonard Manschreck. New York: Oxford University Press, 1965.

Morton, Peter A., ed. *The Trial of Tempel Anneke: Records of a Witchcraft Trial in Brunswick, Germany, 1663.* Translated by Barbara Dähms. Peterborough, Canada: Broadview, 2005.

Naphy, William G., ed. and trans. *Documents of the Continental Reformation*. London: Macmillan Press, 1996.

Noll, Mark A., ed. *Confessions and Catechisms of the Reformation*. Grand Rapids, MI: Baker Book House, 1991.

Pauck, Wilhelm, ed. *Melanchthon and Bucer*. Library of Christian Classics, vol. 19. London: Westminster Press, 1969.

Rummel, Erika, ed. and trans. *Scheming Papists and Lutheran Fools: Five Reformation Satires*. New York: Fordham University Press, 1993.

Rupp, E. Gordon, A. N. Marlow, eds. and trans. *Luther and Erasmus: Free Will and Salvation*. In collaboration with Philip S. Watson and B. Drewery. Philadelphia: Westminster Press, 1969.

Scott, Tom, and Robert W. Scribner, eds. *The German Peasants' War: A History in Documents*. Atlantic Highlands, NJ: Humanities Press International, 1991.

Sharpe, James Anthony, Richard M. Golden, Marion Gibson, Malcom Gaskill, and Peter Elmer, eds. *English Witchcraft, 1560–1736*. 6 vols. London: Pickering & Chatto, 2003.

Sider, Ronald J., ed. *Karlstadt's Battle with Luther: Documents in a Liberal-Radical Debate*. Philadelphia: Fortress Press, 1978.

Spee, Friedrich von. *Cautio Criminalis, or A Book on Witch Trials*. Translated by Marcus Hellyer. Studies in Early Modern German History. Charlottesville: University of Virginia Press, 2003.

Spinka, Matthew, ed. *Advocates of Reform: From Wyclif to Erasmus*. Philadelphia: Westminster Press, 1953.

St. Clair, William, and Irmgard Maassen, eds. *Conduct Literature for Women: Part I, 1500–1640*. 6 vols. London: Pickering & Chatto, 2000.

Strauss, Gerald, ed. and trans. *Manifestations of Discontent in Germany on the Eve of the Reformation: A Collection of Documents*. Bloomington: Indiana University Press, 1971.

Wiesner-Hanks, Merry E. *The Renaissance and Reformation: A History in Documents*. New York: Oxford University Press, 2012.

Wiesner-Hanks, Merry E., and Joan Skocir, eds. and trans. *Convents Confront the Reformation: Catholic and Protestant Nuns in Germany*. Milwaukee, WI: Marquette University Press, 1996.

Williams, George H., and Angel M. Mergal, eds. *Spiritual and Anabaptist Writers: Documents Illustrative of the Radical Reformation, Part I*. The Library of Christian Classics, Ichthus Edition. Philadelphia: Westminster Press; London: SCM, 1957.

Wilson, Peter. *The Thirty Years War: A Sourcebook.* Houndmills, UK: Palgrave Macmillan, 2010.

Yetter, Leigh, ed. *Public Execution in England, 1573–1868.* 8 vols. London: Pickering & Chatto, 2009–2010.

Zell, Katharina Schütz, and Elsie Anne McKee. *Church Mother: The Writings of a Protestant Reformer in Sixteenth-Century Germany.* Chicago: University of Chicago Press, 2006.

Zwingli, Ulrich, Heinrich Bullinger, and Geoffrey William Bromiley. *Zwingli and Bullinger; Selected Translations with Introductions and Notes.* Library of Christian Classics. Philadelphia: Westminster Press, 1953.

Zwingli, Ulrich. *Commentary on True and False Religion.* Edited by Samuel Macauley Jackson and Clarence Nevin Heller. Durham, NC: Labyrinth, 1981.

Index